Ratifying the Republic

Ratifying the Republic

Antifederalists and Federalists in Constitutional Time

David J. Siemers

STANFORD UNIVERSITY PRESS

Stanford, California

Stanford University Press
Stanford, California
© 2002 by the Board of Trustees of the
Leland Stanford Junior University
All rights reserved.

Printed in the United States of America
on acid-free, archival-quality paper

Library of Congress Cataloging-in-Publication Data
Siemers, David J.
   Ratifying the republic : Antifederalists and
Federalists in constitutional time / David J. Siemers.
      p.   cm.
   Includes bibliographical references and index.
   ISBN 0-8047-4106-9 (cloth : alk paper)
   1. United States—Politics and government—
1789–1809.   2. Politicial science—United States—
History.   3. Legitimacy of governments—United
States—History.   4. Constitutional history—United
States.   I. Title.
JK116.S54   2002
320.473'049'09033—dc21   2002003102

Original Printing 2002
Last figure below indicates year of this printing:
11 10 09 08 07 06 05 04 03 02

Designed by Eleanor Mennick
Typeset by BookMatters in 10/12 Sabon and Galliard

For my family,
with respect and affection

Contents

Acknowledgments

This work benefited greatly from the wise counsel of many dedicated scholars. I can only hope to do rough justice in thanking some of those involved.

I owe a tremendous debt to those who oversaw the first iteration of this project at the University of Wisconsin-Madison. Chuck Jones's editing skills are unsurpassed. He made each chapter better, distilling its potential errors without overburdening the work or me with criticism. Chuck's approach to the study of government, emphasizing political process and attention to changing contexts, greatly informed me, and his ability to highlight the lighter side of politics is always enjoyable. Booth Fowler provided steady encouragement throughout, along the way teaching me much about how to communicate effectively. In kind I can only promise him that the next time we go canoeing we won't get lost. David Canon's encyclopedic knowledge of American politics literature is continually impressive and helpful. Likewise his permission to use the Collaborative Research on a Relational Database on Historical Congressional Statistics greatly aided my analysis regarding early congressional committees. The eclectic interests and far-sightedness of these three outstanding scholars enabled me to undertake a project at the convergence of political theory, American history, and American politics. I commend them for encouraging my strengths and remedying my weaknesses, to the great benefit of this work.

John Kaminski's unparalleled knowledge of the ratification period saved me from many errors, but also helped me in a positive sense, guiding and informing me throughout the life of the project. He and Richard Leffler of the Center for the Study of the Constitution have proven both extremely helpful and generous in sharing their resources.

Four other scholars took the time to read the entire manuscript and provided invaluable input. Richard K. Matthews challenged me to figure out how the founding period squared with my own perspective on politics, while enthusiastically endorsing the project overall. Lance Banning encouraged me to pursue more rigorously my theoretical approach to the question of constitutional legitimation. Cal Jillson wisely suggested that I treat Madison's thinking in greater depth and provided needed support in that pursuit. Saul Cornell offered his expertise about the Antifederalists, advised me about how a political scientist might be able to satisfy historians, and suggested numerous ideas and sources that I hadn't previously considered. In their own ways, all four improved the final product. They will surely see their imprint on the following pages, and I hope they gain satisfaction from it, while understanding we all have our different perspectives.

Others read parts of the manuscript, offering valuable suggestions in their particular areas of expertise: James Read, Mark Kann, and Ed Stettner in American political thought; Karen Orren and Sid Milkis in the area of American political development; Ken Bowling and Rick Wilson on the early Congress; and Rudolph M. Bell on political parties in the founding era. Others provided more general advice about my arguments or the presentation of them. Of particular help in this regard were John Coleman, Chuck Cohen, Greg Flemming, David Hendrickson, Laura Olson, Andy Murphy, and Andy Baker.

I also owe much to my students at a rather lengthy list of institutions: the University of Wisconsin-Madison, Bradley University, Wellesley College, Colorado College, and now the University of Wisconsin-Oshkosh. I thank them for their interest, good cheer, and friendliness and hope I've conveyed to them a sense of just how fascinating and quirky politics is. I enjoyed teaching them far more than they will ever know.

In addition to intellectual debts, I have incurred financial ones too. Or rather, through the grants given by the following organizations I was able to avoid financial debts. The Wisconsin Alumni Research Foundation provided a year's funding when this project was in midstream. Research grants at Wellesley College and Colorado College aided my scholarship. So too did funds from the U.S. Capitol Historical Society, the Dirksen Center for Congressional Research, and the Caterpillar Foundation. I thank these organizations and those involved with them.

Finally, this book is dedicated to my family, with respect and affection. As per St. Paul, "Love is patient and kind."

Preface

Jack N. Rakove points out that *The Federalist* gained authoritative status for an ironic reason. With major portions of the work aimed at "demonstrat[ing] that the Constitution had not established the leviathan its worst detractors imagined," early opponents of expansive national power were able to use Publius as an ally in the fight against those who would extend federal authority.[1] The handiwork of Hamilton, Madison, and Jay was thus legitimated as a constitutional authority because of its usefulness in partisan battle. The rancor of the times, rather than its native persuasiveness, cemented the reputation of *The Federalist*. This book argues that the same is true of the Constitution itself: its high reputation and its central position in American political discourse resulted from the partisan fragility of the immediate postratification era.

As much as anything, fear, uncertainty, and political maneuvering allowed the Constitution to succeed. With New Hampshire's ratification on June 21, 1788, the framework of government designed at Philadelphia became law. Yet whether this law of the Federalists and their supporters would be accepted by the politically active public as a whole was an open question. In light of nearly a year of pointed criticism by Antifederalists, many of whom believed the seeds of tyranny were sown in the Constitution, leaders of both camps were unsure whether this system could be authoritative.

By 1788 the American revolutionaries had experienced tragedy along with the triumph of independence. To a person they knew casualties of the war: friends and relatives had been killed, families displaced, women widowed, and children orphaned in a world not disposed to be particularly hospitable toward them. A postwar economic depression spread a less immediate kind of harm, but did so more uniformly. Many reflected on the relatively peaceful colonial times in which they grew up, even if they did not wish to return to them. What must have been particularly striking to the founding generation was how unforeseen and devastating their protracted, internecine war with the British had been. The strident language of the ratification debate gave them pause to wonder if there was to be another eruption of violence.

Antifederalists were forced to ponder this possibility as much as Federalists. They had become a recognizable opposition and were faced with a choice as the much-questioned Constitution limped toward ratification: to endure a highly flawed system of government that threatened to rob Americans of their liberties or to persist in fervent opposition that might precipitate civil strife. The Antifederalists' fear of anarchy and war — informed by their uncertainty that the rule of law rather than chaos would prevail — caused Antifederalist leaders to assent to the Constitution. In turn, they instructed their constituencies to do the same, granting the Constitution at least a trial.

This was acquiescence, however, not a full embrace, encompassing feelings of resignation and a tentativeness that could not by itself be a prescription for sustained legitimacy. As former Antifederalists worked within this suboptimal political order, aiming to prevent the troubling results they had envisioned, they were aided by a remarkable set of circumstances hardly of their own making. To gain ratification Federalists espoused the idea that the Constitution granted the national government only limited and expressed powers, a philosophy that would be adopted by the Antifederalists in their quest to limit federal power. Egregious conditions in Congress served to limit the quality of individuals elected and their tenure served, retarding institutional strength and development. Even the Federalists' overwhelming victory in the earliest federal elections proved to be a boon to the opposition in that aggressive Federalists did not worry about keeping their fracturing ratification coalition together. Antifederalists thus did have a degree of success in the new regime. Moreover, the nature of their postratification argument, emphasizing the inviolability of the Constitution, yielded a strong embrace of the new fundamental law by those whose allegiance had been most uncertain. With both Federalists and Antifederalists championing the young Constitution (albeit in their different ways), an already century-old American belief in written fundamental law as the bedrock of political orders was reinforced and the Constitution became sacrosanct.

In the last twenty years the Antifederalists' thinking has been saved from obscurity, but there is still much to be learned about their contribution to the character of the American regime.[2] A near-exclusive focus on the ratification debates has yielded a portrait of these figures not so much inaccurate as it is single-faceted. Beginning in September 1787 the Antifederalists reacted to a specific political scenario that they believed necessitated a certain kind of response. That scenario lasted all of nine months. Upon ratification they were faced with a new scenario to which they reacted differently. Changed circumstances privileged different aspects of their political beliefs and ideologies than those most prominent in 1787. Federalist policies presented still further challenges, again altering Antifederalist stances. Secretary of the Treasury Alexander Hamilton's fiscal plans in particular created a new set of circumstances, effecting a striking change in coalitional politics and an embrace of partisanship at the national level.

In *The Politics Presidents Make* Stephen Skowronek introduces the concept of "political time" to describe the varied contexts facing American presidents. Some, like Andrew Jackson or Franklin Roosevelt, inaugurate broad partisan coalitions. In succeeding years others administer those coalitions in their maturity. Still other presidents are in the unenviable position of holding aged, fracturing coalitions together, long after what animated their alliance in the first place faded from the political scene. These recurrent "regime cycles" place presidents in a particular context vis-à-vis their party. In turn their particular context helps determine appropriate political strategies and behaviors.[3] In the course of just a few years, the American regime sped through a variety of constitutional contexts. In the mid-1780s, American politicians reacted to an obviously faulty constitution. That context was followed by a time when the Constitution was proposed but not legally sanctioned — the time we often use to define the Antifederalists and the Federalists. That milieu was replaced by one in which the Constitution was ratified, made legal, but not yet implemented, which was superseded by the scenario when the ratified Constitution was initially implemented. A complete view of the constitutional thought of those involved in ratification requires knowledge of how the progression of "constitutional time" triggered different parts of their ideologies and made different behaviors appropriate.

Politics during the founding era, much like any other, was a kaleidoscope of shifting conditions, positions, and alliances. Breathing life into the portrait of Antifederalist thinking requires moving beyond the familiar exposition of the arguments they staked out during the ratification debate to the other scenarios where these same figures applied and adjusted their political knowledge.[4] The same holds true for the Federalists. We can gain a much more well-rounded view of their political thought by devoting greater attention to how they reacted to varied constitutional contexts. The progression of constitutional time revealed a rift among the Federalists, present but submerged in their fight for ratification. That rift appeared most notably in the thinking of James Madison and Alexander Hamilton, the two primary authors of *The Federalist* and the leaders of fracturing wings of their one-time coalition. Much more than a change of heart by either of these individuals or their followers, the progression of constitutional time prefigured their falling out. Madison's group allied with the Antifederalists to become the Republican Party. The complex interaction of these three groups, the remaining Federalists, the Madisonians, and the Antifederalists, more than the Federalists' ideas by themselves, defined the constitutional character of the new regime.

Chapter 1 sets the stage for viewing these groups after ratification. The workability of constitutions depends on fostering a near-consensus that the process they define for formulating statute law is legitimate. In the American context, it seems that that was accomplished very early in the life of the Constitution, but there has never been a definitive picture of how that legitimation occurred. I discuss other scholarly views of the document's legitimation, which have been partial. A fuller picture is needed to round out our knowledge of the political thought of the Federalists and their opponents, as well as to understand how major characteristics of American constitutional practice came to be. The chapter then turns to the Antifederalists. Near-exclusive attention to their arguments during the ratification debate has obscured a substratum of agreement with the Federalists on two items: the need to alter the confederation and the primacy of the rule of law. A variety of scholars perceive that the character of the American regime was planned and successfully executed by the proponents of the Constitution. In reality, the Federalist coalition was much more fractured than most commentators have realized. The Federalist coalition was narrowly focused on ratification — as soon as broader and more detailed projects creep into the picture, members of the coalition break ranks.

The second and third chapters focus on the Antifederalists after ratification. They show that despite the diversity of the Antifederalists they acquiesced to the Constitution quickly and uniformly, even though other options were available to them. Their acquiescence was due to a predisposition to respect the rule of law, something that did not apply to the Constitution when it was a mere proposal, and the fear of potential lawlessness. Despite holding a variety of views, the few Antifederalists elected to the First Congress pledged to abide by the Constitution and work for change from within its bounds. Their numerical weakness dictated that they would lose policy battles; constitutional critiques of the Federalists, by contrast, were of the first order. Even when outvoted, the former Antifederalists could claim that their objections to Federalist policies still held and that such policies were unconstitutional. Unwittingly, the Federalists had provided them with much ammunition to make such constitutional arguments, as the best known of their ratification debate defenses made the point that the national government possessed expressed powers only. The Antifederalists' arguments in the First Congress were scattershot, but they began lines of constitutional argument that the opposition Republicans would hone into a full-blown interpretive philosophy, still espoused by some.

Chapters 4 and 5 deal with the Federalists and the fracturing of their coalition. The fourth chapter outlines the differences in the thinking of Hamilton and Madison. Before and during the ratification debate, they had very different ideas about how to deal with faulty constitutions, how to remedy the problems of the confederation, and how to implement a new national constitution. Madison understood the use of broad discretionary powers as a last resort, violative of a constitution's letter, and only warranted when the fate of the nation was at stake. Although the Confederation Congress was warranted in employing such discretionary power, Madison held the federal Constitution to a much higher standard. In part because he thought the national government possessed sufficient power to be successful and in part because of his respect for the specific understandings sanctioned by ratification, Madison viewed the new Constitution's division of powers between the nation and states as definitive and static. The postratification context triggered a very different impulse for Hamilton. He felt that faulty constitutions could be administered into sovereign existence through the exercise of broad discretionary powers. That had worked in times of crisis under the confederation and it might be made to work again under the Constitution, which unfortunately divided sovereignty, as did the Articles of Confederation, and was thus prone to the same centrifugal tendency. These were disagreements that inevitably became apparent as constitutional time moved forward. As long as each retained influence in the new regime, these differences in their constitutional theories would have important repercussions in the political world. Further, in the months following implementation of the Constitution, Madison would find fault in assumptions that led him to ally with Hamilton. Stripped of certain ideas he held at the time of ratification, Madison's constitutional thinking much more closely resembled many of the Antifederalists' than Hamilton's.

I also focus on what happened to Madison's constitutional thinking in the immediate postratification climate. What changed in Madison's mind was not so much a vision of how to properly interpret a constitution, as most scholars seem to believe, but rather a loss of faith in the benefits of the extended republic, most prominently outlined in Federalist #10. During the second session of the First Congress, Madison became aware that a majority faction was effecting legislation at the national level, precisely what he thought improbable during the ratification debate. The third session of the First Congress confirmed to Madison and his followers that not even constitutional boundaries would stop this self-serving faction from pursuing its desires. This breakdown in what had been such an important part of his recent thinking dictated an embrace of new tactics directed toward the same ends. Events from the First Congress showed that a rights-respecting republic could not be maintained primarily by constructing better institutional arrangements. Such a republic would have to be actively fought for in the realm of public opinion and through a party apparatus in the national legislature. Accordingly, Madison cultivated ties with the former Antifederalists both within and outside of the new government, and the Jeffersonian Republican Party was born. Their alliance was no fluke. In addition to possessing constitutional philosophies that were remarkably similar once Madison was stripped of his unorthodox views about the extended republic, the backgrounds and interests of the Madisonians were more similar to the Antifederalists than the Federalists as well.

The next two chapters treat political alliances and structures in the early Congress. Chapter 6 demonstrates the durability of the Antifederalist-Madisonian coalition and that this coalition remained focused on the proper extent of governmental power. Scholars of political parties have thought the new partisan cleavage indicated that the issue of governmental power receded to a secondary matter in the years after ratification. Their contention is that a new issue cleavage precipitated a coalitional change except on a few votes that explicitly related to governmental power, which reunited the old coalition. But the matter of national power was very much in contention throughout the Federalist era on a whole range of issues. I analyze roll-call votes of each coalition and the issues that were being decided to see whether their assertions are supported. Even when accepting these authors' categorization of votes, the issue-cleavage concept is not validated. Much closer to the mark is John Aldrich, who writes of the "multi-dimensionality" of votes, meaning that they simultaneously activated a whole range of personal, state, and regional preferences, including preferences about the extent of national power. And yet Aldrich's claim that the first impetus for parties came from the Federalists as a means of overcoming a collective action problem seems faulty. In my estimation, the Republicans were the first to organize their partisan apparatus as an electioneering device.

Tenures in Congress were almost uniformly short during the early years of its existence. Despite losing on the term limits issue during the ratification debate, it seems as though the Antifederalists' hope for rotation out of office was satisfied by something like a natural term limit. Conditions in Congress were sufficiently taxing to prevent institutional development and the growth of national power. Federalists and Republicans also agreed, in the main, on the processes and structures to be used in the new Congress. Both groups eschewed the use of standing committees to determine policy matters. At the same time, they used numerous select committees, which allowed them to specialize according to their preferences. Agreement on the legitimacy of the policy process and the slow development of the institution of Congress forestalled any search for radical, extraconstitutional solutions to governmental problems by the opposition party. A final chapter summarizes the events, timing, and causality in the early regime, discusses the enduring contribution of the Antifederalists, and comments on the usefulness of the precedents set in the first years of the republic.

Two great ironies of the American founding take center stage here. The first is that the Antifederalists were as responsible for the legitimation of the Constitution as the Federalists. The second is that the fragility of the times as perceived by its political leaders was the most crucial ingredient in establishing a stable constitutional order. Fear induced stability. Neither of these observations should come as a surprise. Yet what makes these developments ironic from our perspective are our own deeply ingrained assumptions about the founding. Federalists, our assumptions tell us, out-thought and out-maneuvered the Antifederalists with a brilliantly conceived plan for change. So confident are we that the Federalists triumphed that there seems to be little need to consider Antifederalists after ratification, little need to consider that June 21, 1788, provided anything but closure. Yet in this sureness we lose the essence of what animated politics as the new government was coming into being: massive uncertainty. A more realistic grasp of the politics of the era (I am tempted to say of politics itself) can only be attained if the uncertainty and even fear that motivated politicians and citizens on all sides are readily acknowledged. Undoubtedly John Locke and the English Whig opposition inspired the text of the founding; but Thomas Hobbes provided an unacknowledged subtext. The founding was a political process, not a foreordained plan of demigods. That process was full of unexpected turns, reversals, and surprising results, making the founding more fascinating, if less redemptive, than if it were a gift from on high. The regime that evolved from this process did not easily correspond to any particular vision of politics or timetable for it. An accurate description of the founding therefore requires recognizing a kind of Burkean organicism layered on top of the rationalist strivings of three discernible groups: the Federalists, the Madisonians, and the Antifederalists.

Ratifying the Republic

CHAPTER ONE

Consensus, Dissensus, and Interpretation

How the Antifederalists and Federalists Have
Unwittingly Misled Us

Hindsight simultaneously helps and hinders our attempts to come to grips with the American founding. It grants a more expansive knowledge of the era's results than anyone could have had at the time of ratification. This knowledge is problematic, however, as it lures us into a kind of sureness. Lacking a feeling of uncertainty about the era, we assume the founders were as certain about it as we, leading to fundamental miscalculations about their positions and intent. We exaggerate the Federalists' unity and control over the ratification process. We sentence the Antifederalists to an existence as historical footnotes. A necessary step in understanding the political dynamics of the founding is to recapture the uncertainty and fear that so animated action and advocacy during this time. One deeply rooted fear was of utmost importance to both sides: Could a new government foster the level of support required for successful governance?

The ratification debate was extremely divisive. As often happens in politics, moderate voices were obscured by those making more extreme claims. The most memorable arguments of both the Federalists and the Antifederalists presented the public with rather dire scenarios. Proponents of the Constitution argued that popular government could not be sustained without ratification; Antifederalists countered that the document itself was destructive of popular rule. No wonder that leaders on both sides were nervous about the prospects for successful governance even after ratification. Not so very far beneath the surface, however, were the makings for a workable truce. Indeed, a harmonic convergence of political ingredients led to constitutional legitimation.

A discussion of the ratification period must begin with a careful look at the concept of legitimacy as it pertains to constitutions generally and to the United States's version in particular. A distinguishing and functional characteristic of constitutional law is a need to approach consensual support. With constitutions frequently born in times of national strife, legitimation requires acceptance by anticonstitutional groups or parties. In the United States, Antifederalist support was crucial to the Constitution's success. Present-day commentators do not always recognize the Antifederalist role in legitimation, nor that legitimation occurred quickly after ratification. Even among those who do, there is disagreement about the time frame and reasons behind this occurrence. The disagreements result partly from confusion over what kind of actions constitute acceptance. I draw a distinction between acquiescence and something significantly stronger, apotheosis, as two necessary steps in constitutional legitimation. A clearer, more comprehensive picture of these steps can grant purchase on Antifederalist political thought and why American constitutional practice took the shape it did.

Even if it does not seem so at first glance, in 1787 the Antifederalists were prepared for significant reforms that would have strengthened the confederation. They were also poised to accept a ratified Constitution. The Federalists meanwhile were not nearly as cohesive as many have assumed. Or rather, they cohered on a very narrowly focused project — ratification — rather than on some of the much more ambitious plans with which modern commentators have credited them. In overestimating the scope of the Federalist project these analysts have also exaggerated the Federalists' degree of control over the outcome of the founding. Only by confronting these lingering assumptions about the two groups can we come to view ratification as a dynamic political process, one in which compromises and unexpected outcomes that favored the Constitution were commonplace.

Constitutional Teleology: The Quest for Legitimation

Successful popular governance under a constitutional order requires a substratum of agreement about procedural rules. Both constitutional law and statutory law are designed to be authoritative, but the former has a special character that distinguishes it from the latter. Constitutions define criteria for the production and the enforcement of statutory laws.[1] Although constitutional law may designate majoritarian conditions as sufficient for the production of statutes (or a more complicated formula like concurrent majorities in a bicameral legislature with executive approval), majoritarian acceptance is not sufficient for the legitimation of fundamental law. Just as it is difficult or impossible to play a game or a sport with others who cannot agree on authoritative rules, politics in its usual, nonrevolutionary sense is hindered in proportion to the lack of authoritativeness of its fundamental law.[2]

Required to play baseball or bridge or politics is agreement of the "constitutional" rules. When consensus on this structure is achieved then the game can continue despite calls or hands or policies that do not always go one's way, because the people involved have accepted the legitimacy of what is marked as authoritative. By contrast, if there is substantial dissensus over constitutional rules, the possibility of such order greatly diminishes. In the political arena, this consensus is difficult to achieve because the stakes of being on the losing end of policy battles are routinely high. Principles and interests are at stake in legislation, and this being the case, there is frequently little incentive to accept being outvoted. The difficulty of achieving constitutional consensus, or even getting close, is the principal reason so many national constitutions are short-lived.[3]

The United States Constitution faced the same peril. The criterion for ratification in each state was simple majoritarian approval by a popularly elected convention. Ratification proved only that, by late 1788, the Constitution had been acceptable to a majority of delegates in eleven states. North Carolina and Rhode Island were still holding out. Each of the four largest states had formidable groups of political leaders who thought the Constitution highly flawed. In three of these states, Massachusetts, Virginia, and New York, the document passed by bare majorities and then only with the promise of amendments. The success of the new government and the authoritativeness of its policies hinged on the Antifederalists, precisely those who had thought the Constitution inadequate. Only if they acquiesced could a tenuous majoritarian legality become a workable consensual legitimacy. "The problem," write Stanley Elkins and Eric McKitrick, "was not simply that of acceptance [of the Constitution], but the more fundamental one of legitimacy. It was a problem whose resolution ought to begin even before the new government was organized, and could not be seen as complete until some time after it had begun to function."[4]

And yet this crucial transition from legality to legitimacy occurred so quickly, decisively, and seemingly painlessly that it is often overlooked. To be sure, widespread approval of the Constitution bordering on the consensual has not been overlooked; that consensus did not spring seamlessly from ratification itself has. The oversight is an easy one to make, because already in the First Congress the Constitution was called "sacred."[5] Historian Lance Banning relates that by "the Spring of 1791 . . . the Constitution was accepted on all sides as the starting point for further debates."[6] Contemporaneous authors remarked on the strong attachment

Americans had to their Constitution. Loyalist historian Jonathan Boucher, for instance, was baffled at the new order's success, writing in 1797 that "the only very strong point in the present Constitution of these States is in the attachment and partiality of their people for it."[7] Two hundred years later, legality and legitimation seem hardly distinct chronologically, blurring the conceptual distinction between them and discrediting the Antifederalists from perhaps their most important contribution to the American polity. The primary American constitutional habit has been to consider the Constitution as the one and only constitution and to engage in endless dialogue over what it means. Other meaningful constitutional questions are drowned out by this habit, including the fundamental question of the Constitution's legitimacy, how it arose, and how it is (or might be better) sustained.

A nearly consensual, quasi-religious acceptance of the Constitution has, in fact, been a hallmark of American constitutionalism. Among the public and politicians, there is a general trust that it provides the proper bounds within which United States politics must occur, this despite frequent disagreements over what exactly those bounds are. Americans simply have not had to think about how the Constitution was legitimized or how it remains so because it is such an accepted fact of political life.[8] The great mass of constitutional scholarship indicates how seriously Americans take their fundamental law. The words, meanings, and implications of the Constitution matter to Americans. Aiming to present a more authoritative take on the meaning of the document presumes that what it *really* says is critical. Charging a policy with unconstitutionality presumes that the proper bounds for policy are set by it. That we may fill libraries with such materials, both scholarly and otherwise, indicates the powerful hold the fundamental law has on the American mind. It is hardly overstating the case to say that we explain our governing document "just as generations of scholarly exegesis had illuminated the Bible," as the meaning of both documents is of vital importance to the many who have put faith in them.[9]

For all the talk of "culture wars" in current intellectual discourse, the degree to which a constitutional faith deflects major cultural divisions is impressive — or perhaps appalling, depending on one's perspective. H. Jefferson Powell, for instance, laments that U.S. citizens have a pervasive, abiding faith in the Constitution. Americans place faith in "the rationality and ethical quality of legal reasoning," making their de facto moral arbiters the interpreters of the Constitution, the courts, rather than God, church, and conscience. For Powell this is a major failing, yielding the violence of abortion and other state-sanctioned evils.[10] But given an equal number of adamant pro-choice forces, it would seem that this pervasive tradition has kept a nation of those with potentially unbridgeable differences. Powell's observations of 1993 are intended to echo those of Alexis de Tocqueville in the 1830s, that in America moral disputes become legal disputes. The point of difference between the two authors is not whether a constitutional/legal consensus exists in the United States, but whether that consensus is beneficial. De Tocqueville was quite content with citizens who were imbued with a respect for the law sufficient to deflect potential civil strife. Powell finds that this legal harmony has a corrosive effect on the soul.

For well or ill the United States has a constitutional devotion foreign to many nations. A consensual (if vague) acceptance of the ratified document was established quickly and has scarcely abated. But the quick establishment of this consensus raises a conundrum, for in 1787 the ingredients for such a mutual embrace seemed distant indeed.

Michael Kammen discerns (and laments) the cultic embrace of the Constitution in favor of something more rational and measured. In *A Machine That Would Go of Itself*, Kammen disputes that this cultic embrace existed in the Constitution's first decades. He writes, "The cult of the Constitution did not arise as early, nor so pervasively as scholars have believed. Similarly, I do not see a strong constitutional consensus emerging from the start. Instead I find complaints about disloyalty to the Constitution (in 1793, for example), and expressions of hostility verging upon denunciation."[11] Unfortunately, Kammen presents little evidence that hostility was aimed specifically at the Constitution itself after ratification. Those who he cites to support his claim, like Thomas Jefferson and Georgia Senator William H. Crawford, are expressing their dismay that politicians and citizens alike considered the Constitution sacred. These are not denunciations of the Constitution itself, nor do they demonstrate an absence of a "cult of the Constitution." On the contrary, Jefferson and Crawford seem to be complaining about the very cult of the Constitution that Kammen claims does not exist at the time.[12] The next two chapters of this work serve to refute Kammen's assertion, demonstrating that those who might have continued to dispute the Constitution's efficacy in fact embraced it, doing so quickly, uniformly, and wholeheartedly.

Others tend to give the Federalists exclusive credit for the burgeoning public faith in the Constitution. Michael Lienisch's important intellectual history of the Federalist era, *New Order of the Ages*, correctly identifies the challenge of postratification politics. "Legitimacy had to be created," Lienisch writes about the years immediately after ratification, but he proceeds to present the legitimation effort as a Federalist project exclusively: "The critical figures in this effort were those champions of the Constitution who, beginning as early as mid-1787 but especially following ratification, worked relentlessly to win popular acceptance for the new government." Lienisch identifies three developments in Federalist thought that served to "make the Constitution seem somehow second nature."[13] In the five years after ratification, Federalists were able to convince almost all citizens that the Constitution was of a piece with prior American political practice, that they were to be devoted to order (as opposed to practicing the more unruly ever-vigilant-citizen ideal of classical republicanism), and that their proper "psychology" was to be a kind of Aristotelian moderation.[14] These are important developments in the history of ideas, but taken alone they offer a misleading account of legitimation. Continued Federalist advocacy favoring the constitutional system is only half of the story, and a rather predictable half.[15] Whole sections of the country were firmly Antifederalist in 1787, with few or no credible leaders who had advocated ratification. These areas, and ones more evenly divided, did not turn suddenly to accept abstract Federalist political theorizing. Rather, they seem to have gone along with the Constitution because their recognized leaders did.

Those who rightly focus more attention on the Antifederalists' role in legitimation disagree rather markedly on why the Antifederalists came to support the Constitution and when. Behind their differences lies an unspoken dispute over the degree of support required to effect legitimation. Lance Banning has written that the Antifederalist embrace of the Constitution came as a defensive measure in response to specific Federalist policies. Schooled in the classical republican ideal that fundamental law inevitably degenerated, the former Antifederalists clung to the Constitution's stipulations as a means of impeding policies advocated by Secretary of the Treasury Alexander Hamilton. Because their embrace was a reaction, a defense against actual policy maneuvers by Federalists, Banning argues that Antifederalist support for the Constitution emerged during the First Congress, becoming highly recognizable by early 1791, when Hamilton's proposal for a national bank was being debated. At that point, it can be accurately said that the Constitution was "accepted on all sides." During the next two years the opposition organized, and by 1793 the "apotheosis of the Constitution," as Banning calls it, was complete.[16]

Steven R. Boyd looks at things differently in his *The Politics of Opposition*. In a chapter titled "The Capstone of Legitimacy: The First Federal Elections," Boyd writes that "Federalists and Antifederalists believed that the latter could win through the first federal elections what they had lost in the state conventions."[17] Rather than advocating a boycott and not standing for election, the Antifederalists participated in them fully. This willingness to accept the electoral boundaries of the

Constitution was an important step, but not necessarily decisive. For a variety of reasons, Antifederalists did poorly in most races, in contrast to their expectations. Only a handful of them were elected to national office. "Overwhelmed at the polls, deprived of effective leadership, and facing further defections from their own ranks, Antifederalists acquiesced."[18] A combination of the opposition's willingness to play by the Constitution's rules for electoral purposes and the overwhelming confidence placed in the Constitution by the electorate (judging by their endorsement of Federalists) provided the extra increment needed to move beyond mere legality. Since the first federal elections provided the "capstone of legitimacy," to Boyd the Constitution was legitimated by late 1788 or early 1789.

A more traditional view is advanced by Linda Grant De Pauw. In "The Anticlimax of Antifederalism," De Pauw discusses early attempts to amend the Constitution. Many critics hoped for a second convention; New York and Virginia did call for such a meeting. Opposition from Federalists, the innovation of state conventions recommending amendments, and general delays derailed the second convention movement. With no convention on the horizon by the time Congress first met, legislative amendment was recognized by the Antifederalists as the quickest and therefore favored means of altering the document. The successful production of rights-protecting amendments proved more than satisfactory. De Pauw relates that "for most Antifederalists, worship of the Constitution began the day Congress accepted Madison's amendments."[19]

The issue is also treated by Saul Cornell in his recent book on the Antifederalists and their legacy, *The Other Founders*. Cornell draws a distinction between three main kinds of Antifederalists: elite, middling, and plebeian.[20] Shortly after Pennsylvania's state convention ratified the Constitution, plebeian populists rioted in protest in Carlisle, Pennsylvania. The lawless actions of this group of Antifederalists alienated the others, who feared anarchy more than they did living under the Constitution. "The beliefs of the plebeian populists," writes Cornell, "did not provide the basis for building a democratic coalition, but instead split the two most democratic wings of the Anti-Federalist coalition apart."[21] The elite and middling Antifederalists, containing the great majority of their recognized political leaders, agreed to abide by the Constitution to "avert further violence." In the wake of this decision, the plebeian Antifederalists felt a sense of betrayal. Their more radical version of democracy became "muffled," with only periodic outbursts of it becoming public, as in the Whiskey Rebellion.[22]

In part, these disparate positions can be reconciled by deconstructing the different claims they forward. Boyd shows that the Antifederalists were willing to "play by the rules of the game" very shortly after ratification. Banning, meanwhile, describes a much stronger attachment to the Constitution that had arisen by the spring of 1791. Though different in form from Banning's, De Pauw's language suggests the firmer kind of embrace that he describes. Cornell identifies an even more reluctant acquiescence than Boyd, which accepts the Constitution as the lesser of two evils. Sorting out these different accounts can be done partly by treating terms with greater precision. Each recognizes that legitimation of a constitution requires the opposition's acceptance in some way, but how exactly? What does acceptance entail? Boyd implies that Antifederalists backed into acceptance because of a combination of self-interest and a tactical error: they thought standing for election under the rules of the Constitution would benefit them, but badly misjudged the sense of the electorate, doing far worse than expected, leaving them little choice but to agree to abide by the Constitution's framework. Cornell describes a fear-induced acceptance to avoid what was considered a worst-case scenario: anarchy. This kind of tepid, reluctant embrace is sometimes called "acquiescence" by Boyd, and in this case it is a much more precise word than "acceptance." Acquiescence did serve to bolster the Constitution, but not definitively. Boyd leaves the impression that had the Antifederalists triumphed in the first federal elections, or even in subsequent elections, they likely would have changed the Constitution significantly to suit their own beliefs. Cornell hints that if the plebeians had not rioted they could have allied with the middling Antifederalists to form an anti-Constitution party that pressed for democratic change.

It would seem that the more adamant acceptance Banning and De Pauw describe was required to put the Constitution on a solid footing. Arguing that the Constitution provides the unassailable bounds for politics committed the opposition in such a way that its prospects were much more sure. Banning's sometime term for this kind of acceptance is "apotheosis." Again "apotheosis" is a much more precise word than the generic "acceptance," better describing the phenomenon he elucidates. Taken together, these authors discern that constitutional legitimation occurs in two steps. An opposition group that has committed itself against the adoption of a framework of fundamental law must first acquiesce to the legalized constitution for it to work. In the longer term, a constitution must be embraced in a stronger sense by the opposition, reflecting a confidence that it is somehow useful rather than just a problematic expedient to be put up with temporarily.[23] This "apotheosis" might more accurately be called the "capstone of legitimacy" than Boyd's acquiescence. None of these accounts of the Antifederalists' embrace of the Constitution is definitive, as they only deal with one part of the process. I treat both, keeping the two aspects of acceptance distinct, consistently labeling them by their more descriptive terms, and treating them in separate discussions. The next chapter deals with the Antifederalists' acquiescence in depth; the remaining chapters treat the more complicated and multifaceted issue of apotheosis.

The differences between the above authors cannot simply be resolved by greater attention to vocabulary, however. At issue is whether the opposition's acceptance, and thus constitutional legitimacy, resulted from pragmatism or principle. Banning credits Antifederalist constitutional theory as the reason for the apotheosis of the Constitution; Boyd views acquiescence as a pragmatic concession to the realities of politics. Neither of these views is correct in itself. Interestingly, I find both authors mistaken within their own sphere. The Antifederalists' *acquiescence* was much more principled than Boyd believes, while *apotheosis* relied much more on the twists and turns of practical political outcomes than Banning thinks.

Although these authors rightly recognize that Antifederalist actions after ratification are crucially important to the Constitution's prospects, a more accurate, comprehensive picture of their role in constitutional legitimation is needed for two main reasons. First, attention to their post-ratification contribution provides a fuller picture of the Antifederalists, a particularly important group in American political history. Second, through it we understand more fully how the founding era set the tone of American constitutionalism, making the Constitution a nearly unassailable entity. The founders themselves recognized how important early precedents were in defining the nature of the Constitution; there was no more important precedent set in the republic's early years than its consensual acceptance allowed by the Antifederalists' quick embrace of it.

"I Shall Submit with as Much Cheerfulness as I Can"

Antifederalist leaders were a diverse lot, in some cases united only by their negation of the Constitution. Their positive prescriptions were often significantly at odds, particularly concerning the optimum level of control exerted by the democratic populace. Nevertheless, some generalizations may be ventured, both about their reasons for opposing the Constitution and about their prospects for reconciling with it afterward.

For most, the Constitution threatened the achievement of the Revolution. The colonial experience had been proof that a distant centralized government could not be representative. The Federalist plan recentralized government in a distant national capital. Logistical problems that prevented viable American representation in Parliament had been reintroduced. Journeying from North Carolina to New York, for example, often took longer than did passage from Boston to London. Antifederalists speculated that representatives ensconced in this distant national capital would soon lose sight of their constituents' interests because of their physical distance.

In place of the interests of the general populace, members of Congress would favor their own personal interests. The type of people who would be elected from large districts and by state legislatures would be the nation's elite, far more well-off than the average citizen. Aristocratic policies would predominate because there would be no meaningful restraints on national legislators. The necessary and proper clause could be used to sanction anything, the supremacy clause meant that the national government could force policies on the people, and the absence of a bill of rights yielded no assurances that the national government would not tyrannize. The people, jealous of their liberty, would probably not allow for the immediate introduction of tyranny. The national government would accrue power gradually though, eventually leaving the people governed rather than governing.

Vast physical and cultural differences between states were readily apparent to those who did even a limited amount of traveling in the 1780s. The Americans who squared off against each other in the ratification debates were acutely aware of these distinctions. Federalists tried to persuade the public that interstate disparities were not so great as to prevent a collective good. James Madison added the now-famous argument from Federalist #10 that diversity could preclude the formation of harmful majority interests. The Antifederalists felt that frequent clashing of interests proved there could be no nationwide common good. Maryland Antifederalist John Francis Mercer, in a fascinating inversion of Madison's theory, wrote:

We are persuaded that the People of so large a Continent, so different in Interests, so distinct in Habits, cannot in all cases legislate in one Body by themselves or their representatives — By themselves it is obviously impracticable — By their Representatives it will be found on Investigation equally so — for if these representatives are to pursue the general Interest . . . it must be done by a mutual sacrifice of the Interests, wishes, and prejudices of the parts they represented — and then they cannot be said to represent those Parts, but to misrepresent them.[24]

The empirical theory is familiar — it mirrors Madison's. But just as in a real mirror image the view is reversed. Instead of a possible benefit, the compromises inherently a part of the extended republic threatened popular government. Consistently compromising constituent interests, as nationally elected officials would be forced to do, was not proper representation to Mercer and other Antifederalists. State officials, reflective of a much more homogeneous populace, would not routinely have to compromise constituent interests.

These Antifederalist objections are by now familiar and well documented. What is less well understood are their points of agreement with Federalists. Most critics of the Constitution believed that the confederation needed to be altered and were willing to grant it two important powers that probably would have saved it: the ability to raise revenue and to control interstate commerce. Under the Articles of Confederation, Congress could only request money from the states, not demand it and enforce that demand. During the 1780s many states refused to pay the full amount of revenue requested of them. Repayment of war debts and thus economic recovery were made impossible by the haphazard collection of revenue. Several attempts to reform the Articles of Confederation allowing the national legislature to tax failed, but only narrowly. The Articles required unanimous consent of the states to be amended. An "impost" amendment that would have given the Confederation Congress a secure source of revenue was twice approved by twelve of the thirteen states.

Once little Rhode Island had prevented the national government from being put on a sound financial footing; later New York scotched the alteration to the Articles of Confederation. The impost amendments could not have come so near acceptance without substantial support from those who would be Antifederalists. Since an impost would levy a duty on imports only, it did not threaten state sovereignty. Individual states would retain sole power of taxation over citizens and goods inside the state. Thus the impost did not provoke the same reaction from Antifederalists as the Constitution, which they felt left the continued exercise of state sovereignty ambiguous.

Despite not threatening the sovereign powers of the states, the impost did threaten the interests of one state in particular, New York. New Yorkers opposed the impost amendment (and later the Constitution) because it would end the revenue windfall they were receiving from tariffs.[25] A high percentage of imported goods sold in neighboring states passed customs in New York City because of its excellent natural harbor. New York's substantial tariff enabled it to pay off war debts. The costs borne by shippers were ultimately transferred to consumers in neighboring states, meaning that New York was thriving at the direct expense of economically depressed New Jersey and Connecticut. The New York legislature was not about to agree to such an amendment — the financial incentive against doing so was just too great — even if they knew such reform was for the good of the

Union. Thus the Antifederalists as a group were not responsible for preventing centralizing reforms so much as were those in a single state.

The impost amendment was one major component in the effort to grant the Confederation Congress a general power to regulate interstate commerce. Despite the recalcitrance of New York, there was a near-consensus that Congress should have power to prevent discriminatory trading practices. A leading analyst of the economic conditions of the time goes so far as to write, "It is hard to uncover any other issue in American history upon which there was so much general agreement as there was on conferring upon Congress the supreme power over commerce."[26] Or in the words of one Antifederalist, it was "acknowledged on all hands, that an additional share of power for federal purposes ought to be delegated to Congress."[27] Yet the requirement of state unanimity prevented reform.

Remedies to the Articles's failings were readily acknowledged but impossible to achieve. The nation was at a constitutional impasse. Frustration over this impasse produced a call from Virginia for a special convention designed to broker a solution. Though the convention at Annapolis in September 1786 was poorly attended, it alerted nonattending states to the possibility of procuring the necessary changes through a body other than Congress and the state legislatures. The commissioners of the Annapolis meeting recommended another convention be held in Philadelphia the following May to revise the Articles of Confederation. All states but Rhode Island sent delegates to the Philadelphia Convention. Its commission of reform was uncontroversial. What the convention chose to do with that commission, however, became the source of major controversy, but it was not until the delegates went beyond their charge and formulated an entirely new constitution that was not a confederation like the Articles, that a sizable element of the American political community objected.

Another crucial point of agreement with the Federalists was the Antifederalists' reverence for the rule of law.[28] Between the Annapolis meeting and the Philadelphia Convention the agrarian uprising called Shays's Rebellion occurred. Massachusetts farmers had prevented courts in the western part of the state from holding session for several months, delaying foreclosure on their debt-ridden properties. Although this uprising ended without significant bloodshed, it alarmed many Federalists and energized their quest for reform. They feared repeat performances of lawlessness and dire consequences if the national government were not empowered to enforce the rule of law in the states. Future Antifederalist leaders found the actions of the Shaysites more understandable than Federalists, perhaps, but not more acceptable.

Those who would be Antifederalists condemned the Massachusetts rebels. It may be surprising to find Samuel Adams, firebrand of the Revolution, leading forces in the Massachusetts legislature seeking to quell the uprising and harshly punish its leaders, but he did so in his capacity as president of the state Senate. To Adams, agitating for revolution against a distant, tyrannical monarch was far different from participating in lawless activity against a postrevolutionary government elected by the people of Massachusetts themselves. He explained to his cousin John, "Now that we have regular and constitutional governments, popular committees and county conventions are not only useless, but dangerous."[29] The very activities Adams championed and participated in with gusto during the Revolution were not acceptable in a popular government, underscoring the respect for popularly sanctioned "republican" law that even the most incendiary of patriots felt.

George Clinton, governor of New York and future Antifederalist stalwart, assisted Massachusetts by extraditing Shaysites who had fled across the state line. He too felt that it was wrong to rebel against popular governments:

By the free constitutions of these states, the people enjoy the right of electing their rulers, and the elections are as frequent as can possibly consist with convenience; they have it therefore fully in their power by the mere exercise of the right of election, to relieve themselves from the operation of laws which they may deem grievous, or in any wise improper, and cannot justify recurring to violence, and involving their country in confusion and bloodshed, in order to produce a change in public measures.[30]

Yet those who would be Antifederalists also warned against interpreting Shays's Rebellion as more than it was: a troubling example of unrest in the one state where the absence of debt relief had been particularly oppressive. Richard Henry Lee lamented that those who called for extensive nationalizing reforms were overreacting, "too apt to rush from one extreme to another."[31] Reformers sought more centralized power than was necessary, potentially imperiling liberty itself. These leaders believed that in constituted popular regimes flaunting the law was simply unacceptable; it set an anarchical precedent that fundamentally threatened the sovereign people's government. Accordingly, they condemned Shays's Rebellion, even though they were not as greatly alarmed as the Federalists that its events would soon be repeated. America had a long history of political activity by "the people out of doors," and the Antifederalists seemed to recognize that Shays's Rebellion was as much ritual as rebellion, mob action that was familiar but which had gone too far.[32] Their statements about the uprising show Antifederalists to be ideologically ill-poised for a challenge to the Constitution's legitimacy once ratified.

Hints of the Antifederalist acquiescence are actually contained in the ratification debate. Antifederalist leaders frequently predicted what would happen after ratification, since forecasting troubling political results was a necessary part of their critique. Often these predictions related to the problem of maintaining or achieving constitutional consensus. Usually Antifederalists predicted that the people would initially accept the new government only to realize later that it was compromising their interests and slowly accruing power at their expense. With this realization consent would be withdrawn, and civil war or a repressive regime would be the only logical result. Less frequently Antifederalists predicted that the minority would not give up the fight. It is important to note that these predictions were about what the people, not the authors themselves, would do. The wonder is, with many Antifederalists willing to predict that the proposed government would end in tyranny, that personal vows to remain fighting despite ratification were not more frequent.

When Antifederalist leaders foreshadowed their own postratification activities they vowed to accept the Constitution and uphold the rule of law.[33] They would not do so without reservations, but they would do so firmly, out of a sense of duty. In the fall of 1787, Elbridge Gerry of Massachusetts transmitted his dissent to the state legislature along with the observation and pledge, "as the welfare of the union requires a better Constitution than the Confederation, I shall think it my duty as a citizen of Massachusetts to support that which shall finally be adopted, sincerely hoping it will secure the liberty and happiness of America."[34] Maryland's Luther Martin, like Gerry one of the few dissenters who had attended the Philadelphia Convention, was more pessimistic about the future than his colleague, but he also promised to end his opposition. Martin related that he could abide by the Constitution's rules with a clear conscience despite impending disaster, for he had done all that was ethically justified to stop its passage.[35] "Republicus," writing in Lexington's *Kentucky Gazette*, expressed the tacit sentiment of most Antifederalist leaders: "Though I shall always submit to the laws of my country, with as much cheerfulness as I can; yet the voice of the united world shall never persuade me to say it [the Constitution] is right."[36] The Antifederalist leaders' promise to uphold the rule of law was fulfilled.

Amazingly, these professions were written prior to the Constitution's adoption, precisely when the debate was at its most heated. Even then Antifederalists were poised to acquiesce to the Constitution as part of their law-abiding ideology. A few in western Pennsylvania did not give up the fight after ratification and engaged in rioting. This very lawlessness, Cornell stresses, served to alienate Antifederalist leaders from their more radical constituencies, robbing the rioters of any elite sanction or leadership.[37] Without elite encouragement or support, opposition to the Constitution died almost immediately on ratification even in the few communities where citizens did not easily give up the fight. An underlying consensus that the rule of law was tenuous and must be upheld helped preserve an uneasy unity after ratification, as did the acknowledgment that reforms were desperately needed.

Many Antifederalists felt the nation was on the brink of upheaval immediately after ratification. A natural and understandable reaction to potential upheaval is to put up with or even cling to what is established and what is known, despite its less than fully satisfying character. Albert O. Hirschman points out that "brand loyalty" operates in political regimes, just as it does in the marketplace. Consumers often keep purchasing a company's products even as they find their quality declining. Similarly, politicians and citizens may choose to abide by a suboptimal political order, voicing complaints as a way of rectifying problems rather than advocating (or precipitating) a wholesale change of regimes.[38] Hirschman reasons that this kind of brand loyalty has a stabilizing effect, allowing both corporations and political orders to adapt and evolve out of troubled times. If citizens always demanded maximum performance from polities no nation could long survive, as allegiances would switch so quickly as to prevent a stable commitment to any particular political regime.

The Antifederalists were loyal political "consumers" of the new regime — a loyalty indicative of their cautious disposition. It took fortitude, imagination, and even panache to advocate the wholesale changes the Federalists did.[39] They literally aimed to reconstitute the regime, which required throwing away the established legal framework. A good part of what made Antifederalists Antifederalists was their wariness about doing more than patching up an obviously defective regime. After ratification it was clear that the Articles had been scrapped and the Constitution set up in its place. The Antifederalists' caution led them to exchange one faulty political order for another instead of recommitting themselves to an optimal regime. Although they had ideas of what this more optimal regime would look like, there was no single set alternative to the Constitution and little chance of obtaining agreement on any particular alternative. A new political equilibrium had been established, one that the Antifederalists were unwilling to disturb. Aiming for their ideal could only end in fracturing what fragile base there was for governing, a quest that they surmised would yield instability, even anarchy. In Hirschman's terms they chose loyalty and voice over the great uncertainty of "exit."

Yet there were powerful forces that must have tempted Antifederalists to continue a more adamant opposition. Even with recommended amendments the document was ratified precisely as it had come out of the Philadelphia Convention. The Constitution's critics thus still worried that liberty and popular government would be supplanted by an elite-controlled centralized government that would eventually wield unlimited powers. In addition, the new framework had been so vilified by many of their number that acquiescence was politically problematic. Accepting the Constitution seemed to suggest that they had either not believed their own arguments to begin with or were now compromising their heartfelt principles. Both of these scenarios were unflattering and counter to Steven Boyd's assumption: Antifederalists must have realized that their political prospects would erode after their acquiescence.

By the time the first federal elections were held many voters believed the Antifederalists lacked conviction or lacked the courage of their convictions. These beliefs were understandable but almost surely mistaken. The Antifederalists had been so focused on the scenario at hand in 1787 and 1788 that they only rarely articulated parts of their political ideology not triggered by the proposed Constitution. Thus the public was aware of the Antifederalist stance toward a particular unsanctioned proposal for governing but had little idea that they thought popularly ratified fundamental law was inviolable. In short, statements like those offered by Gerry, Martin, and "Republicus" above were too few to prime the public for Antifederalist acquiescence. The tight focus of Antifederalist arguments during the ratification debate painted critics of the Constitution into a political corner once the document was ratified. Federalists, in turn, exploited that vulnerability, harming the opposition's electoral prospects.

A successful interpretation of Antifederalist political thought must simultaneously account for their strenuous objections to the proposed Constitution and acceptance of it after ratification. Rather than a sudden fundamental change in their principles, the passage of constitutional time brought a new context, exposing the aspects of their thinking that I have highlighted here. These ideas, and above all the Antifederalists' devotion to the rule of law, were obscured during the ratification debate. In the months immediately after ratification Antifederalists reacted predictably by acquiescing to the Constitution and did so quite uniformly.

The great bulk of what we know about the Antifederalists deals with a span of only nine months—the length of the ratification debate. This was surely an important time, and an exciting one too because of its high stakes and the clarity of its conflict. Not moving beyond this narrow time frame, however, is akin to a local newscast focusing exclusively on the exciting "visuals" of the day. A report on a five-alarm apartment fire does treat the most exciting aspect of a story and is not fallacious in itself. Yet this focus often fails to address the broader issues involved. Did the owner comply with the fire code? Was the city negligent in inspecting the building? Did a parent leave her young children unsupervised who later became victims? Did she have to because she could not afford day care? Are these problems widespread? Too often these "stories behind the story" are not reported because they are less clear and less exciting than seeing an apartment burn. Antifederalist participation in and influence on the American regime is a story obscured by the more exciting "visuals" of the ratification debate.

A Coalitional Interpretation of the Federalists

The motives of the Federalists have been questioned for nearly a century. Freedom from assumptions of their altruism have allowed for more realistic assessments of their project than the nineteenth century produced. Yet we are only now edging out of an equally pervasive assumption: that the Federalists were a highly unified group bringing a well-articulated vision of politics to the nation. I doubt the ratification process's settlement was what the Federalists foresaw and hoped for. My doubts lead me to a series of questions: How unified were the Federalists? Precisely what did they agree on, and what was internally divisive? Did the plan formulated in Philadelphia unproblematically conform to Federalist preferences? Did they concur on how to implement the ratified Constitution? These questions require close scrutiny because by 1791 the Federalist coalition had fractured. If the Constitution conformed to the preferences of a united group of Federalists and was successfully implemented, this split would be incomprehensible. What makes their postratification division understandable are submerged differences within the Federalist camp, the inherent ambiguity of a complex political process, and slippage between what members of this coalition expected from the new government and what it ultimately delivered.

Despite the brave front offered in their justificatory writings, the Federalists' ability to fully understand and articulate even their own innovations was limited. It is well known that James Madison was initially rather disappointed with the final product of the Philadelphia Convention. Recent evidence demonstrates that Madison's endorsement of the Constitution in *The Federalist* came only after a postconvention revelation that its design could effectively remedy the problems facing the nation. Only several weeks after adjournment did Madison come to believe that the Constitution would inaugurate a sound government.[40] This should give us pause. If the brilliant "Father of the Constitution" himself was only slowly coming to grips with what had been produced in Philadelphia, his colleagues must have been struggling with its meaning and implications too.

Madison also noted that the law only took on a definitive tenor with implementation, writing, "all new laws, though penned with the greatest technical skill, and passed on the fullest and most mature deliberation, are considered as more or less obscure and equivocal, until their meaning be liquidated and ascertained by a series of particular discussions and adjudications." There simply could be no definitive answer about how the Constitution worked or whether it was salutary—until after its implementation.[41] In early 1789 no one was in a position to predict what the new government sanctioned. Perhaps no one was even capable of definitively interpreting what had happened during the last two years.

The Federalists had displayed prodigious talent during the ratification era, realizing a stunning collective achievement. They had not, however, controlled the ratification process in an uncomplicated manner. The document itself was a cobbled-together series of compromises. It was perfectly amenable to none. The best commentaries on the convention emphasize that it took mutual agreements among identifiable coalitions to patch together the Constitution. Thornton Anderson relates that the most important division among the Federalists was the degree of power they felt the national government should possess. This division was so deep that Anderson posits there were three different groups involved in ratification: state sovereigntists, state federalists, and nationalists, the last two forming the Federalist coalition. I employ roughly the same tripartite division in this work, but with different labels: Antifederalists, Madisonians, and Federalists.[42] Despite their differences "the state federalists and several exponents of the New Jersey Plan joined with the nationalists in building a strong central government."[43] Calvin C. Jillson finds the convention's Federalists divided on a wide array of matters. So many were their divisions that in order to write a usable framework for political decision-making conciliation simply had to prevail. Although the outcome was anything but foreordained, Jillson reasons that the delegates were so fractured that standing voting rifts, which might have caused the convention to rupture, were avoided. There were thus significant differences among the Federalists. None of them, nor any cohesive group of them, dictated what the Constitution looked like. Neither were these differences transmuted because of a mutual support of the Constitution, for these differences were rooted in concrete interests and ideological subcultures.[44]

Federalists had also been forced to react to the arguments of their critics. Though some objections to the Constitution were anticipated in the convention, none could predict precisely how the Antifederalists would argue, nor what would resonate with the public. Arguments were often formulated ad hoc. Naturally they also portrayed the Constitution in the least threatening terms possible, promising among other things that the document would sanction no implied powers. Although effective in quelling fears and achieving ratification, these arguments committed Federalists to positions many preferred to forget. The scores of amendments recommended by state conventions were promised consideration, despite fears that they jeopardized the new government. Whether that government possessed (or could accrue) powers that many Federalists thought crucial for national success was unclear. In short, the Federalists did not simply triumph.

Despite their achievement Federalists, like Antifederalists, were sailing into uncharted waters in 1789. Different Federalists had pressed for ratification for differing, as yet unarticulated reasons. The pursuit of ratification required smoothing over potential differences to realize a common goal. Furthermore, Federalists would probably come to divergent understandings of the document once implemented. No one could easily foresee the particular circumstances they would face, and thus they could not perfectly describe the policies they would favor. It was unrealistic to expect this coalition, thinly held together by the hope for a viable federal government, to agree on what the Constitution sanctioned. In short, ratification had been a lengthy, somewhat ambiguous political process. It was not the political equivalent of a situation comedy or a sports contest with their readily defined outcomes. True, Federalists had been more successful than their opponents, but their real accomplishment is that they persevered through all the unexpected twists and turns the ratification process took, not that they dictated the outcome of the process.

Unfortunately for our understanding, major strands of commentary on the American founding have been misinformed by the Constitution's quick success. Many presume that the Federalists were far more unified than they actually were and that their plan was more far-reaching in scope and implication than creating an effective national government. Charles Beard combined both problematic assumptions. Because 120 years of living under the Constitution had allowed the triumph of a Hamiltonian political economy, he and other Progressives were convinced that this had been the Federalist design.[45] But Beard's analysis fails to account for the supporters of the Constitution like James Madison, who actively fought Hamilton's national bank and other proposals designed to foster a more vigorous trade/production-oriented economy.

Hamilton himself surely did have the creation of a trading/production-dominated economy in mind during the ratification debates. Arguably that political economy was the design of the Federalist Party as well. We should take care, however, not to confuse the Federalist Party with the advocates of the Constitution, even though they share a label. The Federalist Party was a narrower, more homogeneous group of leaders (in terms of geography, constitutional philosophy, and policy preferences) than the Federalists of the ratification debates. The Federalists who became "the Federalist Party," Hamilton et al., had restrained themselves from a full expression of their economic preferences during the ratification debates. A full airing of Hamilton's plans would have likely fractured the fragile Federalist coalition by alienating the Southern Federalists with more agrarian constituencies. Hamilton wisely restrained himself, allowing for ratification, the proximate goal necessary for the realization of his treasured political economy. Beard, then, is correct that many Federalist writers were less than fully forthright, but he is mistaken about the reason underlying their obscurantism.[46] Federalists obscured their ultimate goals not because theirs was a well-designed scheme for achieving personal economic gain among a tight-knit group but because theirs was a fragile coalition unified around the significant but narrow and ill-defined goal of creating a strengthened national government. A cobbled-together Constitution was their vehicle, and for it to succeed the Federalists simply could not afford to alienate potential supporters by being fully forthright about their intentions.

The thesis that the American founding signaled a transition to modernity also carries with it problematic assumptions. Some Straussian political philosophers and J. G. A. Pocock have made the case that the mechanism relied on to make government succeed changed fundamentally with ratification.[47] Ancient and medieval republics were designed to cultivate virtue among the populace, they point out, and the Federalists' key innovation was that interests would check other interests, meaning that virtue-cultivation was no longer a priority. Since the proper functioning of the new American polity was not reliant on virtue, leaders felt no need to stress its importance. Their reelection was, after all, pegged to constituent satisfaction rather than any moral standard. The new regime thus encouraged development of selfish interests and their active pursuit in that it tended to be most responsive to those with the clearest, most adamantly stated desires.

Of course the Federalists did not dislike virtue, and that is not the claim of these authors. Rather their questionable assumption is that the Federalists were quite comfortable with the open pursuit of interests and even clashes between those interests. Madison, who offered the idea of interest checking interest in Federalist #10, did not hold that wrangling up as an ideal, but rather as an unfortunate reality that would occasionally have to take place to prevent outright majoritarian tyranny. He and other Federalists were not pleased with this prospect but were willing to live with it. Curiously, many Federalists who lived beyond 1800 critiqued the young government in much the same manner as the Straussians. They felt their experiment had failed in that the selfish pursuit of popular satisfaction was being mistaken for good governance. The cultivation of a self-serving culture might be an accidental outcome of the founding, but it is not one that the Federalists sought.

The clashing of interests in the extended republic described in Federalist #10 was a crucial part of Madison's thinking, but its influence is frequently overemphasized. The best indication that Federalist #10 was not intended as a definitive description of politics at the national level are the eighty-four other editorials Publius felt compelled to write. How resonant the argument was, even among Federalists, is an open question. Madison's beliefs about the extended republic were far from the best-known Federalist justification of the Constitution.[48] Even if Federalist #10 had been more widely read it was too cerebral for many to comprehend and too unorthodox for many to accept. Recently Larry Kramer has argued that few of Madison's fellow Federalists even understood the argument.[49] The Federalists who did understand it probably felt resigned relief at the appearance of this editorial rather than exultation that their position had been definitively stated. The Montesquiean orthodoxy that republics had to remain small in size had been answered in as effective a manner as possible, and the debate could now move on to arguments the Federalists were much more likely to win. The belief that interests checking interests on the national level inevitably produced good policy and was the central component of Federalism would surprise the Federalists themselves.

Still other commentators believe that the Federalists walled off meaningful opportunities for popular participation and influence. Richard K. Matthews, for instance, dubs James Madison's state-building ideal the "heartless empire of reason."[50] Matthews feels that Madison had a dim Malthusian view of human nature leading him to rely on constitutional mechanics rather than democracy in his quest to create a sound regime. Sheldon Wolin and Isaac Kramnick broaden Matthews's claim to the Federalists generally, each stressing the antidemocratic tendencies of the Constitution and its supporters.[51] These authors, like the Straussians, forward a powerful critique of modern American life, but whether that critique is a direct answer to the Federalist project is again questionable. There were Federalists who were extremely wary of popular government and advocated every filter on public input available. Thinking of the people primarily as an obstacle rather than the nation's sovereigns, however, was not a uniform Federalist premise. Madison, James Wilson, and others believed themselves to be (and were arguably) revolutionary in their devotion to popular rule.[52] Characterizing Madison as an opponent of popular input makes his lifelong collaboration with Thomas Jefferson difficult to comprehend. Unless arch-democrat Jefferson recognized Madison as a proponent of meaningful popular rule why would he be in league with Madison? Again, we must be wary of blanket characterizations of the Federalists.

What the participatory democratic critique might really be taking issue with more than the Federalist project are the political effects of two centuries of demographic and social change. At the time of the founding there were only about one million people eligible to participate in politics, about two-thirds of the population being excluded due to gender, ethnicity, or lack of property ownership. States dominated most policy arenas even after ratification, and the number of eligible citizens in them ranged from about 25,000 in Delaware to approximately 230,000 in Massachusetts and Virginia, allowing for meaningful popular input. The exponential growth of the nation's population and the inclusion of formerly excluded groups have swelled the eligible population well over a hundred-fold. The end result is that individual citizens have little direct control or say over political matters, especially as the national government has asserted itself in a broad array of policy arenas. Participatory democrats are not, of course, against the extension of the franchise—that would be fundamentally at odds with their hopes. But their complaints about the Federalists seem misdirected, for the growth and evolution of the American polity far more than the Federalist design have led to the diminution of the individual's political efficacy. Like the Progressives, participatory democrats assume that what happened in America was the Federalist design.

The above theses all make broad claims about the Federalists, a group about which it is difficult to make broad claims. All three are uncomfortable with (their version of) the Federalist project. Beard believed the founders to be the precursors to capitalist robber barons. The later scholars find Federalists responsible for the United States's deepest political pathologies as they variously see them: a virtue-starved nation or an undemocratic one. Despite these negative portrayals the arguments reinforce the Federalists' legend in a curious way, by exaggerating their potency and success. If this narrow group of politicians hatched a plan that has fundamentally defined the United States for more than two centuries, then they rank among the great founders the world has known. When Caesar is cursed for crossing the Rubicon, the protestations indicate that his actions were full of meaning and import. They ultimately reinforce the idea that he altered the Roman republic on his own terms. Caesar thus emerges as a political demigod, even a heroic figure, despite criticism. So do the Federalists in the face of their modern critics. Conversely the myth of Antifederalist weakness is perpetuated.

A few have been more circumspect about the Federalists. Gordon Wood, for instance, believes that the Federalists actually undermined their own quest for a more elite-driven popular government. They did so by "selling" the Constitution as the practical realization of popular sovereignty. Wood stresses the Federalists' devotion to leadership by the nation's best and brightest, a "natural aristocracy." This natural aristocracy would expertly determine the nation's best interest rather than fix policies to public opinion. Too tight a connection between public policy and public opinion was precisely what they hoped to curtail. At the same time, Federalists knew that stressing their doubts about unrestrained popular input would not get the Constitution ratified. So the Federalists emphasized the popular nature of their government instead. All institutions either directly or indirectly represented the sovereign people. The different branches were selected through different means not to stifle popular rule but to provide redundant popular representation preventing any individual or group of political leaders from gaining too much control, allowing none to threaten popular sovereignty.

With Federalists continually emphasizing the popular nature of their proposed regime, citizens believed it to be so. Instead of electing a natural aristocracy, they expected national representatives to faithfully represent popular wishes. Federalists feared institutions dominated by and reflective of popular "interests," precisely the kind of politics prevailing in the United States according to Wood. The real prophets of the founding age, in his view, were the men who came to grips with popular, interest-driven politics on a national scale, like Congressman William Findley, a former Antifederalist.[53] Wood points out that the oft-asserted claim that we live under the Federalists' regime is dubious, because the Federalist preference for policy determined by a national elite of the politically expert did not last. By contrast, the Antifederalist preference for policy reflective of popular interests did come to fruition, even if it was at the national level. The Federalist era's end with the "Revolution of 1800" is indicative of this evolution, for the Federalists were supplanted by the Democratic-Republicans, a group much more comfortable with the representation of raw interests. Wood is keenly aware of the implication. In his contribution to *Beyond Confederation*, he cryptically writes, "The Antifederalists seem forever doomed to be losers, bypassed by history and eternally disgraced by their opposition to the greatest constitutional achievement in our nation's history. But maybe we have got it all wrong."[54]

Maybe We Have Gotten It All Wrong

The Antifederalists, whose acceptance of the Constitution was crucial to its legitimation, were more moderate than has generally been believed. Upon ratification, a new context activated their reverence for the rule of law, even the constitutional law they had strenuously opposed. But few could know that at the time of ratification, because their commentary of the previous months did not seem moderate, written as it was for a different context. The Federalists certainly did not know whether they could count on the Antifederalists to modify their views; neither, probably, did many Antifederalists themselves realize how uniformly their coalition would acquiesce to the Constitution until it happened. Their uncertainty and fear over whether acquiescence would occur are two things that made their acquiescence so public, so uniform, and so air-tight. We too, except for brief glimpses otherwise, have lacked a realization of the Antifederalists' moderation and devotion to the rule of law. Absent an extension of the time frame in studying the Antifederalists, we fail to credit them for its legitimation and the establishment of the Constitution's quasi-religious, consensual acceptance.

Meanwhile the Federalists were more fractured than most of them realized during the ratification debate. James Madison almost surely knew how different his constitutional philosophy was from Alexander Hamilton's, but Madison was reticent—unwilling to air his differences with Hamilton. After all, it was not the proper time to pursue that fight, with the possibility of establishing a viable national government hanging in the balance. That fight would come another day. Given the propensity to think that Madison changed from a nationalist to a "states-rightser" in the 1790s, it is apparent that we are still unaware of the latent rifts in the Federalist coalition. The major strands of commentary on them each rely on a vision of Federalism far more uniform than is actually the case. Their coalition's fracture, already apparent by 1791, ensured that the Antifederalists' opposition would be viable. Their alliance with the Madisonians gave them a chance of being in the majority in Congress and correspondingly little incentive to pursue a radical approach toward a constitution to which they had already acquiesced. That tale, of the Constitution's apotheosis, must wait until after the story of their acquiescence is told.

CHAPTER TWO

"It Is Natural to Care for the Crazy Machine"

The Antifederalists' Postratification Acquiescence

❖

Even after his native Pennsylvania ratified the Constitution, James Hanna, like nearly all Antifederalists, was still apprehensive about its stipulations. Fifteen months passed between Pennsylvania's ratification and the implementation of the new federal system, a time he and other Antifederalists spent uncomfortably in political limbo.[1] With the recommendation of amendments by several state conventions to the inaugural federal Congress, the prospect for changes to the Constitution prior to implementation faded. Certain prominent Federalists had said they would work for amendments, but their pledges were unsatisfactory to the Constitution's critics. The lessons of history advised them that vague promises from prominent leaders were far less sure a method of securing rights and proper representation than written legal guarantees. Some Federalist candidates for the First Congress even campaigned against amendments, lending credence to Antifederalist fears. In many of their minds, the governmental blueprint was as inadequate and dangerous as the day it had become public. This ratification could not change.[2]

But ratification triggered an immediate and significant alteration in the Antifederalist approach toward the Constitution. Their ideology held that citizens had no standing to flaunt the results of proper republican political processes, as disturbing as they might be. A majority of popularly elected delegates had favored the Constitution in most of the states. Accordingly, the Antifederalists in those states felt it would be wrong to dispute the legality of the outcome, despite its deeply troubling implications. So when Hanna wrote to like-minded friends, suggesting a course of action to be taken prior to the impending "crisis" of implementation, he reminded them that "it would be the height of madness and folly, and in fact a crime of very detrimental consequence to our country, to refuse to acquiesce in a measure received in form by so great a majority of our country."[3] Professions of fidelity to the Constitution like Hanna's were not the exception among Antifederalist leaders, but a near-unanimously endorsed norm.[4] In one fell swoop, they declared a whole range of political options, which they might have used to continue disputing the ratified document, off-limits.

Even the most strident critics concluded that it was their obligation to respect the Constitution as law, to urge the populace to do the same, and to work within its bounds to secure change. These are not stances that can be taken for granted when a sizable minority of a nation's political leadership is under the assumption that a new system of government will end in tyranny — particularly when that group's formative political experience was a successful revolution.

Spurred on by Hanna and others, Pennsylvania Antifederalists took the unique step of calling their own convention. This meeting could have proceeded as had some of the Shaysite county conventions two years earlier in Massachusetts, encouraging the thwarting of government procedures, secession, and the taking up of arms to gain satisfaction.[5] But these options were precisely what the Antifederalists hoped to avoid in their professions of acquiescence to the Constitution. Meeting in Harrisburg, the report of the thirty-three delegates representing thirteen of Pennsylvania's eighteen counties contained a list of amendments. But what preceded this list put Federalists at ease: the delegates agreed to pursue amendments through the guidelines set down in the Constitution and urged "the people of this state to acquiesce." The delegates reasoned with James Hanna that "the worst that we can expect from a bad form of government is anarchy and confusion . . . and by an opposition in the present situation of affairs, we are sure of it."[6] This kind of acknowledgment was a necessary step toward the opposition's inclusion in and influence on the new system of government.

To understand the phenomenon of Antifederalist acquiescence, we must explore the reasoning, uniformity, timing, and nature of their immediate postratification position. The system's erstwhile critics followed through on their promises to abide by the result of the ratification process regardless of the outcome. They did so well before the Bill of Rights was formulated or Hamiltonian policies yielded fears of constitutional degeneration. Antifederalists almost uniformly swore allegiance to the Constitution, a ceremony of great importance to them as it signified the transference of sovereignty from state governments to the national government. The few who refused provide examples of political alternatives not taken by the Antifederalists. In contrast, almost all urged accommodation and moderation, providing a flow of information crucial to the popular embrace of the Constitution. Far from aiding Antifederalist prospects for being elected, this position left them extremely vulnerable. In short, the Antifederalists reacted to ratification responsibly, accepting that at least in the short term their acquiescence would hinder their political standing.

Like Lance Banning, I find that the Antifederalists accepted the Constitution from principle. But the evidence I present here shows that acquiescence occurred significantly earlier than Banning believes and for a different ideological reason. Pledges to abide by the Constitution came immediately on the heels of New Hampshire's ratification in 1788. James Hanna's letter, for instance, was written within two months of ratification, seven months before the implementation of the new government. The reasoning employed in these writings suggests that it is more accurate to attribute the Antifederalist conception of the rule of law for acquiescence than it is to cite their constitutional theory, as Banning does. Legal theory and constitutional theory are not unrelated, of course. But when James Hanna and others like him acknowledged that the ratified Constitution should be heeded, they pointed to the document's legitimation via a republican political process as the reason, not its status as higher law. Although the process employed was unique, the Antifederalists felt that it gave the Constitution legal sanction. Had they rigidly adhered to their conception of proper constitutional theory in 1788, they would have insisted that all thirteen states needed to ratify before implementation. The Articles of Confederation still served as America's fundamental law, and it required the unanimous consent of the state legislatures to alter the form of government.[7] At any rate, crediting Antifederalist principles with their acquiescence avoids viewing them either as wholly defeated and shut out of the new political system or as pragmatists who were not really as adamantly opposed to the document as their ratification-era writings seem to indicate.

Steven Boyd's and Saul Cornell's accounts of Antifederalist acquiescence are chronologically closer to mine. Both make important observations about Antifederalist behavior in the immediate postratification climate. Boyd recognizes that this group did not contest the first federal elections in a radical way. However, he does not recognize the principled nature of the Antifederalists' acquiescence. Instead he finds they contested the earliest federal elections because they thought they could prevail. In the wake of ratification, though, it must have been painfully obvious to the Antifederalists that their political prospects would be severely hindered by accepting the Constitution. Unless the public was listening to them very closely, sticking to their principles and accepting the legal nature of the document made them appear like turncoats or alarmists who had not really meant what they had said. Why else would they have produced so much evidence of the kind contained in this chapter, aimed at teaching the populace it was their duty to acquiesce despite their continued wariness? If what Cornell posits is true, that rank-and-file or "plebeian" Antifederalists were willing to continue their opposition outside constitutional bounds, their leaders only disappointed them and lost standing by not doing so. Far from inducing them to acquiesce, pragmatic political concerns pulled the other way, in favor of forming an anticonstitutional party.

Cornell recognizes the Antifederalist leaders' great apprehension of anything smacking of anarchy and perceives their wholly negative reaction against the Carlisle riot. Accordingly he does a much better job of coming to terms with the postratification motivations of men like James Hanna than does Boyd. He also discerns that because the rioting took place relatively early in the ratification process, it galvanized elite Antifederalists against anticonstitutional activity months before any federal elections were held. The Pennsylvanians' Harrisburg Convention is a watershed event to Cornell. "At the very least, before Harrisburg an anti-Constitution party was plausible. But those radical alternatives were decisively rejected" and a loyal opposition emerged, he relates.[8] Although I agree that Antifederalist leaders greatly feared anarchy and were genuinely disturbed by the Carlisle riot, their promises to acquiesce even before ratification occurred indicates that an anti-Constitution party was a virtual impossibility even before the incidents at Carlisle. Rather than an event that changed leaders' minds and became a turning point in Antifederalism, the riots exposed a latent rift within the opposition coalition, reconfirming the "middling" and "elite" leaders' view that laws enacted in a republican manner had to be abided by. The expedient for dealing with potential anarchy was to emphasize the unassailable nature of the rule of law, including constitutional law. That was not an ad hoc response to the Pennsylvania riots but was a part of their mind-set during the ratification process and before it. Thus it is the passage of constitutional time that exposed the Antifederalists' opposition as loyal, rather than specific events from the ratification debate.

The documentary record also leads me to wonder whether the plebeian radicalism Cornell discerns was widespread. It would be easy to overestimate the persistence and virulence of anticonstitutional sentiment in the nation as a whole based on a few cases of popular unrest in one part of Pennsylvania. Nevertheless, it is plausible that popular acquiescence lagged behind that of leaders. Accepting the Constitution was, after all, a fairly sophisticated political act; it may have been difficult for ordinary citizens, not as well versed in the political ideology of the day, to put faith in a document that had been vilified. Cornell's belief is that absent viable leadership, radical plebeian sentiment went underground, only to bubble up again periodically, as in 1793's Whiskey Rebellion.[9] Certainly the actions of the Whiskey Rebels bear some resemblance to the anti-Constitution riots and even Shays's Rebellion. But in between the riots and the Whiskey Rebellion an important transition occurred in popular sentiment toward the Constitution that must be noted: by 1793 the Constitution enjoyed almost uniform popular support as well as elite support.[10] So if Cornell is correct that elite acquiescence drove a wedge between Antifederalist leaders and their constituents generally, I must add that at least in its constitutional aspect the rift healed rather nicely in the months and years that followed.

A plausible explanation for this "healing" is not difficult to figure out, though this account must remain somewhat speculative. Recent research has found a stark difference between public opinions held when there is elite consensus versus elite contention.[11] One recent example is the change in public opinion during the Vietnam War. Before elites criticized the war, protests and public disapproval were minimal. But after countervalent opinions were expressed in the media and by some political leaders popular resistance grew.[12] Political scientist John Zaller finds that in general, popular "resistance to persuasion depends very heavily on the availability of countervalent communications, either in the form of opposing information or of cueing messages from oppositional elites."[13] Upon ratification, Antifederalist newspapers argued that the Constitution should be given a try, as did those who had been "oppositional elites." In light of a nearly uniform stream of information supporting the Constitution, popular resistance did not last long.

Significant evidence leads me to these conclusions, namely, the variety of contexts in which professions of acquiescence were made and the uniformity of that acquiescence exhibited in Federalist sources and state legislative records dealing with loyalty oaths. There were a few Antifederalists who did not acquiesce to the Constitution; they were exceptions to the rule. Their positions and experiences provide a sense of the options open to the opposition that they did not take. Furthermore, "political responsibility" must be acknowledged; the Antifederalists acquiesced despite the political toll in doing so, a fact that reinforces my contention that their initial acceptance of the Constitution was out of principle.

A Union of Acquiescences

The Pennsylvanians' professions, and Hanna's in particular, represent just a small fraction of the Antifederalist pledges of fidelity to the ratified

Constitution. These statements are generally similar in form and language, stating that it is the duty of republican citizens to abide by outcomes sanctioned by popular rule, and that amendments would be pursued in a constitutional manner. What the Pennsylvania example makes clear is that even the critics who were bitterly divided from their Federalist counterparts made these professions, and they did so well before the new government was implemented.[14]

The report of the Harrisburg Convention was printed in a newspaper, but professions appeared in a variety of genres and contexts. Elbridge Gerry, a delegate to the Constitutional Convention, wrote to the Massachusetts legislature to explain why he did not sign the proposed Constitution. Elbridge Gerry's profession of fidelity ("I shall think it my duty as a citizen of Massachusetts, to support that which shall finally be adopted") was contained in a letter he wrote to the Massachusetts legislature stating his objections to the Constitution.[15] Fellow Bay-Stater John Quincy Adams, a young law student and self-identified Antifederalist, confessed in his diary that "[as] I find myself on the weaker side, I think it is my duty to submit without murmuring against what is not to be helped. In our Government, opposition to the acts of a majority of the people is rebellion to all intents and purposes."[16] Nine days later he wrote a fellow Harvard College graduate against whom he had privately debated the Constitution's merits. Adams told his Federalist cousin William Cranch that his transformation was complete, and that he was now "a strong Federalist."[17] Adams's commentary is indicative of the high stakes that Antifederalists believed were involved in their postratification positions and the seriousness with which they took what was procedurally sanctioned as law: either one agreed to abide by it or one was a rebel—there was no middle ground. Because professions like Adams's are from private communications, it would be a mistake to judge them cynically, as a scheme to restore reputations in preparation for elections.

Still others, like Maryland's John Francis Mercer, pledged their fidelity in public letters. Mercer circulated his views in his native Annapolis. With American liberties in peril, the populace energized from the ratification debates, and two states "heretofore united by blood, common interest, sufferings and success" outside the Union, amendments were needed to bring the country together. Unless supporters of amendments were elected as representatives, he reasoned, the nation faced "a very awful crisis."[18] Mercer then offered himself as a candidate for the House of Representatives and pledged to pursue amendments. In addition to that promise, Mercer recognized that "the government being adopted, and the necessities of the union requiring its immediate and energetic execution, all changes that might tend to retard its operations, should be gradually and cautiously effected, and the general sense of the continent previously consulted."[19] Mercer found himself in an awkward position. In the short term, the unamended Constitution would have to be implemented to maintain civil peace, but if the frame of government were not altered it might provoke civil discord itself by stifling liberty. Saving the Union required recognizing and implementing the Constitution while working for change from within.

South Carolina's Antifederalist leaders did not even wait until nine states had ratified to publicize their acceptance of the document. The final portion of the official proceedings of South Carolina's ratification convention contained a pledge from those who had voted against the Constitution. Those erstwhile critics promised to "exert themselves . . . to induce the people to quietly receive and peaceably to live under the new government."[20]

Other concerned activists also acquiesced prior to ratification, because of their particular circumstances. Samuel Adams, for instance, strongly opposed the Constitution privately late in 1787. During the first week of January Adams publicly announced his opposition. The problem with this position was that the Boston tradesmen who served as Adams's constituency throughout his public life adamantly favored the document. These tradesmen met at the Green Dragon tavern "to consider what was to be done in consequence of Mr. Adam[s's] declaration" opposing the Constitution.[21] The final meeting, attended by 380 citizens, unanimously adopted five resolutions in support of the proposed form of government and warned "that any vote by Boston's delegates against the Constitution or support for amendments would be 'contrary to the best interests, the strongest feelings, and warmest wishes of the Tradesmen of the town of Boston.'"[22] Adams, one of twelve Boston delegates to the Massachusetts ratification convention, seemed to take their concerns to heart. Despite his expressed apprehensions, he voted for ratification.

Strangely, even the few Antifederalists who had been Shaysites pledged their support. In the *Hampshire Gazette*, three convention delegates, Consider Arms, Malachi Maynard, and Samuel Field, related that they had opposed the Constitution because it countenanced slavery. In the two years after Shays's Rebellion they had apparently learned a lesson about abiding by established laws. They concluded the explanation of their dissent by writing, "Notwithstanding what has been said, we would not have it understood, that we mean to be disturbers of the peace should the states receive the Constitution; but on the contrary, declare it our intention, as we think it our duty, to be subject to 'the powers that be,' wherever our lot may be cast."[23] That statement was written just two months after ratification and indicates that even many of the "plebeian Antifederalists" were, in fact, aware of a "duty to obey" a ratified Constitution.

Even Patrick Henry's stance changed. According to legend, Henry had refused to attend the Philadelphia Convention because he "smelt a rat," and he fiercely opposed the document in the Virginia Convention. After ratification he still believed that the Constitution needed to be fundamentally altered, going so far as to say that Americans "should seize the first moment offered for shaking off the yoke" of the new government. This was a bolder statement of what the great majority of Antifederalists still believed, that an unamended Constitution was a dangerous framework of government. But how Henry, the most celebrated orator of his time, qualified his position is crucial. The Virginian pledged to "submit as a quiet citizen" to the guidelines that were legally adopted and fight for amendments "in a constitutional way."[24] In other words, the more radical options of ignoring the law, flaunting it, precipitating a revolt, or absenting himself from political affairs in protest were precluded by Henry after ratification. Acquiescences like Henry's indicate that it is misleading to think of the Antifederalists' change in stance primarily as an internal moderation, as many were still firmly against the Constitution's brand of government. It is more precise to think of Antifederalist acquiescence as a turn away from certain forms of political action, a shunning of public actions outside the legally prescribed bounds set by the offending document itself.[25]

Antifederalists in the ratifying states were powerfully affected by the event that made the Constitution law. They could no longer warn the populace about its possible result without adding qualifications—as it had received the sanction of law, good citizens were bound by duty to obey it and to follow its own internal procedures for change. This was far from a belief that everything would "turn out" under the new fundamental law. It was, however, an acknowledgment that certain avenues the Antifederalists might have used to bring about changes were off-limits, declared to be so by the Antifederalists themselves.

"We Are All in Quiet at Present"

The Antifederalists' postratification approach was not lost on proponents of the Constitution. Federalists organizing celebrations took pains to include acquiescent Antifederalist speakers and to encourage yeomen who had opposed the Constitution to march in parades.[26] Private correspondence sent during these months indicated that opposition ended in the ratifying states. At the end of July 1788, George Washington related to James McHenry, "By letters from the Eastern States I am induced to believe the minorities have acquiesced not only with a good grace, but also with a serious design to give the government a fair chance to discover its operation by being carried into effect."[27] In October, John Jay told South Carolinian Edward Rutledge that in New York "the opposition which was violent has daily become more moderate, and the minds of the people will gradually be reconciled to it in proportion as they see the government adminis- tered."[28] Meanwhile news of Southerners' acquiescence spread north- ward. In January 1789, Philadelphia's *Independent Gazetteer* reported that "a gentleman from Virginia, whose information may be relied on, asserts that the controversy between federalists and anti-federalists, which have [*sic*] for some time past distracted and divided the Councils of the several states, has entirely subsided in that quarter, relative to the proposed amendments to the new constitution for the United States."[29]

Not all Federalists were immediately willing to take the Antifederalist acquiescence at face value, however. Virginia's James Gordon, for instance, offered this theory to James Madison: "We are all in quiet at present; there appears to be little or no opposition from the Anties & [I] have been informed they are generally satisfied but I rather think their conduct is intended to lull the friends to the new government into a state of security and then in the fall to make a violent attack."[30] No such attack materialized. For this reason and because professions were contained in private letters, it is reasonable to take them at face value rather than to read a calculating design into them, as Gordon did. Antifederalist elites wanted scrupulously to avoid the stigma of being called Shaysites — a name pinned to any who would flaunt unpopular laws. Admittedly, there was a congruence of principle and interest involved in this avoidance: they fervently believed that laws could not be selectively obeyed; doing so made one a rebel in their minds — a step they were not willing to take. At the same time, Antifederalists knew their reputations and the prospects for amendments might be irreparably harmed if the connection with the Shaysites stuck in the public's collective mind.

Despite Federalist acknowledgments of the opposition's acquiescence in private letters, many pseudonymous newspaper pieces continued to vil- ify the critics of the Constitution. These articles portrayed the Anti- federalists in an unflattering manner to shore up public support for the new system and to ensure Federalist success in the coming elections.[31] The tactics used in these writings shed light on how important respect for the rule of law was to the founding generation as a whole, particularly in the post-Shays's Rebellion political climate. Some pieces intimated that the Antifederalists had not changed their stance after ratification and were considering not abiding by the new system. Others directly compared the opponents to the Shaysites.[32] Faked pseudonymous Antifederalist letters appeared. The most widely reprinted fake letter was one purportedly by "Centinel," the ardent Pennsylvanian who continued to write of "aristocratic conspiracy" in the months after the state ratified. Despite his strident language, the real Centinel never advocated flaunting the law.[33] The fake Centinel reasoned:

Of what service is a man's liberty to him, unless he can do as he pleases? And what man can do as he pleases, who lives under a government?—The very end of government is to bind men down to certain rules and duties; therefore, 'tis only fit for slaves and vassals.—Every freeman ought to govern himself, and then he will be governed most to his own mind. Thus, my friends, you see all government is tyrannical and oppressive.[34]

The impostor Centinel stood for exactly what the vast majority of Antifederalist opinion leaders actively avoided: the notion that laws need not be followed unless they comport with one's individual proclivities. Federalist newspaper salvos like this one were crafted to paint the critics of the Constitution in the worst possible light. It is telling that in it an Antifederalist was portrayed as an unrepentant philosophical anarchist. Many Federalists, no doubt, believed that citizens would find these portrayals credible and, in the process, be repulsed by the Antifederalists' lack of responsibility. The most sensitive political issue during the months between ratification and implementation, it seems, was the frightening potential of selective obedience to the law.

In this climate it was important for the Antifederalists to publicize their actual, changed position, both as a means of saving their own reputations and as a teaching device. Some of them, like the South Carolinians mentioned above, had taken this step immediately after the final vote in their state ratification conventions. Other Antifederalists in positions of authority did likewise. New York Supreme Court Justice Robert Yates, who had quit the Philadelphia Convention in disgust and strenuously opposed unconditional ratification in New York's convention, instructed a grand jury in 1788 that the Constitution's stipulations were law:

We, as good citizens, are bound implicitly to obey them, for the united wisdom of America has sanctioned and confirmed the act, and it would be little short of treason against the republic to hesitate in our obedience and respect. . . . Let me therefore exhort you, gentlemen, not only in your capacity as grand jurors, but in your more durable and equally respectable character as citizens, to preserve inviolate this charter.[35]

Citizens, who for months had been told of the inadequacy of the proposed system, had to be reminded in no uncertain terms that the ground rules had changed, and that with the Constitution sanctioned as law it must be treated as such.

Reminders like Yates's precluded lawless action, but good citizens who still wanted amendments had a recourse: to elect leaders who favored constitutional changes. Thus, as the fall of 1788 progressed, professions of fidelity became coupled with pleas for the election of Antifederalists to the new Congress. "E," writing in the *Boston Gazette*, combined the familiar position that "it has become the duty of good citizens to make a beginning with the Constitution as it is," with this charge:

As the choice of federal Representatives is soon to take place, it is essentially necessary for the good of the Union, that those men be chosen who are most likely to promote the general desire of the people at large — men who are of the persuasion that amendments to the new proposed Constitution are absolutely requisite and necessary to secure the freedom, security, and perfect confidence of every individual throughout the Union.[36]

As a corollary it was argued that Federalists firmly against amendments should be avoided.[37]

Others pointed to the fact that Federalists were not perfectly satisfied with the Constitution either. Why should those who favored amendments be precluded from serving in Congress when Washington, Madison, Franklin, Jay, and Hancock all found parts of the system wanting?[38] Only the unthinking could be perfectly satisfied. Thus the Antifederalist assessments of the Constitution had differed with the Federalists' mainly in degree, not in kind. Many Federalists wanted changes too; the main difference between the two sides was that the Antifederalists had simply urged that defects be remedied prior to implementation. They had risked their reputations in an effort to safeguard American liberty at a time when they could have more safely gone along with the nation's most eminent men.[39]

Many Federalists did not take acquiescences at face value and continued to heap derision on the critics of the Constitution to ensure the success of the new system. To allay fears and reduce uncertainty it was critical that the rather sophisticated Antifederalist stance be disseminated to as wide an audience as possible, so that civil order would be maintained and the fight for amendments from within joined.

The uniformity of Antifederalist acquiescence is best confirmed by their willingness to take oaths in support of the Constitution. The use of oaths and affirmations was crucial to the founding generation — oaths, after all, had been employed extensively to distinguish Patriots from Loyalists in the Revolutionary War. The loyalty oaths taken during the war had been anything but pro forma, and clauses in the Constitution indicate that the founding generation continued to treat these ceremonies with all the seriousness of a "political sacrament," to quote legal historian Sanford Levinson.[40] Taking the oath was a formal acknowledgment of the validity of the transfer of sovereignty from state governments to the new national government. The transference of sovereignty was precisely what the Antifederalists had fought against during the ratification debate. This being the case, Federalists felt oath ceremonies were "linchpins" in making a nation out of a confederated union of states.[41] Once the ratification process had successfully concluded, Antifederalists resigned themselves to the Constitution as law, and so most did not question whether the oaths should be taken, even if it signified a problematic shift of power.

Between ratification and implementation, most states required their elected officials to take oaths in support of the Constitution. The states that had not required their officials to take the oath by August 1789 were told by Congress to do so during their next session. The Oath Act was, in fact, the first law ever passed by the federal government. Refusals to take oaths would likely have been reported in legislative journals, but only very rarely is there an indication that Antifederalists did not comply with the state requirements. The two definitive works on the history of loyalty oaths in the United States barely mention those required of state and national officials in 1789; instead, they skip directly from the Revolutionary War to the nullification crisis of the early 1830s, because almost to a person the Antifederalists willingly took the oaths.[42]

Most extant official records document nothing out of the ordinary during this crucial time period. A typical example is contained in the *Journal of* Virginia's House of Delegates. That body reconvened on October 19, 1789, bound for the first time by the Constitution's stipulations. Their journal simply recorded what it had at the beginning of the previous legislature: "Such members of the House of Delegates as appeared, having taken the oaths prescribed by law, took their seats in the House."[43] The journal of Maryland's House of Delegates similarly reported that with "a sufficient number of delegates being convened, they severally qualified in the presence of each other, by taking the several oaths required by the constitution and the form of government."[44] These journals indicate that the state representatives took multiple oaths. No doubt one of these continued to be to the state oath. Officials in New Hampshire found that their state oath contradicted the one they were to take to the Constitution. Accordingly, New Hampshire removed the words "sovereign and independent" from its state oath and replaced them with the word "confederated." This alteration was not accompanied by controversy, as there was no recorded debate, and the yeas and nays were not called for.[45] Even in Rhode Island, acquiescence was quick and uniform after the state's ratification. After refusing to gather a convention for more than two years, it narrowly approved the Constitution on May 29, 1790. On June 7, acquiescence was unanimous, as the governor, deputy governor, members of the privy council, state representatives, and the state attorney general all took the oath supporting the Constitution.[46]

Two Pennsylvania Antifederalists, John Baird and John Smilie, "required a little time to consider and did not take the oath" at the same time that other members did. Unfortunately, there is no further record of whether they actually decided to take the oath.[47] Smilie, at the very least, became quite accustomed to swearing allegiance to the Constitution, as he became a longtime member of the U.S. House of Representatives. Some months after formulating their oath act, South Carolina's legislature passed a second act stipulating that if officials did not take the required oath to the Constitution they could not engage in official duties. Proponents of the second bill noted that some of their number had not taken the required pledge, and so were not in conformity with the supreme law of the land. Since South Carolina's records named individuals as they took the oath, I determined how much of a problem noncompliance was. I ascertained who was present in the legislative session of 1790 (when the second law passed) by noting all who were present for the final recorded vote of that legislative session.[48] A total of 154 legislators were present. I then checked the daily journal records, making a note of the members who had taken the oath. All but four had complied with the law as of January 20, 1790, when the second measure passed. Just one of these four had voted against the Constitution in the state ratification convention. Two others had been Federalist delegates, and a third was from the same Federalist-oriented district but had not served at the state convention. Those who proposed the South Carolina bill were concerned about noncompliance, but the documentary record indicates that very few failed to comply with the original law, and only one of these individuals was an Antifederalist. On the whole, the Antifederalist willingness to take oaths to the Constitution was so uniform as to be uneventful.

Taking oaths of allegiance was not something the founding generation took lightly. Given their past experience, few Antifederalists felt that pledging to uphold the Constitution as the supreme law of the land was a meaningless ceremony or one they could finesse by performing while simultaneously working to subvert the fundamental law. The Constitution — the unamended Constitution — was not what they wanted, but they felt obligated to take an oath to support it as the law of the land. Almost all who served in an official capacity did.

Exceptions Proving the Rule

Only two other Antifederalists refused to take oaths to the national Constitution, a remarkably small number given the virulence of much of their commentary in 1787 and early 1788. Two who preferred to abandon politics rather than take the oath confirming the Constitution's status as the nation's supreme fundamental law were James Wadsworth of Connecticut and Abraham Yates Jr. of New York, both of whom had served in the Confederation Congress. Connecticut passed its oath act in January 1789, disqualifying any official who refused to swear allegiance to the Constitution. In May, Wadsworth, then a county court judge, resigned from the bench instead of taking the required oath.[49] He wrote Governor Samuel Huntington in October explaining himself. Even though he was flattered by the trust placed in him, the requirement to support the Constitution was too much to bear. Wadsworth "made no Secret of [his] Sentiments touching the Constitution and its Requirements and they are too well known to need any Explanation." He "therefore decline[d] taking the Oath to support the new Constitution."[50] Of course hundreds of Antifederalists had made their sentiments known during the ratification process, but what was unusual was that Wadsworth, unlike his colleagues, felt that nothing had changed after ratification.

The reasoning of Abraham Yates survives in fuller form. Instead of provoking a confrontation with those who would have required him to take an oath, Yates refused to run for reelection to New York's Senate and returned to private life. Yates still hoped that he could convince the people that they had been duped, so he wrote a history of the "conspiracy" that led to the Constitution. Yates argued that there had always been a small but powerful group in American society who favored aristocracy. These men had attempted to control state legislation from the outset of the Revolution, but they had failed, having been consistently outvoted within the states. Realizing that they would never achieve their goals through these accepted channels, the would-be aristocrats orchestrated a change in governments. They did so by converting state leaders to their own aristocratic principles. The conspiracy that culminated in the Constitution began in the early 1780s, when the Continental Congress agreed to entrust the Finance Department to a single superintendent, Robert Morris. Morris proposed that centralized power over finance be significantly augmented. With the war against Britain all but over, he dishonestly argued that major centralizing changes were necessary for the prosecution of the war. Some of his proposals were adopted; others were not, but the idea that the central government could wield uninhibited power over the nation's finances was planted. When the United States slipped into economic depression after independence was achieved, it was good news for the conspirators. By promising that the nation's economy would improve under centralized control, they could justify implementing a wholly new, aristocratically oriented system of government. Undeniably, Yates wrote, this spelled the "death warrant of American liberties."[51]

Though it was not necessarily the norm, it was not unusual for Antifederalists to claim that there were "conspiratorial" actions involved in the formulation of the Constitution. What was unusual in this case was that Yates did not qualify those claims after ratification. He did not weigh the evidence as his colleagues did, finding that popular legitimation outweighed procedural problems and precluded questioning the document's status as law. Instead of pledging to abide by the Constitution while working for amendments, he continued to act as if the document had not received legal sanction. Unlike the great majority of Antifederalist leaders, Yates was so sure that Americans would immediately lose their rights under the Constitution that he figured it made no sense to abide by it or to encourage others to do the same. In his mind, the aristocratic conspirators had already dashed republican government every bit as surely as had the British. With republican government thwarted, the people had nothing to lose and everything to gain by realizing that the new government was a conspiracy. If Yates was persuasive in convincing them, they could at least win back their rights, as they had done in the war for independence. This kind of postratification thinking was so out of step with his counterparts that Yates's biographer writes that he "had all but lost touch with the realities of American politics. . . . The Constitution was a fact, and Abraham Yates would have to resign himself to it."[52]

Yates's history was published for the first time in the *William & Mary Quarterly* in 1963. In introducing the history, neo-Progressive historian Staughton Lynd noted that Yates's perspective on the Constitution's ratification was a lot like Charles Beard's, in that they both focused on economics and upper-class influence. Admittedly, Lynd said, this analysis faltered in some places — but more importantly in his view, Yates's history showed that in 1789 someone was thinking the same way as Progressive thinkers did. "Every essential step in the movement for the United States Constitution as conceived by Charles Beard and Merrill Jensen will be found, dated and footnoted, in this pamphlet of 1789," Lynd excitedly related.[53] There is no doubt that some other Antifederalists were thinking like Abraham Yates and Charles Beard in 1787 and early 1788. But Yates was strikingly alone by 1789.[54]

Though atypical, Yates and the few other Antifederalists who refused to acquiesce in the manner of their colleagues are important in this way: they demonstrate that there were other viable paths open to the critics of the Constitution. Yates, Wadsworth, and the few others like them show that Antifederalists were not invariably forced into an acceptance of the Constitution. The opponents of the new system had the option of refusing to acquiesce en masse. In regions of Antifederalist strength they could have formed their own breakaway republics. Given the highly regional nature of their strength it is quite possible that some of these new states would have survived, and the Union as it had existed since the Declaration of Independence would have been dashed. Perhaps, though, these independent entities would have been forcibly reincorporated into the Union, necessitating civil war. If forcible reincorporation had occurred, there is little doubt that a major portion of the nation's political leadership would have continued to doubt the integrity of the Union and its fundamental law. In this scenario, it is highly unlikely that the Constitution would ever have reached the level of acceptance that fundamental law is designed to achieve. Additionally, instead of urging the populace to peaceably accept what was law, Antifederalist leaders could have encouraged radical protests, like the Carlisle riot. The acquiescent leaders did feel that they had the option of precipitating civil war, but they opted decisively against it.

Alternatively, the Antifederalists could have refused to dirty their hands in the new "aristocratic" system. They could have treated the federal elections as a sham, boycotting them and refusing to send officers to the new government. New Hampshire's Joshua Atherton suggested this tactic.[55] As observers, they could continue to warn against the problematic tendencies of the government and watch as the Federalists either passed the requisite amendments or usurped citizens' rights. If the proper amendments were adopted, the system would become secure. If rights were usurped, as the critics had predicted, it would provide them pretense for a political comeback. When the Federalists trampled the people's rights, the Antifederalists could triumphantly return to restore them, with their political position and historical reputation assured. Although there is evidence that opposition turnout was low, there was no concerted effort to heed Atherton's advice. This frustrated Atherton, who relayed his disgust to New Yorker John Lamb: "In our General Assembly, [where for a] long time there was a decided majority against the new system, opposition has ceased — and the language is 'It is adopted, let us try it.' No slaves could speak a language more agreeable to their masters."[56]

The Antifederalists and Political Responsibility

Antifederalist leaders did not naively trust that popular government would usher in a utopian age, where the citizenry could determine how to govern itself without difficulty. From their perspective, the people were not as well versed in republican political theory as the leaders they chose — Shays's Rebellion had made that clear. So did the rioting in Pennsylvania. Accordingly, during the latter half of 1788, the Antifederalists engaged in a regimen of public education designed to limit the potential for civil unrest in a Union they felt was in a delicate state. In a way, the Antifederalists had contributed to this situation by voicing their grave concerns about the Constitution. Of course they had never meant to inspire civil discord, but they were afraid that their complaints would be taken as a reason to continue opposing the now-legal system. Spurred by their fears and the uncertainty of the times, Antifederalist leaders conveyed a message of political responsibility, which would also make their acquiescence understandable and acceptable. The very fragility felt by these leaders added urgency to their conservative approach to the rule of law, dictating not only a near-uniform postratification acknowledgment of the legality of the Constitution, but indeed a very public one.

To mitigate the possibility of civil disturbance, opinion leaders had to be explicit about the proper response to the changed political scenario. They knew that viable popular government required citizens to accept the legal pronouncements of the community, even when the laws were far from what individual members or factions had wished. A government of the people was qualitatively different from monarchy or aristocracy, where power-holders were sufficiently unitary that governance could well satisfy them. A republic could perfectly satisfy none, for the people were a highly diverse entity. Republican citizenship, the founding generation reasoned, inherently required a kind of "public spirit," which would compel citizens to sublimate their personal desires to the officially sanctioned pronouncement of the polity. This public spirit entailed an awareness of the other voices in the political community and a knowledge that "all particular conceptions and desires will be corrected and restrained by the specific wishes, equal powers, and autonomous conceptions of his fellows."[57] One did not forget one's own political proclivities, nor did the polity simply balance competing interests. Responsible citizens were required in a republic more than altruism or a government that acted as arbiter among those who had no desire or ability to focus on anything but their own goals.

Lance Banning summarizes the attitude of the founding generation toward this "public spirit": "Sound republican decisions were regarded as accommodative in their nature; and after these decisions had been made, the makers were expected to submit themselves to the community's decisions, to obey the law without continual coercion."[58] Banning cites this shared belief as the reason that Thomas Jefferson, democrat and darling of revolutionaries, could be so closely allied with James Madison, advocate of checks on popular rule and friend to conservatives. Their mutual embrace of the public spirit of responsible citizenship softened philosophical differences by leading them to realize that full agreement was not possible, and that those in a free nation needed to come to workable accommodations. That was government. The Antifederalists shared this conception, as evidenced by their acquiescence upon ratification. It is therefore reasonable to extend Banning's conclusion: the very real philosophical differences of Federalists and Antifederalists were mitigated by a mutual embrace of the necessity for accommodation. Peter B. Knupfer concisely states, "Compromise was the expected outcome of republican political action" and "at the heart of the American polity" as the founding generation conceived it.[59]

Given their belief in accommodation and their interest in promoting popular acquiescence after ratification, one might think that Antifederalists were rather blindly wedded to stability as the polestar of politics. But they were not individuals who eschewed every action that might result in civil discord. Most of these figures had actively participated in the Revolution, risking their lives and opting against the tranquility they could have enjoyed under British colonial rule. Colonial government, though, was not *their* government, and the way in which those who became Antifederalists (and others of the revolutionary generation) discerned this was through attention to political process. The legislative process of the English Parliament pronounced policy for the Americans without their input. This was not "republican" according to the founding generation, and so it was illegitimate, worth fighting against and replacing with a governing process that was republican.

In 1787, Antifederalists had feared that the Constitution was aristocratic in its nature and therefore not "of the people." But the process employed in determining whether the Constitution would receive the sanction of law was "of the people" and, therefore, "republican" and legitimate. In the eyes of many opposition leaders, the people had legitimated an aristocratically inclined system. Because the ratification process itself had been sound, there was no recourse but to attempt reform through the newly legitimated system. Outcomes were, therefore, all but meaningless in determining whether law or an entire governmental system was legitimate. In one sense it did not matter how bad the Antifederalists judged the Constitution to be: personal assessments of the law were inconsequential to their status. The only thing that could call a law into question and potentially warrant disobedience was that an improper process sanctioned it.

The Antifederalists deemed the process proper, despite some procedural irregularities: the Philadelphia Convention had exceeded its commission; the backcountry was significantly underrepresented in several state conventions; the press was overwhelmingly Federalist and often unfair in its characterizations of the opposition; mail tampering had occurred, sometimes preventing Antifederalists from disseminating their message; and the proper mechanism for altering the Articles of Confederation had been circumvented. Had the Antifederalists wanted to, they could have selected out enough evidence of this type to make a case against the validity of the ratification process. This position would have saved face for the Antifederalist leaders, as invested as they were in the position that the Constitution was defective.

In accepting the legality of the Constitution, its critics exposed themselves to a charge that is often fatal in elective politics: to use modern language, the Antifederalists left themselves open to being called "flip-floppers." The ratification generation knew these politicians as "trimmers." Trimmers were those who followed the public in its whims to cultivate personal popularity, power, and fame. They eschewed both seeking the good of the nation, which required consistency, and taking unpopular stances. Fear led them to choose what they felt was the only responsible route: moderating their stance despite consequences damaging to their reputations. Ironically, then, the Antifederalists were charged with being trimmers precisely when they were not trimming. Many fell victim to this charge.[60] But in their minds, arguing that the entire ratification process was invalid would have been an irresponsible, selfish, and partial weighing of the evidence, not to mention dangerous in that it would leave the nation without a legitimate framework of governance. Taken as a whole, the validity of the process was not compromised enough to risk civil war.

The preceding statement should not be misunderstood. The Constitution itself *did* risk civil war in Antifederalist minds, but the threat was probably not immediate if they themselves calmed people down and urged compliance. The administrators of an unamended Constitution, even if they were committed aristocrats, would probably not dare tyrannize over the people immediately, for American citizens were too accustomed to civil liberties, and the push for amendments had been too strong to attempt wholesale, usurping changes right away. But surely aristocratic measures would eventually result from an unchanged aristocratic frame of government. Once that happened, the people would likely not stand for it. In the meantime, however, the friends of amendments had a legal recourse: to change the Constitution according to the process stipulated in Article V. And as long as a legal channel existed, Enlightenment-era political theory dictated that illegal action or revolt was not legitimate.[61]

Conclusion

Some time between Massachusetts's ratification, the sixth state to do so, and that of Maryland, Mercy Otis Warren published a pamphlet under the pseudonym "A Columbian Patriot."[62] The pamphlet strongly urged that the Constitution be amended prior to adoption by nine states. Warren, the sister of early Patriot James Otis and wife of the Speaker of Massachusetts's House of Representatives, wrote, "The very suggestion, that we ought to trust to the precarious hope of amendments and redress, after we have voluntarily fixed the shackles on our own necks should have awakened [us] to a double degree of caution."[63] American citizens needed guarantees that they would not be shackled, literally and figuratively, by the new system of government. A second constitutional convention could remedy the nation's troubles by proposing requisite amendments, provided that "a spirit of moderation . . . [prevailed] on both sides."[64]

Warren conjectured that nine states would probably not even approve of the document because the people were too jealous of their rights, but she left the possibility for ratification open. In the event nine states adopted the Constitution as it stood, "A Columbian Patriot" and other Antifederalist leaders would have to turn inward. After ratification the "philosophic lovers of freedom who have wept over her exit" would have to "retire to the calm shades of contemplation." In these calm shades "they may look down with pity on the inconsistency of human nature, the revolutions of states, the rise of kingdoms, and the fall of empires."[65] The refuge of the defeated Antifederalist was not the battlefield, it was the mind. In writing her pamphlet Warren transgressed the eighteenth-century taboo against a woman's participation in political debates. On the issue of political responsibility, however, she was quite orthodox. Like other Antifederalists she believed that opinion leaders who were unsuccessful in persuading free citizens should not provoke civil strife, but resign themselves to the decision of the polity. The progression of constitutional time revealed the Antifederalist movement was as a whole, like Warren, decidedly unradical in nature.

The scenario Warren dreaded did transpire: the Constitution was adopted without prior amendments. Years later, the Massachusetts native reflected that amendments recommended by her state and others were, in fact, tremendously beneficial in restraining "monarchical" influences and in leading to the ratification of a bill of rights. But even with amendments, the first fifteen years under the Constitution were defined by "a struggle . . . between monarchists and republicans."[66] This was not the fault of the Constitution; Warren's epic three-volume *History of the Rise, Progress and Termination of the American Revolution* made that perfectly clear. In these volumes Warren commented directly on the now-amended Constitution she had thought so defective in early 1788. Her embrace turned out to be anything but reluctant. "Perhaps genius has never devised a system more congenial to [the people's] wishes, or better adapted to the condition of man, than the American constitution," she wrote.[67] "It is at present period as wise, as efficient, as respectable, as free, and we hope as permanent, as any constitution existing on earth."[68] Yes, many of the framers of the document had had "monarchical" tendencies. In fact, the forces of monarchy were so prominent at Philadelphia that they created a centralized government without safeguarding citizens' rights or reserving power to the states. But the genius of a republican people reminded these leaders that they could not get away with instituting a monarchical government in the United States. So amendments were passed, and with these changes, America's fundamental law became one of the best, if not *the* best known to humankind, according to Warren. The ten amendments to the Constitution addressed Warren's concerns by guaranteeing the rights Americans had come to find indispensable and by reserving powers not enumerated to the states and the people. With these two major problems remedied, the Constitution clearly became a barrier against tyranny rather than a prescription for one, wrote "A Columbian Patriot." Accordingly, she hoped that nothing would disrupt its operation and reminded her readers that good citizenship required "a strict adherence" to its bounds. If flaunted, the Americans would lose "the best security of the rights and liberties of a country that has bled at every vein, to purchase and transmit them to posterity."[69] Thus the fundamental law that Warren said threatened the United States's revolutionary accomplishment turned into that which fulfilled the Revolution's promise. Even after passage of the Bill of Rights, many, including Patrick Henry, wished to change the structure of the new government.[70] Even so, those like Henry who wanted further changes abided by the Constitution as it was, agreed that the only legitimate method of change was through constitutional means, and ultimately resigned themselves to be bound by the results of the political process — just like their colleagues, and just like the defeated Federalists would eventually do in 1800. Even the most ardent of Antifederalists opted for what they felt was the only politically responsible path and chose to work for reform from within the system they had strenuously opposed as a proposal.

The moderate nature of the Antifederalists' thinking is striking, not only because they had been revolutionaries, but because immediately upon ratification they continued to feel that the Constitution was a prescription for tyranny. This devotion to the rule of law generated by republican political processes was born of a convergence of fear and ideology — government was absolutely necessary and no government could operate without mutually agreed upon rules. The Constitution was accepted as legal, and the event around which that process pivoted was the ninth ratification, not the first federal election, not the Harrisburg

Convention, not the passage of the Bill of Rights or opposition to Hamilton's fiscal program. Ratification advanced constitutional time, changing the context faced by the Antifederalists, prompting a new response to the Constitution. Disagreement over policies and disagreement over what the Constitution meant did not, of course, cease. But disagreement over the Constitution's legal status and the proper method for reforming it did.

The observations of Linda Grant De Pauw and Lance Banning indicate that soon after ratification there was something more to the Antifederalists' approach to the nation's new fundamental law than "acquiescence." Resigned acceptance turned into "worship," to use De Pauw's word, and "apotheosis" according to Banning. The connection between the former Antifederalists and the Constitution quickly became so tight that these authors find only religious terminology successfully describes the connection. As a devout Christian, Mercy Otis Warren might remind these authors that worship was to be reserved for God and not applied to political systems. Yet her sentiments toward the Constitution accurately represent the kind of tight identification that Banning and De Pauw discern. Warren's praise for strict adherence to the document is, of course, no accident. Already by the beginning of the First Congress former Antifederalists were using the Constitution as the measuring stick to determine whether Federalist proposals were legitimate or not. During the "Age of Federalism" government policies were often found wanting by the former Antifederalists, turned "Republicans," because authorization for them was not explicitly contained in the Constitution. They viewed these policies as unconstitutional, coming to believe that they themselves were more faithful to the Constitution than those who had written and championed it. Thus the familiar dialectic between strict constructionist interpretations of the Constitution and their alternative was born. This development is an important part of apotheosis, but it is not the complete story, as Lance Banning believes it to be. One cannot imagine a continued embrace of the Constitution as it kept degenerating absent some hope by the opposition that they themselves might one day right the constitutional ship, for instance. A Madisonian-Antifederalist alliance was virtually prefigured by their constitutional philosophies. Together their combined strength allowed them to pursue an electoral remedy to Federalist politics rather than a radical, unconstitutional remedy. Additionally, the legislative procedures employed in Congress, even by the Federalists, were sufficiently acceptable to the Antifederalists to keep them from contemplating extraconstitutional solutions. On to apotheosis.

CHAPTER THREE

Refuge of the Resigned

The Postratification Constitutional Thought
of Congressional Antifederalists

If late 1788 and early 1789 can be characterized by a reluctant but uniform acquiescence by Antifederalist leaders, the time after implementation brought something different, and for lack of a better word, stronger. These officials began to use the Constitution as a refuge from and a bulwark against activist Federalist policies. Ironically, they did so by employing Federalist theories. During the ratification debate Federalists defended the Constitution by arguing that it granted the national government expressed powers only; any power not specifically written into the document was not to be exercised by the national government. After ratification, the adoption of this philosophy enabled Antifederalists to dispute many Federalist policies on constitutional grounds. This was the first time "strict construction" and "original intent" were used to determine constitutionality. Although Federalists sometimes employed these arguments as well, it was the Antifederalist contingent in Congress that pioneered their application. The opposition generally lost out in trying to determine public policy, but the Antifederalists did establish themselves as major players in the contest to define the meaning of the Constitution. A version of their view that the Federalists had abandoned the doctrine of "expressed powers" was shared by Madison and others who defected from the Federalists. The new "Republican" coalition's constitutional ideas would serve as a dominant paradigm for a generation and still exerts at least a powerful rhetorical and mythological appeal.

In essence, a strong oppositionist ideology based on constitutional argument was ready-made for the former Antifederalists' adoption. It had the distinct advantages of being a critique from within the bounds of the legal Constitution and being endorsed (at least during the ratification debate) by the Federalists themselves.

Table 3.1 lists each of the Antifederalists elected to the First Congress along with some basic information: state of origin, date of election, frequency of speaking in floor debates, the number of committees served on, and electoral fate after the First Congress. Although this information is important for a variety of reasons, one reason is important to note now. The data help to explain why some of the Antifederalists figure more prominently in this chapter than others. Elbridge Gerry, for instance, commented on nearly every subject taken up by the First Congress, often with reference to constitutional theory. John Hathorn, by contrast, never spoke on the floor of the House, nor did he perform significant committee service. In their thinking and writing immediately before the implementation of the Constitution the Antifederalists elected to the First Congress displayed a wide variety of attitudes about the prospects for the government and how to proceed in the national legislature. Despite this diversity, they uniformly accepted the Constitution's legality. Furthermore, the Antifederalists were unusually disadvantaged by the first federal elections. Their weakness, in turn, dictated a reliance on constitutional argumentation that at least theoretically exists above and outside of majoritarian considerations, where they could not successfully compete with the Federalists. Such argumentation also made sense because of past history, particularly the American colonies' experience with charters and the most well publicized argument in defense of the Constitution during the ratification debates. The constitutional arguments made by Antifederalists in the First Congress, though not particularly systematic or philosophically coherent, were "originalist" arguments that set the groundwork for the Jeffersonian Republicans' later elaboration of that constitutional philosophy. The advance in constitutional time from ratification to implementation began the process of apotheosis, the stronger and less revocable embrace of the Constitution, through the articulation of an oppositionist constitutional philosophy offered within the bounds of the document itself.

Congressional Antifederalists:
Ratification to Implementation

Even when contests for the First Congress were in full swing, few records of what individuals thought exist because campaigning was considered unseemly. The Antifederalists who would be elected to Congress were very much divided over what to do about amendments, their level of fear

TABLE 3.1
Antifederalists Elected to the First Congress

	State	Elected	Speeches[b]	Committees[c]	After F.C.
HOUSE					
Jonathan Grout	MA	3-2-89	one	2	defeated
Elbridge Gerry	MA	1-29-89	very many	25	reelected
John Hathorn	NY	3-4-89[a]	none	1	declined
Jeremiah Van Rensselaer	NY	3-4-89[a]	none	5	defeated
Theodorick Bland	VA	2-2-89	many	7	died[d]
Isaac Coles	VA	2-2-89	none	5	declined
Josiah Parker	VA	2-2-89	few	17	reelected
Timothy Bloodworth	NC	2-5-90[a]	few	6	defeated
Aedanus Burke	SC	11-25-88[a]	many	32	declined
Thomas Sumter	SC	11-25-88[a]	few	4	reelected
Thomas Tudor Tucker	SC	11-25-88[a]	many	31	reelected
SENATE					
Richard Henry Lee	VA	11-8-88	many	32	resigned[e]
William Grayson	VA	11-8-88	few	2	died[f]
Joseph Stanton Jr.	RI	6-12-90	none	1	full term[g]
James Monroe	VA	11-9-90	few	7	reelected[h]

SOURCE: Compiled by author.

[a]These elections were held over a two-day period. The day listed is the second day polls were open. Given the era, it was not until days, sometimes weeks, later that a winner was confirmed.

[b]This column contains an assessment of the number of floor speeches given by each member. It is based on categorizations in Bowling's "Politics in the First Congress, 1789–1791" and the biographies in the 14th volume of the *Documentary History of the First Federal Congress*.

[c]The number of select committees served on are contained in the biographies in volume 14 of the *DHFFC*.

[d]Bland died on June 1, 1790.

[e]Richard Henry Lee's health was poor throughout his tenure in Congress. He served the entire First Congress but was absent for most of the second and third sessions. Lee had drawn a four-year term, so his tenure carried over into the Second Congress. Continued ill health led him to resign on October 8, 1792, before his term expired.

[f]Grayson died on March 12, 1790, never having made it to the second session of Congress.

[g]Stanton took his seat on June 25, 1790. His term ended with the Second Congress. He was not reelected.

[h]Monroe, selected to serve the final months of Grayson's term, was "reelected" to a full six-year term early in 1791. He resigned his Senate seat in 1794, having been appointed envoy to France by President Washington.

over disunion and a host of other issues. Additionally, as the nation turned from the more abstracted debate over constitutionalism to the prospect of governing, the pulls of state and region grew stronger. Nevertheless, they remained uniformly acquiescent and prepared to help administer the new government and press for amendments in good faith.

After learning of New York's ratification, Elbridge Gerry wrote to his wife that he was pleased.[1] Above all, Gerry feared the imminent possibility of disunion and civil war stemming from the divisiveness of the ratification debates and the sectional nature of allegiances.[2] New York's accession lessened this danger considerably. It also gave added impetus to the quest for amendments. Ratification had altered his approach. It meant that "every citizen of the ratifying states is in duty bound to support [the Constitution], and that an opposition to a due administration of it would not only be unjustifiable, but highly criminal."[3] Also, the new government had to be successfully launched before amendments could be passed. Gerry was sure that if the new government faltered, union was precluded. Given this view, he boldly stated (during the First Congress) that "the salvation of America depends on the establishment of this government, whether amended or not."[4]

Few of the former Antifederalists would have phrased the young nation's plight quite that way. Rather, they were primarily worried that an unamended Constitution would impede lasting union. The latter view was especially prevalent among Southern Antifederalists, like William Grayson. In the absence of changes, Southerners feared domination by the Northern states, which held an eight-to-five numerical advantage. Some provisions had been written into the Constitution to ease the fears of Southerners; the slave trade, for instance, could not be outlawed by Congress before 1808.[5] But these few measures were not thought sufficient by Southern Antifederalists. Especially troubling was the North's ability, through a simple majority vote, to pass commercial legislation favoring its own shipping interests at the expense of the agrarian South.

Grayson died after attending the first session of Congress. To complete his term, the Virginia legislature selected his dashing young cousin, Revolutionary War hero James Monroe.[6] Monroe had been an unsuccessful and reluctant candidate for the House in the first federal elections. Patrick Henry had prevailed upon him to run against James Madison. Madison was Monroe's friend, and the latter was nowhere near as partisan as Henry, so he confided after the election that it "would have given me concern to have excluded [Madison]."[7] Amendments were the main issue in the Madison-Monroe race. However, as Madison had come to think they were necessary to calm well-meaning Antifederalists, the issue did not fundamentally divide the candidates.

Monroe himself had been something of an oddity for an Antifederalist. He sincerely hoped that a nation could be made of the various states, but he also felt that the time was not yet right, as the states were just too different to be successfully governed by a centralized government. Absent giving the states broad autonomy, which he felt the Constitution did not, a viable union was a chancy proposition.[8] But shortly after Virginia ratified Monroe was optimistic about the Union. Writing to Thomas Jefferson, his former law teacher, Monroe happily reported that Virginia's narrow acceptance was accompanied by a spirit of moderation. The Federalists did not rejoice too much, nor were the Antifederalists depressed, because both sides felt that accommodation would be required.[9] Monroe was also encouraged that eleven states ratified, perhaps finding it evidence disconfirming the theory that the states were not ready for nationhood.

When the federal government got under way, Monroe was back in Virginia, a private citizen. As the first news of Congress's proceedings trickled back from New York, he wrote to Madison: "We are happy to find that both branches of the legislature have formed a house; that the President and vice president are summoned to fill the Executive department, and flatter ourselves that the government will immediately commence its operations."[10] Monroe was not alone among Antifederalists in being relieved that the new government was operational. Since ratification, the Confederation Congress (never known for its efficiency) was a crippled institution. The Congress never attained a quorum in its final session and so could not deal with any of the nation's pressing issues. Since Antifederalist politicians had always been as firmly convinced as the Federalists of the absolute need for government, both groups were concerned about the lack of effective governing by the Confederation Congress in its "lame-duck" session. They hoped a viable government would soon be in place. Administration of the Constitution was an inevitability, and the sooner the new government commenced its operations, the sooner amendments could be formulated and passed.[11]

Not all Antifederalists were as moderate as Gerry and Monroe, but none of those who would populate the First Congress publicly doubted that the Constitution had to be treated as law. South Carolinian Aedanus Burke would prove himself to be the most disgruntled member of the opposition in the initial Congress. Because of malapportionment that underrepresented the primarily Antifederalist frontier areas, Burke estimated that the Constitution had passed despite at least "four-fifths" of South Carolinians being Antifederal.[12] A month after South Carolina's ratification, Burke still felt that a majority of citizens were against the Constitution. Continued popular disgust led him to believe that the "government rests on a very sandy foundation."[13] The people of the backcountry, he was convinced, would try to ruin the new government. They could not do so alone. Successfully thwarting the Constitution required the backing of a prominent state; if either Virginia or New York refused to ratify, Burke was convinced that "the system will fall to pieces." However, he strongly suspected both states would ratify. If they did, he told John Lamb, "you, and I, and all of us, will be obliged to take it, as we take our Wives, 'for better, [or] for worse.'"[14] Apparently, even Burke reminded the disgruntled South Carolina rank-and-file of their duty to acquiesce to a ratified Constitution. A book of *Anecdotes of the Revolutionary War in America*, published in 1822, related that Burke encountered several unrepentant Antifederalist sympathizers in a wagon train bound for Charleston. These men were so insistent that the Constitution would prove harmful that they pledged not to respond if the president were to call out the militia. "When Burke remonstrated on their duty to their country, they forced him to ride alone at the end of the line."[15]

Virginia's Theodorick Bland was similarly resigned. "Not lightly, unadvisedly, or wantonly did I take up my opinion with regard to the new Constitution," he explained. An early proponent of amendments, his predilections received confirmation from those like Richard Henry Lee and Patrick Henry. Bland emphasized that the Antifederalists should present a united front. Working together "may enable us . . . to stem the Torrent, which bids fair to bear down every thing before it." Ratification might mean a change in approach, but it did not dictate a change in Antifederalist principles: "The Virtuous Principles which have dictated our political opinions, I trust, do still remain in full vigor in the breasts of some of us, and will I hope lead us to exertions which will in the end render that government secure and harmless, which in its outset threatens Tyranny and oppression."[16]

Once elected, Bland hinted that South Carolinian Thomas Tudor Tucker should nominate him for the Speakership.[17] Bland arrived too late to be considered for the post, but his chances of being chosen Speaker were slim anyway.[18] Bland was not as moderate as someone like Gerry, and so would have had little if any Federalist support for the post. Gerry, by contrast, might have been selected as Speaker if he desired the position, partly because of his more moderate views, and partly because of his prominence.[19] At the same time, it is important to identify the way in which men like Bland and Burke were less moderate than Gerry or Monroe. The latter two feared that union might prove unsuccessful because new governments were inherently unstable. If the Union faltered, there would be immediate, serious ills — perhaps even civil war. It was imperative, then, that the new government be successfully initiated; when the nation was out of immediate danger, the Constitution could be amended. Amendment was still a prevalent part of their long-term outlook, of course, as they felt representative government could not be maintained without changes. But their rhetoric reflected an immediate interest in successfully christening the new government, which happened to not yet be amended.

Meanwhile Bland and Burke emphasized that the unamended Constitution itself threatened to dash the Union forthwith. Bland was convinced that the descent into tyranny under the new government would be rapid. Every moment without amendments threatened free government. Burke's experience in South Carolina led him to believe that the unamended Constitution was being forced on a still unwilling populace. The only way the new government could gain the confidence of the people was by amending it. One could not set the new government on a firm foundation without first altering it.[20] Antifederalists like Bland and Burke sounded less moderate because they did not think that successful implementation of the Constitution was a necessary prerequisite for amending. Former Antifederalists disagreed, then, over how much a priority amending was early in 1789. What they did not disagree about was the necessity of changing the Constitution. Another matter on which they did not disagree was the necessity of following the law, including the amending procedures spelled out in Article V. No Antifederalist who was elected to the First Congress suggested that amendment (or anything else) be accomplished through extraconstitutional means.

Electoral Results and the Tactics of Weakness

Since ratification had been achieved only with the attachment of recommendatory amendments in five states and two states had refused to ratify, there was reason to believe that opponents of the plan were a nationwide majority, or at least nearly so. But for a variety of reasons, the Antifederalists fared poorly in the first congressional elections. North Carolina and Rhode Island refused to join the new government before amendments were formulated. In so doing, they likely deprived the new Congress of a significant number of Antifederalist votes in the first and second sessions. When they finally did enter the Union, the Antifederalists there were viewed as out of step with political reality and discredited. Voter turnout was low when elections were eventually held, but those who were enthusiastic about the new government did not stay away from the polls, and so were able to elect Federalists to Congress. Both states had but a single Antifederalist in their delegation: Senator Joseph Stanton Jr. from Rhode Island and Representative Timothy Bloodworth from North Carolina. Stanton and Bloodworth took their seats midway through the second session. Two of ten potential members was a very disappointing showing for Antifederalist leaders in the pair of states where sentiment against the Constitution ran highest.

Antifederalists were discredited elsewhere as well, leading to poor showings.[21] Even though they had successfully focused debate on the potential flaws of the plan, Antifederalists were considered the "losers," by many. The Federalist-dominated press, so instrumental in achieving ratification, successfully convinced voters to allow Federalists to administer the new government. They reasoned that those who were in favor of the document all along would be best suited to govern under it. Given their opposition, others might be tempted to sabotage the new government. The results of state elections during 1787, 1788, and 1789 reflected that there had been some kind of "critical shift" in the thinking of the populace. Federalists made advances in almost all of the state legislatures during these years, vaulting into a majority in several states where they had been the weaker group for years.[22] In five states the critical shift was enough to provide impetus for new state constitutions.[23]

So while the Antifederalists initially thought they might do fairly well in the first federal elections, as 1788 wore on, there was reason to become increasingly pessimistic. On June 20, 1788, Jonathan Trumbull Jr. made a comment to George Washington that could be applied to the nation as a whole just a few months later: "The Triumph of Federalism has been great in Connecticut since last winter. The opposition which then existed has dwindled into mere unimportance."[24] The shift to Federalist dominance of state legislatures is best indicated by their selection of U.S. senators. Only one state of the original eleven, Virginia, sent Antifederalist senators to New York City. The two Virginians selected, Richard Henry Lee and William Grayson, were in such poor health that on some days neither was in the chamber. Eventually Rhode Island would add Stanton, and Monroe would come to replace the deceased Grayson, so during the brief third session, as many as three of the nation's twenty-six senators were former Antifederalists.

New York Antifederalists, who had seemed a firm majority until ratification, failed to send any of their number to the Senate. Stubbornness and divided government were to blame. The opposing sides were unable to decide how to elect senators in 1788, when the Federalists held a narrow majority in the state senate and the Clintonian Antifederalists dominated the assembly. Both sides hoped to sweep the 1789 elections, which would have allowed them to appoint both senators. In the 1789 elections, the Federalists retained their majority in the senate and gained a two-thirds majority in the assembly, allowing them to elect Federalists Rufus King and Philip Schuyler.

The opposition's poor showing was not due solely to an attitudinal shift reflected in House balloting and the composition of state legislatures; there were also structural reasons involved. Each state had the option of selecting at-large House delegations or forming representative districts. Selecting one plan of representation over the other had a profound effect on certain states' delegations. Pennsylvania's Federalist legislature chose to hold at-large elections, confident that they were a majority statewide. If the state would have been split up into districts, it was certain that Antifederalists would have been elected from several of the western districts. At-large representation virtually ensured that the Pennsylvania delegation would be uniformly Federalist, as it indeed turned out to be. New Hampshire, which during the ratification period had been nearly evenly split between supporters of the Constitution and detractors, also opted for at-large representation. Antifederalist support had dwindled sufficiently in the months following ratification that Federalists had no trouble sweeping the state's three seats. Although the Antifederalists had been less of a force in Connecticut during the ratification debates, the state legislature ensured an all-Federalist delegation by choosing at-large representation.

In South Carolina, an at-large delegation might have benefited the Antifederalists. If Aedanus Burke's assessment of popular sentiment after ratification was even close to being correct, all five representatives from such an election would have been Antifederalists. But splitting the state into districts, as the state legislature did, almost assured Federalists that representatives from coastal districts would be friends of the Constitution.[25] The newly Federalist Massachusetts legislature opted for district elections as well, conceding that some representatives would be Antifederalists. The Federalists attempted to maximize their presence by making sure that "the districts established favored the eastern part of the state over the populous, rural middle and western counties which had voted against the Constitution."[26] Maryland elected representatives using a unique hybrid system that returned a delegation without Antifederalists. The state was divided into six districts, and each district was to be represented by an inhabitant. Each eligible citizen cast a ballot for every district race, meaning that each cast six votes. Since the Federalists were a decided majority in the state, their ticket prevailed.

The critical shift in the electorate toward Federalists compounded their success. There was the obvious benefit of voters being more disposed to electing Federalist representatives, of course. But the electorate also chose Federalists for state legislatures, who in turn selected Federalist U.S. senators. These same state majorities crafted election laws that benefited their side. The electoral deck was stacked against the Antifederalists from the outset, and only a few well-known individuals and those from solidly Antifederalist regions were able to overcome these impediments. The result was a Federalist landslide that had been unimaginable only a few months before.

The Antifederalists were outnumbered five to one in the House and by an even greater ratio in the Senate. They could not hope to win policy disputes by outvoting Federalists. Even an ability to deliver decisive margins on legislation was in doubt, and with that, any hope of obtaining important concessions. In light of their numerical weakness, pressing for favored alternatives simply by arguing their superiority as public policy could not normally be expected to have a serious impact. Indeed, "strict construction" appeals most often to politicians in a position of weakness who are seeking a defensive refuge. Stanley Elkins and Eric McKitrick write that strict construction "marks the point at which one prefers to see the Constitution not as a sanction for achieving one's own ends but as a protection against those designs of others which have come to be seen as usurping and corrupting."[27] Antifederalists were already disposed to seek "protection" because of their wish to avoid a federal policy altogether on certain matters. Given their acquiescence, finding a way to do so within constitutional bounds was very important. Arguing that the Constitution should be followed strictly served as something of a refuge, allowing the Antifederalists to pursue (in a different and restricted way) what they had attempted to achieve during the ratification debates: the placement of limits on the scope and reach of the new national government.

When former Antifederalists, and occasionally Federalists, endorsed what we now call strict construction and original intent in the First Congress, they made the case that theirs was a closer, more literal, and more faithful reading of the Constitution than that offered (or implied) by their opponents. This gambit of embracing the Constitution in a "strong" sense might seem a strange and perhaps ultimately counterproductive way to attempt to limit the power the Constitution conferred on the national government. Their position might easily be mistaken for an unequivocal endorsement. In fact, they were clinging to the Constitution because they were still wary that it could allow centralized power to be extended and abused. There were, however, several reasons why this "strong endorsement" was logical in the altered context they faced.

Couching one's argument in constitutional terms added a new layer of debate, one less susceptible to being overwhelmed and forgotten. Antifederalists arguing for strict adherence to the Constitution could still expect to be outvoted in the legislature, and thus lose on the policy level, but they could at least momentarily succeed in refocusing discussion to the proper scope of government and the powers that were potentially not authorized under the new Constitution. Even after policies were passed, with their alternatives predictably overwhelmed, their critique lingered, for it was a critique that existed outside of and above the policy realm, as a first-order challenge to the legitimacy of the policy.

The Antifederalist delegation was not only small, it was split internally by the nature of the issues raised in the First Congress. The most crucial of these issues divided members sectionally or along state lines more than they did along the Federalist-Antifederalist ideological divide. No longer could national power be discussed primarily as an abstract concept; state and regional interests necessarily implicated themselves in the representatives' decision-making process, dividing those who had been against the Constitution. The federal assumption of state Revolutionary War debts is a good example. Assumption would require an active federal taxation policy to successfully retire the debt, precisely the kind of precedent Antifederalists would want to avoid setting in the first days of the new administration. But Antifederalist representatives could not ignore the debt burden of their own individual state in assessing their policy options. Because of their state's crushing debt, South Carolina's Antifederalists all voted for assumption, despite its implications for national power.[28] Nor could elected officials ignore the people to whom the debt was owed. Gerry and Grout, the Massachusetts Antifederalists, supported assumption because of the numerous payments owed to citizens of their state.[29] For years these citizens had awaited payment from the states—federal government intervention would ensure they would be paid.

As soon as the focus of political debate switched from more abstract questions to actual, embedded political issues, the Antifederalists were fragmented. This fragmentation accentuated their minority status, reducing any slim hope that they could have a major impact disputing Federalist policy on pragmatic grounds. Being a small, fragmented minority probably reduced incentives to moderate views to gain valuable concessions, because the concessions simply could not be gained. Raising a constitutional issue was the best way that a very small group of representatives, or even a single individual, could make the rest of the chamber take notice and treat their argument seriously, for constitutional arguments had to be refuted. If they were not, the legitimacy of the government's products would not be adequately established. Refuting constitutional attacks inevitably put the Federalists on the defensive, a position they did not deal with as well as their offensive pursuit of ratification. Antifederalist numerical weakness thus led to the adoption of a first-order critique of Federalist policies based on strict adherence to the Constitution's words and the philosophy of expressed powers that Federalists themselves had espoused during the ratification debate. But over and above numerical weakness and fragmentation, the Antifederalists could adopt such a stance because of America's historical experience. From colonial times to their own, a vocabulary of opposition based on strict adherence to a fundamental document had developed.

Developing the Vocabulary of Strict Construction

Besides numerical weakness, there were very good historical reasons why the Antifederalists chose to challenge Federalists the way they did. Although the British thought of their constitution as organic and evolutionary, the Americans had come to believe in constitutions as fixed codes that set the standards of good government.[30] Given this later assumption, deviation from a constitution was a grave political ill. If anything could prevent this deviation, strict adherence to its guidelines could. Such was the thinking of the Antifederalists.

The development of this belief was rooted in the sheer distance of the American colonies from the center of the empire. Instructions took months in their transatlantic voyages. The crown simply could not respond to the political needs of the colonies fast enough to micromanage governance there. Kings could have vested early royal governors with dictatorial powers, but in certain cases they feared that that arrangement would stifle incentives to settle in the colonies, jeopardizing their chances of success from the start. Accordingly, early in their existence some British colonies received royal charters, written documents that sanctioned popularly elected local assemblies and spelled out other privileges of self-government.[31]

Officially these self-governing privileges were always tenuous, because the king claimed that colonists enjoyed them entirely "by royal grace and favor," not as a matter of right.[32] Yet the grants contained in a royal charter seemed permanent to the colonists, the unchanging language of a charter a testament to its immutability. Though it may have been a misunderstanding on their part, settlers believed that royal charters provided a static bulwark against usurpation of their right to home rule. This sense developed in light of periodic attempts to limit colonial autonomy. The most notable of these attempts came in the 1680s, when James II temporarily established the "Dominion of New England" by revoking the charters of Massachusetts, Plymouth Bay, Connecticut, and Rhode Island via complicated legal proceedings, and then combining these four colonies with New Hampshire and New York, already under royal control.[33]

However, King James was deposed from the English throne by the Glorious Revolution. Immediately after James fled, there had been hope in London that close control of the American colonies could be maintained, but events dictated otherwise. James invaded Ireland, and the English were again engaged with France on the Continent, necessitating that the government concentrate its efforts close to the core of the empire. As a way of quickly pacifying the colonies, still unsettled from sympathetic revolts, old colonial boundaries were reinstated, and charters were reissued.[34] Colonists thenceforward felt that the Glorious Revolution was a triumph for the American colonies just as much as it was for England. Charters had proven their worth as barriers; the "rights" contained therein had proven inviolable against a usurper. In short, to the colonists, written charters were "the greatest security that could be had in human affairs."[35]

The colonies with royal charters, Massachusetts, Connecticut, and Rhode Island, were the envy of America. Their citizens' broad freedoms were attributed to their founding document. "It was precisely because the three leading New England Colonies had been founded upon the charter principle and had retained their charters that New England was more secure in her freedom than other sections," thought the colonists.[36] Aggrieved citizens in chartered colonies pointed to the actual wording of their charter and the practices justified by it in their attempts to stave off encroachments on home rule. Colonists elsewhere did not have this same recourse, but attempted to approximate it by framing bills of rights. Because of the perceived success of royal charters, colonial Americans "had a seemingly irresistible urge to codify their rights and privileges," something attempted only under extraordinary circumstances in England.[37] Well before the Constitution was implemented, well before anyone even contemplated independence, Americans were accustomed to the idea that the words of a constitutional document could be used as a limit on unwarranted extensions of governmental power.

When Parliament asserted control over the colonies after 1763, colonists attempted to convince the British of the illegitimacy of parliamentary authority in the New World. Envoys were sent to justify the colonial case, and letters were circulated publicizing the cause. These letters are as remarkable for their constitutional theories as they are for their position on the offending duties passed by Parliament. A public letter written by the Massachusetts House of Representatives in February 1768, for example, states, "In all free states the constitution is fixed; and as the supreme legislative derives its power and authority from the constitution, it cannot overleap the bounds of it, without destroying its own foundation."[38] This was the American orthodoxy in a nutshell. A constitution is distinct from and antecedent to institutions of government. It is very possible that institutions will transgress limits set down in the constitution, and when they do, they annul their proper authority.[39] By corollary, those who properly understand the requirements of the constitution are necessarily in the right.

This kind of argument was never highly convincing to the English, mainly because this constitutional theory simply did not square with that espoused in the mother country. The British felt that acts of Parliament could be unconstitutional if they defied past practice, but there was no doubt that Parliament had the authority to pass such acts. When an unconstitutional act was approved, the people had no "constitutional" recourse, just a political one: they could attempt to elect representatives who took more care with the constitution of England.[40] Americans thought differently.

When it came time to form governments of their own, the revolutionaries realized their ideals by framing written governing documents. They did their best to make state constitutions clear and accessible.[41] Vague and obscure laws would be an invitation for arbitrary rule since neither citizens nor rulers could point to a definite limit on those in power. Rulers would likely take the absence of clear limits as license. And without clear barriers, the kind of arguments that the Americans had used against England, based on the wording of documents they considered fundamental, would be precluded. Fuzzy phraseology was not compatible with constitutional government. Providing clearly expressed limitations on governmental power was its purpose. The first state constitutions were also formed and approved by state legislatures, the lawful representatives of the people.[42] As such, they were considered real social contracts, satisfying the theory of government expressed most convincingly by John Locke.

The norms of clarity, express limitations, and contract were, of course, ideals. They were developed by philosophers and politicians in times of struggle, when they could not be fully realized. When proponents became able to construct governments themselves, important practical matters had yet to be worked out. This was not a matter of naïveté among theorists and revolutionists. Their theories were quite sophisticated. But fully developing the implications of their ideas for governing was premature until a revolution was successful. If unconstitutional actions by institutions were illegitimate, was rebellion automatically authorized? If so, the basis for a lasting government was tenuous. Translating revolutionary norms into a theory of governance required the development of legal processes to determine when the Constitution was being violated and how to remedy such violations. One of these mechanisms, judicial review, was slowly entering the consciousness of those in legal circles during the confederation period.[43] Another went hand in hand with the Americans' colonial experience, and it was more a way of thinking than a legal mechanism per se: if one could argue that one knew definitively, from the language of the document and the aims of those who passed it, what was intended, one could leave the problem of competing interpretations aside, because one necessarily had the answer. This position holds that there really is no need for interpretation at all, and thus other options, those that require interpretation, are precluded.

By 1789, Americans had a century's experience in using language as a barrier against the extension of centralized power. This experience and its importance to the Revolution lead John Phillip Reid to comment that "language . . . [is an] overlooked clue to eighteenth-century constitutional thought."[44] Despite the Enlightenment ideal that legal language be as clear as possible, once governance was actually conducted under written constitutions, there were inevitable discrepancies in interpretation. In this situation, offering a convincing case that one's version of the constitution is definitive is of great importance. One can do this in two ways: by claiming that the wording of the document itself is explicit, or by employing the notion that because it was designed to be immutable, the philosophy and the meaning its framers attached to its wording should be held inviolate.

The core debate during the ratification process was whether the Constitution adequately limited the national government. Antifederalists, of course, argued that it did not. Slowly and by degrees, they thought the national government would implicate itself in every facet of American life. Not surprisingly, the debate hinged on the language of the document. The most celebrated Federalist response to the Constitution's critics provided the rationale for Antifederalist constitutional arguments in the First Congress. Just days after the Constitution was made public, there were already complaints that it lacked a bill of rights, did not acknowledge that the people retained certain powers, would allow Congress to enact whatever it deemed "necessary and proper," and that the document even called into question the validity of the state constitutions.

One of the earliest and the most well publicized Federalist responses to these complaints was offered by Pennsylvanian James Wilson in an October 6, 1787, speech.[45] Wilson refuted several key objections to the Constitution, but the issue he dealt with first was whether state constitutions had been rendered obsolete. According to Wilson, the Antifederalist case hinged on a mistaken assumption: that the national Constitution and the state constitutions were the same kind of contract. The state governments were original contracts, formed from a state of nature. As such, they were given "every right and authority which [citizens] did not in explicit terms reserve." Hence, there was a need to include bills of rights and other barriers against government in them. The Constitution was, by contrast, a federal document. By definition, it respected the existing social contracts of the federating parties. The only powers the national government wielded were those positively expressed, and the national Constitution only superseded state instruments when it expressly contradicted them.

"This distinction being recognized, will furnish an answer to those who think the omission of a bill of rights a defect in the proposed constitution," said Wilson. No federal bill of rights was required, because the rights spelled out in state constitutions were not expressly eclipsed by the Constitution. Wilson made an example of freedom of the press. The Constitution did not grant Congress the explicit power to regulate publications, so state guarantees stood. "The proposed system possesses no influence whatever upon the press," Wilson assured his audience. The only place where Congress would have unlimited power was the yet-to-be designated federal district that would house the nation's capital. A federal bill of rights might be appropriate there, but one was not needed in the rest of the nation.[46]

Antifederalists vehemently disputed Wilson's claims during the ratification debate. Yet after ratification they just as strenuously defended his understanding of the Constitution. Treating the federal document as a grant of expressed powers only was a logical stance for Antifederalists to assume, as it placed the burden of justifying federal actions squarely on the national government itself. Only the policy options that were expressly authorized by the Constitution were permissible. With the Constitution a fait accompli, Wilson's line of thinking provided the best defense against an overly active centralized government — further, this line of reasoning had automatic credibility, as the Federalists themselves had formulated and championed the argument.[47]

Meanwhile, Publius twice penned extensive justifications of the necessary and proper clause. One was written by Hamilton, the other by Madison. The thrust of both arguments was the same: the clause merely confirmed the national government's ability to undertake its explicitly granted powers.[48] It did not add any powers to the national government's repertoire. In Federalist #33, Hamilton asserted that if it had been omitted "the constitutional operation of the intended government would be precisely the same."[49] In essence, the necessary and proper clause was a redundancy. The oft-criticized words merely signified that appropriate means were at the government's disposal in the exercise of its expressly granted powers. Hamilton anticipated the next logical question: If the clause was a mere redundancy, why was it included? The answer to this self-imposed question was that it would "guard against all cavilling refinements in those who might hereafter feel a disposition to curtail and evade the legitimate authorities of the Union."[50] In other words, the necessary and proper clause would prove useful as a barrier against an assault on the national government's authorized powers by hair-splitting state-centered politicians.

Characteristically, Madison's analysis was more regimented. In Federalist #44, he noted that there were four options for dealing with expressed powers besides confirming them with the necessary and proper clause. The framers of the Constitution could have adopted the language of the Articles of Confederation, which "prohibited the exercise of any power not *expressly* delegated." Experience had shown that the word "expressly" was construed "with so much rigor as to disarm the government of all real authority whatever, or with so much latitude as to destroy altogether the force of the restriction." Either construal defeated the intended purpose of the clause. Alternatively, the convention could have tried to enumerate every power necessary and proper "for carrying their other powers into effect," but the list would have been nearly endless, constituting a "complete digest of laws on every subject."[51] An attempt to enumerate the means not necessary and proper would have proven equally long and ineffectual as fundamental law. The framers of the Constitution could also have chosen to remain silent about the means for carrying policies into effect. Like Hamilton, Madison argued that not including the clause would have implied exactly what its inclusion made explicit. "Had the Constitution been silent on this head, there can be no doubt that all the particular powers requisite as means of executing the general powers would have resulted to the government by unavoidable implication." Publius had again confirmed that the necessary and proper clause was an innocuous affirmation that the government could carry out the powers it indisputably held.[52]

The Federalist reasoning while the Constitution was still a proposal that it granted only expressed powers to the national government and that the necessary and proper clause did not add any powers to the government seemed spurious to the Antifederalists. The Constitution's casual and unguarded wording fed their suspicions that many of the Federalists were, in fact, really nationalists. But the Federalist version of constitutional theory prevailed during the ratification debates, along with the Constitution itself. After implementation, the parties exchanged arguments. The Antifederalists, now faced with the Constitution as law, clung to the Federalists' reassuring statements from the ratification debate.

Some of the Federalist's own protestations proved to be the opposition's best ammunition against Federalist proposals. When pressed on constitutional grounds, one wing of the Federalist coalition argued that the necessary and proper clause granted them broad discretionary powers to accomplish the goals set down in the preamble, even if they were not mentioned word for word in the Constitution. When it came time to implement national policies, the Hamiltonian Federalists adopted an approach to the Constitution very close to what the Antifederalists had feared its wording implied in 1787.

Antifederalist Constitutional Arguments in the First Congress

The following summary of the constitutional arguments of the First Congress's Antifederalist members results from a comprehensive study of their speeches given in the first U.S. House of Representatives.[53] Attention to early constitutional debates in Congress has become something of a cottage industry in recent years, with Jack Rakove, David Currie, Harry Jaffa, H. Jefferson Powell, and Joseph Lynch among those writing major works on the subject.[54] While these accounts are valuable, none of the authors focus on Antifederalist constitutional thought per se, being much more interested in how the two early parties formed their constitutional ideologies. Since James Madison took the lead in developing the opposition's constitutional argument, the Antifederalists recede into the background in these accounts.

Saul Cornell helps remedy this oversight by focusing on the way Antifederalist texts were used through the Jeffersonian era. In contrast, this section deals with the general tenor of Antifederalist constitutional arguments in the First Congress alone. The two years the inaugural Congress sat saw the frequent, precedent-setting employment of "originalist" arguments by the opposition. The First Congress is also uniquely situated in terms of constitutional time. In its first months, Federalist ratification pledges served as the only barrier on the extension of national power. These pledges were not legally binding so much as ethically so; Antifederalists continually reminded Federalists of these pledges to shame them into restraint. This scenario changed subtly after amendments were agreed on and delivered to the states for approval, including the two that explicitly reined in the national government (later to become the Ninth and Tenth Amendments). Congressional approval gave Antifederalists firmer legal footing to dispute the constitutionality of certain Federalist policies, but also made clear that the strictest version of strict construction was off-limits.

The first strict constructionist argument made in the House came on April 20, 1789, less than three weeks into deliberations. Though the constitutional precedent at stake was of enormous importance, the issue at hand was trifling. One John Churchman had made an ingenious discovery. He found that longitude could be determined by plugging compass readings into an equation. Churchman petitioned Congress to safeguard this discovery as his intellectual property. He also asked the legislature to fund a journey to the northern reaches of North America, where he could observe firsthand the workings of the magnetic North Pole to confirm his theories. Thomas Tudor Tucker was assigned to chair the select committee considering the petition. He may have maneuvered himself into this role because of the wide-ranging constitutional implications he felt this otherwise minor petition raised. Such purposeful action would not be surprising given Tucker's commitment to limited government and his astute constitutional sense.[55]

Tucker reported that Churchman was entitled to the financial benefits resulting from his discovery. The Constitution allowed Congress to "promote the Progress of Science and useful Arts, by securing for limited Times to Authors and Inventors the exclusive Right to their respective Writings and Discoveries" in Article I, section 8. The House was clearly authorized to pass a bill protecting Churchman's intellectual property. Actively encouraging discoveries by funding expeditions was another matter. The "progress of science" clause did not explicitly countenance any government action beyond protecting inventors' property rights. The only way to justify funding the mission Churchman proposed was through a generous interpretation of powers implied by the Constitution. Since Congress's power to do so was questionable, Tucker "thought it best to err on the safe side."[56] He therefore advised against funding the expedition.

The Churchman petition debate shows that arguments over constitutionality were made on mundane issues as well as monumental ones. That constitutional arguments dominated debate on authorizing a national bank and assuming state debts is well known. But there were also disagreements over the constitutionality of minor issues, like whether congressmen could exempt themselves from militia duty or whether census takers were allowed to record citizens' occupations.[57] There was not a constitutional debate on every issue, of course, but by modern standards it is amazing how often such questions were raised in the First Congress. Constitutional theory was being discussed more in Congress than anywhere else in the new nation, including the Supreme Court.[58] At least one Federalist, Roger Sherman of Connecticut, agreed with Tucker's narrow reading of the progress of science clause. That was not unusual, at least while constitutional doctrines remained unsettled. Practical politics often divided legislators along different lines than ratification.[59]

Antifederalists were divided internally even on matters one would think most likely to unite them, like amendments. Early in the first session, Bland urged that the subject be brought to the floor as quickly as possible. The House did not heed his call, so the next day Bland introduced Virginia's resolution, calling for a second convention. Gerry moved to table the report.[60] A month later Madison offered a set of amendments, the earliest version of what would become the federal Bill of Rights. Gerry again proposed postponement. It was in this speech that he implored his fellow representatives that "the salvation of America depends on the establishment of this government, whether amended or not."[61] Gerry was worried that raising the issue would open wounds that were just beginning to heal. Discussing amendments would prove so divisive and time consuming that effective government would come to a halt, precisely at the time it was sorely needed.

Other Antifederalists, like Burke, favored postponement, ostensibly for the same reason. Given Burke's very different point of view, however, it is likely that he did not fully divulge his reasoning. Since Burke was sure that the new government would be heavy-handed, he felt it was only a matter of time before Americans would be extremely disgruntled. Delay would allow the movement to gain momentum. At the very least, this would prevent Madison and his fellow Federalists from co-opting the issue by watering down proposed amendments. If the issue could be delayed until after the next election, the people might even return an Antifederalist majority to Congress. Burke was probably acting strategically, knowing that the true friends of amendments were substantially outnumbered in the First Congress and trusting that their strength was at its nadir. In August 1789, when Madison's amendments had made their way through a select committee, Burke denigrated them as "little better than whip-syllabub, frothy and full of wind, formed only to please the palate."[62]

Antifederalists had diverse viewpoints and interests, as any group of allied politicians do. Naturally they advocated different positions. Knowing their varied constitutional outlooks and the differing political pressures on them makes many of these disparities understandable. When they argued for strict adherence to the Constitution they argued as individuals on an issue-by-issue basis. Not presenting a united front was not a matter of being disingenuous, particularly before the issue of the Constitution's breadth was legally decided by amendment (though that did not end division either). Even if Antifederalists preferred strict construction, they were not under any legal obligation to rigorously follow that doctrine at every turn, particularly when it would harm their own constituencies. Those preferring strict construction wished for a general climate of restraint. If by contrast there would be a constitutional free-for-all they might reluctantly have to participate to keep their home regions from being disadvantaged.

Almost from the beginning of the Congress, Antifederalists charged Federalists with forgetting the constitutional principles of James Wilson and Publius. Elbridge Gerry accused Federalists of taking liberties with the necessary and proper clause already in May 1789.[63] A few months later, Tucker implied that Federalists were surreptitiously making the preamble into a grant of power far broader than any contained in the body of the document itself. In the second session, Tucker complained, "We have already gone much too far in explaining the constitution; and if we continue on the same plan, there is danger that we shall at length persuade ourselves, that every power which is not expressly refused is given to us."[64] In practice Federalist constitutionalism looked as unlike Wilson's theory as possible to Tucker.

In late-eighteenth-century American usage, the word "construction" was akin to how we use "interpretation," and construction was not looked on favorably by those who had opposed the Constitution. In the first session, Elbridge Gerry argued that legislative construction threatened to make the American Constitution as pliable as that of the British. If members of Congress could provide their own construction of the document, then the Constitution could become precisely what the legislature said it was, just like in English practice.[65] In effect, the very purpose of having a written constitution would be circumvented by the practice of interpretation. During the debate on the president's removal power, Gerry noted that "the gentleman opposite to me from Georgia (Abraham Baldwin) has asserted, that we mean to put a construction on the constitution. . . . I am decidedly against putting any construction whatever on the constitution."[66] Construction was the province of the judiciary according to Gerry, one of the several times that judicial review of congressional acts was explicitly countenanced by a member of the First Congress.[67]

During the debate on amendments, Tucker and Gerry attempted to make strict construction the law of the land. On August 18, 1789, Tucker suggested adding the word "expressly" to the statement that was to become the Tenth Amendment. Tucker's version of the amendment read, "The powers not *expressly* delegated to the United States by the Constitution . . . are reserved to the States respectively, or to the people." Gerry had suggested a similar provision in the Philadelphia Convention. Three days after Tucker's proposal was ignored by the full House, Gerry reintroduced the issue. Few others in Congress insisted that all construction was bad. Most felt that reasonable or "natural constructions" were constitutional; by contrast, there were also "forced constructions," which were not.[68] Even if there was some semblance of agreement on these categories, what was natural and what was forced was a matter of dispute.

Original intent and strict construction are not the same, though the phrases are often used interchangeably. When one tries to recapture the sense of the Philadelphia Convention or the "spirit of the Constitution" one has gone beyond its wording in order to determine its meaning, a tacit acknowledgment that its words are not a sufficient guide in and of themselves. In this view, discovering the true meaning of the Constitution requires supplementing it with knowledge of the founders' understanding of the words and the various practices they thought it justified or prohibited. This kind of endeavor is better described by the phrase "original intent."

Strict construction and original intent are not necessarily mutually exclusive methods of jurisprudence. One might find certain clauses clear, but others sufficiently vague that one needs to look into the intent of those who framed them. It was not unusual for Antifederalist members of the First Congress to use both kinds of argument. Each issue implicated different clauses, the meanings of which could be more or less apparent, perhaps dictating one approach or the other. Additionally, the concepts of strict construction and original intent were not yet clearly defined. The members of the First Congress cannot be expected to have neatly conformed to jurisprudential categories only clearly delineated in the twentieth century. Theodorick Bland, for instance, used both strict construction and original intent arguments on the same issue in one day. The House was debating how to raise revenue. Most members favored raising funds through an excise on ships. The Virginian knew that taxing ships would hurt the South. He also felt that taxing domestic ships traveling to and from domestic ports would violate an interstate commerce provision. "None can go so far as to set aside the words of the Constitution," Bland stated. He then quoted the relevant clause: "'[nor shall Vessels] bound to or from one state [be obliged to] enter, clear or pay duties to another.'"[69]

This strict constructionist argument, based on the wording of a clause, did not convince colleagues. The excise was not being paid to another state but to the national government, after all. Though he still thought "the article was definite, he conceived . . . gentlemen have put different constructions upon it." Bland switched tactics. Despite others' opinions of the clause, none could dispute that "the Convention in framing this article, designed to encourage the coasting trade."[70] The Philadelphia Convention clearly wished to spur interstate commerce (and thus national prosperity) by removing tariffs on goods moving between states. A federal policy taxing domestic ships would serve as a disincentive to interstate commerce, thwarting the original intent of the framers. This second tack proved to be equally unsuccessful.

Occasionally Antifederalists claimed that policies should be avoided not because they were unconstitutional, but because the constitutional order was still so fragile. Using this rationale, Josiah Parker weighed against a liquor excise proposed in the third session. Designed to pay for the assumption of state debts, the liquor excise unduly burdened western farmers. Farmers near the frontier did not have easily accessible markets for their surplus produce. This produce, mainly grain, was bulky and could not be easily transported. It was much easier to transport a product of that grain, distilled alcohol. The farther farmers lived from a population center, the more likely they were to process a crop into liquor. The tax would fall disproportionately on western farmers, who had mainly sympathized with the Antifederalists. Parker phrased his objection to the matter as follows:

It is well known that this government has had many enemies; its measures have in some instances been far from conciliating them all to its operations; perhaps another hasty and improper step may drive some to despair, and raise an opposition to the law, which it will be difficult if not impracticable soon to subdue. . . . I do not urge this objection to an excise on principles of constitutionalism; it is on the contrary, dictated by a desire to support the present government.[71]

Parker's warning was prescient. In three years the federal government would face its first large-scale disturbance, the Whiskey Rebellion, in which farmers from western Pennsylvania flaunted the federal government's excise.

In the First Congress the Antifederalists had not yet settled on what kind of evidence could authoritatively define original intent. Accordingly they used a wide variety of evidentiary sources. They frequently referenced the intent of the Philadelphia Convention. In favoring assumption of state debts, for instance, Elbridge Gerry argued that the topic had been discussed at Philadelphia, and that the delegates generally supported it. If not for a minor technical snag, a provision authorizing assumption would have been written into the Constitution. Gerry urged Congress to follow through on the intent of the convention and assume the state debts.[72] Note that Gerry used the intent of the Philadelphia Convention to press for a position atypical for most Antifederalists. More orthodox members of the opposition were at a disadvantage in using the convention's arguments because they had not attended. It was left to James Madison to argue that the convention's position was, in actuality, different.[73] During the third session's discussion of the national bank Gerry and Madison would again disagree about the intent of the convention.

The understandings of delegates to state ratification conventions were used in constitutional arguments as well. But it was not until after the First Congress that that intent was considered definitive by the opposition. It took time for the Antifederalists and their Madisonian allies to realize that arguments borrowed from state conventions offered more solid support in their quest to limit the scope of the national government. Other sources were also brought forth as authoritative. *The Federalist* was cited a number of times. Cornell reports that Antifederalists strategically "distance[d] themselves from the claims they had made in 1788," quoting more frequently "from the assurances provided by Federalists" than their own works.[74] Occasionally legislators argued that the governing practices of the states should serve as a precedent for the national government. Gerry felt that the president should not be allowed to remove cabinet members without advice and consent from the Senate. To bolster his case, Gerry cited state precedents. Most of the states that had cabinet-like advisory councils did not allow governors to cashier members without outside approval.[75]

Whether the Philadelphia Convention's intent was authoritative beyond the wording they gave to the Constitution seems to have come to a tentative resolution in early February 1791, during the debate over the bank bill. On February 2, Madison pointed out that a convention proposal granting the national government the power to "grant charters of incorporation" failed.[76] If the intent of the Philadelphia Convention were controlling, the national government could not issue a charter of incorporation to a national bank. But on February 7, Gerry responded with the argument that the interpretations and memories of delegates differed. Not all felt that by rejecting the clause in question they were closing off the possibility of chartered entities. Diversity of sentiment being the reality, individual opinions could not be taken as authoritative.[77] Five years later, Madison recalled that discussion as precedent-setting: thereafter the intent of the framers at Philadelphia had not been taken as a proper constitutional authority.[78]

Antifederalist speeches from the First Congress indicate that several different sources were employed to grant authority to one's constitutional arguments: the intent of the framers, the understandings of ratifying delegates, the writings produced during the ratification debates, and state practices. Oddly, their own ratification convention writings took a backseat in these debates.

Though Madison and a few of his Federalist colleagues had opposed assumption of state debts (in the second session) on constitutional grounds, few suspected that their divergence from the Federalist mainstream represented an unbridgeable rift in constitutional philosophy. By the third session, however, Madison's congressional allies were as convinced as the Antifederalists that Hamilton and his supporters had slipped the bounds of Wilson's expressed powers and Publius's benign necessary and proper clause. Madison found himself making the same argument Tucker had in the first session: the preamble was not a grant of powers, just a statement of purpose.[79]

Maryland's Michael Jenifer Stone best described the disappointment the Madisonians felt just one month before the First Congress ended. Speaking against the incorporation of the national bank, Stone pointed out that many of the Federalists were abandoning the constitutional philosophy the nation had seemed united behind after ratification: "Never did a country more completely unite in any sentiment than America in this — 'That Congress ought not to exercise, by implication, powers not granted by the Constitution.'" "This doctrine destroys the principle of your government at a blow." The Hamiltonian philosophy "at once breaks down every barrier which the federal constitution had raised against unlimited legislation."[80]

The Southern Antifederalists ceded leadership on the bank's dubious constitutionality to the former Federalists like Madison and Stone, whose voice would be more authoritative than theirs. In subsequent years, this group would work out several versions of the proper interpretive philosophy. Many Antifederalists retained their philosophical preference for a stricter version of strict construction than Madison and his amendments allowed. And yet these Antifederalists and the Madisonians maintained a close political and constitutional alliance, because the alternative they fought, with the Constitution seemingly providing no limits on the federal government, was radically unlike either of their views and directly at odds with the Bill of Rights.

The most important constitutional developments of the First Congress were these: very early in the Congress Antifederalists felt their opponents were not abiding by the constitutional doctrines of James Wilson and Publius. On an issue-by-issue basis, individuals who had been opposed to the Constitution charged Federalist policies with failing strict constitutional scrutiny. Their cause received support, though not as much support as they would have liked, from the proposed list of amendments Congress approved. In making their arguments Antifederalists used a variety of sources and drew on historical precedents deeply ingrained on the American political psyche. By the third session, an important group of Federalists, including one of the central architects of the new order, agreed with them that the remaining Federalists were not living up to their pledge that the Constitution contained only expressed powers.

Conclusion

The historical antecedents to the Antifederalists' strict adherence arguments seemed to make their position inevitable. At the same time, we must remember that this was something new, and it was a rather amazing occurrence. In a limited span, the Antifederalists went from ardent opposers of the Constitution to a group that laid claim to heeding the document more faithfully than most Federalists. In large part, this development was a result of the logical positions dictated by the Antifederalist philosophy in several distinct constitutional contexts. Even if Antifederalists were still not fully satisfied with the Constitution, they had found a way to live under it (a necessity given their thoughts on the rule of law) that did not relegate them to the historic dustbin. On the contrary, their postratification outlook was sufficiently plausible and moderate to make an alliance with the Madisonians possible. The Antifederalists eventually recovered from the "critical shift" that had so devastated them during the late 1780s, and along with the Madisonians, they formed a viable opposition.

The "strong" endorsement of the Constitution's language used by former Antifederalists should not in itself be taken as an indication that the document had attained full apotheosis, as Lance Banning argues. The originalist arguments made by the Antifederalists were intended, ultimately, to resonate with the public, who would remember the Federalists' pledges during the ratification debate. A prospect of righting the constitutional ship through success in the electoral and policy realms was needed along with their new interpretive philosophy. Had there been no prospect of their constitutional arguments being taken seriously or becoming the accepted manner of interpreting the Constitution, the Antifederalist critique would likely not have remained conservative. Luckily for the Antifederalists, their numbers were bolstered by the Madisonians just one year after implementation, and they did not have to consider taking radical steps outside of legally accepted bounds — at least not until the Federalists took a radical step of their own with the Alien and Sedition Acts passed ten years into the Congress's existence.

The Antifederalist argument for strict adherence was a key step toward constitutional apotheosis. The American electorate knew that the Federalists had championed the Constitution during the ratification debates. By 1791, they were aware that the opposing group was backing the Constitution to the hilt. Its former critics were doing more than mouthing platitudes about its legality, they were insisting on it. The public responded to this cue and went the next step, finding the Constitution "sacred." In turn, politicians heeded the public's stance, and few of them have dismissed the Constitution as unworkable, outdated, or irrelevant since. Although the American approach to constitutionalism is an understandable and logical result of the ratification process, there was nothing inevitable about the long-term apotheosis of this particular Constitution. Rather than a result of meticulous, rational planning successfully executed, this apotheosis has resulted from a rich mix of history and happenstance, political principle and partisan opportunism.

The quest for strict adherence has proved durable. This mode of interpretation lives on in jurisprudential arguments, despite the fact that our Constitution has long been taken to justify governmental action that the founders never intended. Original intent also provides the organizing mythology of the U.S. Supreme Court, as the authority of the framers is routinely a part of the Court's strivings for authoritativeness. The Antifederalists certainly would not agree with all the claims that are made using their style of argument, of course, but their use lent an acceptability to them. The opposition set the tone in the quest to attach meaning to the Constitution's words. As badly as the Antifederalists stumbled during the ratification debates, allowing Federalists to set the nation's agenda, they were as successful at defining the key constitutional dilemma in the postratification period. Help, of course, came from Madison and his colleagues, to which I now turn.

CHAPTER FOUR

Publius in Constitutional Time

A Partnership in Search of Incompatible Equilibria

In Publius's first essay, Alexander Hamilton laid out a plan for the series. He hoped to convince readers of six things, treating them in succession. Five of the six are standard Federalist fare, including an indictment of the Confederation as unable to preserve the Union and a defense of the "republican" nature of the proposed government. One item stands apart: the "necessity of [establishing] a government *at least* equally energetic with the one proposed."[1] Hamilton's phrase suggests that the Constitution may be only barely up to the task, if that, of preserving the Union. One quite easily, and accurately, draws the inference that the author of this phrase would prefer a significantly more vigorous central government. Far from backtracking to allay Antifederalist fears, when he arrives at the topic in Federalist #23, Hamilton repeats the words verbatim, calling for a government "at least equally energetic with the one proposed."[2] Fourteen successive essays are dedicated to demonstrating this necessity; Hamilton wrote them all. The full import of Hamilton's wording is fully appreciated when placed alongside what he did after ratification. As secretary of the treasury he did his utmost to shore up "the frail and worthless fabric," making the government more energetic so that it would not fail.

James Madison took no part in Publius's demonstration that the Union needed "at least" such a vigorous government. Yet the task of reviewing the previous section's work fell to him in Federalist #37. Madison summarizes Hamilton's essays by writing that he has shown "the defects of the Confederation . . . cannot be supplied by a government of less energy than that before the public."[3] Here Madison subtly alters Hamilton's bold declaration to something much more measured and even defensive.

Adopting the new government is a necessity; a government with less "energy" will fail. Although carefully acknowledging that the United States cannot do with a less vigorous government than that outlined in the Constitution, the hint that an even more aggressive one might be needed is consciously dropped, even though Madison himself had arguably pushed for a more vigorous government than that framed in Philadelphia.[4]

Madison and Hamilton are at the same point, as it were, in arguing for adoption of the Constitution, but in doing so they seem to be back-to-back, facing in opposite directions. Hamilton is looking ahead at the terrain he is about to traverse in making a workable national government from a weak, probably too weak, constitution. Madison, meanwhile, is looking back — not nostalgically, but to urge on those who are reluctant to come to that same point where he and Hamilton are. In the early years of the republic, Madison's work is characterized by an effort to forge a rough constitutional consensus approximately at the point he was at in writing *The Federalist*. Meanwhile Hamilton, to Madison's great consternation, had embarked on his own project of placing the national government on a sound footing, taking him well into the territory he gazed at longingly in Federalist #23 through #36.

Earlier I demonstrated that the advancement of constitutional time brought a new Antifederalist approach to the Constitution. Present but largely obscured by their vehement opposition to the document was a pledge to abide by it if ratified. Once implemented, the Antifederalists clung to the Constitution as an expression of enumerated powers only. This new approach only became appropriate — and fully apparent to the nation — once ratification and implementation were effected. Similarly, the full range of Federalist constitutional ideas was not apparent during the ratification debate. Fundamental differences remained submerged while the fight for ratification was on. Implementing the newly ratified constitution was a very different context that laid bare these differences; this was particularly true for James Madison and Alexander Hamilton, coauthors of the bulk of *The Federalist*. In the words of Lance Banning, "Many of the points on which Hamilton and Madison differed most profoundly lay beyond the subject of the series."[5] Careful attention to Hamilton's and Madison's constitutional thinking indicates that their views diverged well before the controversies of the 1790s.

Many have quite rightly emphasized that their respective contributions to the Federalist papers vary, but my focus is different.[6] I draw on sources dealing with constitutional dynamics to discern how these two interpreted the failings of the confederation and how they felt they might proceed more successfully. In short, Hamilton attributed the confederation's failure to the division of power between geographic levels of government—an arrangement he thought to be inherently unstable. The Constitution that emerged from the convention still split powers, even if it did so differently than the Articles of Confederation. The states would probably gain the upper hand under the Constitution, just as they had under the Articles. However, an early, vigorous administration of discretionary powers might allow the national government to prevail over the states. Meanwhile Madison critiqued the confederation more narrowly, allowing him to think that a government that divided powers between states and nation could succeed, provided it was properly constructed. If the division of powers would be clear and the national government able to preserve itself against encroachment, a static federal arrangement could be maintained. Unfortunately, Madison's desired method of protecting the national government against state encroachment, a veto on state legislation, was not included in the Constitution. This omission dictated a heightened reliance on the distinctiveness of the powers wielded by both levels of government and the inherent usefulness of the extended republic to preserve the constitutional system. Thus the specific Constitution they were presented with—though a step in the right direction for both—made Madison and Hamilton think in quite different terms when it came to implementation. Hamilton thought aggressively about the need to quickly mold the government into a shape adequate to solve the problems it was intended to address. Madison thought of conservation; he was touchy about anything that would threaten its recognized equilibrium of power. In the First Congress, both men found themselves in a position to pursue their own favored, but widely divergent, even contradictory, ideals.

Exactly how the events of the early 1790s affected Madison has been discussed by many scholars. Some insist on Madison's overall consistency, others are just as adamant that his constitutional thought underwent a major change. There is some truth to both claims. Greater attention to the changing constitutional contexts in which Madison found himself partially reconciles these views. At the same time, by far the greatest change in his thinking has been entirely overlooked by most recent commentators. They have concentrated on the evolution of how he interpreted the Constitution, a subject on which I argue Madison is fairly consistent. Meanwhile, the most notable proponent of his consistency, Lance Banning, comes to his conclusion only by seriously underestimating the importance the extended republic (as outlined in Federalist #10 and elsewhere) played in his ratification-era thinking. Hamilton's postimplementation project stuck a dagger in two key expectations of Madison: that the Constitution could successfully divide powers between levels of government and that the extended republic would solve the problems of majoritarianism he discerned on the state level. In Madison's mind, Hamilton aimed to erase the meaning of the Constitution through unjustifiable extensions of national power. The latter's cadre of followers in the First Congress proved to be the majority faction Madison thought would not form at the national level. The failure of these assumptions, so crucial to Madison's postconvention mind-set, exposed Madison's core constitutional beliefs as closer to many Antifederalist leaders than to Hamilton's and warranted a new alliance that would save the Constitution by very different means than those he put faith in during the ratification debate.

Looking ahead, we can discern that the terminated collaboration of Hamilton and Madison is a major component of the Constitution's ironic path toward legitimacy. On its face, it would seem that attaining consensual backing for a constitution would be much harder if its two most visible proponents had such an obvious parting so soon after its adoption. Surprisingly, the opposite seems to have been the case. If anything, Madison's dispute with Hamilton enhanced the Constitution's status. If the former Antifederalists had disputed the constitutionality of Federalist actions alone, the united Federalists could have brushed aside their concerns as a misunderstanding of the document proffered by sore losers. In such a scenario, constitutional discourse would not have achieved the central position it did so quickly in the American republic. Madison and friends' split from the Federalists generated more constitutional discourse, reinforcing the importance of the document. It did so by granting the opposition's disputes much greater credence, both philosophically and symbolically. In response to the opposition's constitutional arguments, the Federalist version of constitutionality required vindication. The Federalists' serious response to their opposition completed the development of two fairly well formed methods of treating the Constitution, both arguably in its spirit. The vigorous dispute over what was constitutional, allowed by the defection of James Madison, quickly turned the Constitution into a capacious document in which all could place their hope.

The contingent, almost accidental nature of the Constitution's legitimation is underscored by the realities of this collaboration. In Congress's early years, both sides used *The Federalist* to back up their version of constitutionality.[7] The opposition's solace came mostly from Madison's essays. But Madison's participation in the series was something of a fluke. John Jay fell ill, unable to write during the majority of its press run. Gouverneur Morris, a close confidant of Hamilton's, was approached as a third essayist but declined. William Duer was asked to write and prepared three essays, which were deemed unsuitable for the series. Madison was approached by Hamilton in mid-November 1787, but tried to steer him toward Rufus King as a possible collaborator. All these men were significantly more nationalist than Madison.[8] Knowing the Virginian possessed great talents, Hamilton persisted when he could have recruited others whose nationalist commitments were deeper. During the ratification debate, it became clear that Publius, because of his erudition and thoroughness, was writing the most definitive defense of the Constitution. Madison's contributions to the series lent parts of the work a more temperate air. This helped grant weight to the former Antifederalists' constitutional arguments while giving them the means to perform their very modern balancing act of simultaneously abiding by the Constitution while disputing the government's policies.

[handwritten annotation: Federalist Papers, 85 in total, written by Alex. Hamilton, James Madison + John Jay used pen name "Publius"]

Hamilton's Administrative Politics of Constitution-Tipping

The authors of *The Federalist* pursued their collaboration separately. Alexander Hamilton and James Madison did not routinely consult each other before sending essays to the printer, nor was the writing of them ever a joint effort. In an encrypted letter, Madison acknowledged to Thomas Jefferson that "though carried in concert the writers are not mutually answerable for all the ideas of each other there being seldom time for even a perusal of the pieces by any but the writer before they were wanted at the press."[9] The two apparently shared information on only three essays, numbers 18 through 20, Hamilton providing some notes to Madison.[10] These essays form a running commentary on the political tendencies of confederacies based on historical and contemporary examples. That their closest, arguably their only true collaboration revolved around this subject is very important. At bottom, what united both authors in their quest to construct a viable national government was their belief that confederations were subject to centrifugal forces that, if not checked, would destroy the Union. As soon as one moves beyond that simple assertion to why this phenomenon occurred and what to do about it, Hamilton and Madison part ways in a manner that prefigures their dispute of the early 1790s.

The alliance of Madison and Hamilton was based on an observation of what happened through constitutional time in a certain type of regime. It was impossible to achieve equilibrium in confederations because the sovereignty of component states gradually eroded the powers supposedly lodged in the central government. Already in 1780, Hamilton had diagnosed this centrifugal tendency in the American confederation. In an extraordinary letter to fellow New Yorker James Duane, he stressed the urgency of remedying the situation and laid out potential solutions. Most Americans had been misled by their experience with Great Britain. Still fighting a war that began because a central government exerted increasing control over the periphery of its empire, most thought that the great political problem to be solved was the tendency of centralized authority to encroach on any peripheral authority. That may well be the case in empires not composed of sovereign states, Hamilton conceded, but "there is a wide difference between our situation and that of an empire under one simple government, distributed into counties provinces or districts, which have no legislatures but merely magistratical bodies." In the United States, he argued, the "danger is directly the reverse. It is that the common sovereign will not have sufficient power to unite the different members together, and direct the common forces to the interest and happiness of the whole."[11] Hamilton maintained this attitude through the 1780s and beyond. Madison's account of Hamilton's signature speech at the Philadelphia Convention proclaims that "two Sovereignties can not co-exist within the same limits," and that "the general power whatever be its form if it preserves itself, must swallow up the State powers. Otherwise it will be swallowed up by them."[12]

However, the reason Hamilton gave for the centrifugal tendency of confederations differed from Madison's. Hamilton's explanation was attitudinal; Madison's legalistic. Their remedies differed accordingly. Hamilton hoped public opinion would attach itself to the national government, Madison placed confidence in specific constitutional powers. What follows is an account of Hamilton's thinking on constitutional dynamics and how he hoped to get the Constitution to succeed after implementation.

Like the Scottish philosopher David Hume, Hamilton believed that governments were legitimized more by affective ties than rational consent. States had a great advantage over the national government in fostering such ties because of their greater activity and proximity to the people. Hamilton was particularly impressed that the state's daily administration of criminal and civil justice served as the "great cement of society."

This, of all the others, is the most powerful, most universal, and most attractive source of popular obedience and attachment. It is that which, being the immediate and visible guardian of life and property, having its benefits and its terrors in constant activity before the public eye, regulating all those personal interests and familiar concerns to which the sensibility of individuals is more immediately awake, contributes, more than any other circumstance, to impressing upon the minds of the people affection, esteem, and reverence towards the government.[13]

As states continued to act they became ever more familiar and gained the people's confidence. This confidence, in turn, allowed the states to accrue more power. The populace did not literally consent beforehand to all that the states were doing, but they supported what was done retroactively, seeing that it was of benefit.

Meanwhile, the national government was languishing, barely doing anything visible after the war. As a result, positive affective ties toward it dissolved, replaced by horrible fantasies of what such a government might look like. Such need not have been the case. Returning to his September 1780 letter to James Duane, Hamilton suggestively confided that whenever the Confederation Congress had acted boldly, its actions had been met with approbation:

> [Congress] have done many of the highest acts of sovereignty, which were always chearfully submitted to — the declaration of independence, the declaration of war, the levying of an army, creating a navy, emitting money, making alliances with foreign powers, appointing a dictator &c. &c. — all these implications of a complete sovereignty were never disputed, and ought to have been a standard for the whole conduct of Administration.[14]

The national government might have become predominant had it continued to act decisively. It did not. However, Hamilton took what happened early in the war as evidence that popular sentiment could tip in favor of a national government. An active administration was likely to be met with popular approval. The more visible the national government, the more active its wise administration, the more likely it would be supported, as the state governments were when he wrote. That kind of support would allow the national government to accrue power vis-à-vis the states, which would recede into the background, eventually becoming mere administrative units.

Whether such powers were strictly granted to the nation in a charter of government was not of great importance to Hamilton. The above actions had not been specifically authorized, after all. Neither had all state powers. To Duane he suggested that Congress merely resume acting as it had at the beginning of the war. Congress might regain "powers competent to the public exegencies" he wrote, "by resuming and exercising the discretionary powers I suppose to have been originally vested in them for the safety of the states."[15] In other words, Congress could resuscitate itself simply by asserting that it was fully sovereign and acting as such. Proceeding this way posed some practical difficulties, but did not offend Hamilton's constitutional scruples: most members of Congress likely would not endorse such a bold scheme, and their habitual timidity had accustomed the public to a powerless central administration. Hamilton's practical side told him that simply resuming extensive discretionary powers would come as too great a shock to be successful. Holding a constitutional convention to change the balance of power was preferable. A convention would provide a clear signal that the balance of power between states and nation would change.

Animating the national government required specific structural changes, of course, particularly in its executive capacity. Hamilton suggested that independent agencies headed by "great officers of state" be formed to replace administration by congressional committees or independent boards. Such positions would attract men of great merit who would lend their expertise to the government's administration. As much as this promised long-term administrative benefits, Hamilton was interested in a short-range advantage. Having the nation's most respected men visibly administrate the national government would be of incalculable importance in tipping public sentiment from support of the states to support of the nation. A figure like Robert Morris heading a department of finance "could by his own personal influence give great weight to the measures he should adopt." The prestige of such individuals, translated into administrative action, would let the nation begin to prevail over the states. Thus the benefits of single-headed executive departments "would be very speedily felt" and "give new life and energy to the operations of government."[16] Among the specific measures he suggested the head of finance implement was a national bank. If a bank could succeed in attracting investors, the credit it would make available would help stabilize the currency, spur the economy, and promote nationalist sentiment. The trick was to "engage a number of monied men of influence to relish the project and make it a business."[17]

Hamilton's outlook on the dynamics of constitutionalism changed little in subsequent years. As states increasingly dominated and the national government faltered he found confirmation for his view that sovereignty was strictly indivisible. States were prevailing because their very activity had garnered public support, which in turn reinforced their ability to act. Public support could still attach itself to a national government, though. "Nationalization" required a constitutional convention to grant the national government full sovereign power and a vigorous initial administration by prestigious individuals.

In 1787 his wish for a convention came true. Hamilton's participation was not particularly active, largely because he knew he could do little to coax delegates to his purely nationalist stance. Nevertheless, Hamilton did not hide his position. His marquee speech of June 18 proposed a national government vested with "compleat sovereignty." The speech is often characterized as a thinly veiled ode to aristocracy, because of the suggestion that senators and the president hold their positions for life. And Hamilton might have hoped these positions would eventually yield an American aristocracy akin to the British. In an immediate sense, however, his goal was much different. Life tenures would attract the nation's most respected individuals to the offices. Their prestige and knowledge would allow for an active government. Once the government's activity was felt by the populace it would be supported. With popular support on the side of the national government its sovereignty would be assured and a stable nationalist system would result. In this light, Hamilton's speech takes on a new cast, as an effort to "make the national government look real," to use the words of James H. Read.[18]

Hamilton's speech of June 18 lays bare his differences with Madison. Though Madison disclaimed authorship of the Virginia Plan, there is little question the plan reflected his hopes for the new regime. At the point in the convention Hamilton decided to outline his own preferences, the Virginia Plan had been extensively discussed and the small states' alternative, the New Jersey Plan, had just been introduced by William Patterson. To most delegates, the two plans provided stark alternatives. Clearly this was the case in terms of representation, where apportionment was by population in the former, whereas each state was equal in the latter; something had to give. Additionally, however, the Virginia Plan was thought by most delegates to be a radical nationalist-oriented departure from the Articles of Confederation. It did, after all, cast aside what most thought the hallmark of state sovereignty, that each state have equal say over collective decisions. Hamilton disagreed. The plan merely authorized the national government to act "in all cases to which the separate States are incompetent," presumably leaving most decision-making to the states. Delegates objecting to the Virginia Plan were focusing too narrowly on the new national legislature, not realizing that the formal division of power would still allow the de facto slide toward complete state autonomy that was occurring under the Articles of Confederation. It was at this point that Hamilton offered his observation that two sovereignties cannot exist within the same limits. The Virginia Plan simply would not ensure that the national government would preponderate. Hamilton therefore declared himself "unfriendly to both" plans.[19]

Unfortunately for Hamilton, the members of the convention adopted a constitution resembling the Virginia Plan. Dedicated to compromise and half-measures, timid because of the popular attachment to the states, they split sovereignty between levels of government. Such an outcome was unsustainable from Hamilton's perspective, and at the end of the convention he admitted that "no man's ideas were more remote from the plan than his own."[20] In the same speech, however, he pledged his support and urged all to sign the document. In the next months he fought for adoption of the regime with as much fervor as anyone. But why? Why would Hamilton fight for something he thought would clearly fail? Because he thought it might be possible to make the Constitution fail in the right way.

Even if the convention had not granted the national government sovereignty, it had served one of the vital functions of such a meeting — it signaled to the populace a major shift in the balance of power between states and nation. That signal provided an opening for an administration sufficiently active to make the national government "real" enough to predominate. The yeoman efforts of the nation's most respected individuals would be required. Foremost among them was George Washington, of course, and Hamilton did what he could to make sure that Washington would accept the presidency. Writing his former commander, Hamilton confided that "on your acceptance of the office of President the success of the new government in its commencement may materially depend."[21] Hamilton knew he would probably be part of the Washington administration. He knew it would be a great challenge to administer the national government into reality, but the future of the United States depended on it. Only such a government could stand up to European powers and help build the country into an economic powerhouse, matters that Hamilton knew would prove most salutary to American citizens generally. Shortly after the Constitutional Convention ended, Hamilton weighed future possibilities in a private memo. He held out some hope for an effective national government, as long as its weak constitutional engine was given an initial push: "A good administration will conciliate the confidence of the people and perhaps enable the government to acquire more consistency than the proposed constitution seems to promise for so great a Country. It may then triumph altogether over the state governments and reduce them to an intire subordination." That was, unfortunately, less likely than further centrifugal deterioration. "If this should not be the case, in the course of a few years, it is probable that the contests about the boundaries of power between the particular governments and the general government and the momentum of the larger states in such contests will produce dissolution of the Union. This after all seems to be the most likely result."[22]

After implementation of the Constitution, then, Hamilton clearly had his work cut out for him. He would do his best to administrate the government into a sovereign existence. That work would be disapproved of by those who, like Madison, thought the Constitution's division of power definitive — at least as definitive as language would allow. Hamilton ignored them because the stakes were so high and they were so wrong.

Even though the convention set the cart of government higher on a hill, it would still roll down to a state of rest in the valley of disunion. In the months after ratification Hamilton steeled himself for the Herculean task of pushing the cart over a divide, where it would continue to roll naturally to the valley of national unity. Presented with such a faulty framework that was what a leader in his position was supposed to do — once "passions" would be "turned towards [the] general government" his work would be done and the arrangement "would maintain itself."[23]

Madison and the
Constitutionalism of Suprapolitical Stasis

Hamilton and Madison readily agreed that the Confederation Congress was not up to the task of governing. Both believed that citizens suffered because states retained sovereign power. Both felt the Union at risk because of the centrifugal tendencies of such political arrangements. Thus it is unsurprising to find them collaborating on the great effort to strengthen the national government in 1787 and 1788. Madison and Hamilton were united on the most recognizable constitutional question of the day, whether ratification that would usher in a stronger national government should occur. Afterward, they were both primarily concerned with how to make the constitutional system succeed. What constitutional success meant to them differed and required different approaches. With the advancement of time, their visions inevitably clashed, yielding a major change in coalitional politics.

Whereas Hamilton did not believe the states and nation could ever share extensive powers, Madison felt they could coexist as governments. Federalist #18, the latter's rather tedious relation of the defects of the Achaean League and the Amphictyonic Council, "emphatically illustrates the tendency of federal bodies rather to anarchy among the members than to tyranny in the head."[24] This sounds reminiscent of Hamilton's position. But it is important to note that Madison's use of the word "federal" had not evolved to what it means to us today. He applied the word solely to the kind of government we call "confederal." Modern confederacies were treated in the next two essays. They too tend to be "nerveless," regardless of the constitutional powers granted their central governments. Far from being dangerous to create a more powerful national government, Madison argued it would be dangerous not to. Maintaining the status quo — really maintaining the slide to state dominance — would either bring complete disunion or provoke a usurper to reunite the states and rule them by force. Far better to establish a republican government on the national scale while it could still be done. Concluding his summary of confederacies in Federalist #20, Madison finds that "a sovereignty over sovereigns, a government over governments, a legislation for communities as contradistinguished from individuals, as it is a solecism in theory, so in practice it is subversive of the order and ends of civil polity."[25] Madison expressed similar sentiments both at the Philadelphia Convention and in his private letters.[26]

Madison found the Union in the unfortunate position of having initially adopted a defective kind of constitution. All confederations had inevitably succumbed to the same mortal disease: constituent states came to dominate the central authority, eventually destroying the confederation. The reason behind this type of government's inability to effectively divide power was readily apparent. Constituent states retained full sovereignty while some sovereign powers were also granted to the corporate government. This was the great error of the Articles of Confederation, not that it divided powers between levels of government but that it granted powers redundantly. The Articles "endeavored to accomplish impossibilities; to reconcile a partial sovereignty in the Union, with complete sovereignty in the States; to subvert a mathematical axiom, by taking away a part, and letting the whole remain."[27] State-centric attitudes weren't tearing at the confederation so much as twice-granted formal constitutional powers. The solution to the specific problem Madison identified was not to grant the nation an exclusive right to wield all coercive power but to divide powers as clearly as possible between the states and nation. Substituting what we call a federation for the confederation would do the trick. Madison could not yet articulate this remedy as succinctly as we can, but he had made the conceptual distinction and was devoted to a federal arrangement. Hamilton made no such distinction; all regimes that attempted to split powers were prone to centrifugal failure.

Accordingly, Madison revealed his "strong bias in favor of an enumeration and definition of the powers necessary to be exercised by the national Legislature" very early in the Philadelphia Convention.[28] He also revealed this anti-Hamiltonian stance to Jefferson shortly after the convention adjourned, writing that one of its great objects was "to draw a line of demarcation which would give to the General Government every power requisite for general purposes, and leave to the States every power which might be most beneficially administered by them."[29] If this was indeed the purpose of the convention, then Madison was aware Hamilton aimed to subvert it. He knew that for Hamilton no such line could be drawn. Differences within the convention did not end there. To Jefferson he outlined no less than five different positions for dealing with the federal relation. He characterized Hamilton's preference as abolishing the states altogether. Others proposed that Congress be granted indefinite powers to legislate, either with or without a veto on state legislation. Madison's own hope was to grant Congress limited powers to legislate and provide it with an ability to veto state laws. A fifth alternative was finally agreed to: granting Congress limited powers to legislate with no negative on state laws.[30] Clearly, the Federalists were not of one mind on the proper constitution of the federal relation.

The negative on state laws was crucial to Madison. As he understood it, this provision lodged sovereignty in the national government. It allowed the national government to guard its own power against state encroachments and be the ultimate arbiter of constitutionality. Unlike Hamilton, then, Madison's conception of national sovereignty did not entail possession of the full range of coercive power, just the guarantee that when disputes arose between governments the national government would have the final say. An added benefit of the veto was that state laws that infringed on the rights of individuals could be voided. Madison touted the negative as the least coercive (and thus probably the most effective) way to ensure national sovereignty.[31] His leap of faith in proposing the veto, one that others at the Philadelphia Convention readily pointed out, was that the nation would abide by its formal constitutional powers. For Madison, constructing fundamental law that was sufficiently meaningful that its stipulations would be respected would be the hallmark of a successful constitution — precisely what he believed the convention could accomplish.

Unfortunately, the convention voted down his treasured veto. This was a blow to Madison's hopes for constitutional stability; without the veto, he was unsure the national government could protect its powers. In response, Madison threw himself into the effort to construct a definitive list of national powers.[32] Perhaps an equilibrium of power could be maintained in a federal system if the national government's responsibilities and powers were defined with sufficient clarity. His response to what he perceived as the convention's greatest blow against national sovereignty was directly opposite Hamilton's. The loss of the veto caused Madison to cling all the more tenaciously to a static vision of defined powers. This very enumeration of powers was what Hamilton found to be the convention's greatest blow to national sovereignty. It made Hamilton come to realize that he would have to stretch the Constitution's specific stipulations by asserting broad discretionary powers, pursuing its nationalizing spirit rather than its sovereignty-splitting letter.

The reasons Madison feared dissolution of the Union were similar to Hamilton's. He concurred that it would be impossible for individual states to defend themselves against outside aggression and that disputes between and within states could not be settled absent national arbitration and in extreme cases the use of force. Madison added his famed analysis from Federalist #10 that states were poor respecters of rights left to themselves.[33] Since both men were quite sure the nation was headed for disunion under the Articles of Confederation, the gravity of the problems that would result dictated that they bury their differences. But if things were to take an unexpected turn, toward an assertive national government, there promised to be no agreement between them.

Both men contemplated the potential results of an assertive national regime before the events of the 1790s. In his 1780 letter to James Duane, Hamilton had entertained the idea that an aggressive national government wielding broad discretionary powers could be the nation's salvation. Madison knew just as well as Hamilton that much of what the Confederation Congress had accomplished was "done without the least color of constitutional authority."[34] In Federalist #38 Madison condoned those actions, but only because Congress was forced to work under such a faulty constitution. Congress faced a "dreadful dilemma" in choosing whether to flaunt the Articles or let the Union founder. They chose to administer the national government despite the unfortunate extraconstitutionality of their actions. In contrast to the breezy Hamilton, Madison never considered the assertion of broad discretionary powers by the national government as anything more than the lesser of two evils to be undertaken in an emergency brought by a defective constitution overly stingy in its grant of national powers. In a properly formed government, transgressing constitutional bounds by wielding broad discretionary powers was taboo. A frequent mischaracterization of Madison is that he changed from advocating broad discretionary powers to being a "strict constructionist." More accurately, the constitutional context changed around Madison, requiring an altered response. A constitution so faulty that the national legislature had to assert broad discretionary powers gave way to a better constitution that could be treated as such fundamental laws should, with reverence for its specific meaning.

Madison hoped for nothing less than to create a definitive fundamental law that would "last for ever."[35] Gary Rosen writes that Madison's understanding of a successful charter of government was "a kind of godless civil religion, with the Constitution serving as an altar."[36] If the Constitution was to be the religion's altar, it was also to be its written language, its scripture. In general this constitutional scripture would provide widely understood and recognized parameters for the actions of each level and branch of government. There would inevitably be disputes over its interpretation, but with a well-written constitution these disputes would not be so severe as to erode the sense that its provisions meant something and could not be transgressed. Constitutional malleability was the great evil to avoid. From Hamilton's perspective, the trouble with this view is that Madison chose an inherently unstable arrangement, one that divided powers between levels of government, as his preferred constitutional scripture. Hamilton had no doubt that Madison's preferred government would never achieve the latter's ultimate goal: timeless stability.

To ensure its sacred character, Madison's constitutional scripture would receive its form above and outside normal acts of legislation. Its power would be officially sanctioned by clearly recognized acts of popular consent occurring in historical time. The constitution would also be "popular" either directly or indirectly in all its aspects. Each of these matters were inimical to Hamilton's thinking.

One reason Madison thought the states flaunted the Articles of Confederation was that it had not been treated extraordinarily. In each particular state, its authority rested on the sanction of the state legislature, just like any other law. Thus there was no reason to believe, nor foolproof constitutional argument to claim, that the Articles trumped state laws opposed to it. Madison strongly advocated that the Constitution be ratified by ad hoc conventions. This extraordinary arrangement would mark the Constitution as an exceptional legal entity, a true act of popular sovereignty outside, above, and unalterable by mere statutory law.[37] The convention adopted this "indispensible" provision, but probably more because it thought getting state legislatures to ratify would be more difficult.

The ratification process gave Madison some scares, particularly when states threatened to ratify conditionally. Accepting the Constitution on a contingent basis was unacceptable to Madison for similar reasons as legislative ratification: it perpetuated the debilitating idea that individual states could dictate the content of fundamental law. That possibility led right back to the problem of confederations. Ratification occurred without anything more than recommendatory amendments, however, gratifying Madison that the quest to create a constitutional law superior to statutory law had begun auspiciously. An amendment mechanism was in place that incorporated legislative sanction, but it required supermajorities in both houses of Congress and approval by three-quarters of the states. None could mistake the message: the legislature alone could not alter the Constitution, nor could even the entire national governing apparatus. Hamilton's postimplementation project would directly flaunt this principle. Formulating legislative plans that would favorably modify the balance of power seemingly expressed in the Constitution is what Hamilton set out to do and did. One could not have struck a more direct blow at Madison's static constitutionalism. At the end of his life, Madison acknowledged as much in an interview with Nicholas Trist:

In a word, the divergence between us took place — from [Hamilton's] wishing . . . to administer the Government . . . into what he thought it ought to be; while on my part, I endeavored to make it conform to the Constitution as understood by the Convention that produced it and recommended it, and particularly by the State conventions that adopted it.[38]

"Produced," "recommended," and particularly "adopted" — past events all, upon which any legitimate political action in the present hinged. Hamilton was no less interested in the people's consent, but for him the time sequence was reversed by practical considerations. Having been presented with an inherently unstable Constitution not adequate to remedy the confederation's problems, he could only try to administrate it to perfection with consent coming once the nation's citizens saw its benefits.

Denying an Earlier Version of Himself?
On Madison's Constancy

Recent works in political thought and the history of ideas offer widely disparate versions of how the founding era affected James Madison's thinking. These competing accounts have proven confusing to those aiming to discern why politics took the shape it did in the early republic. At the risk of adding to the confusion, but with the hope of limiting it, I will offer an alternative view.

The first assessment of Madison, the one with the most proponents and the longest history, is that his thinking changed dramatically in the years after ratification, in large part because Virginia's interests and the influence of Jefferson moved him from a fervent nationalizer to a champion of states' rights. Madison's two most widely read biographers, Irving Brant and Ralph Ketcham, share this view. A renewed scholarly interest in modes of constitutional interpretation has led recent variants of this theme to focus on Madison's interpretive theory. Stanley Elkins and Eric McKitrick find that it served Madison's purposes to make a 180-degree turn shortly after ratification. By the end of the First Congress, Publius's "loose construction" had given way to Madison's "strict construction" in an attempt to minimize Hamilton's influence. Although his political partner "Jefferson could move into strict construction with rather less strain than Madison, . . . Madison's position was now fully reversed. In denying Publius, he was denying an earlier version of himself."[39]

Recently, this position has split into two distinct strands. Joseph M. Lynch views Madison's approach to the Constitution as inconsistent even within a narrow time frame, indicating that he cynically fit constitutional arguments to the subject at hand.[40] Lynch relates that "in the first session of the First Congress, Madison placed the membership on notice that when the interests of his state and region, and . . . of his own career, were involved, and when the stakes were high enough, he was capable of subtle, sometimes substantial, shifts in constitutional positioning." His maneuvering "served only to diminish his personal authority . . . tarnish[ing] his reputation as a disinterested expositor of the constitutional text."[41] Meanwhile, Jack N. Rakove describes a much more intellectually honest Madison, but one who groped his way toward an effective concept of *originalism* through the 1790s. Madison's protestation that the understandings of state ratification conventions were definitive did not exist at the founding and only reached full flower with the debate over the Jay Treaty. Developing this interpretive strategy was manifestly political, according to Rakove, in large part because constitutionalism and politics proper were not so conceptually distinct then as we now think them to be. In contrast to Lynch, Rakove emphasizes the defensive nature of Madison's interpretive strategy and his consistent use of it once developed. "By 1796," Rakove notes, "the politics of opposition had placed Madison in a position he had never expected to occupy."[42]

A second set of interpretations point to Madison's consistency.[43] This view is most forcefully stated by Lance Banning. Banning believes the above scholars have been misled by Federalist attempts to portray Madison as a turncoat and they don't really understand his full preratification position. Banning makes the case that, rightly understood, Madison was something of a strict constructionist throughout his career, even during his service in the Confederation Congress. "His respect for written limitations of authority and charter boundaries between the powers of the nation and the states did not develop after 1789. It was apparent during the Confederation's darkest years." True, Madison sometimes allied with those in favor of nationalist reforms, but only selectively. He was "simply not a 'nationalist' during the early 1780s — not, at least, in several of the senses commonly suggested by that term. He was not an early or enthusiastic friend of radical reforms. His cooperation with the Morrisites did not reflect a concord of opinion."[44] If Madison's preratification nationalism is as exaggerated as Banning claims, then his mode of constitutional interpretation, stressing the understandings of the state convention delegates, is far from a radical departure. Banning believes a big part of the reason why Madison's nationalism has been overemphasized is a "reductionist fixation on the absolute centrality of *Federalist* no. 10," which proffered a nationalist solution to state problems, but was never intended as a full exposition of his political theory.[45]

James Read underscores Madison's overall consistency as well, but also points out that the threat to liberty he perceived as most grave dictated how he acted. "What especially distinguishes Madison, besides the seriousness of his commitment to civil liberties," according to Read, "is his appreciation of the extremely broad range from which threats to liberty can proceed."[46] Sometimes liberty is threatened from one quarter and sometimes another. Madison's attempts at putting out fires where they occur is why many view him as inconsistent; sometimes preserving liberty meant throwing one's weight to the federal side of the equation, at other times to the states. During the confederation period, preserving liberty dictated augmenting national power against the usurping states; during Hamilton's tenure as secretary of the treasury, it meant shifting to protect the states from nationalist encroachment.

Instead of illuminating James Madison's thought, these competing interpretations serve to obscure it and confuse scholars who study the era. For instance, in an otherwise masterful account of how the U.S. Senate transformed from a Federalist-envisioned "American House of Lords" to a much more democratic institution that actively worked as the House's partner in formulating legislation, Elaine K. Swift remains agnostic about why forces favoring the latter kind of institution prevailed as early as they did. Specifically, Swift cannot account for why the group fighting a more elitist conception of the role of the Senate included Madison and his colleagues. Swift calls the Madisonian-Antifederalist axis "an unlikely alliance."[47] She wonders aloud whether the supporters of the Constitution who became Democratic-Republicans "had genuinely changed their minds" or just "pragmatically sought the support of the lower rank in building a strong partisan base in a more democratic political environment." Either way, "they deprived the Senate of the consensus it needed to fulfill these [Federalist] purposes."[48]

The democratization of the Senate that Swift observes would certainly not have occurred when it did without the Madisonians reinforcing the former Antifederalists. Further, that important development may not have taken place at all if Madison and his colleagues remained in the Federalist fold, setting a far different tone for the regime. Since Madison led this sizable, critical faction, we cannot understand why the American government took the shape it did without understanding his reasoning. Absent such knowledge, political scientists and historians may provide important descriptive analyses like Swift's, but the logic behind the evolution of the American polity remains elusive.

My alternative to these seemingly contradictory analyses has been hinted at but never fully articulated. Without elaborating, Marvin Myers tantalizingly states that after ratification "the analysis of *Federalist No.* 10 disappeared for a season. The mortal disease of majority faction ceased to trouble Madison."[49] Forrest McDonald gets a bit more specific in figuring out a reason for this disappearance in a footnote: "Madison *could* not have believed in the efficacy of the faction-checking machinery described in *Federalist* number 10 after the spring of 1791, when it had become evident to his way of thinking that the Hamiltonian 'faction' had captured total control of the national government."[50] For a season in Madison's life, the themes of Federalist #10 were crucially important. Just as abruptly, its main premises seemed to crumble. This development forced a change in Madison's thinking about how to safeguard rights in republican governments. The ends of popular government did not change, but the means of obtaining these ends did. The magnitude and importance of this alteration in Madison's constellation of ideas were much greater than any in his interpretive stance toward constitutions.

Jack Rakove's deft treatment of Madison's gradually articulated theory of originalism is well-taken. How much of a departure this formulation was from his earlier stance is the key question, however. There are several instances from the Confederation Congress where Madison refused to endorse a measure because Congress lacked constitutional authority to deal with it, precisely what he aimed at in the 1790s in arguing that the understandings of state ratifying conventions were definitive. The most important instance of Madison's refusal to loosely construe the Articles of Confederation was in response to Robert Morris's proposal of a national bank in May 1781. Madison's initial opposition foreshadowed his dispute with Hamilton: Congress lacked the power of incorporation and so could not commission a bank.[51] The year 1781 was a desperate one financially for the fledgling republic, though, and by the end of it Madison endorsed the bank, but not without experiencing the kind of "dreadful dilemma" he described in *Federalist* #38. In changing his stance, the young Virginian acknowledged that the powers set down in the national constitution were not decisive because they were so paltry as to threaten the Union. This concession would prove misleading to Hamilton, who assumed Madison would once again see the necessity for a national bank a decade later, despite its discretionary nature. For Madison, attention to a changed constitutional context trumped his own personal conviction that a national bank would be beneficial. Setting a proper tone for the new regime required respecting the Constitution's division of powers, a stance that would have destroyed the Union under the Articles. The power of incorporation had been proposed and rejected in the Philadelphia Convention, and if the Constitution were to succeed, its specific division of powers had to be respected, dictating rejection of the bank proposal. Madison might have worked harder to clarify this contextual distinction during the ratification debate. Instead his efforts focused on refuting the Antifederalists, who were intent on narrowing national discretion as much as possible.

Madison's reaction to the first national bank proposal also shows that any effort to portray him as a consistent strict constructionist fails. Nevertheless, it indicates that he took seriously the linguistic bounds set down in charters of fundamental law and that he was loath to extend discretionary powers. Additionally, Madison had demonstrated a reluctance to loosely construe the Constitution well before the debate over the Bank Bill. In the first month Congress met, some Federalists suggested that representatives of the national government administer loyalty oaths to state officials. Madison objected on constitutional grounds, saying that the national government "ought to avoid an assumption of power" — requiring state officers to take an oath was authorized; having the national government administer the oath was not.[52] Given the other issues facing them, this must have seemed a trivial distinction to most in the First Congress. And it is hardly the kind of parochial or self-serving measure that Lynch describes as animating Madison's constitutional positions at this time. Someone intent on molding the Constitution to his own narrow purposes would hardly expend political capital on such an issue. To be sure, Madison took the stance he did to mold the Constitution — but in a way that comported with his constitutional principles rather than his immediate interests. Opposing federal power to administer oaths was important because of the precedent it would set, thwarting the first of many possible discretionary powers that the national government could assert for itself.

Madison's constitutionalism is vexing because he adheres to a middling philosophy in a series of bipolar environments. While we often think in the polar terms of strict construction and loose construction or their other labels, Madison would have rejected such a dichotomy in favor of a threefold typology. Just as in the First Congress, through the 1780s, many members of Congress, Madison included, used the phrases "natural construction" and "forced construction" to describe proposals that were not specifically sanctioned by the wording of a constitution. A natural construction might include something not specifically enumerated but logically and closely implied by it. Forced constructions went beyond the phraseology and the logical intent of specific enumerations.[53] At the other extreme was the kind of crabbed Antifederalist-style construction Madison fought in the Confederation Congress and objected to in the Federalist Papers, which required "expressed" words as authorization. Madison continued to oppose that kind of strict construction, voting against its inclusion in the set of amendments Congress endorsed. In Madison's mind, then, there were three broad types of constitutional interpretation from which to choose: strict construction, natural construction, and forced construction. Madison consistently favored the middle option against the other two. The language he used to defend natural construction and the settings he found most authoritative in discovering "natural construction" changed, but Madison never strayed from the idea that constitutional clauses provide meaningful bounds that should not be transgressed and grant a certain amount of discretion to lawmakers. Far from being a great departure, the interpretive theory Madison developed in the 1790s was very much in line with his earlier thinking. The perceived failure of the extended republic forced a much more pointed departure and led directly to the particular changes we see in Madison's behavior during the 1790s, foremost among them his embrace of partisan politics.

The cynical maneuverings that Lynch describes, between the assertion of implied powers and a very narrow reading of clauses, can be explained largely by his own inability to come to the same conclusions as Madison about "natural constructions." This is an understandable but faulty result of Lynch's habit of viewing constitutional arguments primarily as instrumental, post hoc rationalizations — something not unknown in Madison's time but inimical to Madison's own hopes of endowing a document with specific meaning. Despite this, Lynch's work provides a significant critique of the Madisonian project. Like many in the 1790s, Lynch fails to see Madison's positions as "natural constructions" — even after meticulously considering his justificatory speeches. Coming to agreement on what is a natural construction and what is a forced construction is far harder than Madison anticipated.

By contrast, the coherency that Lance Banning carves out for Madison can only be accomplished by pushing Federalist #10 into a dark corner. Describing the essay as only a part of Madison's thinking is a necessary corrective to overly broad interpretations offered by Charles Beard and Robert Dahl. Going beyond that correction to question its significance around the time of ratification is a serious misstep in gauging Madison's mind-set. While I edge toward Banning and Read in thinking that Madison was more consistent in his constitutional philosophy than not, I simultaneously quarrel with their assertion that very little changed after ratification. Establishing this position requires further attention to the themes of that famous essay.

The Kaleidoscopic Majoritarianism of Federalist #10

Although few Federalists apparently even understood the benefits he claimed for the extended republic, Madison himself relied heavily on its logic for a time. Larry D. Kramer finds that the ideas contained in Federalist #10 came to Madison in distinct revelations occurring in the twelve months before the Philadelphia Convention first met. Before the summer of 1786 Madison's thinking was quite conventional, lacking "any notion that reform at the national level might have something to do with solving problems in the states." Only in preparation for the Annapolis Convention, Kramer finds, did Madison "uncover a startling pattern: the fatal weakness in all [confederations] was the tendency of the provincial governments to quarrel with each other and encroach on the central authority."[54] A "second breakthrough" occurred in April 1787, when he realized that extending the sphere of government could solve the centrifugal tendency of confederations.[55]

Kramer's language suggests just how enamored of these new ideas Madison must have been. As is typical of someone who has undergone a revelatory experience, Madison would repeat his new, treasured ideas over and over. Articulations of the benefits of the extended republic appear at several critical junctures: in the "Vices Memo" Madison wrote in preparation for the Philadelphia Convention; in one of his first major speeches there on June 6; in his October 24, 1787, letter to Jefferson explaining the proceedings of the convention; in his first contribution to *The Federalist*, its tenth installment; and for good measure an abbreviated version is wedged into Federalist #51. Madison articulated his discovery of the benefits of the extended republic at almost every turn. Responding to Jefferson's objection to the national veto, Madison argued that the faction-solving mechanism of the extended republic would make the veto power benign.[56]

The national veto had disappeared by the time Madison wrote to Jefferson and with it one of the key mechanisms on which he felt he could rely to make the national government work. In its absence, Madison rested his faith on two remaining pillars: the theory of the extended republic and the distinctness of national and state powers. For Madison's own vision of the new constitutional republic to come to fruition, his predictive statement of how the extended republic would work would need to come true. There is every reason to believe that Madison thought it would.

In the first sentence of Federalist #10, Madison writes of the "violence of faction." It would be easy to misconstrue that short phrase to mean that factionalism is inherently violent, but we are shortly introduced to the precise set of circumstances in which it is. Factionalism is violent where a majority group can consistently get its way. "When a majority is included in a faction, the form of popular government . . . enables it to sacrifice to its ruling passion or interest both the public good and the rights of other citizens."[57] If governments can be arranged to ensure there will not be a majority faction, the violence is automatically broken. Government will not turn utopian under such circumstances, but it will be much less likely to trample rights or spill beyond constitutional bounds.

The brilliance of Madison's remedy to majoritarianism is that it employed already widely held assumptions being reinforced daily by Antifederalists. A national republic was not viable, they claimed, because the uniqueness of each particular state could not be represented in a national republic. That position contains three distinct ideas, and Madison built his argument around two of them. First, Madison agreed with the Antifederalists that states were relatively homogeneous internally. One could easily discern a particular political culture in each. Madison faulted that political culture for being overbearing. Secondly, both the Antifederalists and Madison found the states to be heterogeneous when compared with one another. Each state was distinctive. Madison used this heterogeneity to posit that majority factions would be very unlikely at the national level. Thus a plan for preventing debilitating majoritarianism emerged from readily accepted assumptions about the states. The Antifederalists' third assumption was that states were altogether too different to successfully coexist within a sovereign structure. Madison disagreed; out of disparate states a national regime could be forged that would curb the problematic majoritarianism extant in the relatively homogeneous states.

What is less clearly stated than Madison's distrust of semipermanent majorities is the assumption of a tight link between mass opinion and the preferences of representatives. This statement may come as a surprise, for it is easily remembered that Madison feels the extended republic will broaden the field of candidates who possess "the most attractive merit" and can "refine and enlarge public views."[58] Representatives cannot refine and enlarge public views without there being some disjunction between public opinion and legislative decisions. Yet the premise that national representatives will serve as a buffer to public opinion is not only qualified in the essay, it is also covertly contradicted. Madison himself acknowledges that "enlightened statesmen will not always be at the helm."[59] He also compares the act of representing with adjudicating a case directly involving the judge. In that situation, actors are likely to err because they are personally interested in the outcome. The analogy presumes the interestedness of representatives. Legislators — essentially judges in their own cases — will be driven by favored concerns averse to a more common good, the hallmark of factionalism. The interestedness of legislators is such an obvious fact to Madison that he asserts it simply by posing a rhetorical question: "What are the different classes of legislators but advocates and parties to the causes which they determine?"[60] Legislators, just like factions, generally act in an interested manner. Does the representatives' interestedness mirror that of their constituency, though? Madison certainly thinks that is the case in the state legislatures. In them "the most numerous party, or in other words, the most powerful faction must be expected to prevail."[61] This descriptive statement moves quickly and seamlessly from assessing the strength of a faction among the populace to a conclusion about what one can expect from public policy in such a state. Madison here observes that state elites accurately reflect mass preferences. That is precisely the problem, for popular majorities are electing legislative majorities whose policies turn out to be disruptive. But the long-standing assumption has been that Madison believed representation would be substantially different on the national level. Federalist #46 puts a serious dent in that assumption. If anything, writes Madison, "the members of the federal legislature will be likely to attach themselves *too much* to local objects." He still believed that "a local spirit will infallibly prevail much more in the members of Congress, than a national spirit will prevail in the legislatures of the particular states."[62]

Further, the extended republic's success is predicated on the likelihood that national legislators *will* advocate the causes of their constituencies — to a point, of course, with each needing to compromise to effect policy. Not only will national representatives be "interested," they will reflect the very factional interests displayed by the public. The multiplicity of popular factions extant among the populace will prove beneficial, thinks Madison, because that multiplicity will also be present in the halls of Congress. Compromise in the national good will be brought by the mixture of the Virginia tobacco planters with Massachusetts mercantile men and South Carolina rice barons, each with their own distinct set of interests. If anything, what makes national representatives more refined is that despite their localist bent, they will more happily compromise than their brethren on the state level.

One of Madison's concealed assumptions in Federalist #10 is that issues will be treated discretely by the new regime. That is, for the new republic to work as Madison says it will, majorities must be cobbled together from among several minority factions on each particular issue in turn. We might call this view *kaleidoscopic majoritarianism*, as alliances between groups will be ad hoc and temporary. Any sort of durability in alliances threatens Madison's institutional remedy. If a majority alliance persists through time and encompasses a variety of issues, then it would replicate the damage caused by a unified majority faction. The groups in alliance would still be seeking particularistic interests averse to the common good, after all. The persistence of an alliance would spell one of two things. First, the groups might not be so different after all, meaning that they would not have to compromise much. In that case, legislation produced would not approximate the common good much better than that produced by a majority faction. Those in the majority could count on the durability of their alliance and proceed to trample those not in the majority.

Alternatively, a durable alliance could mean that disparate groups were colluding to obtain something of great importance to each of them. Imagine three minority groups, each having a single primary objective not at odds with the other groups' objective. Each could easily achieve their objective through a simple quid pro quo arrangement if their combined membership equals a majority. In that scenario, three issues would be "captured" by minority groups that would not have to compromise at all to achieve their interested objective. Needless to say, when self-interested minority groups can pass legislation unchanged there is little hope of approximating the common good. The extended republic was designed to foster legislative bargains on a broad array of issues. But as soon as legislative bargains occurred across issue domains, the template for republican compromise presented in *The Federalist* is stretched to the breaking point. To refute their critics, Federalists might have noted that logrolling in Congress could ensure that key local interests would be satisfied. None made that argument. Madison himself surely could not, for it would mean admitting that particular factions could still predominate in the extended republic.

Madison's presumption of a lack of connectiveness between groups was not simply naive. The view was almost surely based on his experience in the Confederation Congress where durable national parties had failed to form. It was entirely logical of him to presume that national representatives would remain factionalized, allying on a particular issue only to fall out of alliance on the next. Despite his fear of majority factions, Madison did have a deep commitment to majoritarianism as the proper legislative decision rule. The kaleidoscopic majoritarianism envisioned in Federalist #10 would approximate the common good because it would force substantial compromises from a variety of factions on each issue. In 1787, Madison believed that kaleidoscopic majoritarianism would allow for republican government at the national level; any more connective kind of majoritarianism threatened republican government. That is the idea he would jettison in the early years of the new regime.

Because Madison's analysis is of popular groups, one could easily think of him as a sociologist. And surely he is engaged in studying the "development, structure, interaction, and collective behavior of organized groups of human beings," as sociologists do. Yet Madison's argument in Federalist #10 is unsociological in a crucial way: he specifically rejects social solutions to the social problems he discerns, relying instead on institutional and structural remedies. In 1787, Madison believed that the most pressing social problems could be remedied through political engineering. The reason pure democracies fail to remedy their social problems is that their governments are equivalent to their social world — they can't alter the raw factionalism found there. State constitutions have made "valuable improvements" on direct democracy by moving beyond a literal representation of all things social. But a superior sovereign structure, provided by the Constitution, definitively contains "the social" without stifling it.

During the course of 1787 and 1788, Madison would become enamored of his pet idea, the extended republic. He came to believe in the logic of Federalist #10 so much that it quelled his initial disappointment over the lack of a veto power over state legislation, something he had initially considered essential for the government's success. The assumptions Madison carried into that essay and into the First Congress were very much a product of his experience in the Confederation Congress, with shifting alliances and very little cross-issue discipline. Madison logically assumed that this kaleidoscopic politics was the only kind possible at the national level.[63] The events of 1790 and 1791 would prove him wrong. A majority faction, pursuing their particularistic interests, formed at the national level. Madison's response would be to seek a social solution to this political problem, precisely the reverse of what the extended republic was supposed to accomplish.

Conciliatory Hints

James Madison knew the Federalist alliance was a tenuous one. Certainly it was apparent to him that Hamilton's nationalism went far beyond his own position. But he also knew more generally that "Federalism," the label uniting their group and separating them from the Antifederalists, was thin and misleading in that his constitutional philosophy taken as a whole was closer to that of many Antifederalist leaders than to a major portion of the Federalists. Thomas Jefferson relayed such a view in a letter to George Mason during the First Congress. Mason had written to Jefferson asking him to bridge any rift between him and Madison, which Mason feared may have resulted from his refusal to sign the Constitution. Jefferson reassured Mason that Madison had not "turned cool" toward him. On the contrary, reported the secretary of state, "I have always heard him [Madison] say that tho' you and he appeared to differ in your systems, yet you were in truth nearer together than most persons who were classed under the same appellation."[64]

Mason and Madison both had a "system," to use Jefferson's term, or full constitutional philosophies, to be more specific. Their constitutional philosophies appear much different to the indiscriminate eye because at a particularly crucial time they were caught on opposing sides of a very public question. Their stance on this public question labeled them — for all time. Yet the two simple labels do not capture the full range of their constitutional thinking. Just as diverse views within both camps separated Mason and Madison from those who happened to share the same label, a full exposition of their constitutional thinking yielded important similarities between the two Virginians. And if Madison knew that his own constitutional philosophy was far closer to Mason's and his kind than Hamilton's, then he surely contemplated that they might very well be on the same side on many issues treated by the new national regime, including the crucial question of what powers were appropriate for the national government to wield.

Latent similarities in the thinking of Madison and the Antifederalists did lead them to ally in the years after ratification. Surely their thinking evolved somewhat as time progressed, and that is particularly true for Madison. But more than any change in his thinking, the progression of constitutional time exposed the constitutional preferences Madison held in common with the Antifederalists well before ratification. His thinking on a whole range of constitutional matters was closer to that of men like Mason and Thomas Tudor Tucker than that of Hamilton. Tucker, the same man who represented South Carolina in the first two Congresses, was a Bermuda-born, Edinborough-educated physician. Tucker wrote a commentary on South Carolina's constitution under the name "Philodemus" three years before the national ratification debate would get under way. The pamphlet, entitled "Conciliatory Hints Attempting, by a Fair State of Matters, to Remove Party Prejudices," was written before anyone could anticipate what the federal Constitution would look like, but its range of constitutional commentary reveals an outlook strikingly similar to Madison's in certain ways.[65]

Philodemus's pamphlet does not directly comment on the work of Publius, nor on the specific phrases of the Constitution. But those specifics are precisely what might serve to obscure their similarities, because they include the matters on which Tucker and Madison disagreed and led them to be on opposite sides of the ratification question. Tucker's pamphlet, written for a different context, raises other issues where the two agreed, revealing that the alliance that Tucker and Madison would help forge was far from accidental. On the subject of how constitutions should be formed and dealt with in practice, these two were much closer to each other than either was to Hamilton.

Tucker believed that the greatest problem with South Carolina's constitution was that it had been formulated and adopted by the state legislature. Though there was a single written document of fundamental law, Tucker still thought this practice too close to the British model, where the sum of parliamentary decrees *were* the constitution. If the legislature could form a constitution and change it at will, as it had in both 1776 and 1778, then in theory its power was as unlimited as Parliament's. Tucker called for a specially convened constitutional convention, which would act as a genuine "social covenant entered into by express consent of the people."[66] The main purpose of this convention would be to define the powers granted to the people's representatives in a way that was "unalterable by the legislative, or by any other authority but that by which it is framed."[67] In his placement of "the constitutional" outside and above the legislature, Tucker's vision for South Carolina is very reminiscent of the kind of suprapolitical stasis Madison hoped the national Constitution could provide. Both sought constitutions that meaningfully defined limited governmental powers legitimated by a clear expression of popular approval prior to implementation. These goals, central to Tucker and Madison, were not of concern to Hamilton.

Tucker also objected that the state constitution set up governing institutions too much like the British institutions, in that it attempted to replicate estates-style representation. Under the provisional constitution of 1776, members of the very small upper house, or Legislative Council, were selected by the lower house. The constitution of 1778 allowed for popular election of a senate, but it had just twenty-nine members and a high property qualification for eligibility. The Charleston elite who continued to dominate politically after the Revolution were clearly in favor of an upper house that would act as the House of Lords did in England, restraining the democratic excesses of the people at large. Jerome Nadelhaft relates that Governor John Rutledge was even against the reforms of 1778, justifying his position against the new constitution by saying "'the people preferred . . . a compounded or mixed government to a simple democracy, or one verging toward it' because the effects of democratic power 'have been arbitrary, severe, and destructive.'"[68] Tucker was appalled that the state's aristocracy assumed it should possess so much power.

State politics was resembling Britain's, not surprisingly, with parties inherently pitted against each other engaged in a precarious balancing act: the British government "is, and always has been a government of contention," wrote Philodemus, "in which the opposite parties have been for a length of time by chance so nearly balanced as not yet to have destroyed each other. How long that will last, it is difficult to say; but it may be affirmed that there is nothing of stability in their constitution."[69] Such contention was to be replaced by a "pure republican" government, where each institution would represent the citizenry as a whole rather than a particular subset of it. Bicameralism was to be retained as a check on elites, ensuring that if one branch of the legislature would become self-serving it would be checked by the other.

Though Madison was less vocal about it he was no less opposed to the British estates-style of representation. In contrast to Hamilton, who was particularly impressed with Britain's representation scheme and wished to emulate it as closely as possible, Madison did not think the British government worthy of imitation. In Federalist #39, Madison lumped it with other faulty governments that combined republicanism with aristocracy, writing "the government of England . . . has one republican branch only."[70] Private correspondence confirms Madison's distaste for Britain's institutional arrangements. John Adams's *Defence of the Constitutions of the United States* was written in 1786. Adams's book defended the state constitutions against their European critics by emphasizing that the institutions they commissioned did indeed resemble the British mixed constitution. Madison lamented to Jefferson that Adams's book was so well written it would probably "revive the predilections of this Country for the British Constitution." In the same breath he hoped "many of the remarks in it, which are unfriendly to republicanism, may not receive fresh weight from the operations of our Governments."[71] Madison's father also read Adams's *Defense*, which his son had sent him early in 1787. James Madison Sr. proclaimed Adams "has not made a Convert of me, any more I trust, he has of you."[72] His father believed Adams's design to be insidious, that "under the Mask" of defending the American constitutions, he intended to subvert their republican nature. There is no evidence that Madison thought his difference on this point with Adams or Hamilton was anything but an honest disagreement. Yet it was a disagreement of profound importance. The outcome of this dispute would determine if the United States was truly a republic or not. Unlike many Federalists, Madison never intended the U.S. Senate to be an "American House of Lords." Madison did not make his views against the British institutional setup entirely clear during the ratification debate, so as not to alienate his Federalist compatriots. A few years later Madison judged congressional policies reflective of upper-class interests, and he rededicated himself to a purely popular regime where all institutions represented "the people" as a whole.

In their view of constitutions as inviolable social contracts, in their belief that past popular consent yields present constitutional bounds, in their emphasis on stability and immutability as a necessary requisite of successful fundamental law, in their hope that "constitutionalism" existed outside and above normal legislative politics, and in their rejection of British-style mixed republics, Tucker and Madison shared much that would separate the latter from Hamilton. Even what led them to endorse a new constitution in their differing contexts was similar. Tucker decried the minor rioting that had occurred in Charleston in response to the legislature's leniency in treating Loyalist merchants. In the same way Madison's quest for constitutional stability had been energized by Shays's Rebellion.

Madison's relationship with Tucker was never particularly close — they were acquainted but apparently never corresponded. Tucker did serve alongside Madison in the first two Congresses, however. It is there that Madison opposed Tucker's attempt to insert the word "expressly" into what was to be the Ninth Amendment.[73] Madison was dead-set against reincorporating this word that had led to the "dreadful dilemma" faced by the Confederation Congress. In Federalist #44 Madison first explained why he was against this provision. Were it to be contained in the Constitution, "the new Congress would be continually exposed, as their predecessors have been, to the alternative of construing the term 'expressly' with so much rigor, as to disarm the government of all real authority whatever, or with so much latitude as to destroy altogether the force of the restriction."[74] Tucker's proposal was well intentioned, in that it was aimed at producing an inviolable constitutional order, but it would backfire, either producing another "nerveless" government or one where the wording of the Constitution had to be routinely transgressed and thus was without meaning. Madison spoke against the amendment, more as an exercise in clarifying the nature of the new government than an effort at persuasion. Given the composition of Congress he was sure the amendment would not pass.

Tucker also had a democratic enthusiasm that was foreign to Madison. But this is the same enthusiasm Jefferson possessed, which never dictated a serious rift between him and Madison. Despite these differences, after 1790, Madison and Tucker were political allies as long as both remained alive. Tucker served twenty-eight years, the entire Jeffersonian era, as treasurer of the United States. Madison recommended Tucker for the post in 1801, writing to Jefferson, "I have always regarded him as a man of the greatest moral & political probity, truly attached to republican principles."[75]

Alexander Hamilton and James Madison never truly saw eye to eye on constitutional matters. For a season, the most pressing constitutional question brought them together. Beneath their important belief that confederations failed because of their centrifugal tendencies lay a host of significant differences. Among them was Hamilton's cocksure assessment that all governments attempting to divide powers between levels of government would fail, baldly contradicted by Madison even during the formulation of the Constitution. Despite the latter's acknowledgment that perfectly delineating powers was impossible, Madison jealously guarded the Constitution's specific division of powers between nation and states as he understood it. This difference prefigured the conflict of the 1790s. Implementation of the particular Constitution they were working with brought them into inevitable conflict because Hamilton pressed for broad discretionary powers while Madison resisted any movement from the equilibrium ratified in 1788.

Most politically active Americans marveled at the wealth of constitutional commentary produced during the ratification debate, both in range and erudition. Later scholars have done likewise. In my view, what the partnership of Madison and Hamilton shows is how much was left submerged and unsaid during the ratification debates. It is no wonder with so much left unsaid that Madison's split from the Federalists of a Hamiltonian stripe has been difficult to come to grips with. It certainly was for many Americans, including the Federalists themselves, Hamilton not being an exception. In the years after ratification, each of the three groups involved in that landmark event would find the political world collapsing around them. The Antifederalists lost the battle over ratification and subsequently found Federalists pursuing policies even outside of what the loosely written Constitution sanctioned. The Madisonians found members of their own coalition reneging on their most visible promise from the ratification debate and in so doing threatening the concept of a national government that wielded only limited powers. The Federalists found their coalition inexplicably ripped apart by one of their own. These occurrences kept all on edge. Fear of upheaval prevented each group from advocating wholesale change at the same time that constitutional discourse remained front and center. During the 1790s, varied visions of constitutionalism were fleshed out, and the Constitution became capacious, something in which members of each group could place their hopes. Its own vagueness, its own ability to be interpreted in multiple ways, allowed the Constitution to become the unassailable entity to which all looked for hope.

As we will see, Madison lost faith in the institutional mechanics of the extended republic but gained faith in partisanship, linking him in a stronger way than he ever imagined he would be with those like Thomas Tudor Tucker.

CHAPTER FIVE

The Unbearable Transience of Federalist #10

James Madison always had a timid, nervous quality to his character. The news he received from Thomas Jefferson, his much more assured political colleague, in early October 1792 must have made him nearly apoplectic. At the very end of a letter complaining about the Virginia legislature's reaction to the Bank of the United States chartered by Congress, Jefferson mentioned that he dropped Madison's last letter to him somewhere on the road between Mount Vernon and Alexandria. Jefferson satisfied himself by casually noting that he sent a messenger to recover the missive.[1] A rare bit of pique shows through in Madison's nervous response:

> The accident mentioned . . . has caused no small anxiety; which wd. be much greater were it not hoped from your not writing to repair it, that a safe train had been laid for the purpose, & particularly that the article had been put under seal. The possibility of its falling into base hands at the present crisis cannot be too carefully guarded against.[2]

Here, coupled with his agitation about the immediate situation, is a much more far-reaching fear. Despite the successful effort to achieve ratification, the benefits Madison thought would accrue from the extended republic were proving elusive. Indeed, the future president had become gravely concerned about the character of the new republic very quickly after the Constitution had been put into practice. The regime materializing around Madison in the 1790s was very different than that he had projected.

Political developments of 1790 and 1791 forced Madison to reassess key assumptions that underlay his political theory during the ratification fight. Madison's reassessment did not constitute a wholesale change in his approach to politics, even though it appeared as such to many of his erstwhile Federalist colleagues because it led him to part ways with them. What is particularly notable about these alterations is that they occurred in what has often been considered the heart of Madison's political thought: the ideas of Federalist #10. In *The Federalist*, Madison's analysis is that of an institutional engineer; his later writing takes a sociological turn, acknowledging the primacy of public opinion in determining a regime's character. Madison's keen wariness of majorities that persist through time and across issues is replaced by a wholesale effort to cultivate the right kind of semipermanent majority. What he believed would occur on the national level, a kind of kaleidoscopic majoritarianism where majorities were pieced together on individual issues, was supplanted by a connective majoritarianism where relatively stable alliances existed across issues and through time. Instead of simply lamenting that unanticipated development, Madison altered his approach to cultivate the proper connective majority. His thinking evolved because what he had downplayed as improbable in Federalist #10 came to be: a majority faction in the legislature, representing only a minority of citizens, was passing policies of benefit to them at the expense of the general populace.

This "crisis" scenario led Madison to alter his behavior in a number of more pedestrian ways. Even before Jefferson's mishap, both men had been numbering their letters to each other to discern if any fell into hostile hands. Since Jefferson had been embarrassed the year before by the publication of an impolitic private note about John Adams, both were making more oblique references. Madison, for instance, did not openly acknowledge exactly what was missing in his reply to Jefferson. Key letters written to close political confidants, responding to their inquiries about strategy and philosophy are, not so curiously, missing. Among these items is an assessment of political process in the new Congress where Madison comments on whether popular majorities were being thwarted, a note to Jefferson probably confirming that Madison's Princeton classmate, Phillip Freneau, was willing to found an opposition newspaper, and a response to Henry Lee discussing the debt-funding system constructed and administered by Secretary of the Treasury Alexander Hamilton.[3] Madison likely asked the recipients of these letters to destroy them. Uncharacteristically for Madison, at crucial periods during the emerging crisis, whole months go by without any of his correspondence surviving.

Despite these holes in the documentary record, a fuller picture of Madison's thinking immediately after ratification emerges from his extant correspondence, personal notes, and the essays he wrote for the *National Gazette* in 1791 and 1792, the paper he persuaded Freneau to found.

Madison himself greatly valued consistency and stability, both in regimes and in individuals. As a shrewd politician he also knew his opponents would exploit his apparent inconsistency in parting with the Federalists. Thus Madison always insisted on his own consistency. That self-assessment is correct to a point. Madison remained committed to a popular regime that approximated the common good and preserved rights as far as possible. Yet the means of achieving and maintaining such a regime underwent a profound change. Fisher Ames, in a character portrait of Madison written early in the First Congress, related that the Virginian was a formidable politician with one important fault: "He is too much attached to his theories."[4] Ames is correct in discerning that Madison always retained a theoretical bent to his political analysis. Madison was clearly attached to his theories, because he thought they were correct. But when events annulled his expectations of how the extended republic would work, Madison realized that his political theory required amending and he did so.

A representative sample of Federalist, Madisonian, and Antifederalist figures from the early Congress shows that the Madisonians were significantly more like the Antifederalists than those in the Federalist Party. The new alignment, joining Madisonians with the former Antifederalists, was not accidental or constructed on a whim. It was grounded in the congruence of principles and interests and thus proved durable. Even a third of a century later, during the Missouri Compromise, this alignment was still a recognizable part of the new government.

Already by the end of the First Congress, Madison's confidence that there would be no dominant faction in the national legislature was shattered. Alexander Hamilton's fiscal proposals were being passed, largely by Northern congressmen, men who, to Madison, constituted an interested majority. This unexpected development led to an unanticipated role for the so-called Father of the Constitution. Instead of acting as something of a prime minister, shepherding common-good–oriented administration policies through the House as he had done in the first session, Madison found himself the leader of an opposition group populated by a few friends and his former Antifederalist opponents. Though few realized it at the time, Madison's stunning break from his *Federalist* coauthor Hamilton, and with him the Washington administration, would become a fixed characteristic of the national political landscape. Madison's break from the Federalists helped the former Antifederalists both symbolically and substantively. The Antifederalist-Madisonian coalition's opposition to the constitutionalism of the Federalist Party became increasingly viable, as did their prospects of becoming an elective majority in Congress, crucial factors in the transition to apotheosis.

How Madison Became a Partisan of the Common Good

"Had a respite from [Madison's] public duties permitted him in the fall and winter of 1789 to write a treatise in political theory, he would have been at the peak of his power to do so," writes his biographer Ralph Ketcham.[5] James Madison's theories of government and justifications for the Constitution written in *The Federalist* seemed bolstered by the events of 1788 and 1789. But as a new decade turned, Madison found national politics increasingly at odds with certain of his ideas from those essays, leading to a reassessment of political tactics and constitutional philosophy necessary in the new republic.

However, before the bad news came the good. First there was his own election to the newly formed national legislature. Madison squared off against his friend James Monroe (who had opposed ratification) for a House seat in the February 1789 election. The citizens in Virginia's Fifth District had been predominantly against the Constitution, the district having been gerrymandered for the benefit of Monroe by the Virginia legislature led by Antifederalist Patrick Henry. Madison promised his constituents during the campaign that he would help obtain amendments to the Constitution to secure personal rights.[6] But he did not pander to Antifederalist hopes by promising structural changes in the new government itself. The promise of personal-rights amendments, furthermore, was not a concession in Madison's mind. His goal in forming a new constitution was, after all, to safeguard rights. During the ratification debate he thought an enumeration of them was not strictly needed, as the system of factional checks would prevent minority rights from being trampled. After ratification he felt that attaching a bill of rights would calm well-meaning but misguided Antifederalists.[7] So while Madison maintained his Federalism, Antifederalist-oriented constituents elected him to the House. Federalists across the nation were heartened to find Madison's constituents voted for him regardless of their differences of political opinion. The results of the first federal elections as a whole were an indication that citizens would recognize and elect men of "sense and discernment," because there was a Federalist landslide.

In addition to the Federalists' electoral success, Madison's conception of the extended republic seemed confirmed as well. Despite the legislators' differences, Congress successfully established a federal judiciary and executive departments, secured a source of revenue in duties placed on imports, and offered a bill of rights to the states for ratification. The last accomplishment was no small feat, as the great majority of representatives favored postponing the issue — many Federalists still thinking it absolutely unnecessary and Antifederalists hoping that they could successfully press for substantial structural changes in a future session or second convention. Madison spearheaded all these efforts but the bill on the national judiciary, which originated in the Senate. Of course even Madison had been disappointed by some things: the Congress was at an impasse over the location of a permanent capital and had not gone along with his proposal for higher duties on imports from nations (like Britain) that did not have commercial treaties with the United States.[8] Even so, the country had a revenue bill, and compromise in the common good had been accomplished, just as Madison had predicted. In these actual political developments, he found evidence that his theories of government were more correct than those of the Antifederalists: for "great moderation and liberality" prevailed, which "disappointed the wishes and predictions of many who have opposed the Government."[9]

While Madison felt vindicated by the first session of Congress, he became disturbed during the second session, where the main items on the agenda were Hamilton's fiscal proposals. Hamilton suggested that the United States promptly pay off all foreign debt, that the national government assume the wartime debts of the states, and that the national government pay in full the holders of government securities that had been issued to help fund the Revolutionary War. Paying the foreign debt was uncontroversial, but assumption of state debts and Hamilton's suggestion for remunerating holders of war securities made Madison extremely uneasy. Virginia was one of the states that had nearly paid off all its war debts. So Madison argued that assumption would be unfair, not only to Virginia, but to all of the states that had responsibly serviced their debts since the end of the war. In addition, Madison noted that during hostilities with Britain accounting procedures had been sketchy and many records were lost. The level of debt in some states was still not entirely clear and needed to be clarified before the national government could take on this burden.

On federal securities issued during the war, Madison was not at all averse to paying the full sum of what the government had promised its soldiers. Any government that was to have sound credit needed to follow through on such obligations. However, due to the lack of revenue under the Articles of Confederation, these securities were many years old, and many of their original holders had been forced by necessity to sell them to speculators at a fraction of their face value. Madison wanted the government to discriminate between the original holders of the securities and those who had bought them at bargain prices. Paying in full those who had bought the notes from original holders would reward idle speculators at the expense of those who risked their lives and fortunes in the service of their country. The speculators should get a fair market value for the notes they held, but those who had been engaged in military service should get the bulk of the payment. Madison had hoped that the extended republic's policies would much more closely approximate a common good. In the case of assumption, that meant a policy that would credit individual states to the degree they had paid off their debts. In the case of discrimination, that dictated a policy that would recognize and reward the sacrifices for which the certificates had been issued in the first place. The policy proposals to which Federalists clung tenaciously clearly contradicted Madison's sense of the common good.

Instead of endorsing Madison's "discrimination," both houses of Congress elected to pay the current holders of the securities their full face value without any compensation for those who sold the issues. Madison was deeply disheartened by this result. The injustice of the situation was clear. What was not clear to him, at least at first, was that this kind of injustice might be deeply embedded in the system he helped found, rather than a discrete occurrence brought on by the quirks of this particular issue. Immediately after the defeat of discrimination, Madison assessed the result in a letter to his father. In it he blamed defeat on practical matters that had led to an honest disagreement with other representatives. "The proposition for compromizing the matter between original sufferers & the Stockjobbers, after being long agitated was rejected by a considerable majority, less perhaps from a denial of the justice of the measure, than a supposition of its impracticability."[10] Just two weeks later, by mid-March 1790, Madison had become much more circumspect, foreclosing the possibility that the outcome was due to an honest disagreement over practical issues. As the House discussed the assumption of state debts, Madison was beginning to discern a pattern in its behavior and presented a very different view to his friend Edward Carrington than he had to his father: "There must be something wrong, radically & morally & politically wrong, in a system which transfers the reward from those who paid the most valuable of all considerations, to those who scarcely paid any consideration at all."[11] Madison was coming to the realization that national representatives were not acting as he had thought they would. Instead of favoring local interests but compromising to reach an approximation of the national good, they were legislating as a majority faction, favoring a much narrower set of interests than he thought they would represent.

Madison led the floor debate for those against assumption of state debts. Not surprisingly, those from states burdened with substantial debt, like Massachusetts and South Carolina, favored assumption, but so too did many other Northern representatives. Madison suspected that they saw assumption as a means of cementing federal power over states. Even with these reinforcements, proponents of assumption were not a majority. Several votes were taken in succession in the House and on each assumption failed. But those in favor would not let the issue die. In a letter to James Monroe, Madison chided "Eastern representatives" for pressing the issue too hard, not accepting the will of the legislative majority in doing so: "It [passing assumption] will be tried in every possible shape by the zeal of its patrons. . . . We shall risk their prophetic menaces if we should continue to have a majority."[12] Here Madison alluded to the speeches of some assumption proponents, which despaired of a continuation of the Union if the national government did not help them by taking on their debt.[13] Madison, always protective of the Union, was increasingly prone to allow a distasteful compromise to occur.

Still on the First Congress's legislative agenda was that other controversial issue that was at an impasse: determining a permanent site for the national capital. With every representative stubbornly favoring either his own home area or the closest logical site, there looked to be little chance to broker a result. Absent a decision, the temporary capital would likely become the permanent capital by default. Since Congress had determined that the temporary capital would be Philadelphia (beginning in the third session of the First Congress), Virginia and the South would have no chance of housing the capital, the advantages of which were readily apparent. The possibility of allowing assumption in exchange for a Southern capital was too great an opportunity for Madison to pass up.

A dinner meeting with Hamilton at Jefferson's rented home was the result. There the secretary of state attempted to bridge the gap between the most influential member of the House and the secretary of the treasury. Apparently a bargain was struck: state debts would be assumed by the national government as they stood in 1790, in return for the placement of the permanent capital on the Potomac.[14] The two most critical issues facing the national legislature had been resolved in one fell swoop; not a bad evening's work. And yet the result was not what Madison had expected from the new government. To approximate the common good, Madison had counted on issues being treated discretely. Linking issues to facilitate bargaining threatened to allow interested minorities to get their way. During the residence debate, it seems Madison still did not contemplate that broad coalitions would band together on a variety of legislative subjects. Madison related to Monroe that "if the Potowmac succeeds . . . it will have resulted from a fortuitous coincidence of circumstances which might never happen again."[15] Likewise he wrote to Edmund Pendleton that "if any arrangement should be made that will answer to our wishes, it will be the effect of a coincidence of causes."[16] Madison still was not counting on groups getting their way by logrolling across issues, much less a semipermanent coalition that would stick together on a broad range of issues.

In the third session of the First Congress, there was to be no compromise on the most pressing issue at hand: the establishment of a national bank. The national bank, in addition to further impugning the Federalist majority's sense of fairness, called into question their commitment to the Constitution itself. The bank was designed to bolster the nation's credit, spurring the economy by offering a ready source of funds to be borrowed by entrepreneurs. Madison did not oppose that goal in the abstract.[17] He had, after all, endorsed such an entity in 1781, despite his qualms about whether the Confederation Congress possessed the power to incorporate one. Madison had also pressed for an incorporation clause to be included in the Constitution, which would have removed a key objection to the bank's constitutionality. The convention had excised the incorporation clause from Article I, section 8, however. Because of that omission, and because Madison could not find any other expressed power that, naturally construed, allowed the national government to found a bank, he opposed it on constitutional grounds.

Madison's argument was sufficiently reminiscent of the Antifederalists' postratification arguments that it seemed to many that his constitutional philosophy had made a full turn. Like the Antifederalists, he reasoned that nowhere was the power to establish a national bank explicitly mentioned in the Constitution. He went beyond them, though, in arguing that the bank was not logically implied by any other powers, most notably the powers of taxation and borrowing mentioned in Article I, section 8. What Madison was defending, at least in his own mind, was the middling interpretive position he had fought for all along. Requiring every action of Congress to be expressly validated by the words of the Constitution was too narrow a reading. Congress could pursue an objective set down in Article I, section 8 through any method logically implied by the language of the appropriate clause. Congress could not, however, legislate out of thin air without a specific constitutional sanction for its purposes. The power to charter a bank was not an expressed power nor sufficiently related to any expressed power to be justified. The bank was only justified by "remote implications, which strike at the very essence of the Gov't as composed of limited & enumerated powers."[18] Several Federalists attempted to justify incorporation by saying it was authorized by the preamble's charge to promote the general welfare, directly contradicting James Wilson's claim that all of Congress's powers were enumerated in Article I, section 8.[19] Madison's view was that the Constitution would not have been adopted without that widely known assurance and thus the nation and political figures were bound to it.[20]

The passage of the Bank Bill confirmed what Madison had discerned midway through the debates on assumption. The extended republic was not working as planned. Legislative majorities were not reflective of the common good. Rather, a majority faction in Congress was passing legislation in its own interest, a scenario he had thought improbable when writing Federalist #10. The Bank Bill had upped the ante considerably, because it showed that this interested faction would not even stop at the bounds the Constitution had set. If legislative outcomes consistently benefited only a small minority, citizens would come to conclude that the Federalist structure, not just its initial administration, had failed. Since Madison thought that the government was advantageous to only a very narrow class of individuals, what he called a "praetorian band" of "stockjobbers," he feared that the public's loss of confidence would be nearly total.[21] If a near total loss of confidence were to occur, the people would either have to regain control of their government by revolutionary means or submit to one that abused them. Either scenario would prove more painful than trying to salvage the present Constitution. To salvage the Constitution, Madison's tactics had to be modified considerably. He did not doubt that there was a common good, nor that it could be reached under the right circumstances. But successfully pursuing the common good required abandoning the premise that institutional arrangements would yield this result more or less automatically and adopting the tactics and zeal of partisans. Madison could not abide merely serving as a vocal minority within the legislature. His influence would have to be felt publicly, as he thought the viability of the Constitution and the life of the nation were at stake. Furthermore, he was willing to risk the stigma of partisanship for that common good, a stigma he felt he could beat precisely because he was working for the Union as a whole instead of a selfish interest.

There is no better example of Madison's new efforts as partisan of the common good than his successful attempt to persuade Phillip Freneau to establish a newspaper in the nation's capital. Jefferson and Madison clandestinely approached Freneau about serving as editor in the same month that the Bank Bill passed. The mission of the paper was to counter the Hamiltonian information and editorials printed in the *Gazette of the United States*. Freneau's *National Gazette* was, in other words, designed to be an opposition newspaper from its inception. Given the highly accusatory, almost bawdy nature of the press during this era, there is little doubt that Madison viewed this step as one from which there was to be no return to the halcyon days of the first session.[22] Madison was no longer trying to persuade his fellow congressmen to compromise their localist interests to form majorities; he had given up on that vision. He was now engaged in a war for the hearts and minds of American citizens.

"Your Arguments Have More
Force Out of Doors than Within"

The protection of rights in a free, popular regime remained Madison's goal. Thus his claims of consistency are not mistaken, properly understood. But goal-directed consistency is only part of the story. The original plan of how to achieve those ends was scrapped. Madison's tactics changed dramatically, based on observations about how the new regime was operating. Madison decided he could help solve the problems of the new regime by cultivating a connective majority within constitutional bounds. A good number of Madison's friends were prepared to abandon the Constitution. With Madison's leadership they might have joined willing Antifederalists to become an anti-Constitution party. Madison's revised thinking would not allow such an outcome, however. Rather than turn on the Constitution, Madison turned toward partisanship, something that had been highly suspect, as a vehicle for ensuring that the republic would remain a popular, rights-oriented regime. This new solution represents a stark change in Madison's "social science." Whereas the Madison of Federalist #10 offers a political solution to a social problem, the later Madison offers a social solution to a political problem.

Madison received confirmation that there was something "radically & morally & politically wrong" in the system of government from political confidants. Henry Lee was a frequent correspondent, and his assessment of the new regime was very unflattering. By early March 1790, just after the defeat of discrimination, Lee wrote to Madison, who was in New York at the time, about Virginian attitudes. "Enmity was rather encreasing, than otherwise" toward the general government, observed Lee.[23] Shortly thereafter, he scolded Madison for not better protecting the interests of Virginia: "Is your love of the constitution so ardent, as to induce you to adhere to it, tho it should produce ruin to your native country?"[24] Madison and Lee agreed on the specific matters that had been badly decided. The absence of "discrimination" had benefited New York and Philadelphia speculators at the expense of many Virginians. Assumption threatened to disadvantage the Commonwealth as well. Unlike Lee, Madison was not prepared to indict the Constitution itself. "I cannot feel all the despondency which you seem to give way to," he wrote, "though in several respects they [policy decisions] do not comport with my wishes."[25]

After passage of the Bank Bill, Madison more frequently heard disheartening assessments from friends. Particularly upsetting was the sentiment that the government did not even come close to approximating the common good. Lee told Madison that "in the various doings of Congress . . . it plainly appears that very little regard is paid to the minds of their constituents."[26] The sentiment that the new government was not reflective of popular wishes was confirmed by John Beckley. "Our domestic affairs," Beckley related, "seem to me, to be fast verging to the issue of a contest between the Treasury department and the people."[27] Given Hamilton's successes in Congress, it went without saying that "the people" were losing the contest. This thwarting of popular rule led some to think that the whole effort spent in changing governments had been wasted, and worse, counterproductive. Writing to Madison in September 1792, George Nicholas predicted that the government "will probably end in monarchy." The ultimate cause was the well-meaning Federalists' failure in bringing positive change: "Revolutions have become hateful in my eyes; when they are effected by honest men on good principles, they are made to serve rascals and bad purposes."[28] Like Lee, Nicholas was prepared to chalk up the effort to form a new government as a failure. Madison was not willing to make that move.

Nevertheless, these consultations confirmed many of Madison's own observations. Surprisingly to him, in the new regime there was only a very loose connection between national representatives and their constituents. Given the assumptions of the tenth *Federalist*, Madison probably imagined he would expend most of his energy holding the forces of local prejudice at bay in order to forge effective compromises approximating a more general good. Instead, Madison frequently found himself in the unexpected position of pleading with representatives to heed constituents. In the debate over amendments, he asked fellow representatives to take seriously the large number of citizens with qualms about the new system. In the discrimination debate, Madison wondered aloud what people would think if America would "erect the monuments of her gratitude not to those who had saved her liberties, but to those who had enriched themselves in her funds."[29] Not paying soldiers in full would strike a blow at the fragile optimism that had prevailed since ratification. In the debate over assumption, he tried to persuade representatives to his position by a simple statement of its popular strength: "If we could ascertain the opinions of our constituents, individually, I believe we should find four-fifths of the citizens of the United States against assumption."[30]

If local prejudice did not account for legislative behavior, what did? Unfortunately, not an attempt to "refine and enlarge" the public views. Instead it was the transposition of the private motives of political elites onto public policy, precisely that which Madison had looked past in Federalist #10. Writing to Edmund Randolph about assumption, Madison lamented that the advocates' perseverance was a result of individual "motives."[31] Outright self-service was clearly apparent to him once the national bank issued shares. Letters written to Jefferson in July 1791 confirm that many representatives who had favored the bank were working to secure a personal windfall. "Of all the shameful circumstances of this business," read the secretary of state, "it is among the greatest to see the members of the Legislature who were most active in pushing this Jobb, openly grasping its emoluments."[32] Shares supposed to have been sold in Boston, New York, and Baltimore were quickly bought up by members of Congress and their friends in Philadelphia, where more than half of all shares were sold.[33] Not only had a majority coalesced much too easily on the national bank given the assumptions of Federalist #10, but the majority seemed "interested."

Madison would come close to overtly repudiating Federalist #10 in January 1792. His anonymously written essay in the *National Gazette* titled "Parties" begins with the assertion that "in every political society, parties are unavoidable."[34] If the word "parties" was meant to be interchangeable with "faction," then Publius would certainly agree, for in Federalist #10 factions were found to be sown in the nature of humankind. In the essay, however, it becomes clear that Madison is not simply replacing one word for the other. Among the things that might "combat the evil" of partisanship is that "*one party*" can act as "a check on *the other.*" Madison thus has in mind a specific kind of factional arrangement not contemplated in his earlier essay, a two-party system where both parties compete for majority status across time. His own definition of faction was rather narrow: a group of people united behind some particular interest. A political party of the kind that Madison envisioned would have to be united on a broad array of matters—potentially every matter treated by the public sphere. Madison, then, is saying much more than that parties are inevitable; he is saying that connective alliances are inevitable. The assumption that each issue would be treated discretely had subtly given way to the realization that multiple factions would be bound together in a semipermanent partisan structure that would take positions on a broad array of issues.

Instead of a multiplicity of factions checking each other, Madison now hoped the emerging two-party system would act to check the selfish designs of either (read the Federalist) party. The apparent wish of some was to try to broaden the number of interests through government policies. That option is ridiculed: "Let us then increase these natural distinctions by favoring an inequality of property. . . . We shall then have more checks to oppose to each other: we shall then have more scales and the more weights to perfect and maintain the equilibrium. This is as little the voice of reason, as it is that of republicanism."[35] "More checks to oppose each other" was precisely why Madison had thought the extended republic would produce better political outcomes than the states. He might have clung stubbornly to this his primary theoretical discovery by pursuing policies designed to increase factionalism. But Madison, in what seems like a quarrel with his former self, rejects that option in favor of cultivating a majority party, a connective majority reflective of the public good.

Since Madison felt that the faction in control of Congress was so narrow, there was great opportunity to organize a party that more closely approximated the public good. At the end of the First Congress, Madison's father, James Madison Sr., told his son, "It appears to me that your Arguments have more force, out of Doors, than within."[36] To James Madison Jr. the assertion that his ideas had more broad-based public support than support within Congress was a major understatement. Back in Virginia during a recess of the Second Congress, Madison wrote Benjamin Rush who remained in Philadelphia: "The complexion of federal policy, is so generally condemned, that there is not eno' of disagreement to disturb the ordinary calm."[37] Given gross and legitimate public dissatisfaction, a course of action was clear: organize a party that would gain majority status by publicizing its differences with the elitist Federalists. In other words, the theoretical embrace of connective alliances was supplemented by Madison's own active cultivation of partisanship. Madison himself would be quick to add that if he was being a partisan of anything, it was of the public good. And yet pursuing that goal by cultivating a bipolar domestic sphere was far different from brokering legislative compromises from the inside.

Promoting the new connective majority entailed a variety of activities. Madison himself named the organization the "republican" party, to indicate that it was in service of the general good. To publicize the group's positions and activities he helped found the *National Gazette* and actively solicited subscriptions, making sure that the paper did not fail for lack of funds before its message was disseminated.[38] With Washington hinting of retirement in 1792, Madison did his best to make sure that the party was prepared for a presidential campaign. Jefferson would surely be the party's standard-bearer, but the vice presidential slot was of some concern. When he believed that Aaron Burr was the best recruit they could muster, Madison wrote Rush that "it is to be regretted also that an antagonist . . . could not be found, who would better unite those of every party who have at bottom the same object, and by that means a more decisive proof of the republicanism of the people."[39] Even after Washington had decided to stand for reelection, Madison hoped to embarrass the Federalists by electing a republican vice president. Madison wrote to elector William Overton Callis that he should vote for George Clinton over John Adams because "antirepublicanism is now a greater danger than antifederalism."[40] Within Congress, Madison was making sure that the republicans stuck together. In short, Madison's hope was to disseminate the information that would allow republicans to win a legislative majority. That majority, which would be instrumental in steering the nation back to a republican track, was the same kind of connective majority that he had not contemplated would even form in the extended republic, with its kaleidoscopic treatment of issues.

Additionally, Madison contributed the series of essays to the *National Gazette* quoted here. In so doing he was heeding the advice of James Monroe, who, like Madison, believed that "the scale will soon preponderate one way or another" to a government that would be permanently elitist and self-serving or one that would right itself and approximate the general good.[41] "Certain it is that the field is open for a general discussion of the measures of the government," wrote Monroe to Madison, "turn your attention to it."[42] The essays, eighteen in all, were published between late November 1791 and late December 1792. Several objectives were pursued: first, early essays, like "Parties," primed the public for a partisan battle; second, Madison brought forth "wedge issues" in seemingly apolitical pieces; and third, three late essays overtly argued for the Republicans against the Federalists.

The essay "Parties" had girded readers for a partisan battle. If parties were inevitable, then there would have to be a partisan fight and those involved could not be blamed for their participation alone. Rather, they should be judged on the political positions they espoused, a contest that Madison believed republicans would not lose if the public was informed of their quest to right the republic. In the essay "Consolidation," Madison goes beyond saying the government should not promote a multiplicity of interests. He reverses his presumption that the greater variety of interests among the public is somehow beneficial. Rather, greater congruence of public opinion is desirable:

The less the supposed difference of interests, and the greater the concord and confidence throughout the great body of the people, the more readily must they sympathize with each other, the more seasonably can they interpose a common manifestation of their sentiments, the more certainly they will take the alarm at usurpation or oppression, and the more effectually will they consolidate their defence of the public liberty.[43]

In "Public Opinion," the political effect of the republic's size is discussed. In 1787, Publius had not only attempted to reverse the Montesquieian wisdom that large republics were impossible, he reasoned that only they could promise stability. Now Madison raised a qualm about large republics that made him sound more like an Antifederalist than Publius: "The larger a country, the less easy for its real opinion to be ascertained, and the less difficult to be counterfeited." Government could help remedy the problem of size by building good roads, promoting commerce, and facilitating the circulation of newspapers. These policies were "equivalent to a contraction of territorial limits, and [thus] favorable to liberty."[44] Suggesting that newspapers be widely circulated and that roads be well built and maintained seems innocuously apolitical. Yet heeding these suggestions would provide a crucial conduit for information to the republican constituency, the bulk of whom lived away from the coast. Madison was hoping to forge a tighter connection between the majority of citizens and their government. He backed this position up with action in Congress, fighting for months to reduce the cost of mailing newspapers.

Also seemingly nonpartisan were discussions of immigration and fashion. Yet Madison hoped these "wedge issues" would divide the populace to the benefit of the republicans. In "Population and Emigration," the first essay of the series, Madison argued that European countries were growing well beyond their carrying capacity. America's success was based on the flow of such emigrants to the New World. In short, people were a valuable import for which the country did not have to pay. Allowing surplus populations to immigrate was humane as well. Such a position was likely to be greeted with favor by much of a potential republican constituency, many of whom were not far removed from their own migrations.[45] In the long-term, Madison counted on most migrants and their kin to support the Republican Party. In "Fashion," Madison pointed out that an economy based on manufacturing items for consumption was prone to upheaval. Those employed making shoe buckles, for instance, were at the whim of popular tastes. Twenty-thousand buckle manufacturers were out of work in England, Madison wrote, because it had become the fashion to wear shoes fastened by strings. An agrarian economy was much more stable and much less likely to leave its population starving.[46] Madison here appealed to the farmers that made up the bulk of the nation. The argument was intended to be commonsensical and not invoke overtly political feelings. And yet it clearly drove a wedge between those in favor of a mercantilist economy (and not coincidentally the national bank) and the vast majority of Americans.

The three final essays cast off all semblance of objectivity. In "The Union, Who Are Its Real Friends?" Madison answers with an unmistakable indictment of the Federalists. Those who "pamper[ed] the spirit of speculation" and promoted "unnecessary accumulations of the debt" that created "pretexts for new taxes" were not its friends. Such individuals based their policies on "arbitrary interpretations and insidious precedents" that served to "pervert the limited government of the Union."[47] Conversely, those favoring a "republican system of government" are its friends. In the next essay, "A Candid State of Parties," he asserted that it is "the duty of the citizen at all times to understand the actual state" of parties. Those who follow through on this duty will discern that Federalists, or the "Anti-republican" faction as he brands them, believe "government can be carried only by the pageantry of rank, the influence of money and emoluments, and the terror of military force." Madison finds:

The other division consists of those who believing that mankind are capable of governing themselves, and hating hereditary power as an insult to the reason and an outrage to the rights of man, are naturally offended at every public measure that does not appeal to the understanding and to the general interest of the country.[48]

This definition of the two sides was tautologous, but it reflected Madison's belief that one party was clearly republican and the other clearly not. It is not surprising, then, that Madison thought the vast majority on the republican side. Their "superiority of numbers is so great," he predicted, "that no temperate observer of human affairs will be surprised if the issue in the present stance shall be reversed, and the government be administered in the spirit and form approved by the great body of the people."[49] The final essay consists of a pretended conversation between "Republican" and "Anti-republican," with the latter figure taking positions as offensive as his pasteboard name would suggest. In these final three essays Madison is overtly partisan and even demagogic. He who had presented public opinion as inherently problematic in Federalist #10, prone to too much passion and interestedness, was engaged in stoking popular passion for the Republican Party.

Madison's postratification actions and writings indicate that he significantly modified his political thought to preserve its purpose. The political mechanics of the extended republic had not worked as planned. Legislative majorities were forming, but they did not consist of multiple factions compromising to approximate the national good. A looser connection than anticipated between the public and elites allowed a self-serving, connective majority to form in Congress. To combat this usurpation, it became Madison's mission, and that of "republicans" throughout the nation, to cultivate a connective majority that could "take the nation back." Madison was a man of many roles in politics, including president, secretary of state, and trusted adviser to Washington. During the founding, Madison had acted as a political engineer, overseeing the erection of a political structure he thought would solve the nation's most pressing problem. Just months into the life of the new regime he would adopt an outsider's role. The new, unanticipated threat to republicanism coming from inside the government itself required Madison to cultivate public opinion. In more abstract terms, Madison had turned from offering a political solution to a social problem to offering a social solution to a political problem, trusting that properly cultivated, the "holy zeal" of public opinion could reassert the Constitution's limited and defined grant of powers to the national government.[50]

Characteristics of Madisonians,
Federalists, and Antifederalists

Madison's turn away from the Federalists was shocking, but more importantly from a political standpoint was the group of representatives who accompanied him in defecting. Seventeen of the sixty-five-member House of Representatives initially supported administration proposals but found themselves in the opposition before the conclusion of the First Congress. Even combined with all the Antifederalists they did not constitute a majority, but they did make up a substantial opposition, commanding twenty-eight of sixty-five votes. Together they were able to affect policy decisions on which the Federalists were not united. Further, the new alliance gave them hope of gaining majority status relatively quickly and righting the constitutional ship. They were already a formidable bloc, and the way Federalists were legislating, seemingly benefiting the well-to-do without regard to the average citizen, gave the opposition great hope that a majority could be gained sooner rather than later. In the Senate, there was a less punctuated, dramatic turn to the opposition, but the turn was no less substantial. Though they defected piecemeal, eventually eight of the twenty-six members of the first Senate who had voted in favor of the Constitution became Republicans.

The alliance of the Madisonians and Antifederalists was not a fluke, particularly after Madison dropped his unorthodox ideas about the extended republic. But the alliance was not just based on relatively compatible constitutional philosophies; it also seemed to reflect a congruence of backgrounds and interests. Data on the three groups indicate that in some important ways the Madisonians were significantly more like Antifederalists than Federalists. The information compiled here does not treat all members of the early Congress, just those who had voted in state ratification conventions. By definition this sample eliminates any ambiguity about constitutional positions taken at the time of ratification.

Additional data from these individuals and a further discussion of the method of constructing this sample is contained in Appendix B.

Table 5.1 differentiates Federalist and Antifederalist ratification convention voters in all Congresses (not just the First) by their partisan affiliation. Nearly all of the Antifederalists remained in the opposition, with only two of forty-nine identified by Kenneth C. Martis's *Historical Atlas of Political Parties in the United States Congress* voting with the Federalist Party. Meanwhile, those who supported the Constitution were split between the Federalist and Republican Parties, with a few more populating the former. Considered by state, this sample generally approximates relative populations, with a few notable exceptions. North Carolina convened two ratification conventions (the first refused to ratify), both of which were very large. A greater percentage of those with political aspirations was able to participate in North Carolina's ratification process than in any other state; therefore those elected to national office had almost inevitably attended one or the other state convention. South Carolina is somewhat overrepresented for this same reason. New Jersey, by contrast, is the most underrepresented state, because its convention was small and ratification was hardly contested. Since New Jersey's ratification was a foregone conclusion, the state's most formidable politicians, ones who would be considered for national office, did not need to attend. The proportion of ratification convention delegates who voted in favor of the Constitution (65 percent) nationwide is reflected by the composition of the sample (63 percent). The ratio of Federalists to Antifederalists in individual states is also generally reflective of their overall strength, with a few exceptions: New Hampshire's convention was closer to even than a Federalist landslide, while Maryland's and South Carolina's Antifederalists were not quite as strong in their respective conventions as might be thought given the information in the appropriate rows from Table 5.1. Considering these numbers by region, each unsurprisingly has more who voted in favor of the Constitution than Antifederalists. While the Antifederalists are clearly outnumbered in New England, they are close to the total number who voted to ratify in the mid-Atlantic and the South. The regional difference in the presence of Madisonians is also great. The great majority of New England ratifiers remained Federalists, while the division between Federalists and Madisonians in the middle Atlantic is nearly even. In the five Southern states, there are twice as many ratifiers who joined the opposition as there are Federalists. Although the split between the supporters of the Constitution was not purely regional in nature, regional ties seem to have played a significant role in the division.

On page 125 is a map of the First Congress where each district is

TABLE 5.1

Party Affiliation of Ratification Convention Delegates to Congress

State	Profederalist Convention Vote		Antifederalist Vote		Total
	Federalist	Republican	Federalist	Republican	
MA	11	3	0	5	19
NH	2	1	0	0	3
CT	9	0	0	0	9
RI	2	0	0	2	4
NY	1	1	1	4	7
PA	4	3	0	5	12
NJ	2	0	0	0	2
DE	0	1	0	0	1
VA	5	6	0	12	23
MD	3	2	0	2	7
NC	3	13	1	11	28
SC	3	5	0	6	14
GA	0	2	0	0	2
Total	45	37	2	47	131

SOURCE: Compiled by author. Two supporters of the Constitution, John Langdon and John Sevier, supported the Washington administration through the First Congress, but switched party affiliation some time after. John Langdon is identified by Kenneth Martis as switching from an administration supporter to the opposition by the Third Congress. He served in the Senate through the Sixth Congress. John Sevier left Congress for more than twenty years after the First Congress but was elected to the House to the Twelfth and Thirteenth Congresses as a Republican. Both men are counted as Republicans. Three of the Antifederalists, two from New York and one from North Carolina, are "ratifying Antifederalists." These individuals were clearly against the Constitution but voted to accept it once it became clear that the state had to agree to the Constitution or be left behind by the new government. The two Antifederalists who were elected as Federalists are John Williams of New York who served in the Fourth and Fifth Congresses and William F. Strudwick of North Carolina who served in the Fourth Congress.

shaded by the legislator's group membership: Federalist, Madisonian, or Antifederalist. Proadministration "Federalist" forces controlled thirty-seven seats, a clear majority. But the seventeen Representatives who populated the Madisonian bloc combined forces with the eleven Antifederalists by the third session of the First Congress. This map suggests that the Antifederalists and Madisonians tended to hail from similar areas, usually expansive districts that were either away from the coast or isolated for some other reason, by North Carolina's Outer Banks, for instance. Though there are some notable exceptions, like North Carolina's Fifth District — present-day Tennessee — and Virginia's First — the northern half of what is currently West Virginia, Federalists were concentrated in coastal areas, representing the more dense and thus smaller districts. Twelve of the seventeen Madisonian districts and seven of the eleven Antifederalist districts were in the South.

The map suggests the possibility that Madisonians and Antifederalists share similar backgrounds, backgrounds that differ from those in the Federalist Party. One possible difference might be in level of education. By virtue of their election to Congress, all these individuals are political elites, which dictates that a much greater percentage of those in each group attended college than among the public generally. But we might also expect a disparity in college attendance between those who were from more well-to-do urban and coastal districts (and families) and those from backcountry regions. The map indicates that those in the Federalist Party were much more likely to be from the more established and afflu- ent coastal areas. Thus we may expect a greater percentage of those in the Federalist Party went to college than the Antifederalists or the Madison- ians. College attendance naturally did not dictate the Federalists' position on the Constitution, but the same set of antecedent factors that allowed them to get their education in the first place, that they were from estab- lished families in coastal regions, tended to prefigure support for the Constitution. A difference in backgrounds between the Federalists and their one-time allies, the Madisonians, should be reflected in the percent- age of them who attended institutions of higher education.

To discern where and whether individuals in this group went to col- lege, I first consulted *The Biographical Directory of the American Con- gress.* If there was no record of an individual attending college there, I checked further in the biographical files contained at the Center for the Study of the Constitution in Madison, Wisconsin. When one disaggre- gates "the Federalists" into Federalists and Madisonians, we do find a disparity in their educational backgrounds. A clear majority of Federalists in the sample (58 percent) attended college, while only about a third of Madisonians (35 percent) and Antifederalists (31 percent) did. College attendance is far from a perfect measure of wealth at the time of ratifica- tion, of course. Yet this measure raises the possibility that the Madisonians' socioeconomic characteristics were similar to the Antifederalists, helping to explain the rift in the ratification coalition. Even if the Madisonians were equally as well-off as the Federalists in 1787 it stands to reason that their material experiences were quite differ- ent. Federalists came from families already well established and wealthy enough to afford the luxury of a college education. Most Madisonians had not come from such families; so if they were as wealthy in their adult- hood as Federalists, then they were "self-made men," a socializing expe-

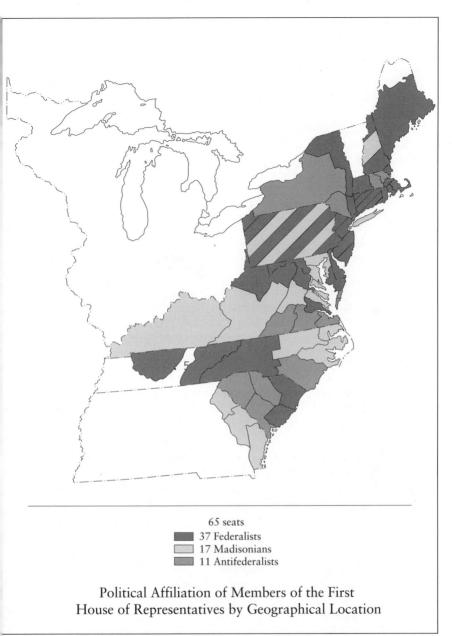

65 seats
37 Federalists
17 Madisonians
11 Antifederalists

Political Affiliation of Members of the First
House of Representatives by Geographical Location

SOURCE: Kenneth C. Martis, *Historical Atlas of U.S. Congressional Districts.*

TABLE 5.2
College Attended

	Federalists (n=45)	Madisonians (n=37)	Antifederalists (n=49)
Harvard	11	1	2
Yale	7	0	1
Princeton (N.J.)	5	3	2
William and Mary	1	3	5
European	2	4	4
Other	0	2	1
Total	26	13	15
	58%	35%	31%

SOURCE: Compiled by author using *The Biographical Directory of the American Congress* and biographical information housed at the Center for the Study of the Constitution in Madison, Wisconsin. If individuals attended more than one institution, the college they last attended is the one counted.

rience very different from the Federalists'. If one aggregates the sample, the overall percentage of those attending college is 41 percent, almost exactly the percentage found by Allan Bogue et al. in their study of the Congress as a whole during these years.[51] Nearly a century ago, Charles Beard rested his revisionist argument about the Federalists on the fact that they owned more "personalty" than did their opponents. Through the decades, researchers have discerned that though Beard was generally correct in his assertion that Federalists were more well-to-do than their opponents, his implication that Federalists were motivated primarily by the wish to protect a specific type of property was faulty. Robert Brown, Forrest McDonald, and others found more significant disparities in Federalist property holdings than Beard acknowledged.[52] The large difference between the college attendance rates of Federalists and Madisonians suggests the possibility of a systematic disparity in background and socioeconomic conditions within the coalition that pushed for ratification. At the very least, the Madisonians' educational background is more like the Antifederalists' than the Federalists'.

Speaking more directly to the question of socioeconomic position at the time of ratification is one's profession. Table 5.3 provides support for the hypothesis that the socioeconomic position of the Madisonians was more like the Antifederalists' than the Federalists'. Many more Federalists were lawyers than were those of the other two groups. If those who were judges before being elected to Congress are combined with those who

TABLE 5.3

Profession Immediately Prior to Congressional Service

	Federalists	Madisonians	Antifederalists
Lawyers	28 (61%)	10 (26%)	14 (29%)
Judges	2 (4%)	3 (8%)	1 (2%)
Planters/Farmers	5 (11%)	7 (18%)	12 (24%)
Unknown/ No Information	4 (9%)	7 (18%)	13 (27%)
Mercantile Pursuits	4 (9%)	3 (8%)	1 (2%)
Medical Doctors	1 (2%)	2 (5%)	2 (4%)
Others	2 (4%)	6 (16%)	6 (12%)

SOURCE: Compiled by author from *The Biographical Directory of the American Congress* and the biographical files at the Center for the Study of the Constitution in Madison, Wisconsin. I have double-counted one Federalist and one Madisonian. *The Biographical Directory* relates that Benjamin Edwards made a living through agricultural and mercantile pursuits and that Hugh Williamson was both a medical doctor and engaged in mercantile pursuits.

practiced law, we find that almost two-thirds of the Federalists came from a legal background (65 percent), while only about one-third of the Madisonians (34 percent) and Antifederalists (31 percent) did. This result again points to a difference in socioeconomic status. It also probably explains the Federalists' greater familiarity and comfort with common law than their Madisonian colleagues, whose penchant for statute law was shared by the Antifederalists. Aggregated, these findings once again correspond closely to the findings of Bogue et al. for all representatives elected during the first twenty years of Congress's existence.[53]

One of the reasons many favored the Constitution was because it eliminated tariffs between the states. Free trade was bound to benefit those who were involved in mercantile pursuits and associated trades. Therefore, one would expect a greater percentage of Federalists and Madisonians would be engaged in commercial activity. This expectation is borne out by the evidence, though not with the same certainty because of scanty numbers. Only one Antifederalist was "engaged in mercantile pursuits" compared to four Federalists and three Madisonians. It is probable that quite a few of those who were planters or farmers sold their crops commercially, as did plantation owners like James Madison. But it is difficult to find information on the size or scope of commercial farming. Nevertheless, the image that the Antifederalists were primarily small farmers is a powerful one. And it is true that more Antifederalists were farmers than either of the other two groups. Yet only one-third of these political elites whose professions are known were farmers. This is a greater percentage than either the Madisonians (a quarter of those whose professions are known) and the Federalists (about one in eight). The only other significant disparity between the groups is that nearly all the Federalists' professions are listed in *The Biographical Directory* itself, which is not the case for the other groups. This may be an indication that, on the whole, Madisonians and Antifederalists are more obscure—not necessarily in their own time but in what later generations chose to record and remember about them.

In sum, when one analyzes those who favored ratification as two separate groups, based on their postratification affiliations, we see significant disparities. Even from among the relatively small amount of systematic evidence available about their lives we see that the Madisonians were closer to the Antifederalists in some ways than the Federalists. These patterns were submerged during the ratification debate. As politics turned away from abstractions to more practical matters, these differences in background, place, and occupation helped break the Madisonian-Federalist coalition and secure the new Madisonian-Antifederalist one.

Conclusion

On Tuesday, February 15, 1820, the United States Senate was again occupied with the long-standing controversy over whether the Missouri Territory would become a "slave state" or a "free state." That day the senators assembled to hear a three-hour oration by William Pinkney of Maryland. Pinkney argued that the federal government could not dictate certain terms to a state entering the Union: slavery or its prohibition was a "domestic" policy of the individual states already established and therefore could not be federally mandated in newly admitted states if they were to be coequal members of the Union. If Missouri were not allowed to decide the question for itself, then it and those to follow would be second-class states. Those who would end the spread of slavery were well intentioned, but their attempt at reform came at the expense of state sovereignty, and their precedent would jeopardize the theory of a limited central government.[54]

Pinkney's speech was a direct response to New York Senator Rufus King, who had forwarded a different constitutional interpretation the previous Friday. King reasoned that since Article IV, section 3, clause 1 of the Constitution stressed that "New States *may* be admitted by the Congress into this Union," Congress had ultimate authority over the conditions of entry. The Confederation Congress had set an important precedent in this regard, prohibiting slavery in the Northwest Territory through the Ordinance of 1787. By a logical extension, justified by the wording of the Constitution, Congress could determine whether a state would be allowed into the Union "slave" or "free," argued King. The national legislature had passed on exercising this discretionary power when admitting states like Tennessee and Alabama because slavery was already established in them, their territories having been carved from already existing slave states. But the Congress was not similarly constrained in the case of Missouri, as it consisted of land acquired by the federal government after ratification, with no slavery policy at the time.[55]

In the next month Pinkney's exhortation to find a compromise to save the Union was fulfilled, and Maine was parceled off from Massachusetts as a free state to "counteract" the admission of Missouri as a slave state. However, in historical terms King, the nascent "free soiler" and the one who argued that ultimately there was to be no compromise on slavery, "won the war," despite not surviving to see that outcome. A third of a century before the Missouri Compromise, these two men had both been called on to help decide another question at the center of American political life, whether the Constitution should be adopted. In 1787 the thirty-two-year-old King, then a resident of Massachusetts who served as a delegate to the Confederation Congress and Philadelphia Convention, had been elected to the Massachusetts ratifying convention from his hometown of Newburyport. Likewise Pinkney, a twenty-four year old just admitted to the bar in Harford County, Maryland, was entrusted by his fellow citizens to decide on this weighty issue. Just as they had opposing positions on the extension of slavery, the two voted differently on ratification, King one of the architects of the bare majority that approved the Constitution in Massachusetts (with recommendatory amendments), Pinkney part of a small minority who opposed the document in Maryland.

These two men, and the rest of those who were called on to vote on the Constitution in state ratifying conventions, did much more than merely decide whether a new frame of government was acceptable or not. They helped set the course of American constitutionalism. They also continued to play a leading role in the political life of the new nation for a generation, setting policy both in their states and in Congress, concurrently interpreting the Constitution. These men were not just "founding fathers" frozen in time and distanced from the rough and tumble of real politics, these men were politicians actively involved with the pressing issues of their day. Accurately gauging the impact and the importance of the founding generation requires understanding how the Constitution's template was applied in practice to the nation's politics by many of the same individuals who were involved in the ratification process.

The King-Pinkney debate of 1820 is indicative of the future relations of former Federalists and Antifederalists for a number of reasons. These two senators framed arguments like their colleagues, simultaneously dealing with what might be called "politics proper" and issues of constitutionality. Both men wished to see a certain policy outcome on the Missouri issue, but couched their arguments in constitutional terms in order to grant them authority. Two plausible versions of what was constitutional were available to these men in large part because of the competing philosophies developed by the opposing parties in the years immediately following ratification. Their debate suggests that those who squared off during the ratification debates continued to oppose each other in recognizable ways. Pinkney, the Antifederalist, hoped to define a limit on the extent to which the national government could encroach on state sovereignty even in 1820. King argued that the long-term good of the Union required another control on state discretion. But this vignette might prove misleading if taken too far. Care must be taken not to draw the conclusion that an unaltered bipolar political landscape continued uninterrupted from 1787 to 1820 and beyond. The primary venue for their arguments had shifted from the newspapers to the halls of Congress and from whether the Constitution was salutary or not to what it meant. But the composition of the two sides changed as well. Bipolarity continued, to be sure, yet it was a new bipolar arrangement, now dividing against themselves those who supported the Constitution.

While the nationally renowned King and Pinkney squared off in the Senate, across the uncompleted Capitol toiled four others who had voted in their state's ratification conventions. Only one of these U.S. representatives, Martin Kinsley of the soon-to-be-created state of Maine, had voted against the Constitution. James Johnson of Virginia, John Rhea of Tennessee, and South Carolinian Charles Pinckney had solidly backed the proposed frame of government in their respective conventions. They had not, however, remained in the Federalist camp. Each of these three were Republicans, like James Madison. Needless to say, in this highly charged sectional debate they did not support King's proposal. Neither did they agree with his interpretation of the Constitution.

In a far less polished speech than either King or William Pinkney (no relation) delivered, Charles Pinckney outlined what might be called a Madisonian stance, stressing the importance of dual sovereignty rather than "states' rights" or federal primacy. Pointing out that he was the only representative who attended the Philadelphia Convention, Pinckney aimed to cloak his insights in the veneration that most representatives, younger by a generation, felt toward the founding.

Between pro-Southern arguments where his reasoning is suspect, a

Madisonian constitutional argument is offered.[56] What prevented domination and tyranny, according to Pinckney, was the division of power between the national government and the states. When there were but thirteen states a combination of three or four of the largest could threaten the nation, but "with twenty-four or more States it will be impossible, sir, for four or five States, or any comparatively small number, ever to threaten the existence of the Union." The increased number of states served as a bulwark against possible aggrandizement by the federal government. This was a far different mechanism than the national veto Madison had originally proposed to ensure that the balance of powers agreed upon would be maintained. The intent was the same, however. If there were no states at all, Pinckney related, a national majority could simply prevail, forcing its will on the others. To Pinckney, "it is this system [of dual sovereignty], which is not at all understood in Europe and too little among ourselves, that will long keep us a strong and united people."[57]

It is not difficult to imagine who Pinckney thought ignorant of dual sovereignty: the Federalists, of course, who wished to impose their will on a new state. Yet he may also have thought some of his Republican colleagues were in need of a lesson in American constitutionalism as well. Pinckney reminded his listeners that certain powers and responsibilities were given to the federal government, and others were retained by the states. That delicate arrangement could be threatened from either side. Just as it was possible to exaggerate federal primacy it was possible to err in overemphasizing state powers. Realizing and embracing the separation of powers agreed upon in the Constitution were key to figuring out who may properly act in this (or any other) instance. Pinckney thus employed his own version of the tried and true Wilsonian formulation: "The Constitution, being a frame of government consisting wholly of delegated powers, all power not expressly delegated [is] reserved to the people or the States." Since determining the populations of states was not in the federal arsenal, the national government could not dictate whether Missouri would be slave or free.

Within the decade Pinckney, King, and Pinkney would all be dead, symbolizing the passing of the revolutionary generation. The nation lived on, but the sectional dilemma facing politicians remained, even beyond the Civil War. The options for solving this dilemma and the constitutional arguments behind those options would have been quite familiar to these leaders.

As indicated by the latter-day positions of the above speakers, one's constitutional approach was more than a transient stance; it was a disposition — an ideology — unlikely to dissolve with the acceptance of the Constitution or in light of alternate interpretations. With the advancement of constitutional time, the Hamiltonian Federalists' faithfulness to their conception of constitutionalism required an aggressive push for extensive discretionary powers at the national level. Faithful to their own conception of constitutions as static and limited grants of power, the Madisonians bolted from the Federalist fold and joined with the former Antifederalists who had a similar preference for constitutional stasis.

Coexistence was not easy, but a variety of factors allowed it. One was that the two sides shared certain goals and beliefs. Most importantly, each group felt convinced that union was preferable to disunion. Mutual preferences that were less apparent were also important. For instance, each favored democratic, highly accessible procedures and structures under which to conduct legislative business. Another factor allowing coexistence was historical happenstance. Several matters conspired to keep national office from being desirable early in the nation's history. Many of these reasons, like the arduousness of travel, were beyond the control of politicians. The relative undesirability of national office kept congressional tenures short. Short tenures served as something of a de facto term limit. So despite the fact that rotation in office was not mandated, the Antifederalist preference for it was largely satisfied, arguably with results similar to what they had envisioned. At the very least, the government did not quickly transform into what the Antifederalists feared, a purely national regime.

When the Antifederalists recovered from their dismal showing in the First Congress and their numbers were bolstered by the breakaway Federalists, the opposition could and did have a significant effect on national policy. A final reason that those who came to different conclusions concerning the proposed Constitution were able to coexist under it as law was the nature of the regime they founded. The nation was both Federalist and Republican, to paraphrase Thomas Jefferson's first inaugural address; both Federalist and Antifederalist. No permanently disgruntled minority party materialized among the nation's early political actors. None were so dissatisfied or politically disadvantaged as to seriously question the Constitution itself, and thus its nascent legitimacy was bolstered.

The juxtaposition of theory and practice in the early republic has a good deal to tell us about American political thought. By his own estimation, empirical events went against the grain of Madison's prior thinking and thus greatly limited the applicability of what has been taken to be the centerpiece of his political theory, Federalist #10. The incongruousness of subsequent events should, however, not lead us to ignore it. Rather, understanding the argument of Federalist #10 and the political developments that made it inapplicable in the mind of its author is a first step in the realization that the founding was a process and not the product of a single mind or event. Accordingly, any accurate treatment of the founding must be well-versed with many points of view from the ratification debates and must expand the chronological horizon beyond 1787 to discern how theory fit with practice. If we do not seriously assess what Publius argued with what transpired afterward, there is little hope that we can truly understand the dynamic process of America's founding.

A fuller knowledge of what happened to Madison's argument provides us with a specific example of two principles that have achieved mantralike status in the field of political theory: the time-bound nature of political thought and the limitations of theory without a corresponding knowledge of practice. Too often these ideas are offered as disclaimers, to hold at bay the contention that those who study political theory are ahistorical and impractical. Madison's experience should give us pause to consider that the thinking of major figures in the field can undergo changes both sudden and vast, even at times when they seem at the height of their craft. The modifications in Madison's thinking were spurred not only by the imprecise fit between theory and political practice but also by his irreconcilable differences with the Hamiltonians. Neither party adequately understood the fundamental nature of these differences, a matter that one might have thought a joint project of political theorizing would make apparent. Perhaps the particular nature of the essays written are responsible — they were, after all, designed to effectively argue the case for the Constitution and were written before its framework was a matter of practice. But we must at least pause to wonder whether these problems afflict political theory generally.

Even with major alterations, much of Madison's thinking remained intact, of course. His famous contention from Federalist #51 that "men are not angels," for instance, and so *The Federalist* as a whole is surely not for the scrap heap. What my research indicates is that the essay usually considered the most important work of political theory from the founding, Federalist #10, was the first to become irrelevant and obsolete in the mind of its author. The theories of the other actors involved, the Hamiltonians and the Antifederalists, seemed, despite some modifications brought about by the new political reality, to have remained fairly intact.

No single group of the founders foresaw or controlled the outcomes of the historical process to which they were party. Thus what has been proclaimed to be the most calculated, rational founding the world has ever witnessed falls short of the goal of foolproof societal engineering. But how could it be otherwise in a nation whose leaders uniformly felt that compromise was necessary in a viable republic? The one-time foes of the Constitution agreed to abide by its formal requirements, and its supporters allowed them to freely participate. What resulted was a political hybrid, where the Federalists got their nation, the Antifederalists got a closer link between policy and public opinion, and both were able to advance competing versions of how to treat the Constitution. The ratification was a process, punctuated by a point of implementation that altered the debate, but did not change the fundamental questions or their need to be addressed. The rational, contractual model of liberal government is stretched even by its wildest success, the American founding. For in a United States almost uniformly devoted to the principles of Locke and other Enlightenment figures there was something of a Burkean element, where political development took on a life of its own. America's founding was not entirely subject to calculation, but did have a rationality in that it worked itself out. The results were related to but not dictated by the various strands of thought found there, and in "working itself out," these approaches worked their way into the national psyche.

CHAPTER SIX

Continuity and Change
in the Transition to Partisanship, 1789–1801

Two versions of constitutionalism divided those who had pressed for centralizing change in 1787. This rift was not readily apparent during the ratification debates, even to many of the principal actors involved. The two individuals who would become known as the leaders of their respective parties, Alexander Hamilton and James Madison, were in tight collaboration on the effort to secure ratification. The fruit of their joint effort is one of the few collaborations to be considered a major historical work of political theory. But within eighteen months of the Constitution's implementation, these same men were engaged in a partisan struggle over its meaning that was to be to the political death.

When Madison found that Hamilton's followers in Congress were aggressively and successfully pursuing policies that he believed were not in the national good and beyond the powers granted to the national government in the Constitution, a shift in mental terrain was required — for Madison faced what he had believed to be impossible in the extended republic, a majority faction of legislators unresponsive to the common good. This shift in thinking included an embrace of partisan tactics that had heretofore been strongly proscribed. Three things heartened Madison: the faith that he was helping to restore meaning to the Constitution, his confidence that he was pursuing the common good, and the significant number of representatives and senators who followed his lead into the opposition. Republicans of all stripes engaged in cultivating popular opinion, confident that the popularization of politics would more closely approximate the common good. And so the Madisonians' link with the former Antifederalists in Congress was anything but accidental, as many critics of the Constitution had urged that policy needed to be kept tied to public sentiment. True, this popular politics was on a scale that the Antifederalists had originally thought impossible, but they, like their allies, were learning by doing, adjusting their thinking to square with the empirical reality they found after implementation of the Constitution. This group was saddened if less shocked that the Hamiltonians proffered so wide-ranging and active a role for the government, particularly in economic affairs. As they had predicted, the necessary and proper clause was allowing license to self-interested officials who constituted a congressional majority. So together the Antifederalists and the Madisonians adopted the tactics of partisans and the philosophy of strict construction.

This coalitional change was readily apparent to political observers, particularly the remaining Federalists. Most were disgusted with and confused by Madison, because they did not fully grasp how different his constitutional ideas were from Hamilton's and their own. Lulled into believing that Madison's hopes for the new government were not far different from theirs, they branded him a turncoat when he left the Federalist fold. Theodore Sedgwick, for example, called Madison "an apostate from all his former principles," in an early 1790 letter to his wife and expressed consternation at his being a "convert to anti-federalism."[1] Abigail Adams, meanwhile, expressed her disgust that Madison brought with him to the opposition a good number of votes in Congress, primarily from his own region. Writing to Cotton Tufts in May 1790, Adams noted that "Madison leads the Virginians like a flock of sheep."[2] These reactions to Madison's defection, based on an incomplete knowledge of his constitutional philosophy, have been incorporated in assessments of him for more than two hundred years.

In this chapter, I gauge the strength and durability of the Antifederalist-Madisonian coalition through the Federalist era and analyze voting behavior during that time to comment on other works that deal with the emergence of political parties in the United States. Many students of political parties have viewed this time as the first era in which true political parties governed a nation in turn, a crucial development in modern politics. To make their point, these scholars have overemphasized the discontinuity of the party politics of the 1790s with the controversy over ratification. A recent corrective to this view is provided by John Aldrich in his book *Why Parties?* There Aldrich rightly emphasizes the continuity of the ratification debates with the partisanship of the 1790s. Nevertheless, his view of the birth of political parties stresses that the Federalists, particularly Hamilton, inaugurated the party system within Congress to gain the upper hand in forging a strong national government. More accurately, the Madisonians precipitated party formation as a means of gaining an electoral edge.

Below, data on the cohesiveness and alignment of the three groups drawn from roll-call votes are used to assess the validity of the accounts of party formation. I find little support for the views of party scholars who posit that the 1790s inaugurated a new issue cleavage. While this finding squares with John Aldrich's, I also find it necessary to correct in certain ways the picture of early party formation offered by him. Subsequently I discuss the major issues of the Second through Sixth Congresses, again presenting roll-call data that illuminate the three groups' positions. I conclude that the Congress itself likely did not meet Federalist expectations because there was little institutional memory or incentive for the nation's most respected individuals to populate the institution. The advancement of constitutional time brought both partisanship and an institutionalized weakness to Congress, both of which the Republicans could readily accept.

Fitting Theory and Practice: Interpretations of the Early Congress

Compared to the landslide of commentary and analysis on *The Federalist* and other ratification debate essays, the early U.S. government has received scant attention. This is less an indication of the inadequacy of research on this era than it is a signifier of how important scholars have taken the ratification debates to be. Despite certain differences of interpretation, the literature on the first decade of U.S. politics firmly establishes a trend toward increasing partisanship. Furthermore, several authors have determined that in conjunction with this increasing partisanship leaders turned more and more to popular appeals to justify policies. This is perhaps the most crucial transformation of form American politics has ever taken, from the republicanism envisioned by many of the founders, to something not anticipated or hoped for by most of them, the Jacksonian democracy described vividly by Alexis de Tocqueville in the 1830s. Finally, these studies have discerned and commented on the eclipse of Federalism, the sudden and nearly total disappearance of Federalism after the "Revolution of 1800."

Stanley Elkins and Eric McKitrick skillfully weave a relation among all three of these findings in *The Age of Federalism*. In a partisan atmosphere, Federalists were forced to appeal to the public to sanction their policy alternatives. In the first few Congresses, "one sees them [the Federalists] doing a surprising number of things right, at least from day to day."[3] In other words, the Federalists did quite well in appealing to popular opinion to legitimate many of their specific policies. For example, they were able to convince a largely Francophile public that a closer relationship with Britain (arranged by U.S. envoy John Jay in 1794) would be in their material interest.[4] But in repeatedly appealing to popular interests to sanction policy, the Federalists unwittingly sowed the seeds of their own destruction, for the Federalist hope was not for policy driven by popular interests, but rather for policy discerned by a select natural aristocracy. In the climate of politics they themselves helped to create, the Federalists' elite conception of politics was doomed in the long run.

Likewise James Roger Sharp, in his *American Politics in the Early Republic*, finds that partisanship led to unanticipated consequences. Partisanship was not considered acceptable and was taken as an indication of a dispute so pervasive and grave as to threaten the nation's existence. Politicians in this era felt that they were close to the brink of the Union's dissolution. In this crisis atmosphere, partisanship almost spun out of control, as one felt one's opponents were playing fast and loose with the nation's very existence. No wonder, then, that the division between the Federalist Party and the Republican Party steadily increased, as both sides became more distrusting of each other, to the point where partisan divisions were almost ironclad by the Fifth Congress, when Federalists felt sufficiently threatened to pass the Alien and Sedition Acts. In the absence of elite consensus there was an understandable turn to popular, interest-based politics. This disturbed the Federalists, who considered themselves republicans and not democrats, so much that they felt their experiment had failed.[5] Gordon Wood concurs in *The Radicalism of the American Revolution*, finding that the American people took the rhetoric of the Revolution in a way unintended by the Federalists. Federalists wanted to break the hold of Britain's artificial aristocracy and replace it with a homegrown natural aristocracy; those who deserved to govern by their superior talents would be elected to office. By contrast, the people believed that the American Revolution signaled an end to aristocracy altogether, to be replaced by a politics based on popular interests. There are some fine shades of difference between these arguments, but these authors are in agreement about the phenomena they discern in the early American republic and are quite close in their perceptions of the mechanisms of our early political development.[6]

Whereas the above theses deal with the broad scope of American politics in the 1780s and 1790s, others have focused more exclusively on the Congress. Many of these later authors have been drawn to the study of the early national legislature by the intriguing question of whether the differences displayed there were of the character of modern parties. That development is important because the early American republic might be the first time and place where true competing parties envisioned ruling a nation in turn, a development of crucial importance to the practice of modern politics. Accordingly, these studies move beyond discerning a rise in partisanship, to a more sophisticated analysis of how pervasive that partisanship was and whether the requirements for true political parties were satisfied in the era. William N. Chambers finds in *Political Parties in a New Nation* that by the Third Congress the four hallmarks of political parties — structure, function, following, and cohesion — were in place, and so he finds that the United States's first party-system was indeed the first true system of party politics in the world.[7]

Rudolph M. Bell refines Chambers's thesis by categorizing congressional roll-call votes from the first six Congresses. On roll calls that dealt with the scope of governmental authority, Bell found that two factions were consistently at odds through the first three Congresses, but these factions were not necessarily split on other categories of issues. This being the case, the requirements for true partisanship were not satisfied early on. However, once the central government successfully put down the Whiskey Rebellion in western Pennsylvania, Bell says that the issue of governmental authority was largely settled; and with the "first-order" question of governmental authority established, two parties with opposing views on a wide variety of issues coalesced.[8] John F. Hoadley, by contrast, writes that parties developed more quickly, this despite the fact that the factions that formed were not the same as those that took sides on the Constitution. Issues of governmental authority still provided the major cleavage of the first session of the First Congress. But by the second session the Congress had moved on to other issues, and with that a new cleavage, more closely approximating the sectional disagreement that intensified and persisted through the year 1800.[9] Despite the difference in time frame, Hoadley agrees with Bell and Chambers that the early American Congress was the site of the first viable party system.

Some recent work has been critical of these partisanship studies, however. John Aldrich and Ruth Grant argue that

focusing on party development has distorted the picture of the politics of the immediate post-ratification period and has led to a serious misunderstanding of the continuities between the politics of the 1780s and those of the 1790s. The distortion can be attributed in part to a concentration on institutional development that excludes political ideology.[10]

Instead of a break from the old divisions and the forging of party coalitions around a new set of issues, Aldrich and Grant point out that the Antifederalists made up the bulk of the opposition party, and that they were opposed by a group that was almost uniformly Federalist. The development of a new partisan form was notable, but "the origin of parties was rooted in the continuing nature of the conflict between federalist and antifederalist understandings of republican government."[11] Developing the practices and institutions of partisanship on the fly was an effective means for Federalists and Republicans of continuing the debate over the power and scope of national government.

Aldrich expands on this idea in his recent book *Why Parties?* There he points out that the Constitution itself was formulated to provide a tentative answer to what he calls the "great principle," or how powerful the central government should be. Preferred solutions to the great principle were spread "along a dimension that ranged from the Articles at one end to a powerful, unified national government at the other."[12] Although the Constitution clearly sanctioned a more powerful government, just how powerful was still an open question upon implementation. If issues activated only the representatives' views on the great principle, the median view in Congress would likely have defined the great principle, but other considerations intervened. With state and sectional interests thrown into the mix, there was no majoritarian solution to be had. Chaotic vote cycling resulted, best exemplified by the inability to decide on a site for the capital and on assumption, on which there were numerous inconclusive votes before the famed dinner party agreement. This instability threatened to expose the national government as unable to address the very problems it was designed to solve. Hamilton, realizing that more representatives favored a strong national government than not, knew that political parties could suppress secondary concerns and yield a favorable equilibrium on the great principle. The Federalists, and Hamilton in particular, engaged in party-building behaviors, successfully inducing an equilibrium that ended the voting chaos apparent in the first two Congresses.

Aldrich suggests that Madison was positioned between Hamilton and the Antifederalists on the great principle continuum. He points out that while "ardent Anti-Federalists might see power lurking behind the decision to buy George Washington a desk, Jeffersonians and Hamiltonians might not. But when it came to Hamilton's ambitious fiscal policy, Jeffersonians might well disagree." In response to Hamilton's fiscal policy and accompanying party-building activities, which sanctioned a more nationalist regime than Madison wished for, he and Jefferson engaged in party-building activities of their own. "At the end of the Second Congress," Aldrich writes, " 'Madison and Jefferson decided they must organize an opposition.' "[13] The Madisonians (Aldrich occasionally uses this label, but more often uses "Jeffersonians") allied with the Antifederalists to provide a counterpoise to the nationalists as they threatened to define the great principle.

To be fair to the studies of partisanship, their primary concern is over the early development of a viable party apparatus; their commentary on the continuities and discontinuities of politics during this era is antecedent to this primary goal. Nevertheless, there does seem to be a difficulty posed by their collective approach. It is apparent to Chambers, Bell, and Hoadley that the debate over the Constitution can in no way be called a struggle between two real parties. The issue at hand did not remain live long enough for true partisanship to occur. But more importantly for them, there were not two distinct partisan organizations that were able to coexist within one framework of political rules, because that which was being debated was the framework of rules itself. It is only when two (or more) "sides" can abide by the results generated within a particular framework of government that parties can be said to exist. Thus, if the requirements for viable parties are satisfied in the 1790s, as these authors find, then there *must* be discontinuity with the ratification debate, when parties could not exist. They find that the old question over the Constitution was replaced by a new issue cleavage that divided the parties in a new way. So Hoadley, for instance, proclaims that unlike in the ratification debate, "it is clear that philosophical differences were not the immediate basis for the division into opposing parties."[14] But those who split into Republican and Federalist factions in the 1790s were convinced they were following defensible principles every bit as much as when they were debating over the Constitution itself.

Aldrich is closer to the mark in many ways. His understanding that the issue of national power remained front and center in the representatives' minds is allowed by an acknowledgment that the Madisonians had much different ideas on the issue than the nationalists. Earlier party scholars, working under the long-standing assumption that Madison had been a nationalist, could only logically account for his alliance with the Antifederalists by positing that the issue of national power had receded. Aldrich also stresses how important the early years of the republic were in setting lasting precedents, something abundantly clear to both Madison and Hamilton. With the Constitution "purposefully ambiguous" about the great principle "the first few Congresses would be critical, for actions taken—or refrained from—in its earliest years would set the clearest precedents for just what power resided in and would be acted upon by the new national government."[15] At the same time, Aldrich mistakenly sees party formation in this context as a tool used within the legislature to end vote cycling. Although politicians did realize that parties could be useful in achieving their favored collective outcomes, it was the Republicans who inaugurated party activity.

Postratification Cohesion and Alignments

By now it is clear that viewing politics in the early national Congress with one eye on the ratification debates yields three distinct groups: the Constitution's supporters who with Hamilton became the Federalist Party; Madison's breakaway group of administration foes; and the former Antifederalists, almost all of whom opposed the administration and became Republicans. One advantage of studies on partisanship during this era is that there is no longer much mystery about the partisan alignment of national representatives. Kenneth Martis has compiled the determinations of various authors and cleared up discrepancies between them in his *Historical Atlas of Political Parties in the United States Congress.* Martis relates that by the Fourth Congress, citizens clearly knew if candidates were Federalists or Republicans, and the polarization between them was pervasive enough that each member clearly falls into one party or the other. Even in the first three Congresses, though, members were recognizably in one camp or the other based on their voting records. The difference is that party labels were not used extensively, and the populace thus did not employ them as a voting cue. Therefore, following the practice of several other scholars, Martis labels members either pro-administration or anti-administration for these Congresses.[16]

Table 6.1 combines Martis's determinations of partisanship with stances on the Constitution taken by members of Congress who had voted at state ratification conventions. Combining these two positions enables us to get a sense of the strength of the three aforementioned groups through time. This juxtaposition indicates that the Constitution's proponents broke into two camps already in the First Congress. While the "Madisonians" were significantly outnumbered in the first two Congresses by their pro-administration counterparts, their numbers relative to Federalist forces subsequently grew. In the Fourth and Fifth Congresses, this breakaway group outnumbered Federalists in the House. And from the Seventh Congress to the Eleventh, there were still many of those who had made the "switch" to the Republican side, while the Federalist Party was moribund. On the other side of the ledger we see that but for an occasional anomaly, the Antifederalists were uniformly anti-administration/Republican. I use this sample of individuals, readily recognizable in terms of group affiliation, to analyze roll-call votes. But of course this again is a selected sample of those who populated Congress in its early years, not the entire population. Although the positions many members of Congress took on the Constitution is unclear, what is clear is how many individuals were pro-administration and anti-administration or later,

TABLE 6.1

Party Affiliations of Ratification Convention Voters in Congress

	Federalist				Antifederalist			
	Pro-Administration/ Federalist		Anti-Administration/ Republican		Pro-Administration/ Federalist		Anti-Administration/ Republican	
Congress	House	Senate	House	Senate	House	Senate	House	Senate
1	15	9	7	2	0	—	6	3
2	13	10	6	2	1ᵃ	—	5	2
3	11	11	10	2	0	—	10	1
4	6	10	14	3	2	—	8	2
5	5	6	8	4	1	—	12	2
6	10	3	4	3	—	—	10	2
7	2	0	6	2	—	—	12	2
8	1	1	8	2	—	—	16	3
9	1	1	7	2	—	—	14	2
10	1	1	8	2	—	—	7	2
11	1	1	6	0	—	—	7	2
12	1	0	3	1	—	—	6	1
13	2	2	3	1	—	—	3	0
14	2	2	1	1	—	—	2	0
15	—	1	2	—	—	—	0	0
16	—	1	3	—	—	—	1	1
17	—	1	1	—	—	—	—	1
18	—	1ᵇ	—	—	—	—	—	—
Totals	71	61	97	27	4	0	119	26

SOURCE: Compiled by author. Categorization is based on an individual's vote on the Constitution in a state ratification convention and their subsequent partisan affiliation as determined by Martis's *Historical Atlas*. I colloquially refer to pro-administration/Federalists as Federalists, and anti-administration/Republicans who voted in favor of the Constitution as Madisonians.

ᵃWilliam Pinkney, an Antifederalist who had pro-administration leanings, was elected to the Second Congress, but never cast a vote.

ᵇBy the Eighteenth Congress, Federalists like Rufus King are identified as "Adams-Clay Federalists."

Federalist and Republican. Table 6.2 shows the partisan composition of both the House and the Senate in the first eight Congresses. As in the sample of those who voted in ratification conventions, Martis's determinations of partisan affiliation are used. Although the Federalists clearly outnumber the opposition in the First Congress and the Republicans clearly dominate the Federalists by the Eighth Congress, in between there is rather close competition between the two parties. This close competition

TABLE 6.2

Partisan Composition of the First Eight Congresses

	Senate		House	
Congress	*Pro-Administration/ Federalists*	*Anti-Administration/ Republicans*	*Pro-Administration/ Federalists*	*Anti-Administration/ Republicans*
1	18	8	37	28
2	16	13	39	30
3	16	14	52	54
4	21	11	47	59
5	22	10	57	50
6	22	10	60	46
7	15	17	38	67
8	9	25	39	102

SOURCE: Compiled by author using Martis's *Historical Atlas.*

allowed for a relatively conservative approach by the opposition party. Instead of risking the stigma of repudiating the Constitution, they chose to seek majorities through electioneering.

The lack of a viable Federalist Party population after the Sixth Congress makes a comparison of the dynamics between these three groups difficult after 1800. One could say that the Federalists were no longer as they had existed previously, and so there is not a vital Federalist-Republican dynamic to explain after 1800.[17] Accordingly, the data I analyze are from the first six Congresses. They derive from roll-call votes in the House, as significant numbers of all three groups served there. Each member fitting the criteria of my sample was grouped into the appropriate category (Federalists, Madisonians, and Antifederalists), and the alignment of these groups on every recorded vote in the first six Congresses was analyzed in two ways. One measure is based on where each group's majority was aligned, and the other is based on yea/nay percentages by group. But first, as an overall measure of group cohesiveness, I added the number of votes cast in a group's majority for each roll call of a given Congress and divided it by the total number of votes that group cast. This gives a percentage figure of the total cohesiveness of each group by Congress, a group-unity score.[18]

Given the increased polarization through time discerned by various authors, one would expect that each group would show increasing cohesiveness. In addition, cohesiveness should be quite high. If the "Madisonians" were just a little more unified than what we would expect by

TABLE 6.3

In-Group Cohesion: Percentage of Group Members'
Votes in the Group's Majority, by Congress

Congress	Federalists	Madisonians	Antifederalists
1	79	70	78
2	76	83	82
3	80	80	83
4	83	82	90
5	89	91	92
6	88	89	95

SOURCE: Compiled by author using roll-call data from the Inter-University Consortium for Political and Social Research, data set #0004.

chance, then we must question whether it is correct to label them Madisonians or to treat them as a distinctive group at all. Similarly, if the Federalist Party members and Antifederalists are not very cohesive, then we must seriously doubt whether the traditional view of politics in the first six Congresses is correct, and by extension whether we can draw any conclusions from looking at them as separate entities. One would also expect that the Madisonian and the former Antifederalist majorities would align very often, particularly after the First Congress, while alignments of the Federalist Party with either of the two groups that formed the Republican Party would be less frequent. I also expect that the Madisonians would rarely be alone in their majority alignment, as it would require that they strike out on a course where neither the Antifederalists nor the Federalist Party members agreed with them. Table 6.3 supports my expectations. The groups do indeed show a great deal of cohesiveness, each averaging well over 80 percent.[19] These figures do increase over time, rising from the 70s and low 80s in the First and Second Congresses, to high 80s and low 90s in the Fifth and Sixth. The former Antifederalists seem to be the most cohesive group overall, but not by a great margin. This measure of cohesiveness confirms that each group was highly unified.

The question remains how these tight-knit groups aligned with each other. The first measure of alignment simply considers where the majority of each group voted on each individual roll-call vote. If all three majorities were on the same side, then I consider the vote "consensual." If majorities did oppose one another, then I determine which groups sided together and which group was isolated. Table 6.4 gives the percentages of

TABLE 6.4

Group Majority Alignments

Alignments on All Votes

Congress	Total Roll Calls	% of Consensual Votes	% Federalists Oppose Antifederalists	% Madisonians Alone
1	109	33	58	9
2	102	21	74	6
3	69	16	77	7
4	83	31	67	1
5	155	22	74	4
6	96	23	77	0

Alignment of Madisonians When Federalists Oppose Antifederalists

(by percentage)

Congress	Madisonians with Federalists	Madisonians with Antifederalists	Madisonians Neutral
1	30	60	10
2	9	88	3
3	4	91	6
4	7	91	2
5	3	97	0
6	4	84	12

SOURCE: Compiled by author using roll-call data from the Inter-University Consortium for Political and Social Research, data set #0004.

votes that were consensual, which divided the Federalists and Antifederalist groups, and on which the Madisonians were alone. Table 6.4b deals exclusively with the votes from the column of 6.4a where Federalists opposed Antifederalists, indicating where the majority of Madisonians aligned on these votes.

The number of consensual roll calls, where no two groups' majorities were opposed to each other, peaked in the First Congress. But for a slight anomaly in the Fourth Congress the amount of consensual roll calls remained lower, about the rate of one in five votes taken.[20] The number of votes where the Antifederalists' majority was opposed to the Federalists' is high, as anticipated. Nearly three-quarters of all votes cast after the First Congress are of this nature. The Madisonians are rarely alone in their majority alignment. Or another way of characterizing the alignment is that absent substantial agreement on all sides, there were few issues on which a majority of Antifederalists and Federalists agreed. After the inaugural Congress, the Madisonians rarely sided with the Federalists against the Antifederalists, doing so less than 10 percent of the time when Federalist and Antifederalist majorities opposed each other.

This kind of analysis can speak further to the conundrums of continuity or discontinuity and timing that separate the various interpretations discussed above. If one can characterize the early Congresses by the introduction of a new dominant issue cleavage, then one would expect there to be frequent alignment of the Madisonians with the former Antifederalists. But Bell and Hoadley also find that the new cleavage was not all-pervasive at first. Issues of governmental authority were still being decided in the new Congress, and these votes initially revived the old alignment. This being the case, one would expect that the alignments on "government authority" roll-call votes would be different from the normal alignment where the Madisonians sided with the Antifederalists. The main difference between Bell and Hoadley in this regard is how long they think the residue of the old cleavage remained, Bell arguing that it lasted into the Third Congress, Hoadley thinking it dead after the first session of the First Congress. If Bell is correct, we would expect to see Madisonians voting with Antifederalists except on votes pertaining to governmental authority into the Third Congress. If Hoadley's contention is more accurate, we would see Madisonians shifting between camps during the early days of the First Congress only.

A glance at the figures in Table 6.4b seems to lend more credence to Hoadley's view than to Bell's, as a major, durable alteration in alignments seems to have occurred roughly between the First and Second Congresses. The low percentages of this kind of vote in the Second and Third Congresses would seem to bode ill for Bell's thesis, unless those votes are exclusively about governmental power.[21]

In order to more fully discern the relative positions of the groups, I introduce a second tool for looking at alignments. In this second type of alignment analysis, I compare the percentages the groups voted yea/nay on each bill and use the differences in those percentages to place each bill in one of four categories. The first category, which I will call the *Ratification Alignment*, consists of votes where both the Federalists and the Madisonians acted significantly unlike the former Antifederalists.[22] We would expect these kinds of votes on governmental authority roll calls if Hoadley and Bell are correct. In the second category, the *New Alignment*, are those bills where the percentage difference between Antifederalists and Madisonians is small, but that between Antifederalists and Federalists is large. The majority of bills should fall in this group. By contrast, there should be very few *Anomalous* votes, a third variety,

TABLE 6.5

Percentage of Roll Calls by Alignment Category

Congress	Ratification Alignment	New Alignment	Anomalous Alignment	Consensual Alignment
1	16	34	13	38
2	13	46	12	29
3	4	75	3	17
4	5	70	0	25
5	1	79	2	17
6	7	77	0	16

SOURCE: Compiled by author using roll-call data from the Inter-University Consortium for Political and Social Research, data set #0004.

where the percentage difference between Federalist and Antifederalist votes is not great, but that between Antifederalists and Madisonians is. These votes do not correspond to either the old cleavage or the new alignment, and thus should be rare. Finally, the fourth category consists of those votes where the percentage differences between Antifederalists and Madisonians, as well as Antifederalists and Federalists, are low. This last category roughly corresponds to the consensual votes found above, and therefore I will call this the *Consensual Alignment*.

The overall results of this analysis are presented in Table 6.5. As expected, the majority of votes fall under the New Alignment category, but surprisingly, not before the Third Congress. The number of Ratification Alignment votes are very low after the first two Congresses, as are the Anomalous Alignment votes. However, there are a higher number of Anomalous Alignment votes than expected in the first two Congresses.[23] The level of votes in the Consensual Alignment category never differs from the amount of consensual votes found in the earlier analysis by more than 8 percent. This measure of alignment seems more reminiscent of Aldrich's view than the others', with a relatively chaotic voting pattern characterizing the first two Congresses and a much more stable arrangement subsequently.[24] But it is in the area of specific issues, and particularly by comparing governmental authority roll calls with others, that it may help to know which of the various theses discussed is closest to discerning what actually took place. If there is not a substantial difference of alignments between those votes that are deemed to be about governmental authority and those that are not, then there is little reason to side with Bell or Hoadley and conclude that the politics of the 1790s was defined by a different issue from that which animated the ratification debate.

The Formation of the First American Party System

I have reconstructed the votes that Bell and Hoadley considered government authority votes, comparing those votes against all others. Although Hoadley bases his categorization of votes on Bell's, there are a few differences, as well as the aforementioned disparity in time frame. Accordingly, the analysis is tailored to the author's individual thesis. Even so, the similarities of their arguments yield similar expectations. One would expect few if any consensual votes on government authority issues, because these matters were still prone to the old conflict. As such, these votes would reflect the Ratification Alignment, where the Madisonian majority sided with the Federalists and opposed the Antifederalists. By contrast, nongovernment authority votes should predominantly reflect the New Alignment, with the Madisonians voting with Antifederalists instead of the Federalists. These differences should be valid through the Third Congress for Bell, but only through the first session of the First Congress for Hoadley.

The evidence does not square well with the contention that the old division over the Constitution existed on a certain set of votes into the Third Congress. None of the government authority roll calls during the Second or Third Congress reflect the old alignment. On only two of thirty such votes in the Second Congress did the Madisonian majority side with the Federalists.[25] No such alignments occurred in the Third Congress. The Madisonians did, contrary to expectations, side with the Antifederalists on many of the governmental authority votes. Even in the First Congress nine of twenty votes are of this variety. Nineteen of thirty votes were this way in the next legislative term, while all government authority votes but one in the Third Congress found the Madisonian majority with the Antifederalists. Furthermore, there does not seem to be a great disparity between the government power roll calls and others. There should be many more New Alignment votes on other issues, with Madisonians joining with the Antifederalists, but this is not the case. By these measures the contention that a distinctive new cleavage took hold of the legislature except on a certain category of votes where a different and older cleavage held sway is not supported.

Hoadley's conception of the issue cleavages in the early Congress seems, at least initially, to be closer to the mark. In the first session of the new legislature, Ratification Alignment votes occurred six times out of eight votes on central authority issues. The majority of votes on other matters reflected the New Alignment. But in the analysis of majority alignment, matters are less clear. Madisonian majorities did side with pro-

TABLE 6.6

Alignments of "Government Authority" Votes
(as determined by Bell and Hoadley)
Compared to Alignments of All Other Votes

a) Bell	Government Authority	All Other Votes
1ST CONGRESS		
Alignments by Category		
Ratification Alignment	6	11
New Alignment	8	29
Anomalous Alignment	0	14
Consensual Alignment	6	35
Alignments by Group Majority		
Madisonians and Federalists		
Oppose Antifederalists	4	15
Federalists and Antifederalists		
Opposed, Madisonians Neutral	3	3
Madisonians and Antifederalists		
Oppose Federalists	9	29
Consensual	3	33
Federalists and Antifederalists		
Oppose Madisonians	1	9
2ND CONGRESS		
Alignments by Category		
Ratification Alignment	0	17
New Alignment	12	25
Anomalous Alignment	7	7
Consensual Alignment	11	23
Alignments by Group Majority		
Madisonians and Federalists		
Oppose Antifederalists	2	5
Federalists and Antifederalists		
Opposed, Madisonians Neutral	0	2
Madisonians and Antifederalists		
Oppose Federalists	19	47
Consensual	5	16
Federalists and Antifederalists		
Oppose Madisonians	4	2

(continued)

TABLE 6.6
(continued)

a) Bell (continued)	Government Authority	All Other Votes
3RD CONGRESS		
Alignments by Category		
Ratification Alignment	0	3
New Alignment	6	46
Anomalous Alignment	0	2
Consensual Alignment	0	12
Alignments by Group Majority		
Madisonians and Federalists		
Oppose Antifederalists	0	2
Federalists and Antifederalists		
Opposed, Madisonians Neutral	0	3
Madisonians and Antifederalists		
Oppose Federalists	5	43
Consensual	1	10
Federalists and Antifederalists		
Oppose Madisonians	0	5

b) Hoadley	Government Authority	All Other Votes
1ST CONGRESS		
Alignments by Category		
Ratification Alignment	6	6
New Alignment	1	15
Anomalous Alignment	0	0
Consensual Alignment	1	6
Alignments by Group Majority		
Madisonians and Federalists		
Oppose Antifederalists	3	3
Federalists and Antifederalists		
Opposed, Madisonians Neutral	2	2
Madisonians and Antifederalists		
Oppose Federalists	2	15
Consensual	1	7
Federalists and Antifederalists		
Oppose Madisonians	0	0

SOURCE: Compiled by author using roll-call data from the Inter-University Consortium for Political and Social Research, data set #0004.

administration Federalists three times, but they also went along with the Antifederalists twice and were evenly split on two other votes. By this measure we see that the relative proportion of votes across categories is still as expected, but it is no more than a proportion. The concept of *issue cleavage* presumes the strong reliability of positions and alignments. When two different cleavages exist simultaneously depending on the issues being discussed, one expects alignments to be quite distinct. In this case one is hard-pressed to explain why Madisonians sided with Anti-federalists on some governmental power bills, and why only three of eight votes (by this measure) were aligned as predicted. This evidence calls into question the applicability of the issue cleavage concept and the contention that two competing cleavages were at work even in the First Congress.

Instead of applying the issue cleavage concept, it seems more appropriate to conclude that in the First Congress alignments on government authority issues varied from vote to vote. Discerning how these votes related to the ratification debate is critical to our understanding of the positions taken. This point may be illustrated with three individual votes from the first session of the First Congress that are labeled as government authority votes by both Bell and Hoadley. The first is the well-known bill containing the provision stipulating that the president had the power to remove executive branch officers without Senate approval. It was approved consensually. But when former Antifederalist Aedanus Burke brought a measure to the floor designed to prevent the national government from interfering in elections (a little remembered but important fear of the Antifederalists), Madison's forces aligned with the Antifederalists and against pro-administration forces. On the very next vote, a bill that would have prohibited Congress from levying direct taxes (Antifederalists again sponsored the bill), the Madisonians sided with the Federalists.[26]

These three matters, all decided in the summer of 1789, show the limitations of Hoadley's argument. From the perspective of each group the votes are quite understandable; but from the perspective of an issue cleavage that should yield one particular kind of alignment they are not. During the ratification debates, most Antifederalists were less worried about a domineering president than they were of a Senate that was too powerful. They were fearful that certain shared powers, like treaty-making and appointments, were rightly executive in nature. They argued that to prevent corruption these powers needed to be separated between branches, not shared among them. Sharing these powers was granting the Senate too much control. Giving the president the right to cashier his own cabinet secretaries, as the first bill did, was a small step toward ensuring that the chief executive would have power independent of the aristocratic Senate. Meanwhile, members of the other groups were satisfied that the

Senate's power to confirm would be an effective check on a rogue executive branch, and so the Senate's approval to remove officers was not necessary. So on this bill, it is not surprising that the Antifederalists voted with the supporters of the Constitution.

On the second issue, the Antifederalist position is obvious, as the proposal was designed to prevent the nation from encroaching on the states. Madison and his colleagues sided with them, feeling the states were up to the task of determining the time, place, and manner of election for federal representatives. Like the Antifederalists, the Madisonians were uncomfortable with the national government having exclusive control over congressional elections. The more nationally oriented Hamiltonian Federalists did not join these two groups and saw nothing wrong with the national government prescribing conditions for the states, as it was one way to help make a nation out of what had been a confederation. Finally, the fear of excessive direct taxes was a persistent Antifederalist theme. The two groups that had supported the Constitution had a single position on taxation: in order to be a successful nation the central government had to have a secure source of revenue. Although both Federalists and Madisonians looked to taxes on imported goods as the major source of revenue for the country, they were not willing to rule out direct taxation of the populace. Eliminating the possibility of direct taxation would have been an indication to them that the new government faced the same key infirmity as the Confederation. So the Federalists and Madisonians combined to defeat that proposal.

In looking at these three bills we see that votes that pertained to governmental authority in the First Congress were decided on a measure-by-measure basis, not in a manner consistent with the concept of issue cleavage as presented in Hoadley's *Origins of American Political Parties*. Further, the issue cleavage concept is based on the premise that a watershed event in politics changes stances. The preceding votes do not indicate or prefigure a profound change in any group's thinking but are based on stable patterns extant before ratification even occurred. In addition, labeling some roll calls "government authority" votes while cleanly fitting others into different categories is suspect. That which laid bare the divide between the Madisonians and the Federalists was, after all, Hamilton's fiscal program. The votes on assumption of state debts, on discrimination between securities holders, and on establishment of a national bank are categorized by Bell and Hoadley as pertaining to "domestic economics," rather than "governmental power." But one cannot even touch the debate on the national bank and these other issues without running across the Madisonians and the former Antifederalists questioning aloud whether the national government had the authority to act as they proposed.

In a way, issues were always "constitutional" in the early years of the republic. For as yet, there was no firm conceptual divide between what was "merely partisan" (a very modern way of thinking) and what involved a first-order question about the good of the nation. True, many of the trappings of a modern party system were in place; but the modern attitude was missing, as these leaders were never comfortable with the idea of opposing sides ruling the country in turn. National leaders themselves thought that a modified version of the ratification debate was being played out in the U.S. Congress. Even the interpreters who employ the concepts and language of later-day party scholars hint at this continuity by finding "government authority" votes even past the Third Congress. But they do not claim that the Madisonians were inclined to side with the Federalists on these issues. Roll-call data show that did not happen.

John Aldrich, meanwhile, acknowledges the "multi-dimensionality" of votes. Each vote could trigger preferences about a variety of things, most notably regional and state considerations and personal preferences, as well as the great principle. The variety of matters being considered by representatives led to vote cycling and prevented any one of them, including the great principle, from being definitively decided. Absent some sort of structure-induced equilibrium, little could be done without leaders stepping in to forge solutions issue by issue (as they did at the dinner agreement), a very taxing way of getting things accomplished. A party apparatus was needed, Aldrich says, to limit the number of considerations in the representatives' minds, thus forcing a definitive solution on the great principle. Hamilton in particular saw the advantage in forging a party, as "he could count a majority in both chambers who supported his plan and, presumably, his vision of the proper role of the national government. . . . Hamilton, whose goals were closest to realization and therefore most at risk, had the most to gain by taking new initiatives."[27] According to Aldrich, Hamilton therefore initiated partisan organization as a way of ending vote cycling within Congress to concentrate the public agenda on the great principle and promote nationalism.

That scenario makes logical sense. Clearly Alexander Hamilton realized how important it was to establish early that national powers were expansive. Yet whether this is the way parties really began is an open question. Aldrich relies primarily on secondary accounts to make the point that Hamilton initiated party formation. Aldrich himself does not go far beyond observing that Hamilton recruited Fisher Ames, Theodore Sedgwick, and Jonathan Trumbull as lieutenants on the chamber floor. There is no detailed explanation of what these individuals did to limit the pull of considerations other than the great principle. The analysis of roll-call votes in chapter 3 of *Why Parties?* does indicate that secondary and tertiary considerations did fade by the Third Congress, allowing the great principle to come to the fore as the primary consideration in key votes. Such evidence confirms that "parties in government" were effective by the Third Congress. However, just because parties were proving useful in "structuring equilibrium" within the Congress does not mean that the Federalists, or Hamilton in particular, initiated partisan organization.

At the very least, Madison and his colleagues, including Jefferson, were engaging in partisan organization long before early 1793, when Aldrich thinks they began doing so. Madison himself was convinced there was something radically wrong in the new government that could be remedied through party organization even as the assumption issue was being debated, three years before Aldrich thinks he turned to partisanship. We know that Madison and Jefferson were recruiting Philip Freneau to found the *National Gazette* in the summer of 1791. They had likely settled on doing so during the third session of the First Congress.[28] Madison and the Republicans had a logical reason to engage in party formation, as Aldrich points out: "Failing to reach majority size, the minority would naturally turn to the public, seeking to elect more of its members. That is essentially what the Jeffersonians did when facing a Hamiltonian majority."[29] Absent more compelling evidence that Hamilton or other Federalists worked to forge a party apparatus as early as the Republicans, it seems that parties got their start in a different manner than Aldrich cites. The first parties did not arise "as institutional solutions to the instability of majority rule," a Federalist tool to overcome a collective action problem, but as electioneering devices by the minority in Congress.[30]

There is much to commend in Aldrich's work. He possesses a more accurate picture of the early republic's dynamics than those who believe a new issue cleavage took hold shortly after the Constitution's implementation. He also acknowledges that Madison and his colleagues were not nationalists, that they could be alienated by the Hamiltonian Federalists, and that when they organized, they focused on electioneering. Yet in his quest to demonstrate that parties are primarily useful *inside* a legislature, to solve collective action problems, one crucial ingredient is missing: evidence that the majority organized first. More likely, the legislative minority was the first to begin organizing, realizing as they did the discrepancy between their numbers in the legislature and the support for their ideas among the electorate. Of course the total membership of Congress during this time was miniscule. No doubt it was much easier to effect political change in an organization of roughly one hundred political sophisticates than to effect change among the populace. I suspect that the relative difficulty of forming an external party organization, with party labels offering meaningful cues to the public at large, has misled

Aldrich into assuming that the initial design behind the move toward parties was an insider strategy rather than an outsider strategy.

Issues and Voting Behavior in the
Second through the Sixth Congresses

Although events in the First Congress exposed the rift between the Hamiltonian Federalists and the Madisonians, the character of the conceptual divide between these groups only becomes fully clear with an understanding of their approach to events in the Second Congress and beyond. In order to shed light on the major contours of politics in the Second through the Sixth Congresses, I highlight issues and positions that will aid in furthering an understanding of the mind-set of the groups involved and shed particular light on the divide between Federalists and Madisonians.

The results of the 1790 census commissioned by Congress were coming to light in the early months of 1791, so reapportionment was on the minds of the nation's politicians. During the Second Congress several votes were taken that posed the question of how many constituents per representative there should be. This was, of course, a major issue during the ratification debates, where Antifederalists had suggested that the ratio should be much lower than the minimum 30,000 constituents per representative in the Constitution. This time the options considered were in a much narrower range: for instance, an amendment to the apportionment bill that was voted on on December 19, 1791, would have set the ratio at one representative for every 33,000 inhabitants. Similar amendments were considered. One would expect that the Federalists would agree to higher ratios while Antifederalists would prefer the lower ratios. And this is indeed what occurred on each vote of this nature. Antifederalists were unanimous in their support of lower ratios, while Federalists were three times as likely to vote for the higher ratio than the lower.[31] But the position of the Madisonians is of most interest. Given the view of Elkins and McKitrick and Gordon Wood, stressing that the supporters of the Constitution wished for leadership by a natural aristocracy, one might expect that many of these former Federalists would be content with high ratios. But on these bills Madisonians cast a total of thirty-three votes with the Antifederalists and only two with the Hamiltonians. Either the Madisonians did not share the Hamiltonian Federalists' hope for a natural aristocracy or they quickly changed their minds about it after implementation of the Constitution. In the Second Congress they supported a larger House that they hoped would produce political results closer to the people's sentiments, and not uncoincidentally the common good.

The same Congress received news that France had ratified a new republican constitution. Many of the members of Congress, themselves revolutionaries, wished to congratulate the French on their achievement. And while an innocuous resolution "expressing interest in the future of the French nation" passed the House nearly unanimously, a second resolution "wishing the French nation wisdom and happiness" was controversial.[32] Antifederalists and Madisonians were uniformly in favor of this second resolution, but the Federalists balked, a majority of them voting against sending these sentiments to Paris. They were wary of the French approach to republicanism, which seemed to them to sweep away all established "estates" in favor of a government that was wholly popular. This was not a government that even attempted the classical balancing of the interests of the one, the few, and the many, like the British system did. Instead, it was a government wholly (and dangerously) devoted to the interests of the many. But to the Republicans generally — as it was to Madison in particular — the British model was at best an incomplete version of republicanism. The French plan was closer to the ideal, where all institutions were attached to and served the people. Hence the Republicans could hardly contain their exuberance. They hailed the new government of France as the first in a long line of sympathetic revolutions that would remake the world.

At the end of the Second Congress, serious charges of misconduct were leveled at Secretary of the Treasury Hamilton. He was accused of flaunting instructions from President Washington on governmental borrowing. Even more troubling accusations were in the air, namely, that there were accounting irregularities at the Treasury Department, with the possibility that Hamilton himself had benefited. The secretary worked furiously in the last weeks of the Second Congress to clear his name. Hamilton explained the supposed accounting errors in a report to members of Congress a few days before several misconduct resolutions were decided. On six resolutions Federalists voted sixty-four to two to exonerate Hamilton. Some Antifederalists chose not to embarrass themselves in light of Hamilton's apparent innocence and abstained. But of eleven votes cast ten were against exoneration. The Madisonians alone were of a divided mind on the matter. They cast fifteen votes with the Antifederalists and twelve in favor of exonerating Hamilton. At the very least, some Madisonians were reluctant to put Hamilton through a sham trial to stem his pursuit of a vigorous mercantile economy.[33]

By the Third Congress relations with Great Britain had soured. The peace secured by the Treaty of Paris was in jeopardy because of British refusal to relinquish the forts they held in the Northwest Territory and by their commandeering of American ships. The House therefore passed several embargo resolutions in the spring of 1794 and considered two measures to strengthen the nation's military. In eight votes relating to the embargo, Federalists voted against the various sanctions by a combined total of fifty-two to nineteen.[34] By contrast, Antifederalists strongly favored sanctions, voting for them sixty times against eight nays. The Madisonians were also firmly behind the embargo, with forty-six votes in favor and just six against. The Republicans were put into something of a bind by the British threat, as they greatly feared the influence of a standing army, but felt the need to increase the nation's preparedness. An initial proposal to significantly augment the national military was defeated because the Antifederalists and Madisonians were uniformly opposed; but eleven days later a more modest bill came over from the Senate to which both groups unanimously agreed. On both measures the Federalist majority opposed the Republicans.

Domestically, there was unrest in the western counties of Pennsylvania, where locals were refusing to pay the high excise taxes Congress had imposed on whiskey stills. By late 1794, the insurrection had run its course — without substantial violence — but President Washington had been greatly alarmed. In a public address on the disturbance the chief executive blamed what he called the "self-created democratic societies" for the nation's troubles, and he expressed concern that several of these societies both inside of Pennsylvania and outside it had conspired to encourage lawlessness and would do so again. The House resolved to reply to the president's contentions. In three separate measures they determined that they would not refer to "self-created societies" in their reply, that the insurrection had in fact begun in western Pennsylvania, and that democratic societies outside of Pennsylvania had not been involved.[35] These majorities were formed by the familiar coalition of Madisonians and Antifederalists, who disputed Washington's version by a combined count of forty-four votes to one. Against the efforts of these Republicans, the Federalists could not successfully carry the president's version of events on any of these votes, despite opposing them on twenty-six of twenty-seven votes cast. In their reply to the president the Republicans condemned the Pennsylvanians, but they were careful to avoid blaming the nationwide populism they were helping to create.

The Jay Treaty made its way to the United States in the recess between the Third and the Fourth Congresses. Though all were relieved that an accord had been reached and war averted, the Republicans were incensed — at first by the secrecy surrounding the treaty, and then by part of its content. For five months the nation waited on tenterhooks, knowing that there was a treaty, but not knowing its terms, as the Senate debated it in secret. This secrecy brought freshness to the Antifederalist fear of a domineering, elitist Senate. The upper chamber was withholding vital information from the people, whose government it was, after all. What could be the motive for such concealment in popular government, unless treachery were involved? When the treaty's provisions actually came to light, there was more consternation. Britain reserved to itself the right to carry goods to and from the West Indies, a trade of great importance for America. Unfortunately the House had no say in treaty-making, and so members were not even sure if they could debate the matter. Early in a series of highly partisan votes the House decided that it could indeed discuss treaties as long as they were related to legislative business. In subsequent votes the House determined not to call the treaty "objectionable" by a bare majority and to vote funds for its implementation.[36] In all eight votes taken, the Republican majority opposed the Federalist majority by objecting to the treaty and its funding. Republicans cast 156 total votes, of which 152 were cast for their majority. The Federalists were slightly less cohesive, with 30 of 37 votes opposing the Republican majority.[37] In this Congress there were also frequent proposals that aimed at adjusting the composition and size of the military. On these votes, the Federalist majority was consistently opposed to the Republicans.

By the beginning of the Fifth Congress, relations with France had chilled. The French felt betrayed by the Jay Treaty, as envoy James Monroe had promised them that there was little chance of reconciliation between the United States and Great Britain, with which France was once again hostile. The French began raiding American ships, and the Republicans' close connection with them became something of an embarrassment. The embarrassment turned severe with the revelation that the American diplomatic mission in Paris had been offered the opportunity for a settlement in exchange for a large bribe to the French foreign minister. In light of the "XYZ Affair," newly elected President John Adams called Congress into a special session. Adams proposed an extensive new commitment to military preparedness, but his concerns were largely dismissed as "war fever" by the Republicans. The slim Federalist majority was not initially unified to deliver what Adams wanted. But dismissing Adams's concerns turned out to be a rather grave miscalculation by the party of Jefferson and Madison. Although his actions were not always clear, the president genuinely wished to avoid hostilities with France. And the nation sensed that the Anglophiles were more right than their Francophile counterparts on this matter. Around the country Republicans were losing popular support.

Sensing a weak moment for the Republicans, the Federalist Congress passed the Alien and Sedition Acts in the summer of 1798, toward the end of the Congress. The impact of these statutes is well known: there were very few people affected by or prosecuted under either, but they were an unmitigated public relations disaster for the Federalists. The Alien Act served to estrange immigrant groups that had been part of the Federalists' successful electoral coalition, and the Sedition Act suddenly proclaimed by fiat that the partisan arrangement that had a tenuous but pragmatically successful run in the nation's first ten years was criminal. The Federalists first employed the Sedition Act late in the session on a pesky but ineffectual member of the House, Matthew Lyon.[38] When news spread that Lyon had been expelled from the House for sedition he became something of a martyr. Word about these clumsy Federalist attempts to outlaw the newly developed form of popular/partisan politics did not permeate the country until after the elections for the Sixth Congress, so a Federalist majority was returned to Congress for a final time in 1799.

The Sixth Congress was the most partisan of all, with issues of military preparedness and economic sanctions against France taking center stage. The Federalists, not surprisingly, led the charge for both, again consistently opposed by the Republicans. Despite several reconsiderations of the Sedition Act, the law was not repealed. On two occasions the Speaker of the House, Theodore Sedgwick, broke a tie vote that preserved the act. But this was not only the most partisan of early Congresses, it was also the most uneasy, as the Federalists tried to force a change in the political arrangements the national government had worked with since the early days of the Second Congress. But there was to be no turning back.

The great majority of stances taken by these three groups are understandable given their preratification ideologies. There were new developments to respond to and a sense among each party that they had to stick together across issues, of course. But the new partisan alliance was not brought about by any fundamental change in any group's thinking. The most major change discernible was Madison's jettisoning of the highly unorthodox ideas of Federalist #10. It is telling that he and others of his group could quite successfully retain the remainder of their constitutional philosophy while doing so. The Constitution changed the rules of the game and the terms of engagement, precipitating a new alliance for the Madisonians, but it was not productive of wholly new ideas in governance.

Conclusion

One final factor must be mentioned in conjunction with partisanship to round out our view of why the Antifederalists did not pursue extraconstitutional politics in the 1790s. Recall that in the early 1780s Alexander Hamilton speculated that the national government could be transformed into a fully sovereign entity if the nation's preeminent men were allowed to administer executive departments. He and the other nationalists thought likewise about the new government: if it could attract preeminent figures, then it might predominate. Critics of the Constitution feared that preeminent figures would set up shop in the national capital and never leave. They frequently proposed "rotation" out of office, what we call term limits, to prevent legislators from becoming too comfortable in their positions.[39] Although they did not make the argument explicitly, they probably understood that the more and the longer that the nation's "best and brightest" populated Congress, the more likely the national government would accrue power. The Articles of Confederation had a provision for rotation, but the Federalists had chosen not to retain it in the Constitution. One of the key defects of the Confederation Congress, they felt, was a lack of continuity in membership. This lack of continuity hindered the ability to develop expertise and work efficiently. Federalists hoped for a continuity in the national legislature that would allow the national government to firmly establish itself. Table 6.7 presents data about the length of congressional tenures for the sample of members who voted in ratification conventions.

For each group, the modal tenure served is just one term. Nearly two-thirds of the members served less than four years in Congress. Only a handful of individuals served more than three terms. What these tenure averages indicate is that in the early years of the republic there was something of a natural term limit in effect. Travel was so egregious and the rewards of serving in the national legislature so meager that there was little incentive to be a career politician at the national level. In personal economic terms, serving in Congress was a sacrifice for the vast majority of those elected during this time, as they had to abandon their primary occupation. Members of Congress did not receive a salary, instead relying on a skimpy per diem. Land travel was particularly arduous, and representatives from the backcountry hazarded life and limb to get to the nation's capital. Ocean travel was faster, but hardly more safe.[40]

Once in the capital conditions were little better. Epidemics ravaged Philadelphia during the 1790s, the nation's capital from 1791 to 1800. Once the new federal city of Washington was established as the home of the national government matters turned even worse. Poor sanitary conditions and the stagnant water of the Potomac and Anacostia Rivers caused numerous infections, the most common being malaria.[41] In Philadelphia, members of Congress who brought slaves as personal servants were harassed by Quakers, who encouraged the slaves to run away.

TABLE 6.7

Length of Tenures in Congress[a]

	Federalists	Madisonians	Antifederalists
1 Congress or less	16 (33%)	18 (36%)	30 (49%)
2 Congresses	13 (27%)	14 (28%)	10 (16%)
3 Congresses	7 (15%)	8 (16%)	6 (10%)
4 Congresses	6 (12%)	5 (10%)	4 (7%)
5 Congresses	— —	1 (2%)	3 (5%)
6 Congresses	4 (8%)	2 (4%)	3 (5%)
7 Congresses	1 (2%)	— —	3 (5%)
8 Congresses	—	1 (2%)	— —
9 Congresses	1 (2%)	— —	2 (3%)
10 Congresses	— —	— —	— —
11 Congresses	— —	1 (2%)	— —
Totals	48	50	61
Mean Congresses Served	2.65	2.52	2.58

SOURCE: Compiled by author using data from *American Leaders*.
[a] Tenures are considered separately if served nonconsecutively. Fractions of terms after one term in Congress are counted as a full term. For purposes of determining the mean number of Congresses served, "less than 1 Congress" equals 0.5 terms. The total number of tenures is larger than the total number of members of Congress who voted in ratification conventions because some individuals served multiple tenures.

In Washington, there was no such difficulty, but boredom seemed to take its place. Social life was all but nonexistent there, because there were virtually no inhabitants other than government officials (who were not numerous). At least New York and Philadelphia could be fun and interesting. Combine these factors and one can readily understand why congressional tenures were usually short. Each group of politicians followed a pattern of legislative service amenable to the Antifederalist way of thinking in the early years of the republic, often making the capital little more than "a way station in the pursuit of a career."[42] With so few legislators serving more than a term or two, Hamilton's hopes of surreptitiously creating a strong national government by translating the prestige of elected officials into national power was thwarted.

The irreconcilable views of what was constitutional threatened to dash the Union to pieces by inaugurating partisan politics, which the founding generation thought of as a mortal disease. Ironically, while the Constitution's vagueness generated this dilemma, it also provided just enough common ground, accepted as it became on all sides, to allow the nation to survive that which many thought it could not. To avoid the great stigma of blatant partisanship, leaders from both sides clung to the document, justifying their approach to politics as constitutional. Partisan politics and constitutionalism were intimately intertwined in the early years of the republic, but importantly the political figures of the age did not attribute the growth of partisanship to the Constitution itself. Had they acknowledged that the Constitution was responsible for the birth of party politics it would never have achieved the consensually legitimate status it did. Instead, both sides blamed their opponents for the turn to partisanship, ironically shielding themselves with that which contributed to the confusion as much as anything. Coupled with a healthy dose of fear and a rough partisan balance, the opposition did not consider an anticonstitutional strategy. Rather, they worked concertedly from within the new governmental framework, hoping to take its reins rather than to overthrow it.

No one can accurately claim that things were not different after ratification. Discerning exactly how things were different is the key. Antifederalists had to come to grips with an adopted Constitution. Madisonians were forced to make alterations in their political philosophy by the perceived rogue nature of the Hamiltonian majority. And even those in the Federalist Party felt compelled to appeal to the people on matters of policy. But they were dealing with the same matters they had discussed theoretically in 1787, such as how strong the national government should be and how best to stave off corruption in a republican system. To say that these matters were decided once and for all with ratification, with the passage of a bill of rights, or even at the resolution of the Whiskey Rebellion, is to seriously mistake the mind-set of the founders and their goals. The physical trappings of two distinct parties were indeed evident after the First Congress. Missing, however, was the attitude of partisans in the modern style: that parties may successfully rule the country in turn. And just as the partisans of the age believed, their battle *was* to the death, for the Federalist Party suffered a blow in 1800 from which it never recovered. Many Republicans hailed this event as the recovery of the common-good politics Madison had envisioned, only to become bitterly disappointed again in the mid-1820s when their own party split into irreconcilable factions.

CHAPTER SEVEN

The Founding Generation and Political Process

Structural Arrangements in the Early Congress

Less accidentally satisfying to the Antifederalists than short congressional careers were the structures and processes the new Congress adopted. Federalists did not impose a committee system or procedural rules that were unacceptable to their opponents; nor did the Republicans after the "Revolution of 1800." Rather, there was a high degree of congruence between Federalist and Republican organizational preferences. When the Republicans finally gained control of the legislature they did not need to tear down the institution's structures, because those they were comfortable with were already in place.

To the founding generation, establishing a legitimate legislative process was crucial. The concern over legitimacy trumped norms of efficiency, coordination, and the development of expertise. The focus on legitimacy led the early Congress to adopt that with which it was familiar: the very cumbersome organizational rules of the Confederation Congress. Thus the initial structure of the Federalist's revolutionary regime was not revolutionary at all, but rather defined by stasis. In their uncertain times, it made sense to adopt a set of rules that had already been agreed on previously, even if it was far from ideal. Although both parties' organizational preferences had their roots in similar concerns, their differing situations and political ideologies led them to support the same structures and processes for different reasons.

That legislative organization in the early Congress can be better characterized by mutual agreement than partisan rancor contradicts or significantly adds to the findings of other scholars. Many have noted the Republicans' satisfaction with the extensive use of a Committee of the Whole and ubiquitous, short-lived select committees, but fail to emphasize that the Federalists were a majority when this committee system/legislative process was adopted. Similarly, there has been little mention of the Federalist wariness of standing committees and the logic behind their slow growth. Examining committee formation with primary reference to the Republicans only cannot fully account for the structures employed in the first twelve years of the federal Congress. Furthermore, this frame of reference may lead to the erroneous impression that committee structures may have been adopted primarily for partisan advantages or pragmatic reasons rather than for a commitment to organizational norms. I find that the form and usage of the early legislative process are reflective of some combination of the political thinking of the supporters of the Constitution and those who had been Antifederalists and are not solely based on the assumptions of the Jeffersonians — or the Federalists.

A plausible explanation for the process used in the early Congress to formulate laws requires juxtaposing the political thought of each group with the facts we know about its early rules, norms, and committees. I concentrate here on the House because significant numbers of those who were Federalists and those who had been Antifederalists met there.[1] Our main sources of information on early committees in the House portray a system undergoing slow, evolutionary change. Select committees gradually were granted more autonomy, and some graduated to the growing fold of standing committees. By the 1820s the founding generation had passed from Congress, and with them their preferred method of organization.

Determining legislative rules and procedures was potentially a severe stumbling block in creating a governing system where all acted within constitutional bounds. The American Revolution was, after all, based on an assessment by colonists that British legislative procedures were illegitimate, as they affected the colonies. Detailed legislative procedures had not been set down in the Constitution. The progression of constitutional time thus yielded the necessity of formulating patterns of legislative conduct. It could not be taken for granted that the two sides would agree on proper legislative rules. If Federalists and Antifederalists could not agree, the governing system was unlikely to produce legislative outcomes that both groups (and by extension the American public) would consider legitimate.

The Classic View: Federalists Down a Whole

Federalist and Antifederalist writings have long been held up as a model of practical political theorizing that adeptly deal with how fundamental changes in governmental form affect a polity. But for these thinkers the internal rules of institutions warranted little attention.[2] The committee structures to be employed by Congress, for example, did not command Federalist or Antifederalist pens. Neither was the Constitution directive, as it dictated only the barest organization, designating a presiding officer for both the House and Senate. Article I, section 5, clause 2 simply states, "Each House may determine the Rules of its Proceedings." This open-endedness has led to vast, defining changes in the American legislative process, the most important of which was the adoption of a system of standing committees.[3]

Although some nuance has been added to our knowledge of early legislative organization in recent years, the assumptions about why Congress adopted the initial structures it did are decades old. These assumptions are descriptively accurate, but the account of why these structures were used is partial. Early in the first session, the House adopted its inaugural set of rules. The most striking feature of these early rules was the prominent role designed for the "Committee of the Whole House on the State of the Union," a feature carried over from the Confederation Congress. In the classic study *Congressional Committees*, Lauros Grant McConachie notes that the Committee of the Whole was really a misnomer, in that it consisted of the entire membership of the House merely operating under different procedures than it used for final consideration of measures.[4] The hallmark of proceedings in this committee was that the number and length of speeches a member could deliver were not limited in the normal manner. The possibility of wide-open debate led McConachie to call the Committee of the Whole "the favorite committee of the minority," because it gave them a free forum.[5] At the very least, dissenting opinions could be publicized in the Committee of the Whole (with one's constituents appeased), but ideally objectors won converts or tired out members in the majority, gaining valuable concessions or postponements.

Although only the House sitting in its official capacity could pass legislation, the Committee of the Whole determined subjects and guidelines for policy. Debate in the committee was detailed and often tedious; the House jealously guarded its prerogative to direct the course of legislation from potential alteration by subordinate committees.[6] Only after the Committee of the Whole had approved legislative guidelines would a temporary select committee be convened to write a bill corresponding to those guidelines. But many did not appreciate this mode of operating, according to McConachie, and the division was along partisan lines, with pro-administration forces (later Federalists) disliking the opportunities the Committee of the Whole gave their anti-administration (later Republican) foes.[7] Why the Federalists put up with a dominant Committee of the Whole the entire time they were in the majority is left unclear. If they had been solidly against this method of proceeding, they could have easily changed the House rules to limit its role.

Ralph Harlow reemphasized McConachie's findings, but also studied state procedures in *Legislative Methods in the Period before 1825*. He speculated on what influenced members of the early Congress to so liberally employ the Committee of the Whole. Legislators from several states were well acquainted with it, despite its differing functions in various states. Three of the four largest, Virginia, New York, and Pennsylvania, used the committee extensively.[8] The crucial role the Committee of the Whole played in the U.S. Congress corresponded most closely with Virginia's practices.[9] These procedures were inefficient according to Harlow, frustrating his Progressive spirit, which favored governments that could accomplish public matters with more dispatch. Harlow wondered aloud why Congress chose the inefficient methods of the Old Dominion over the more up-to-date and streamlined procedures of other states, most of which had developed standing committees by 1789: "With the wealth of precedents available in journals of contemporary state legislatures, there was really no definite reason why the first Representatives should not have formulated rules of procedure which would enable them to go ahead smoothly and rapidly in the transaction of business."[10]

Similarly, Joseph Cooper writes that the House of Representatives was "overextended" in its reliance on the Committee of the Whole "both in theory and in fact."[11] The overextension was due mainly to Jeffersonian enthusiasms, which privileged rational discussion and a highly egalitarian process. In this view, good legislation was not to be forged by a narrow team of experts in committee, but by the whole legislature in its deliberative capacity. Using the Committee of the Whole prevented distortion of policy by committees that could not fully reflect the sentiments of the majority or discuss the ramifications of public policy effectively. But in a triumph of pragmatism, the Congress slowly retreated from its principled objection to autonomous committees, particularly after 1809, and in doing so diminished the power of the Committee of the Whole. By the 1820s legislative material was routinely referred to standing committees directly rather than by order of the whole House.[12] Here, as in earlier works, it is left unclear why "Jeffersonian" preferences of committee structure prevailed at a time when the Jeffersonian Republicans were a minority.

Together these classic works on the early Congress portray a system of great inefficiency. Initially, even the most mundane tasks had to be debated by the whole House and only then parceled out to a committee designed especially for the purpose. Gradually but surely this cumbersome way of operating gave way to the system of standing committees organized around separate policy fiefdoms still familiar today. Nevertheless, these authors all find that Congress suffered through a barely workable organizational structure for at least the first dozen years of its existence. Clearly a good deal remains to be explained about the Committee of the Whole, primarily why the Federalists chose not to radically limit its role if they felt it was a tool of the minority, stifling their vision of good government.

Eschewing routing business through standing committees meant relying on hundreds of short-lived select committees that followed the House's detailed instructions and then disbanded. Each of the first twelve Congresses convened more than one hundred such bodies (see Table 7.1). House rules stated that no bill could reach the floor except via a committee specifically authorized to bring in a bill. Members were appointed by the Speaker except in unusual cases when the House decided otherwise by special order.[13] Initially no select committee performed any more than one well-defined function, which was stated in outline as the title of the committee. These tasks ranged from the utterly trivial to framing the most important legislation. Once a committee reported back to the House it was almost without exception disbanded, but there was no rule requiring automatic dismissal. In time, House rules stated that a member could excuse himself from serving on a committee if he was on two others at the time of appointment, evidence that service was indeed considered a burden. One reason committee work was onerous was that meetings generally took place in the evenings, as they were not to be held when the House was in session. McConachie was again the first to systematically study select committees, discerning that they were a necessary adjunct to a powerful Committee of the Whole. As an institution the House slowly grew less wary of entrusting certain matters to committees, and by 1800 it sometimes referred new subjects directly to select committees before discussing them as a body.[14] The House also began to parcel out more than one task to certain committees, allowing them to continue in existence for a whole session, or even an entire Congress.[15] As the tenures and responsibilities of select committees grew, their number fell dramatically. Certain select committees took on the characteristics of standing committees and were in fact their direct precursors. But one could still distinguish between the two types. Membership on standing committees was designed to be representative of the entire Union, while select committees were generally made up of sectional interests or policy partisans who clearly identified with the task at hand.[16]

When the Committee of the Whole requested that a bill be drawn up, the inchoate legislation was expected to conform to its guidelines. It was

TABLE 7.1

Number of Committees by Type
in the First Twenty Congresses

Congress	Select Committees	Standing Committees	Year Began
1	212	1	1789
2	180	1	1791
3	250	2	1793
4	110	5	1795
5	115	5	1797
6	112	5	1799
7	123	5	1801
8	142	6	1803
9	130	7	1805
10	133	9	1807
11	187	9	1809
12	155	9	1811
13	88	12	1813
14	116	19	1815
15	93	19	1817
16	64	21	1819
17	47	25	1821
18	58	26	1823
19	38	27	1825
20	16	27	1827

SOURCE: Compiled by author from data collected
by the Collaborative Research on a Relational Database
on Historical Congressional Statistics, 1788–1992, and
McConachie, *Congressional Committees*, Appendix A. I
include data from Congresses Eleven through Twenty to
demonstrate how complete the eclipse of select committees was by their standing counterparts after the founding generation passed from the scene.

easy to tell who favored a measure (and presumably would be most likely
to follow the guidelines set) from the deliberation that had preceded the
call for a select committee. Usually the member who moved that a committee be raised was an ardent proponent of the measure, willing to serve
on the committee and work for his favored legislation. He was generally
appointed chair.[17] Normally the representative who seconded the call for
a committee was nominated for service as well. No attempt was made to
balance policy partisans with members who were of a different opinion.
Cooper quotes Thomas Jefferson's *Parliamentary Manual*, which

metaphorically describes a committee guideline as a child of the House, who "is not to be put to a nurse that cares not for it."[18]

There have been several recent projects that have delved into the nature of early select committees. Thomas Skladony studied the evolution of these structures by examining all the select committees raised in five separate sessions of Congress, each separated by approximately ten years. His work emphasized that ad hoc committees were not created equally. Instead, an informed picture of select committees differentiates them by purpose.[19] Select committees that were commissioned to do several tasks were in existence at least by the Fifth Congress and seem to have been relied on for very significant legislative work. Historian Norman Risjord buttresses Skladony's argument that select committees must be distinguished in purpose and importance and cites the Committee for Protection of Commerce and Defense convened in the second session of the Fifth Congress as an example. Sitting for nearly eight months, this committee reported out the infamous Alien and Sedition Laws as well as several major proposals strengthening the American military establishment. This committee was stacked with Federalists, helping to make Risjord's general point that early committee membership was composed for partisan advantage.[20] A top echelon of "reliable men" garnered more than their share of appointments from the outset of Congress's existence.[21]

In conjunction with a congressional research project designed to catalog all committee participation throughout the history of Congress, Charles Stewart and his coauthors tested several hypotheses about select committees prior to the Civil War. Stewart et al. found that the numerous select committees that dealt with private claims tended to be referred to committees that had members from the claimants' state or region, raising the possibility that members of the early Congress were engaging in a form of constituent service or pork-barreling.[22] Risjord's thesis that committees were stacked in favor of partisans is supported, with the exception of the Third and Fourth Congresses.[23] Finally, Calvin Jillson and Rick Wilson broaden the study of select committees to include the Confederation Congress. Despite several organizational experiments, Jillson and Wilson find that members of the Confederation Congress inevitably returned to their inefficient system of select committees. The two authors conclude that a select committee system directed by a dominant Committee of the Whole was a serious design flaw that "alone would have been sufficient to lead to [the Congress's] collapse."[24]

Taking these sources together we see that select committees were evolving in the early years of the nation's existence, and that it is important to distinguish them by role and purpose. A few came to draft multiple bills of great importance later in the Federalist era, but the vast majority of committees were still convened for a single task and quickly disbanded. Even the important select committees (called "semi-standing" by Skladony) still received their instructions from the Committee of the Whole. In fact, no bills or reports could be introduced without permission from the House itself. Committees were designed to favor the tasks presented to them and were usually tilted in favor of the majority party. This was a cumbersome system compared to one that could be constructed of standing committees.

How this inefficient system of select committees prevailed for so many years requires explanation, particularly if this same system doomed the Confederation Congress. Although Jillson and Wilson's research points to a more plausible reason than McConachie's of why this system was adopted — not because the Virginians wanted it but because the general membership was familiar with it from the Confederation Congress — their assertion that Federalists pressed for change in 1787 partly to alter the structures of the legislature is unsatisfying.[25] The House of Representatives had a larger membership than the Confederation Congress or the Senate, thus lessening the burden of committee membership on individuals. But the burden was still great, and other problems, like the lack of ability to coordinate or develop expertise, were not remedied. If institutional efficiency was a goal, the Federalists failed miserably. More likely, it was not their intention to fundamentally alter legislative procedures, otherwise they would have done so. Although the purpose of a select committee was indicated by its title, the specific roles established for standing committees were spelled out in the rules of the House itself. Even the number of members these committees would have was established by standing rule. In the First Congress only one permanent committee was formed, Elections. It was designed to certify the qualifications of members and gather information on any disputed contests. For more than five years Elections remained the only standing committee. In November 1794, a second was established, Claims. One year later, during its first weeks, the Fourth Congress established three new committees, titled Commerce and Manufactures; Revisal and Unfinished Business; and Ways and Means. After this flurry of creation, no new standing committee was established for nearly ten years, until midway through Jefferson's presidency. Committees on Accounts and Public Lands were then created, followed by two formed in the last full year Jefferson was chief executive (1808), District of Columbia and Post Offices and Post Roads. The first term of James Madison's tenure went by without any further establishment, but aggressive institutionalization in his second term more than doubled the number of standing committees (see Table 7.1 above). Before 1813, however, the dominant characteristic of the standing committee system is their paltry number.

TABLE 7.2

Standing Committees Established in the First Twelve Congresses

	Date (Congress)		Members	Suggested By
Elections	April 13, 1789	(1)	7	Rules Committee
Claims	Nov. 13, 1794	(3)	7	Rules Committee
Commerce and Manufactures	Dec. 14, 1795	(4)	7	Williamson (NC)
Revisal and Unfinished Business	Dec. 14, 1795	(4)	3	Rules Committee
Ways and Means	Dec. 21, 1795	(4)	14	Gallatin (PA)
Accounts	Nov. 7, 1804	(8)	3	Leib (PA)
Public Lands	Dec. 17, 1805	(9)	7	Findley (PA)
District of Columbia	Jan. 27, 1808	(10)	7	Key (MD)
Post Offices and Post Roads	Nov. 9, 1808	(10)	17	Rhea (TN)

SOURCE: From McConachie, *Congressional Committees,* Appendix A. There is one error in this table: North Carolina's Hugh Williamson could not have suggested that the Commerce and Manufactures Committee become a standing committee because he was not elected to and did not serve in the Fourth Congress.

Of nine standing committees created in the first two decades Congress met, three sprang directly from select counterparts: Revisal and Unfinished Business in 1795; Ways and Means also in 1795; and Post Office and Post Roads in 1808.[26] The first three entries were formed at the suggestion of the Committee on Rules, but after 1794 it became common for individual members to suggest new committees. Just like with their select counterparts, the Speaker controlled the membership and appointed chairs.[27] Initially, Speakers appointed an entirely new membership for each session. But by the turn of the century it was not uncommon for members to be reappointed from the previous Congress.[28] A major concern about standing committees then, as now, was their ability to be truly representative of the whole nation.[29] To inhibit their autonomy, standing committees could not report bills out without authorization until 1815, and only by the 1820s were matters referred to them without approval from the Committee of the Whole.[30]

McConachie cryptically accounts for the addition of early standing committees by saying their growth was "forced . . . by the broadening of the sphere of the general government through causes external to the House."[31] Whatever those external causes were, it is clear that McConachie felt that the House had little choice in increasing its repertoire of standing committees. Rather, standing committee formation is depicted as something of a natural process with a life all its own: "From the chaos of the beginning, from the nebular dust of scattered business, select committees group themselves into huge growing nuclei, the first standing committees."[32] This evolutionary outlook gives little sense that the initial formation of standing committees was controlled in any way by Congress's membership. There is a sense of the inevitable in Harlow's book as well, and a frustration that the main contribution of the founding generation was to postpone it. Cooper stresses that the growth in standing committees can be accounted for by a triumph of pragmatism over theory, a view implying that standing committees were formed despite the logic of the founding generation, rather than because of it. Jillson and Wilson posit that rules already in place put severe constraints on members in their efforts to formulate new rules. While they do not directly comment on the early federal period, it stands to reason from their analysis that members may have wanted an effective system of standing committees but were unable to establish it in the Confederation Congress because of its preexisting rules. None of these authors ultimately believe that the early committee system was particularly responsive to member ideals and preferences.

I view the early committee system as significantly more reflective of the wishes of its members. True, the mode of organization they chose makes little sense in other historical contexts, but it made sense in theirs because the regime was so fragile. Eschewing legislative leadership and expertise within a representative institution can be highly functional, if the membership feels that their development would compromise representativeness. The initial membership of Congress, having logged ninety-nine years in the Confederation Congress, was well aware of its organizational problems, yet they voluntarily readopted its most cumbersome features. Yet at the same time, the legislative procedures employed in the early Congress were not simply dictated by one of the key groups involved in the founding.

There is no doubt that standing committees were exceptions in the early House. The question is whether these were exceptions to the founding generation's entire way of thinking or exceptions understandable within their mind-set. If we confine our view to the first two decades of Congress's existence, we can clearly discern a logic behind the development of the standing committees.

So three questions, one corresponding to each of the major structures discerned in the early House of Representatives, beg for adequate explanation. What accounts for the dominance of the Committee of the Whole through the Federalist period, when that party was in the majority at the national level? Why were members willing to abide by a tedious, inefficient system of select committees that took up a great deal of time without rewarding them with much discretion? Finally, was there any logic behind the establishment of the early standing committees that corresponded to the founding ethos or was this development a "natural" institutional force driven primarily by the inevitable need to become more efficient? Answers to these questions provide a window on how apotheosis was achieved. Structures and procedures had to be amenable to both sides for them to keep "playing by the rules" of the constitutional game.

Founding the Committee of the Whole

Unfortunately, these questions are more easily stated than answered. My goal is to provide plausible explanations to the above conundrums that more fully square with the factual record than prior interpretations. I do not contend that scholars such as Joseph Cooper are wrong and have nothing to teach us about the early congressional committee system. On the contrary, these works still account for the Republican preference for a dominant Committee of the Whole. At the same time, there are other aspects of their collective interpretation that are less than satisfactory. The contention that the Federalists uniformly chafed under the operation of the Committee of the Whole, based primarily on a few well-heeled quotes of Federalist stalwart Fisher Ames, is suspect.[33]

Ames's comments were written in a private letter during the first session of the First Congress. The Massachusetts lawmaker related that business proceeded slowly and sloppily in the Committee of the Whole, but that very little could be done to streamline the system because of the Virginia delegation's near paranoiac reliance on the whole House. Ames's letter has achieved prominence primarily because it is one of the few contemporaneous commentaries on early committee workings. Internal organization was simply not a normal topic of conversation between members of Congress and their contemporaries. Patrick Furlong, in a dissertation on the organization of the House during the Federalist era, notes that "with rare exceptions, the members said nothing of committee work in their private letters, except to repeat that it was a constant affliction."[34] With a shortage of firsthand accounts, Ames's observations have been taken to be a general Federalist lament. But several factors make this reasoning spurious.

Foremost is the stark fact that the Committee of the Whole remained the dominant organizational structure through the Federalist period. This was an impossibility without a healthy amount of Federalist support. In addition, the frustration Ames expressed was with Virginians, not administration opponents. If the nascent opposition had been responsible for the delays he probably would have called them "Antis" in his letter, Ames's routine epithet for those who opposed the Washington administration.[35] To the contrary, roll-call analyses indicate that most members of the Virginia delegation were routinely voting *with* Ames during the first session.[36] Ames's assessment occurred before Madison and his colleagues defected and parties had coalesced, meaning consistent partisan divisions (whether over policy or organization) could not yet be discerned at the time of his comments, even by an insider.

In fact, Ames himself did not believe that partisanship animated the push for a dominant Committee of the Whole. In the same letter, Ames mentioned that "there is less party spirit, less of the acrimony of pride when disappointed of success, less personality, less intrigue, cabal, management, or cunning than I ever saw in a public assembly."[37] Had the opposition attempted parliamentary maneuvers to favor their causes, Ames surely would not have felt the way he did. Furthermore, the young congressman's prior legislative experience in Massachusetts had not acquainted him with the use of the Committee of the Whole, and it is likely that Ames's initial frustration subsided once he became accustomed to its operations. Furlong found that "after the first session there seem to have been no further complaints about doing business in the Committee of the Whole" from Ames or his colleagues.[38] In the absence of other explicit observations, Fisher Ames's comments have taken on an inflated meaning that they do not genuinely convey.

The silence of members of Congress about committee structures is a serious impediment to our understanding. But instead of privileging the few comments that exist, we should take this silence as a key piece of evidence in and of itself. Those who revolted from Great Britain and founded the nation's government were not shy about expressing themselves, particularly about the proper construction of political institutions. Had there been a deep-seated, prolonged disagreement over the organization of the House along partisan lines, it is more likely that researchers would be inundated by commentary than face a lack of it. During this same time there is no shortage of primary evidence detailing the growing, and by the mid-1790s bitter, partisan rift between Federalists and Republicans. While the basis for partisanship was rooted in disparate philosophies of government, the lack of a record of rancor over organization indicates that the two parties, for whatever reason, found the House's structural arrangements mutually satisfactory.

While they were still in alliance in the earliest days of Congress, James Madison — one of the Virginians frustrating Fisher Ames — likely convinced his colleagues to adopt the set of legislative procedures he believed would be considered most legitimate by critics of the Constitution. This process had the dual advantage of being familiar, having been accepted under the Articles of Confederation, and highly democratic. This legislative process was virtually unassailable and presumptively legitimate. Once Madison and his colleagues defected, inertia and perhaps a heightened concern about legitimacy kept the remaining Federalists from changing the legislative process.

But there may also be ideological reasons behind the Federalists' acceptance of the Committee of the Whole. The founding generation was well aware that the course the American Revolution took would have been unthinkable without committees. Committees of correspondence were early and effective publicists of the violation of American rights and were at the forefront of the movement to cut ties with England; before they could formulate their own constitutions colonies established committees of safety as interim governments; the Continental Congress coordinated the war effort as an ad hoc committee of states before official adoption of the Articles of Confederation in 1781. But the very quality that made these structures so useful to the Patriots during revolutionary times also made them suspect under a republican government. As revolutionary bodies, the committees mentioned above were "self-styled": no government or constitution commissioned them to do what they did. When the colonial government was not safeguarding rights or representing citizens, self-styled bodies became quasi-legitimate means of achieving those ends. Under a government that was representative and did protect rights this kind of committee autonomy was inappropriate.

If there was any difference of opinion on the matter, the potential rise of self-styled subgovernments was more of a concern to Federalists than Antifederalists. A primary reason for their push to establish a viable national government was the feeling that control was slipping away from states and into the hands of self-appointed groups like those at several unofficial New England conventions. During the Federalist era this concern was still acute. For example, many Federalists blamed "self-styled Democratic Societies" that had sprung up across the country for inspiring the Whiskey Rebellion in western Pennsylvania. Although the Federalists were generally less apt than Antifederalists to fear conspiracies of duly-appointed political leaders, they were not naive about the possibility of individuals circumventing the established legislative process. Having the House maintain strict and explicit control of committal and bill introduction was a way for this constitutionally legitimate body to ensure that committees would not become self-styled. Strictly limiting the number of standing committees helped maintain control as well, because it sent the message that no subordinate grouping of the legislature had autonomous existence or jurisdiction.

Students of the Federalists have often noted the centrality of their concept of *natural aristocracy*.[39] Stanley Elkins and Eric McKitrick tell us in

The Age of Federalism that "this principle—men of the right sort— comes close to holding the key to the entire Federalist idea."[40] So along with privileging the exclusive ability of legitimized institutions to govern under a constitutional order, many Federalists presumed expertise was essential to good government, and that both citizens and lawmakers would have the good sense to be guided by men of discernment. Those who framed the Constitution relied so heavily on expertise according to the Antifederalists that they endangered the principle of separation of powers. Article II, section 3 of the Constitution requires that the president recommend to the Congress "such Measures as he shall judge necessary and expedient" in State of the Union messages. This requirement was intended to (and from the outset did) provide the president a major role in policy formation, an injection of the executive into legislative matters unacceptable to many critics of the Constitution. The complaint that the Constitution did not sufficiently separate powers was one of the Antifederalists' most common.

So while Antifederalists fretted about legislative bodies receiving advice or information from the executive branch, Federalists sought to gain expertise where they could, without, however, compromising institutional legitimacy. When the First Congress established executive departments, each was commissioned to prepare plans instructing Congress on "the improvement and management" of the policy area they administered.[41] The Congress, the vast majority of whose members had favored the Constitution, asked the heads of the executive departments to file reports on how to make sound policy, much as it did its ad hoc committees. Department secretaries like Alexander Hamilton welcomed this opportunity and were deeply involved in the formulation of policy. Hamilton worked closely with the initial Congress, and on his recommendation the national legislature assumed state debts, organized a system of public finance, and established the Bank of the United States. In arguing for reference of a particular legislative question to Hamilton, pro-administration Congressman James Hillhouse related that his constituents

expected their business to be done in the best manner possible, and that he should not rely on his own information only, but endeavor to avail himself of the information of others. He said he should consider himself unequal to the task of taking a share in legislating for the Union, if he was to depend on his own information alone. He expected to derive information from every source.[42]

This was a pointed rejoinder to the opposition, which seemed to privilege a formulaic deference to separation of powers over the opportunity to receive policy expertise from department secretaries, and in so doing create the best legislation possible.

It is likely that the Federalists did not feel the need for standing committees organized around policy areas because in their perception, sound advice on a legislative agenda was flowing from executive departments.[43] Evidence in support can be seen in the first Committee on Ways and Means, established as a select committee on July 24, 1789. Ways and Means was quite active in the weeks before Alexander Hamilton was nominated and approved as the first secretary of the treasury, but disbanded six days after he took his post.[44] While the Madisonians had deep reservations about the soundness of Hamilton's vision for the country's economic future, few if any doubted that the secretary's plans were expertly designed to achieve this vision, and the remaining Federalists relied heavily on that expertise. Ways and Means was only reestablished as a select committee in March 1794, with Hamilton hinting of resignation. He officially left the Treasury Department at the end of January 1795, replaced by his subordinate Oliver Wolcott, a solid administrator, but one who lacked Hamilton's brilliance and stature.[45] Congress recessed a month into Wolcott's tenure, but when it reconvened it took just two weeks to unanimously turn Ways and Means into a standing committee. Federalists most likely approved of the new structure as a means of restoring the policy leadership they missed in Hamilton's absence.

Those who had been Antifederalists very much disapproved of the secretaries' influence in legislation.[46] But a practical effect of this reliance was that the Federalists felt little need for standing policy committees and so were as willing as the Republicans to maintain the position of the Committee of the Whole. But the Federalists probably did not come to favor the same structures as Republicans merely by accident. It is also quite possible that the Federalists, sensing their opponents would react severely against standing committees, opted for a vigorous Committee of the Whole in part to placate them, knowing that they were in a majority, that they could pass their preferred policies anyway, and that executive departments would aid in policy formulation.

Had Federalists disliked the Committee of the Whole as much as several scholars assert, they would have routinely objected to or eliminated "first reference" of legislative matters to it. But during the entire Federalist era, legislative business was almost always referred to the Committee of the Whole first. Only by the second session of the Fifth Congress was passage of one part of the legislative agenda through it a mere formality: the subjects brought up by the president in his State of the Union address were automatically parceled out to select committees after 1797.[47] And recall that it was 1815 before bypassing the Committee of the Whole became standard procedure.[48]

Neither McConachie nor Harlow documents instances of partisan fights over committee reference.[49] Cooper extensively cites congressional debates in which Republicans explained their principled stances on reference, but in keeping with his focus on the Jeffersonians he does not extensively comment on what the Federalists were arguing. When the debates Cooper includes in his footnotes are examined, positions on reference prove not to be as partisan as earlier research implied. There are many instances where Federalists called for further deliberation in the Committee of the Whole and several times when Republicans advocated forming a select committee.[50] In most of these cases partisan lines were crossed. Cooper himself finds that "after the fall of Hamilton some Federalists, notably William Smith of South Carolina, became vehement champions of the committee of the whole."[51]

A member's reference preference often depended on concerns that were incidental to partisanship. If a lawmaker felt that the whole chamber had insufficient expertise to pass good legislation, he would call for a select committee to gather information. If he felt that open debate would clarify the issue, then deliberation in the Committee of the Whole was suggested. Nor were members inflexible about these referrals. Madison, for instance, opined that discussion of a bill of rights was sufficiently important that it should be undertaken by the whole chamber. Federalists objected that much was left to be done in the initial session of Congress and that it could not be accomplished if such a major topic was debated fully in the Committee of the Whole. Considering their objections, Madison successfully moved for a select committee, was promptly named a member, and thereupon guided his preferred amendments to floor consideration.[52]

During the entire time that Federalists controlled the House, they made only one definitive move against the Committee of the Whole. On May 18, 1798, the same Federalist Congress that passed the Alien and Sedition Acts agreed to a rule that any individual could deliver only one speech on any subject in the Committee of the Whole, temporarily effecting a fundamental change in its business. This rule was directed at Albert Gallatin, the Republican's vigorous floor leader. But just two weeks later, the Federalists rescinded the rule.[53] At any point from 1789 on, a simple majority of the House, Federalist, Republican, or a combination of the two, could have passed a similar rule and effectively ended the dominant role occupied by the Committee of the Whole; other than for two weeks in 1798, they did not do so for an entire generation.

The Republican attachment to the Committee of the Whole based on a preference for democratic and deliberative procedures has been made clear by Joseph Cooper. I would add that extensive use of the Committee of the Whole fit the opposition viewpoint well for another reason. The

Republicans were convinced that their outlook was closer to the sentiments of the people than the elitist Federalists, who were convinced that only they were the "right men." Yet for the reasons detailed in previous chapters, the Antifederalists' showing in the first federal elections was very poor. The early opposition group did not despair, because they were convinced that all that stood in the way of their own legislative majority was a lack of public knowledge about their philosophy vis-à-vis the Federalists'. Proponents of the Constitution had dominated the newspaper war during the ratification process, a critical factor in their success.[54] The opposition group had learned from this experience: with the help of Madison they had commissioned Phillip Freneau to edit the *National Gazette*.[55] Freneau's *Gazette* printed the news from Congress, and he could report the speeches delivered in the Committee of the Whole, a primary vehicle for highlighting the differences between the Federalists and their opposition. Committee sessions, by contrast, were private and could not serve to benefit the Republican cause. Though it did so slowly, this "outsider strategy" seems to have worked, as the Antifederalists, joined by the Madisonians, became the dominant force in American politics for a generation, beginning in 1800.

At any rate, *both* Federalists and Republicans accepted the procedures adopted in the House as legitimate. With a legitimate process in place, the philosophy of the day dictated that the law produced had sanction and viability, provided that it did not transgress constitutional bounds. This development was absolutely essential to the apotheosis of the new regime.

Living with Select Committees: Developing a Niche

Relying on the Committee of the Whole with numerous select committees as adjuncts was cumbersome for two reasons: first, it was more time consuming to debate and form policy guidelines in a group of several score than it would have been with ten or fifteen others; and second, ad hoc committees hindered members from developing routinized methods or expertise in dealing with particular kinds of legislative business.[56] An additional reason these groups chose to live with the Committee of the Whole is that these select committees did allow them to specialize. Examination of select committee participation makes clear that the roles Federalists, Madisonians, and former Antifederalists played on them were significantly different. This difference corresponds with their distinct conceptions of representation.

In the last several years the Collaborative Research on a Relational

Database on Historical Congressional Statistics, under the direction of Elaine K. Swift and eight others, has cataloged a comprehensive listing of select committees and their memberships based on the House *Journals*. I have used the titles of the committees to categorize them by purpose. Four types of select committee may be distinguished: claims, policy, institutional/administrative, and ceremonial. The first type of committee reported on the legitimacy of private petitions or reported in a private bill of compensation. Policy committees either researched and suggested action on a matter of public policy or brought in a bill to that effect. Institutional/Administrative committees took care of the internal business of the House and administered the governmental apparatus under legislative discretion. Finally, a small number of ceremonial committees handled things like the erection of a mausoleum for George Washington after his death.

I again analyze those members of Congress who voted in ratification conventions, identifying those who voted for the Constitution and later joined the opposition as Madisonians. In 1995, Stewart et al. raised the intriguing possibility that "Jeffersonians were more disposed to push private claims in Congress" while their Federalist counterparts concentrated on formulating policy.[57] The data compiled by Swift and her collaborators enable a test of this hypothesis. Stewart and his coauthors' speculation makes a certain amount of sense when coupled with the Federalist and Antifederalist ideologies. With Antifederalists generally more interested than Federalists that government accurately reflect and respond to public opinion, it would seem possible that they would be more disposed (within reason) to accept the legitimacy of claimants who petitioned government. With many Federalists emphasizing that the expertise of the natural aristocracy rather than a satisfaction of popular wishes makes for sound policy, it is likely that we would see them working together on policy committees and paying comparatively less attention to claimants.[58]

Tables 7.3a, 7.3b, and 7.3c, respectively, show the number and type of assignments received by Federalists, Madisonians, and Antifederalists. The tables indicate that Federalists received significantly more assignments per member in the first six Congresses than did their Antifederalist counterparts. The average Madisonian also received fewer assignments than the average Federalist, but not as few as the typical Antifederalist. Nevertheless, none of the groups were shut out of select committee participation, with the possible exception of the Antifederalists in the highly contentious Sixth Congress. For all groups the number of claims committees served on drops significantly after the Third Congress, mainly because of the formation of the standing Committee on Claims. But this is also a function of the Congress increasing in size, so individual mem-

TABLE 7.3A
Federalist Participation on Select Committees by Type

Congress	Members	Assignments per Member	Claims	Institutional/ Administrative	Policy	Ceremonial
First	15	11.7	39	34	100	3
Second	13	10.8	56	20	65	0
Third	11	10	35	6	65	4
Fourth	6	5	4	7	17	2
Fifth	5	2	1	1	8	0
Sixth	10	4.3	10	14	14	5
Seventh	2	2.5	0	1	4	0
Eighth	1	2	1	1	0	0

TABLE 7.3B
"Madisonian" Participation on Select Committees by Type

Congress	Members	Assignments per Member	Claims	Institutional/ Administrative	Policy	Ceremonial
First	7	12.8	23	20	45	2
Second	6	8	22	5	19	2
Third	10	6.1	18	5	36	2
Fourth	14	2.4	11	6	17	0
Fifth	8	2.9	4	3	16	0
Sixth	4	2.5	3	2	4	1
Seventh	6	3.5	7	3	10	1
Eighth	8	5	10	9	21	0

TABLE 7.3C
Antifederalist Participation on Select Committees by Type

Congress	Members	Assignments per Member	Claims	Institutional/ Administrative	Policy	Ceremonial
First	6	7	14	6	21	1
Second	5	6.4	23	1	8	0
Third	10	5.7	36	1	20	0
Fourth	8	4.6	8	11	18	0
Fifth	12	1.8	5	5	11	1
Sixth	10	0.5	0	1	3	1
Seventh	12	2.9	6	6	22	1
Eighth	16	3.1	18	12	20	0

SOURCE: Assignments per member is an averaged figure. Criteria for categorization are one's vote in a state ratification convention coupled with later party status. Compiled by author using the Collaborative Research on a Relational Database on Historical Congressional Statistics.

TABLE 7.4
Percentage of Assignments by Select Committee Type
(Percentage Claims/Percentage Policy)

Congress	Federalists	Madisonians	Antifederalists
First	22/57	26/50	33/50
Second	40/46	46/40	72/25
Third	32/59	30/59	63/35

SOURCE: Compiled by author.
The two numbers in each cell do not add up to 100 because the percentage of Ceremonial and Institutional/Administrative select committees are not included here. After the Third Congress the standing Committee on Claims handled the bulk of the House's claims work.

bers were less heavily taxed through time. Although the Federalists and Madisonians did serve on many claims committees, it seems that before the Claims Committee was established this was something of a specialty of the former Antifederalists.

If we compare the percentages of committee type served on in the first three Congresses, claims versus policy, we find that Antifederalists served on more claims committees than they did on all other types combined (Table 7.4). In the first six years of the federal Congress, 56 percent of Antifederalist assignments were to claims committees contrasted to 31 percent for Federalists and 32 percent for Madisonians. During the same time the majority of Federalist participation (55 percent) was on policy committees. Just over half of the Madisonian assignments dealt with policy in these six years, but by contrast only 37 percent of the former Antifederalists' assignments were to such groups. That this difference in committee-type participation is due to chance strains credulity, because members could practically appoint themselves by calling for or seconding a call for a committee, and because Federalist Speakers rounded out the committee membership. The relatively nonpartisan Frederick Augustus Muhlenberg, who would be counted as a Republican by the Fourth Congress, was Speaker for four of these six years. Muhlenberg saw his role as collegial rather than partisan, and so it is likely that partisan advantage accounts for only part of the wide disparity in assignment percentages.[59] Once Claims became a standing committee the Republicans were allowed a majority of seats. It is therefore possible that Antifederalists willingly gravitated toward claims committees and Federalists allowed them to do so because they were more interested in policy committees.

This is not to say that the opposition was happy with its minority role in Congress; ideally they would have liked to have a greater say in policy matters, or at the very least kept the Federalists from having their way. But one of the things that may have kept the Antifederalists in Congress moderately content with the new constitutional system was that it allowed them to fill a role in the new Congress that suited them and aided in their efforts to "serve the people." At the same time, the Federalists were able to act much as they had envisioned representatives working on the national level, as a meeting of the minds, discerning what was best for the nation without fundamental reference to popular whim. It is also notable that the ratio of committee types Madisonians served on was much closer to the Federalist ratio than the Antifederalist ratio. When the Madisonians combined with them, their coalition attended to both concerns of representation and policy formation, the balancing act that Congress continues to perform today.

Standing Committees: The Logic of Development

For different reasons both Federalists and Antifederalists felt standing committees were sufficiently taboo that they suffered under an alternate, inefficient mode of organizing the House. But as time wore on exceptions to the taboo increased. Here, I attempt to address whether the exceptions made corresponded to the same logic that kept the Committee of the Whole a dominant force. The founding generation employed standing committees almost exclusively to aid in processing administrative tasks rather than formulating policy in the first twenty years after ratification.

The sole committee designed to help formulate public policy before 1808 was Ways and Means. There are special circumstances behind this unique treatment of a policy realm, but four committees were established before Ways and Means. To preserve a proper sense of development I treat them in chronological order. Just two weeks into the inaugural Congress and one week after the first enumeration of House rules, a standing Committee on Elections was created. The purpose of the committee was to "inspect the credentials of members, and to investigate facts in connection with contested elections, but strictly speaking it performed no legislative work."[60] Thus a Committee on Elections did not transgress the taboo against standing committees. Plus it performed a vital function. Certifying the elections of members was a necessity; polling procedures were far from routinized, and information about election returns was not always readily available or reliable.

Despite the fact that most state legislatures had such committees, it is likely that the federal Committee on Elections caused the former Antifederalists some trepidation. During the ratification debates some had warned that if Congress (rather than the states) was able to certify its membership, the power would be abused. And the first appointments to the committee likely did not prove heartening, as all seven committee members were solidly in the pro-administration majority. But contrary to predictions, the committee quietly went about its work and was satisfied with the credentials of all who had been elected. In the Second Congress only one member was unseated, James Jackson of Georgia.[61] And although his ouster in favor of General Anthony Wayne shook out along partisan lines, it is worth noting that the House chamber debated the competing claims of the two men and ultimately voted on the issue; the Committee on Elections had researched the matter and presented its report, but it was still up to the whole House to make a final decision. Only the most touchy of administration foes could feel that this committee's work fulfilled Antifederalist prophecies. After the First Congress anti-administration forces gained entry to the committee, further allaying their fears. If the Committee on Elections began in controversy, the House *Journal* does not record it; neither is there any evidence that the former Antifederalists did not accept its role.

The early Congresses were flooded by claims of individuals, groups, and businesses, because the national government assumed state debts and responsibilities. Most of the claims stemmed from the Revolutionary War, petitioners asking the government to compensate them for services rendered or grant them pensions because of disability. In the first three Congresses alone 280 select committees were convened to investigate and report on the legitimacy of petitions or to author bills to compensate claimants. Congress's close attention to these matters had the unintended purpose of encouraging even more petitions, and by the mid-1790s the workload caused by private matters threatened to derail the legislative agenda. So at the suggestion of the select committee on rules, the House formed a Claims Committee, the purpose of which was "to take into consideration all such petitions and matters or things touching claims or demands on the United States . . . referred to them by the House, and to report their opinion thereupon, together with such propositions for relief therein, as to them shall seem expedient."[62] Note that it still took referral by the House itself for Claims to act, and private bills still needed to be passed in regular session for compensation to occur.

One reason establishment of the Claims Committee met with no opposition was that the vast majority of claims had no effect on public policy. In fact, this administrative committee would free the House as a body to concentrate more on policy and less on investigating concerns of individuals. But every so often claims work edged into the policy realm, as when a certain group of manufacturers asked that taxes on their goods be reconsidered because of their detrimental effects. The committee did exactly what it was designed to do in these cases, report on the legitimacy of the claim. This could entail suggesting that tariffs on cloth, for example, were too high, but the committee was not involved in drafting the legislation that would reduce the tariffs. Instead, a select committee would be established with that specific purpose in mind. Again, the policy role of this committee was minimal, and so its establishment did not strike the founding generation as improper. Republicans formed a majority there during parts of the Third and Fourth Congresses, and for the entire Sixth Congress, when Federalists dominated the other standing committees.[63]

The title of the next standing committee formed, Commerce and Manufactures, makes it sound like a policy-oriented one, but it was actually a division of the Claims Committee. Claims continued to investigate petitions of individuals, but Commerce and Manufactures looked into the petitions of businesses. Accordingly, the House rules' commission for it is almost identical to that of Claims: "It shall be the duty of the said Committee of Commerce and Manufactures to take into consideration all such petitions and matters or things, touching the commerce and manufactures of the United States, as shall be presented, or shall or may come in question, and be referred to them by the House, and to report, from time to time, their opinion thereon."[64] Once again it is apparent from the standing rule that the whole House controls reference of subjects to the committee, and that the matters referred would primarily be claims.

On the same day the House established Commerce and Manufactures it granted the Committee on Revisal and Unfinished Business standing status. The House assigned it three functions: to investigate which laws were nearing expiration and needed to be renewed; to examine the House *Journal* from the previous session to determine the tasks commissioned by Congress that were not accomplished by select committees; and to suggest revisions in laws that authorized national offices. The first two tasks were exclusively clerical in nature, providing committee members with no legislative discretion. They simply determined which laws were expiring and which select committees had not reported back regardless of their own preferences. The last task required them to bring the law up to date with the offices that had been created in the new federal bureaucracy, dealing them into the game of government management, but providing them with no discretion over policy. Of the committees established by December 1795, it is likely that members of Congress were least wary of Revisal and Unfinished Business, because there were only three members assigned to it instead of seven or fourteen. The fewer the members, the less likely the committee represented the whole country, but in this case representativeness did not much matter because of the purely clerical nature of its business.

Turning to Ways and Means, its business cannot be characterized as routine or clerical. Instead, the committee was designed from the outset as a policy-formulating body. Ways and Means is therefore the most significant exception to the normal organizational preferences of the founding generation. Nevertheless there are good reasons why both Federalists and Republicans accepted its existence and made it the only policy-oriented standing committee. Transforming the select committee on Ways and Means into a standing committee was suggested by former Anti-federalist-turned-Republican Albert Gallatin late in the Fourth Congress. Early historians like Henry Adams and Ralph Harlow reasoned that Gallatin suggested standing status in order to thwart the Federalist penchant for forming policy in the Treasury Department.[65] The Federalists, however, did not treat Gallatin's suggestion as a partisan threat; none of them offered any objection or voted against the Pennsylvanian's proposal.[66] This unanimous endorsement was not due to surprise, as Gallatin had raised the matter twice in the previous week, only to have it tabled both times. The Federalists were quite comfortable with a standing Committee of Ways and Means, likely because the Federalist Speaker would appoint its members, and because it was a vehicle to replace the retired Hamilton's herculean efforts in financial policy formation.[67]

The Antifederalist reasons for proposing and favoring such a committee were more complex and rooted in America's colonial past. The critics of the Constitution greatly feared government's economic power and the potential that this power would be misused. They had a "country party" mentality inspired by the English Whigs who had reacted against the innovations of the crown and Sir Robert Walpole in the early part of the eighteenth century. Walpole had used his position as first lord of the treasury and chancellor of the exchequer to create the role of prime minister. And though this title was not yet an official designation, Walpole's influence in the House of Commons was, for twenty years, immense. In conjunction with the crown extending its power vis-à-vis Parliament through an aggressive system of patronage, the Whigs theorized that the English constitution, and with it representative government, was perishing.[68] As the Hamiltonian system unfolded in America, "the Walpolean parallel at every point was too obvious to miss."[69] The Republicans were quite simply afraid that Hamilton had become so powerful a center of influence that he limited the representative quality of American government.

Strict watchfulness had to be maintained over the government's economic power according to the Antifederalists. During the 1790s, Hamilton and the Federalists had been tripping warning signals, and this dictated an unprecedented and perhaps radical move in the thinking of the opposition: they had to risk forming a policy committee in Congress to prevent Hamilton or his successor from becoming an American version of Walpole. The Republicans held a slight majority in the Fourth Congress when all members were accounted for (absenteeism was a major problem), and perhaps party-leader Gallatin felt that they could win the speakership in the next Congress, and with that control the committee. At any rate, both parties took pains to ensure that Ways and Means would be representative of the whole country, setting its membership at fourteen, with the expectation that one member from each state would be on the committee. Again the two sides' reasoning was different, but it led to the same workable structure. And even on this most exceptional of exceptions to standard operating procedures the logic of the founding shows through. This is not the logic of a single group or individual, but the logic of a hybrid regime that contained Federalist, Madisonian, and Antifederalist elements.

The next standing committee formed, nine years later, was considerably less important. Its role can again be described as clerical, because it took over a task formerly performed by the Clerk of the House, its accounting procedures. Just like Revisal and Unfinished Business, the power and scope of the Committee on Accounts were considered innocuous enough that a group of three could be trusted with its work. By the time Accounts was established in 1804, the Republicans were firmly in control of the House and Senate, and the Federalists would never again achieve a majority there. But despite this partisan dominance Republicans still did not shift policy formation from the Committee of the Whole to standing committees. The next year a Committee on Public Lands was convened to aid in the administration of territorial land that had more than doubled because of the Louisiana Purchase. The committee helped to form territorial policy to be sure, but granting this power over unorganized land was far from allowing them to make policy for the great majority of citizens in the states already formed. Nevertheless, Public Lands does represent an incremental step toward the future organizational system Congress would adopt.

Another "special administration" committee was formed in 1808, designed to administer the District of Columbia. This committee performed a function similar to Public Lands in that it was granted some autonomy in a strictly proscribed policy arena that affected a limited number of citizens. Of seven members at least one was from Virginia and another from

Maryland in order to properly represent the interests of the citizenry. This is another incremental step toward policy committees, but a rather small one when the totality of public policy is considered. In contrast, the last standing committee created before the Congress's twenty-fifth year was organized around a major arena of public policy in the young nation. In this respect the Committee on Post Offices and Post Roads was much like Ways and Means and unlike the clerical committees. Its decisions significantly affected transportation and communication throughout the nation, policies that had required the convening of numerous select committees in each of the previous Congresses. Because of its substantial policy role its membership was large, designed to approximately represent the Union by including one representative from nearly every state. This, the last of the standing committees created while Jefferson was president, was a portent of what was to come in the next few years. By 1825, standing committees would serve as the House's primary mechanism for policy formation.

To 1813 there were only two brief recorded discussions surrounding the establishment of these standing committees: one over whether seven or fourteen members should constitute Ways and Means, the other a few justificatory speeches given in favor of the Committee on the District of Columbia. All in all this is hardly the picture of partisan rancor that many have suggested.

Both Federalists and their opponents eschewed using standing committees to formulate policy for more than twenty years. During this time a few standing committees were convened to take care of clerical and administrative concerns. Toward the end of the era a handful of committees edged into policy arenas, but the only major exception to the normal mode of organization to 1808 was the Committee of Ways and Means, which for idiosyncratic reasons made sense to both sides. Joseph Cooper emphasized that after 1809 the Jeffersonian philosophy about committees gave way to a more pragmatic approach. At first this appears a concession to expedience, perhaps even hypocrisy. However, loosened individual standards were not responsible for this institutional change; that responsibility fell to the passing of the founding generation and with it their preferences of legislative organization. Joseph Cooper writes, "The generations of Republicans who entered the House after 1809 made no effort to rethink or reapply the old Jeffersonian concepts," for better or for worse.[70]

Conclusion

Political scientists who have examined the Congress in historical perspective frequently treat a period of many decades. Although this method is often useful in discerning the broad operational contours of a highly complex institution, at times enough detail is lost to distort the accuracy of our picture of the legislature. If one is told that the Congress "quickly" developed a set of standing committees, then the time frame of the analysis must be made explicit. The change from a dominant Committee of the Whole to dominant policy-forming standing committees was quick perhaps when viewing all of congressional history, but the Committee of the Whole was the nation's prime legislative mover for a long time, an entire generation. This was the founders' generation, when the same people who had debated the propriety of making a nation out of the Confederation populated Congress. The era was bisected by the "Revolution of 1800," before which the Federalists maintained a legislative majority, and after which the Republicans dominated. The whole House was preferred to standing committees as the engine of policy direction both before and after 1800, something not possible without significant Republican *and* Federalist support. The Federalist reasoning for embracing the Committee of the Whole presented here should be taken as a supplement for Joseph Cooper's thesis on the Republican side.

The mutual preference for legislative direction by the House disguised disparate motivations, rooted in the differences of the Federalists and Antifederalists. Federalists opted against standing committees due mainly to their conception of good public policy formation: the Committee of the Whole helped mitigate the problem of faction, allowed for enhanced coordination with the executive branch, and prevented the appearance of self-styled subgovernments. The former Antifederalists, resigned to the fact of national government, wanted assurances that the people's representatives as a whole rather than elite-controlled, back-room "juntos" would control policy. Thus, in the reasoning behind the embrace of the Committee of the Whole, the rivalry of the two sides continued. At the same time, a mutual understanding of proper procedure served the vital function of endowing a fragile infant institution with some semblance of legitimacy. It also gave two factions, both of which thought they and they alone held the proper philosophy of government, some common ground. And so together the Federalists and their opponents constructed the legislature — another indication that though the Antifederalists may have lost the ratification battle, their ideas and preferences were not ignored afterward.

The organizational theories of both the Federalists and the Antifederalists anticipated the most major concern that has arisen about standing committees: whether they can be representative of the nation and thus produce good policy. For both groups the answer was that they could not. The Federalists' fear of state or regionally based factions and the

Antifederalists' concern that small groups of elites would dominate a national government led to a mutual avoidance of policy-oriented committees, other than in the exceptional case of Ways and Means. The alternative structures chosen by the House fulfilled goals of both sides. The pro-administration Federalists were able to establish a policy-creation role for the executive, an arrangement that subsequent history has proven useful, and likely necessary. And at the same time, open debate in the Committee of the Whole aided the opposition in publicizing its ideals, eventually contributing to the eclipse of the Federalists.

But the Antifederalists in particular may have miscalculated in eschewing the use of standing committees. Their fear of elite usurpation led them to forego an opportunity to mend by statute what they found to be a fatal flaw in the Constitution, its tendency not to properly separate powers. The creation of policy-forming structures in the legislature paralleling the executive departments might have endowed the Congress with an independent spirit that would have challenged the executive branch, even with unified Federalist control. In studying the period from 1800 to 1828, James Sterling Young notes that this rivalry is precisely what did develop when Congress formed policy-oriented committees. Young finds that after Jefferson left office, the operation of the American government turned dramatically from one that had been executive-led to one where the president's leadership capabilities were quite limited.[71] This executive-legislative rivalry developed under a unified Republican government, and so it is possible that the same phenomenon would have occurred under Federalist administrations.

In forming a new and unique legislature, the Federalists themselves admitted they were participating in a great experiment. Those who know precisely what they are doing, those who are certain, need not experiment. By the Federalists' own admission, then, the new government was a source of significant uncertainty. One of the ways uncertainty was minimized, fear allayed, and legitimacy bolstered in this experimental legislature was the adoption of familiar rules and procedures that corresponded with long-standing preferences. This familiar legislative process was not simple. On the contrary, one can hardly think of a more cumbersome system. What stands repeating, though, is that the founding generation did make a conscious choice in sacrificing efficiency for authoritativeness. They were not naive in doing so. Theirs was a context that bordered on the revolutionary, one in which the success of the new regime was far from certain. Adopting familiar rules gave the new institution a cast of legitimacy and a workability it otherwise would not have. Change in political context can place politicians in awkward positions. In the critical realm of legislative procedure, it was thought best on all sides to deal with the passage of constitutional time by reverting to past practices that were tedious but uncontroversial. A dominant Committee of the Whole was a highly functional part of the founders' experiment — at the same time that it was a part of the experiment not written into the Constitution, leaving to future generations the possibility of organizing the legislature in ways more responsive to their concerns.

CHAPTER EIGHT

The Antifederalists

Ironic Legitimators of the American Regime

The need to transition from legality to legitimacy is an inherent but unspoken and often unfulfilled requirement of modern constitutionalism. Though legitimation was accomplished quickly in the United States, it resulted from a complex mix of ideology, practical politics, and happenstance. It was also far from apparent to the individuals involved that this transition would, in fact, occur. Ironically, one of the key reasons that the Constitution did succeed was the very fear that it would not. These fears, along with their law-abiding conservatism, led those who had criticized the proposed Constitution to a first stage of acceptance: acquiescence. Upon ratification the opposition pledged to abide by the newly sanctioned fundamental law and to work from within its bounds for their favored changes.

The fear that induced acquiescence is just one part of the story of the Constitution's legitimation, however. Long-term success required a much more adamant embrace than tentative acquiescence provided. Adopting the Federalists' own argument from the ratification debate that the national government was granted only expressed powers moved the Constitution in the direction of apotheosis, but only in conjunction with the opposition's perception that they could gain a majority in the national legislature. The defection of the Madisonians from the Federalist fold, unanticipated by those who populated the Federalist Party, allowed the opposition to contemplate taking control of the new government and righting the constitutional ship. In an atmosphere of tight partisan competition, both the Federalists and the Republicans did their best in claiming the constitutionality of their actions, something that reinforced the Constitution's central position in American political life. Meanwhile, the lack of continuity within the legislature hindered Federalist attempts to translate their prestige into national power, and the cumbersome, chamber-driven legislative organization adopted by the founding generation satisfied the opposition, who were sticklers for procedural orthodoxy.

Although the Antifederalist leaders' acceptance of the Constitution was far from sufficient for legitimation to occur, it was something without which it could not occur. In accepting the ratified Constitution, in assiduously urging citizens to do likewise, in constructing a constitutional philosophy tightly associated with the fundamental law, in engaging in partisan competition within its bounds, the Antifederalists were the Federalists' partners in the Constitution's success. For most of American history, patriotic historiography obscured any conclusion but that the Constitution's critics were weak in organization and argument, bested by the superior talents of the Federalists. This historiographical approach is understandable, if still inaccurate: knowing that the nation as a whole had little in common other than a uniform embrace of the Constitution, historians emphasized its sacredness, the genius of its Federalist framers, and the failures of its opponents. Just as in the era immediately following ratification, the solidity of the Constitution was built on a fear that the United States was in danger of crumbling.

Modern historical research is more nuanced than the patriotic scholarship, but also more segmented, in chronology and perspective. There is a body of knowledge on the confederation period, another dealing with the ratification era, and yet another covering the "age of Federalism." Students of history learn important lessons from each: the confederation was inefficient and indecisive by design, but that design increasingly did not meet the political needs of the citizenry; the Constitution was written and shepherded through the ratification process by an extremely able group, but the process was highly divisive, centering around whether the proposed document partook of popular government or not; the nation's first party system formed quickly after the Constitution was implemented, growing to a near ironclad and dangerously divisive phenomenon by the Fifth Congress. This and much more detailed knowledge may be culled from in-depth work confined to each distinct period.

Yet one cannot adequately discern how the United States's constitutional politics was shaped during this era, nor appreciate the influence of both the Federalists and their opponents, without taking a longer view, and a more integrative look, paying attention to the time before, during, and after the ratification debates. Such an integrative look takes us through several constitutional contexts, what I have called a progression of constitutional time. This progression has much to tell us about each of the groups involved in the ratification fight. The Antifederalists were more conservative than most have previously thought and were poised to accept the Constitution on principle if ratified. Hamilton and his followers in Congress differed markedly from the coauthor of *The Federalist* on how to successfully implement a constitution. Madison, the leader of a crucial swing group, was forced to abandon his hope that institutional arrangements in the extended republic, familiar from Federalist #10, could solve the problem of factionalism. The progression of constitutional time exposed what was present but largely obscured by a particular constitutional context that we often think fully defines the thinking of the individuals within that context. The more rounded view afforded by heeding the several contexts these individuals faced refutes some of the most long-standing myths of the founding era, including Madison's supposed switch from a nationalist to a states-rightser, the Antifederalists' impotence, and the Federalists' degree of control over the ratification process and the course the nation has taken since.

What follows provides a detailed picture of the events, timing, and causality in the process of constitutional legitimation. I assess the Antifederalists' impact in three ways: discerning their influence on the American regime, recounting the positions of influence occupied by individual Antifederalists, and examining their prescience in discerning the course of American constitutionalism. I conclude by offering some final comments on the three groups involved in ratification and the constitutional regime they founded. There I attempt to correct one of the most common misconceptions about the Antifederalists, point out what this episode tells us about political theory, and point to the strengths and weaknesses of the American constitutional consensus.

Events, Timing, and Causality in the Process of Constitutional Legitimation

During the ratification process, the Federalists were like a chess player one move ahead of their opponent, consistently outflanking the Antifederalists. Those who were most motivated to seek nationally oriented reforms were more willing to populate the Annapolis Convention and, later, the one in Philadelphia. Because of their limited enthusiasm for extensive reforms, prominent figures who became Antifederalists tended to select themselves out of service in the Constitutional Convention. The convention was, therefore, highly motivated to achieve centralizing changes, changes more substantial than most political leaders envisioned. Among their number was George Washington, the nation's "indispensable man," who granted immense prestige and credibility to their cause.

The new framework for government was offered to the states as an either/or proposition: they could ratify, or the country would continue to labor under the Articles of Confederation. Since there was a consensus that government under the Articles was defective, engineering a forced choice between the Constitution and the Articles was quite a coup — not because this choice led to a quick and inevitable ratification, but because it backed the Constitution's opponents into a corner, making them seem to defend the indefensible.

For several states the advantages of the Constitution were unmistakable. These states ratified quickly and in so doing imparted more positive momentum to the movement. Yet the ratification process sputtered a bit after this initial flurry, and it was not clear that other states favored the Constitution given a "take it or leave it" option. Federalists thereupon skillfully switched the terms of debate away from the all-or-nothing proposition. In Massachusetts, they arranged for the convention to recommend to the new Congress specific changes that would win over the mildest of the Antifederalists. The tactic worked. Massachusetts ratified, and in the remaining states approval with recommendatory amendments became the norm. Without these amendments, winning over enough Antifederalists to achieve nine ratifications was a doubtful proposition. The recommended changes also forestalled the possibility that a second Constitutional Convention would meet and scrap the work of the first. Because alterations were recommended, rather than legally binding, the Constitution would not have to be altered prior to implementation, nor exactly as any particular state wished.

That nine states, instead of seven or thirteen, were necessary to effect ratification was a brilliant move. If the requirement had been higher, ratification could not have been achieved; had it been lower, the opposition's claims of illegitimacy would have been fiercer, more defensible, and resonated all the more. In sum, the Federalists' effort during the ratification process was a classically executed example of controlling the agenda and dividing one's opponents to conquer them. Despite a great deal of opposition, the Federalists were able to effect ratification with minimal concessions and without relying heavily on procedural shortcuts or political shenanigans; at the end of the process even the Antifederalists realized that the Federalists had won the day.

Nine states, a two-thirds majority, ratified by June 21, 1788. Four days later Virginia, the largest, wealthiest, and most influential state followed suit. While most Antifederalists were not simple majoritarians, they did believe that what was clearly the will of the collected citizenry could not and should not be ignored. Accordingly, when faced with a Constitution that was legally sanctioned by a large majority of states, almost all

Antifederalists accepted it as the legitimate framework for government in America. This acceptance entailed a voluntary renunciation of any and all radical political moves — defined as those outside the sanctioned bounds of the Constitution itself.

Antifederalists knew that republican government was an experiment that could go awry. One of the dangers of popular government, they discerned, was that citizens encouraged to think of the government as their own might get greedy, and when they found the law imperfectly corresponded to their wishes they might not obey it. To limit this possibility, the Antifederalists engaged in an extensive campaign to publicize their position: the legally sanctioned pronouncements of the community could not be violated no matter how egregious they seemed, as long as there were viable procedural remedies. In constitutional terms, this development was monumental. Despite a preponderance of diverse and divisive views among political leaders, as of mid-1788 there was consensus that the Constitution provided the legitimate bounds for government — acquiescence — a key criterion of constitutional success.

Federalists did not rush to implement the new Constitution after the ratifications of New Hampshire and Virginia. During these months word of the Antifederalists' acquiescence did indeed reach the public while, simultaneously, the Federalist-dominated press continued to tout the benefits of the new national government. Early in this interim period New York, the one key holdout, fell into line with the ten other ratifying states, fearing that it would lose the national capital. The two states that remained outside of the Union, Rhode Island and North Carolina, were isolated and without prestige. Both sides realized that it was only a matter of time before they joined too.

Even while the Antifederalists acknowledged the Constitution as law, they did not exit the ratification fight empty-handed. The passage of recommendatory amendments and Federalist assurances that the Constitution granted the national government only expressed powers gave the Antifederalists less to fear about the new Constitution than about Federalist duplicity, which potentially could forestall amendments and dash the doctrine of expressed powers. After ratification the Antifederalists expected of Federalists — and held them to — what the Antifederalists were doing themselves, abiding by the will of the collected community. Since the Constitution would not have been ratified without recommendatory amendments, the will of the community was neither strictly Federalist nor Antifederalist, but some combination of the two that neither side considered ideal, but both were willing to accept — a far cry from total Federalist vindication.

The Federalist and Antifederalist attempts at disseminating information about the ratified Constitution worked. This uniform information flow to the public about the Constitution's status helps to explain how it so quickly achieved such a dear place in the hearts of American citizens. Thus established as the nation's unassailable political bedrock, those who had opposed the Constitution suffered by implication, ironically at least partly due to their own efforts at confirming its legitimacy. The results of state and federal elections in the years immediately following ratification provide evidence of a popular backlash against the Antifederalists. Their stance on the Constitution was wrong, judged the public in retrospect, and initially there was no compelling reason to trust the new government to any but those who had formulated and favored it.

While many Federalists urged caution and accommodation in the uncertain months after ratification, others attempted to marginalize their opponents rather than include them, particularly as it became clear that the Constitution was a resounding popular success. Many in this latter group of Federalists only reluctantly went along with the Bill of Rights, the first public indication of the divide that would place the proponents of the Constitution in two opposing camps. Doggedly urged on by James Madison, as crucial to the Constitution's success in his own way as Washington, a set of amendments that addressed their opponents' main concern was agreed to in the first session of the U.S. Congress. Federalists passed amendments that secured rights, but without incorporating any of the Antifederalists' suggested structural changes in national institutions. Although some in both camps disliked this compromise, in the main, the Bill of Rights served to bolster the nascent constitutional consensus.

Even with the Bill of Rights, the former Antifederalists who were elected to Congress led an uneasy existence. Substantially outnumbered, they could not hope to determine public policy at a time when crucial precedents would be set. The best they could do, from their perspective, was to remain vigilant against the exercise of powers not contained in the Constitution. In several Federalist policies, various individuals discerned unwarranted expansions of national power. The Antifederalists' response to these policy proposals was tailor-made for them by previous American experience with governmental charters and by the well-known ratification-debate protestations of Federalist James Wilson. An understanding of the Constitution had been ratified along with the document itself, Antifederalists reasoned: its language granted only expressed and limited powers to the national government. These were the first examples of the form that constitutional contests were to take in the new regime, centering around its proper interpretation, one side espousing something akin to what has been called strict construction and the other claiming to follow its spirit in pressing for substantial discretionary powers by the national government. The philosophy of strict construction, the Antifederalists' contribution to American jurisprudence, helped to cement the Constitution's place at the heart of American civic religion. In arguing that the letter of the fundamental law was crucial, their constitutional theory focused debates on justifying political moves under its language. The group closest to the true meaning of the Constitution would supposedly prevail, irrespective of what modern times or the twists and turns of public opinion dictated.

During the second and third sessions of the First Congress, a significant contingent of Federalists came to the conclusion that their colleagues were extending national powers beyond what was justified by "natural implications" of specifically granted powers. This group was led by James Madison. Madison himself could not have helped but been struck by the failure of his hopes for the extended republic. In Federalist #10 he postulated that there would probably not be a self-interested majority faction in Congress. With Congress's assumption of state debts, refusal to discriminate between original holders of government securities and their present owners, and the foundation of a national bank, Madison found that a majority group was aggressively and successfully pursuing self-aggrandizing policies contrary to the national good and not justifiable under the Constitution. By the end of the First Congress, the Madisonians were organizing an opposition newspaper, signaling a definitive break from the Hamiltonian Federalists.

In the short run, the Federalists who remained were successful. Those who favored the Constitution had polled such a decisive majority in the first federal elections that they did not need to accommodate Madison and those who followed him into the opposition's camp. Still a clear majority in both houses, they were able to pass their preferred policies. President Washington considered vetoing the national bank on constitutional grounds, but Hamilton's brief defending the enterprise proved more persuasive to the president than Jefferson's and Madison's arguments against. Even so, the Federalists' success came at an immense long-term cost, permanently alienating the Madisonians when they might have been kept in the fold by moderating Hamilton's proposals. In a way, then, the Hamiltonian Federalists were victims of their own overwhelming success and their eagerness to set the tone for the new government early, paying more heed to what their majority could pass than to what would hold their original coalition intact. That very reticence to compromise was based in large part on the Hamiltonians' hope to administrate the national government into a fully sovereign existence as soon after implementation as possible, a disposition that only became fully apparent with the passage of constitutional time.

Secretary of State Thomas Jefferson became the new opposition's standard-bearer. Jefferson attempted to win President Washington to his side by explaining what had transpired:

The Antifederalist champions are now strengthened in argument by the fulfillment of their predictions; that this has been brought about by the Monarchical federalists themselves, who, having been for the new government merely as a stepping stone to monarchy, have themselves adopted the very construction of the constitution, of which, they declared it unsusceptible; that the republican federalists, who espoused the same government for its intrinsic merits, are disarmed of their weapons, that which they denied as prophecy being now become true history; who can be sure that these things may not proselyte the small number which was wanting to place the majority on the other side?[1]

To Jefferson, developments in the First Congress made clear that there were actually three key groups involved in ratification: Federalists who like him and Madison were predisposed to favor a defined and limited national government and took James Wilson's protestations seriously; another set of Federalists who privately favored a much stronger central government than that enumerated but who publicly backed the document to the hilt, hoping that under it they could extend national power; and finally the Antifederalists, who had presciently warned against the latter kind of Federalist. Jefferson, in relating that the "republican federalists" were "disarmed of their weapons," hints at the collapse of "well-meaning" Federalism. Unfortunately for Jefferson, the group he called "Monarchical federalists" formed a clear majority in Congress. Their majority spurred them to vindicate broad discretionary powers almost immediately after implementation of the Constitution. The only option available to republican federalists like Jefferson and Madison was to ally with the Antifederalists. In doing so they presumed that the Antifederalist portion of their coalition would not be so obstinate as to prohibit the restoration of the constitutional balance the republican federalists had envisioned and had enshrined in the Constitution. In short, Jefferson and Madison quickly came to realize that the Antifederalists were more likely to abide by the Constitution as it was ratified than the Hamiltonian Federalists.

If well-meaning republican Federalists could convince the populace that the "Monarchical federalists" were edging the regime into one that served their own interests, then the republicans could prevail. But this required embracing new tactics, partisanship in the service of the national good. Given the eighteenth-century belief that the existence of political parties indicated a profoundly dysfunctional regime, the turn toward partisanship was a drastic step indeed. It indicated a conviction among the Madisonians that their former political partners were attempting to put an end to republican government itself. For Madison personally, the change in tactics was stunning, as he scrapped his assumption that kaleidoscopic policy formulation would predominate and solve the problem of factions, embracing the connective majoritarianism of partisan politics wholesale.

Those in the Federalist Party continued to deride opponents through the 1790s with the simple epithet that they were "Antis," an indication that among the public many still judged them to be disgraced obstructionists. The effectiveness of this charge diminished through time, however. By the Third Congress the House was nearly evenly split between Federalists and Republicans, the latter enjoying a slight advantage in the rare times when almost all members were present. William Findley, commenting on Federalist tactics in his *Review of the Revenue System*, noted that "the artful cry of the danger of antifederalism is gradually ceasing to have its effect. The more people examine, the more they are convinced, that no body of antifederalists exists in the United States, and that no design for overturning the government has been entertained since the commencement of its operation."[2]

The claim that "no body of antifederalists exists" was indicative of the postratification tactics of those who had criticized the Constitution. Because the Constitution was so universally popular, those who had opposed it did not attempt to defend their stance during the ratification debate so much as submerge it, instead emphasizing that they and the nation had moved on. The Antifederalists' affiliation with the new Republican Party was what mattered now; through it they were fighting to preserve the popular government that the people had ratified in 1788 and preserved through the adoption of the Bill of Rights.

The potential for lawlessness also continued to be an issue. Antifederalists found the potential for unrest a validation of their premise that the people would not consider national policies their own. The heavy-handed nature of Federalist policies, as they saw it, contributed directly to the Whiskey Rebellion. In instances of actual or threatened disobedience, Republican leaders repeated the same instructions to citizens they did after ratification: obey the law while pressing for redress, doing so through legal channels without resorting to mob action or collective lawlessness. Findley, for instance, in his *History of the Insurrection in the Four Western Counties in Pennsylvania*, writes that Pennsylvanians were perfectly justified in questioning government policies, just not in the manner that they did. Preventing courts from holding session to block the execution of a law, for example, was indefensible in a popular regime. "The great error among the people," he related, "was an opinion that an immoral law might be opposed and yet the government respected, and all other laws obeyed."[3] Findley reminded his readers that "we are under a moral obligation to respect government, not only as a divine ordinance, but also as a moral compact, binding the people to one another for its support."[4]

Federalists were inclined to see the continued potential for unrest as a failure of their plans. Not that the failing was theirs; the people were disrespectful of lawful government and were encouraged to think in terms of their own interests rather than the nation's. Federalists who thought these tendencies would be overcome by the new Constitution came to blame the "active and designing leaders" of the opposition for encouraging such behavior. Little could be done to stifle these leaders in the Third or Fourth Congress because the Federalists did not firmly control the House. But by the Fifth Congress, Federalists had regained a clear majority there and had retained control of the Senate and the executive branch. They were therefore in a position to put the most troubling Republican leaders in their place; they attempted to do so by passing the Sedition Act. With the Sedition Act, the Federalists attempted to turn back the clock to the brief time before parties existed on the national scene. In essence they were trying to outlaw the style of politics that had become familiar in the new regime: policy contests overseen by rival parties. This had been a key part of the ratification's settlement, but was, from the Federalist perspective, an unintended nuisance. The Sedition Act would help national leaders formulate policy — in their minds the Constitution's purpose from the beginning.

Not surprisingly, Republicans found the Sedition Act violative of the Constitution. In their view, outlawing criticism of the government was clearly despotic. If the Federalists were successful, the government would not be republican at all. Republicans did not, however, fully agree on the tactics to be used in combating the new policy. Some, like former Antifederalist John Dawson, advocated seeking redress through the courts and then by constitutional amendment if necessary. In a July 19, 1798, broadside printed in Philadelphia, Dawson argued that the Sedition Act was unconstitutional. "And this, I trust, will be the opinion of the Courts. Should it not, it behoves . . . every citizen to endeavour, in the mode prescribed by the constitution, to obtain its repeal, as it will have a tendency to curtail one of the first and dearest privileges which we enjoy; that of freely expressing our sentiments on all public men and measures."[5]

Madison and Jefferson, meanwhile, took a different route, penning the Virginia and Kentucky resolutions, respectively. These resolutions asserted that it was the right and duty of state governments to interpose themselves between the national government and the people when the former passed an unconstitutional law. These resolutions attempted to shift the locus of constitutional interpretation from the federal courts to the state legislatures. Although these tactics were very different from Dawson's, their effort was also intended to dispute the renegade Federalist regime in a nonviolent manner. Additionally, all Republicans emphasized to the electorate that the national government could not stifle the free exchange of ideas about the government. Trying to eliminate the rival party could not be done without destroying the outcome of the ratification process. The constitutional rift over the Constitution wrought by its implementation yielded partisan politics, which while still not respectable, had come of age.

Federalists in the Fifth Congress seriously miscalculated. Enforcing the Sedition Act to the degree that it would have fulfilled Federalist hopes was impossible. The few sedition cases prosecuted under its guidelines backfired. Men like Matthew Lyon, jailed in October 1798, became martyrs in the Republican cause, symbols of Federalist tyranny. The Alien Act, also passed in 1798, estranged immigrant communities, some of which had been important portions of the Federalist electoral coalition. The Fifth Congress also prepared for war with an increasingly hostile France. But the military buildup that Federalists authorized was not seen as an effective deterrent to war. Instead it was considered another hallmark of tyranny: the dreaded standing army in peacetime, about which the Antifederalists had been so exercised in 1787 and 1788. Federalists in the Fifth Congress "somehow manage[d] at each turn to do everything wrong."[6]

The end result of Federalist blundering was a Republican landslide, the so-called Revolution of 1800, through which the Republicans firmly gained control of the national government, never to relinquish it to the Federalists. With the Federalists a shadow of their former selves in subsequent years, the Republican conception of interest-oriented politics flourished. James Sterling Young reports that in the years from 1800 to 1828, "the power-holders on the Potomac fashioned a system of surpassing excellence for representing the people and grossly deficient in the means for governing people."[7] This is a Federalist lament.

Federalists constituted a slim minority on the national scene through the War of 1812, though their strength was concentrated in New England. Relations with Great Britain turned sour late in the first decade of Republican rule. This development was troubling to Federalists, who still hoped for close ties with England. A second war with Great Britain threatened to undo the prosperity they had worked so hard to foster. But the Federalists were no match for the young Republicans in Congress, the so-called War Hawks, who succeeded in having Congress declare war. Two years into the War of 1812, Federalist delegates from every state in

New England met in Hartford, Connecticut, to draw up resolutions criticizing Republican policies and to plan how to hold the Republican majority at bay. The Hartford Convention called on Republicans to end military conscription and rescind trade restrictions. Ironically, they also adopted a strong states' rights perspective, attempting to employ the Republicans' own argument, honed when they were the minority, against them.

The Federalists' timing was unfortunate. Their resolutions were made public just before news of the Treaty of Ghent reached the United States. Peace gave the Republicans a great public relations boost at the direct expense of the Federalists. Because Federalists had met in secret and did not support the war, the public was ready to believe Republican misinformation that they had advocated breaking up the Union, or worse, conspired with Britain. The Federalists did not recover from this blow and never came close to challenging the Republican majority again.

Nevertheless, certain prominent Federalist individuals hung on. Many of them allied with Andrew Jackson in the 1820s. No doubt these Federalists, most of whom thought stifling rampant democracy was part of their project in 1787, were not entirely pleased to ally with the arch-democrat. Shaw Livermore has explained why this alliance occurred: Federalists were inextricably wedded to the idea that they themselves were the nation's rightful leaders. In the late 1820s and early 1830s they discerned that the only way to stay in a position of authority was to court Jackson.[8] Having to ally with such a figure reinforced to the Federalists how imperfectly their hopes for the new government were realized. The Antifederalists gradually faded from the political scene as well; time took its inevitable toll. But they did not depart bitterly disappointed, nor did they have to grope for a party that would take them. Antifederalists had a home, the Republican Party, which was not the same as Antifederalism to be sure, but as close as these figures could have hoped in the earliest days of the national republic.

The Antifederalists were major players in the Constitution's success and definition. What is strange is that this group could for so long be considered overwhelmed. After all, they were close to, if not a majority in 1787–88, and included in their number were many influential politicians who did not disappear on ratification. One politician who knew something about the influence of "losers," Samuel Tilden, best expressed the influence of groups like the Antifederalists. The New York governor who lost the disputed presidential election of 1876 once wrote that "in shaping the policy which emerges from the conflict, the minority acts a part scarcely less important than the majority; and the dissentients are thus prepared to accept the result. Such is the process by which the will of all parts of the community is collected, averaged, and represented in the policy finally agreed upon."[9]

Individual Influence,
Political Precedents, Theoretical Prescience

Antifederalists were important to the American regime after the founding in three ways. First, the former Antifederalists themselves continued to be influential figures in national, state, and local politics. Second, the fight that they waged against the Federalists set important, enduring precedents in the conduct and nature of American politics. Third, key portions of their prescriptive theory are validated by subsequent events. These influences are far from absolute, of course, but they are significant. When the entirety of their political contribution is considered, the Antifederalists were much more important to American political development than has been realized.

A list of the most prominent critics of the Constitution is impressive, even when one limits it to those active and influential on the national scene. Two presidents, James Monroe and John Quincy Adams, opposed the Constitution. Both were major figures in national politics for more than a quarter century. Monroe was the last president, the only one other than Washington, to be elected unopposed. He is also one of the few early presidents still widely known for a policy, specifically the foreign policy based on his Monroe Doctrine. Adams was elected chief executive by the House of Representatives when no candidate received a majority in the four-way race of 1824. His selection was a compromise, settled on partly because of his strong ties to the founding period. Adams served as an important transitional figure, holding the highest office in the land when the nation seemed not quite ready to embrace Jacksonianism and the new level of partisanship and democracy that came with it.

The accomplishments of James Monroe and John Quincy Adams show that Antifederalists were not precluded from the nation's highest political office because they were on the "wrong side" at a crucial time in national history. Rarely are members of opposition groups so successful in revolutionary settings — when they are, it is more often because they have overthrown the regime their rivals instituted than successfully incorporated themselves into it.

Even so, two Antifederalist presidents may seem like a small number — small until one pauses to think about the affiliations of all the presidents in the three-group typology offered by Jefferson above and that I have used in much of my analysis. Washington was strictly antipartisan in philosophy, but the tenor of his administration can safely be described as Federalist. John Adams tried to remain above the partisan fray like Washington. This proved to be his chief weakness, though, as he failed to unite his own party even though he was a firm Federalist. Jefferson had been out of the country during the ratification debate, serving as the American envoy to France. He embraced the Constitution but not wholeheartedly, as he wished for amendments. Jefferson split from the Federalists along with Madison during the First Congress. Thus, of the six presidents who took a public stance on ratification, the first two were nationalist Federalists, the next two were "republican federalists" or Madisonians, and the last two were Antifederalists.

Three vice presidents had been critics of the Constitution: Aaron Burr, George Clinton, and Elbridge Gerry. Burr attempted to gain election to New York's ratification convention but was easily outpolled in Federalist-dominated New York City. His exploits after ratification are infamous. A shameless self-promoter at a time when political self-promotion was universally disdained, Burr nearly became our third president through a curious mix of realpolitik and constitutional accident. When the election of 1800 was thrown into the House because of a tie in the Electoral College, a shift of three crucial votes would have elected Burr instead of Jefferson. Burr seemed to court Federalist votes in the House, permanently alienating him from Jefferson and the Republicans.[10] Burr's disgrace was not due to his Antifederalism, but rather was a result of his almost uncontrollable ambition, which led him to grasp at the nation's highest office clumsily and too soon. That he was in a position to seek the presidency is a further testament to the fact that criticizing the Constitution was not an insurmountable political impediment.

George Clinton is one of only two men to hold the office of vice president under two different presidents.[11] The longtime governor and favorite son of New York was selected to replace Burr on the Republican ticket in 1805. Failing in his bid four years later to follow Jefferson as the nation's chief executive, Clinton reluctantly agreed to serve in the office under Madison as well. As president of the Senate, Clinton cast the deciding vote in at least one major policy controversy. When the charter of the national bank was about to expire, there was a closely contested debate over whether to recharter it. When the votes were counted, the proponents of rechartering had tied with those against. Clinton voted not to recharter, citing the bank's dubious constitutionality.[12] Clinton died in the spring of 1812, an election year. To replace him, Madison chose Elbridge Gerry, the man who fought tooth and nail on almost every point at the Constitutional Convention only to oppose the document in the end. Gerry's tenure as vice president was short. He, like Clinton, died in office.

Although Clinton and Gerry finished their political careers in national office, clearly the time of their greatest impact and influence was earlier, when they were state leaders. Clinton was elected governor seven times, first in 1777 and for the last time in 1801. His political dominance of the state earned him the nickname "Pharaoh of New York." It was Clinton who allowed the Constitution to be ratified at the appropriate time despite his own opposition.[13] He controlled patronage and forged alliances that characterized his state's politics for more than thirty years. Gerry's role as an agitator for national independence was second only to Samuel Adams, Thomas Paine, and Patrick Henry. Gerry was a leading organizer of the committees of correspondence and coordinated relief efforts for Boston, aimed at softening the blow of the British siege. For ten years, he was a member of the Continental Congress. Gerry (like Clinton) was considered in the top echelon of national leaders by contemporaries, one who could not be ignored or taken lightly. Prior to his service as vice president, Gerry served two terms in the U.S. House of Representatives and was twice elected governor of Massachusetts.

Like vice presidents today, Gerry, Clinton, and Burr were chosen partly for their ability to balance a ticket. Their selection paired a favorite-son Northerner from a key state with a Virginian. But these combinations also united a former Antifederalist with a former Federalist, and not accidentally. These pairings served as a symbol for the Republican Party, which considered itself the party of all the people, Federalists and Antifederalists alike, possibly excepting only those Federalists who were bent on subverting the Constitution. The latter belonged to the Federalist Party, which attracted almost no Antifederalist support. Uniting those who had opposed each other on ratification was of practical importance too, as it helped Republicans at the polls. Putting a prominent Antifederalist on the ticket virtually guaranteed that Republicans would carry certain areas, enough to tip the balance in their favor in certain states, and perhaps nationally.

Many members of Congress and several cabinet secretaries were also Antifederalists. Albert Gallatin, for example, served prominently as both. After Madison retired from Congress in 1797, Gallatin took over as leader of the opposition in the House. In 1801, President Jefferson chose Gallatin to serve as his secretary of the treasury, a post of immense importance to the founding generation. Britain's prime ministership had evolved from the head of the treasury, and Hamilton had set the tone of the Federalist government in his capacity as treasury secretary. Unlike the vice president, the holder of this position wielded real power on a daily basis. At the first opportunity Republicans had to fill this post, it was entrusted to a former Antifederalist.

There were many members of the U.S. Congress who opposed the Constitution during ratification. Each of them had a vote and made an impact with it to some degree. Most of these politicians are now obscure, but at the time many were influential policy-makers. The list of congressional Antifederalists in Appendix B is not exhaustive, as it includes only those who had also voted in ratification conventions. The total number of Antifederalists who served in Congress is significantly larger.

On the state and local levels, especially, Antifederalists wielded a great deal of influence after ratification. This is a difficult matter to document or grasp, because the state and local officials of the ratification era are now almost all obscure. The postratification electoral shift away from the Antifederalists was, like all electoral shifts, a marginal, time-bound phenomenon. Criticism of the Constitution was concentrated in certain regions and localities. Political elites in many of these areas were almost uniformly Antifederalist. Citizens within these areas selected local and state representatives after ratification, and often the only viable candidates were Antifederalists, many of whom served in state and local offices without interruption. As a result, the lopsided ratio of Federalists to Antifederalists in the first two Congresses was not indicative of the ratio of the same two groups in most state houses, which was much closer to being even. The Antifederalists were, therefore, not as marginalized in most states as they were on the national scene in the earliest years of the republic.

Plus, in the years after 1790, the balance of power in individual states shifted back away from the Federalists, and many states they had captured in the late 1780s elected new Republican majorities during the 1790s. State legislators and town officials whose names mean nothing today allowed Antifederalism, in its modified, postratification form, to exist and thrive after June 21, 1788. Most of these officials never served at the national level. The most prominent, like Samuel Adams and Patrick Henry, were towering figures of the age, but even more important were the thousands of now-anonymous figures who held office after ratification; they were the politicians who had the most impact on citizens' daily lives. Cumulatively, their political contributions had a great effect on national politics too: state officials elected Senators, campaigned and organized for national candidates, and provided the political opportunities allowing others to move up the political ladder.

The Antifederalists influenced politics indirectly as well. The Bill of Rights provides a good example, a taste of the complex mixture of political influence in the ratification's settlement. Omitting a bill of rights proved to be the Philadelphia Convention's most major oversight. Explaining what might result from this omission was easily the most effective argument in the Antifederalist arsenal. The Constitution simply would not have passed without Federalists promising that amendments would be considered; moderate Antifederalists had to be won over. Thus recommendatory amendments were tailored by both groups to address the concerns of the moderate critics. Though none of these recommendations were binding, many of them were incorporated into the amendments formulated by Madison.

Not surprisingly, the Bill of Rights turned out to be the Antifederalists' favorite part of the fundamental law. Its tenor was different from the main body of the Constitution. In delineating rights, it posited that there were areas upon which the national government could not encroach. In other words, it recognized that the American national government was to remain limited. The Bill of Rights has played a profound, if not dominant, role in American jurisprudence. Although the Antifederalists were the first to emphasize it in their jurisprudence, certainly much of what has been made of the Bill of Rights was not foreseen or intended by them. It is highly unlikely, however, that the rich but checkered history of individual rights in the United States would have developed in the same way without the Bill of Rights, or without the Bill of Rights as it is. At least indirectly, the Antifederalists are responsible for the first ten amendments.

The Antifederalists should also be credited for their role in the Constitution's quick legitimation. Since they knew the tenuousness of constitutionalism as a mode of governing, they strenuously emphasized that accepting the legal Constitution was a citizen's sacred duty. The populace took their leaders' admonitions to heart, and thus no anti-Constitution party formed. A definitive step toward apotheosis was taken immediately after implementation, when the former Antifederalists embraced the Constitution in a strong sense, formulating the doctrine of strict construction. In attempting to combat activist policies, they helped cement the bond between the populace and the Constitution. Not only was the importance of constitutionalism reinforced and strengthened by the nature of the Antifederalists' postimplementation argument, but popular devotion to this particular Constitution was cultivated, a key characteristic of the American regime. Privately some public figures may dislike its framework, but in the public arena, the Constitution as a whole is all but unassailable. Energy that might be put into championing a new constitution in other regimes is here put into the quest to define the meaning of the one and only Constitution. A certain political stability has resulted. This is not to say that American politics has not or cannot change — it has tremendously in more than two hundred years. Rather, it is to say that sudden, drastic changes rarely occur, as they are difficult to support, not having the sanction of prior constitutional practice.

Strict construction also provides the Supreme Court with its organizing mythology. When push comes to shove, the High Court does not justify its interpretation of the Constitution by pointing to the dictates of modern practice. Nor do its opinions rely on the seemingly commonsense fact that its decisions are authoritative in and of themselves. Instead, Supreme Court decisions are portrayed as justified by the Constitution and even required by it. Thus in its quest for authoritativeness, the Supreme Court often revisits territory first staked out by the Antifederalists: they say their reading of the Constitution is definitive, because it is not a reading so much as it is what the Constitution itself demands. Officials in black robes are not the only ones who have employed this argument, of course. Elected politicians have often employed strict construction or original intent arguments.

Additionally, the Antifederalists/Republicans did a great deal to ensure that local and state political practices would survive ratification. Yale legal scholar Carol M. Rose has written convincingly on the subject.[14] Rose argues that local political customs and practices are as much a part of the American constitutional tradition as the Constitution and its historical jurisprudence. To put it in Rose's terms, she believes that the United States has an unwritten, ancient constitution in addition to our written version. America's ancient constitution consists of locally based culture and law, precisely what the Antifederalists were trying to defend. Localism has indeed played a crucial part in U.S. politics, despite the fact that the national government is sovereign. Even with the spectacular growth of the national government, some modicum of federalism has always been preserved. That the states did not wither into mere administrative entities is at least partly due to the Antifederalists, who made it abundantly clear that the Constitution did not authorize pure nationalism and provided a counterweight to Hamilton's design to administer the national government into full sovereignty.

There are also contributions that have been less successful historically, but which have provided grist for political debate. In attempting to limit the tendency of centralized power to grow and retrench, Antifederalists offered numerous suggestions. Chief among them was the quest for rotation out of office. The Antifederalists were not the inventors of rotation, but they were its most articulate advocates. What the Antifederalists hoped to achieve through law was accomplished almost by accident. Today, incentives for politicians are such that the majority of national representatives wish to serve for longer periods than they did two hundred years ago. Many Americans today find the legislature rife with the kinds of problems that Antifederalists believed would result from long tenures. Accordingly, the idea of term limits has been revived. More than twenty states have imposed term limits on their state officials. But for a Supreme Court decision to the contrary, many would certainly restrict their national representatives from serving without interruption as well.[15] Not to be outdone, many national officials have imposed an unofficial term limit on themselves. And of course the Twenty-second Amendment imposes a two-term limit on the nation's chief executive.

Additionally, the initial mode of congressional organization reflected Antifederalist preferences. These organizing principles have long passed from the scene, but through the years many reform movements aim at resituating power closer to the floor majority, which is where the Antifederalists believed it belonged. The great challenge of a Congress organized into standing committees, to frame authoritative policy reflecting national preferences, was the primary concern of the Antifederalists.

The Antifederalists deeply influenced the generation of politicians that came after them. This influence cannot be easily quantified or appreciated in the aggregate, but it is readily apparent on an individual level. The biographers of many important "second-generation" American politicians like John C. Calhoun, Martin Van Buren, and John Tyler have noticed the Antifederalist influences on their subjects.

Irving Bartlett's recent biography of John C. Calhoun notes the striking similarity between his father Patrick Calhoun's stance toward the Constitution with that of his son, despite Patrick's death when John was a small boy: "John Calhoun had internalized his father's independent spirit and basic political convictions long before he entered public life. His father's principles in opposing the Constitution would be his own as he sought to reshape the Constitution a half century later."[16] Calhoun also learned about politics from his extended family and his fellow backcountry South Carolinians; almost all of them had been Antifederalists. John likely looked up to his older cousin Joseph, who had voted against the Constitution as a delegate to South Carolina's ratification convention and later served in Congress.

Martin Van Buren's father was a minor Antifederalist official in Kinderhook, New York. Though Abraham Van Buren had been "an anti-Federalist in a Federalist town and county, [he] held the post of town clerk for ten years."[17] The elder Van Buren was a tavern-keeper, whose business served as a political meeting place. As the parents of politically successful individuals often do, Abraham "taught his son how to get along with people and introduced him to politics."[18] President John Tyler's father was a much more prominent figure than the elder Van Buren, capping his political career with a term as Virginia's governor and service as a federal judge. John Tyler Sr. had been a delegate at the Annapolis Convention. He ardently wished that the Confederation

Congress would gain the power to regulate commerce. Yet he opposed the Constitution, saying that "it contains a variety of powers too dangerous to be vested in any set of men whatsoever."[19] President Tyler's biographer, Robert Seagar, says that "the most important single fact that can be derived from John Tyler's formative years is that he absorbed in toto the political, social, and economic views of his distinguished father."[20]

Calhoun, Van Buren, and Tyler are simply the most prominent politicians who were influenced by Antifederalism. Hundreds of other political officials in the early nineteenth century were the sons of Antifederalists or grew up in places where the work of the Philadelphia Convention had not been popular. The heroes and mentors of many boys interested in political service were Antifederalists-turned-Republicans. It is likely that the first political questions these boys asked of their elders centered on the Constitution and ratification. Learning the nuances of the Antifederalist position, and how it was transformed but not destroyed by ratification, was thus an important part of political socialization in the early republic. The Antifederalists, and the Federalists who joined them to constitute the Republican Party, apparently did something right, as that party dominated American politics after 1800.

I have emphasized that the ratification process created a hybrid regime. After ratification, not everything went the Federalists' or the Antifederalists' way. For the latter group, the two most troubling aspects of the new order were the irksome clauses still contained in the Constitution, particularly the supremacy clause and the necessary and proper clause. Included among the ratification debate commentaries were predictions about the character of politics in the "nationalized" regime and how the growth of national power would be justified. These predictions turned out to be surprisingly accurate. So in addition to their own influence, personally and conceptually, the Antifederalists are important because of their theoretical prescience.

In the letter to President Washington quoted above, Jefferson pronounced the Antifederalist predictions true already by 1792. He was far from alone in his thinking. Antifederalists who had predicted that powerful leaders in a distant national capital would have the incentive and the ability to accrue additional powers believed their predictions were coming true before their very eyes, policy by policy. The opinion of Spencer Roane was indicative of what many Republicans thought during and immediately after the Federalist era: "Notwithstanding the opinion of the Federalist, the prophecy of the opponents of the Constitution turned out to be true."[21]

Time and again during the ratification debate, Antifederalists stressed that a few offending constitutional clauses would allow the national government to expand. Federalist assurances to the contrary seemed either highly technical, as was Madison's explanation of the necessary and proper clause in Federalist #44, or glib, like James Wilson's protestations that the Constitution granted only limited, expressed powers. In the rough and tumble of politics it seemed doubtful that the fine distinction Madison was making (that the clause applied only to powers already expressly granted to Congress) would hold. On the other hand, Wilson's argument seemed disingenuous to the Antifederalists, as it did not square with the tenor of the document. When Publius and Wilson were critiqued in this way by their opponents, Federalists chose to remain silent instead of offering counterarguments.

Judging from hindsight, it is apparent why the Federalists could not adequately respond. Taken as a whole, the American experience vindicates Antifederalist predictions about the nationalization of politics. The federal government has indeed accrued power, often without benefit of constitutional amendment. The growth of national power has been mainly incremental rather than wholesale, just as most Antifederalists believed it would be. And there is little doubt that the clauses that caused the most consternation in 1787 and 1788 are at the heart of the growth of national power. One legal scholar puts it this way: "The most accurate predictions . . . actually came from Antifederalists. It was they who foresaw that the 'general welfare' and 'necessary and proper' clauses in the Constitution could readily legitimize sweeping changes in the balance of national versus state powers."22

Antifederalists believed that the growth of national power would have a corrosive effect on the relationship between citizens and their government. Above all, the success of a republic depended on the belief among citizens that the regime was *theirs* in the collective sense. This "confidence," as many Antifederalists called it, could not be sustained or cultivated without common citizens serving as representatives, their preferences receiving significant consideration in the formation of government policy. The Constitution would inevitably shrink confidence, its critics argued, because on implementation it would limit the political opportunities of average citizens and produce policies that only slightly corresponded to their hopes if at all. Unfortunately, confidence would continue to decrease as the national government accrued more and more power. In time, they despaired, confidence would be so low that citizens would not think of the government as their own.

This loss of confidence was not just an unfortunate occurrence in the minds of the Antifederalists; it was dangerous. A widespread popular belief that the government's products are collectively "ours," at least in a figurative sense, helps a nation to function. Laws are inevitably not to all citizens' liking, even in the most homogeneous state. If citizens retain a sense of confidence in the regime, they feel an obligation to obey laws that they may not agree with, partly out of deference to their fellow citizens and partly because they are sure that other policies will be more to their liking. By contrast, when citizens lack confidence in the regime, they are disgruntled; the only incentive for them to follow government mandates is to avoid the retribution that would be visited on them if they do not obey. Execution of a government lacking the people's confidence relies on coercion and force rather than voluntary compliance. The necessity of government coercion was a key sign for the Antifederalists that the government was not "of the people."

If Antifederalists were able to view American politics today, they would likely be struck with how little confidence citizens have that the United States government and its policies are theirs. There is plenty of patriotism, to be sure, and a sense that the United States is a great country, if not the greatest country in the world. But often these sentiments are divorced from the national government and its policies. At most, the national government is defended as providing necessary and beneficial services. Rarely is it cited as a key factor in America's successes. Even though citizens identify strongly with the nation, they arguably do not feel a part of national governance.

Many Americans are convinced, sometimes with good reason and sometimes not, that the policies of the federal government do not reflect their wishes and hopes. Antifederalists would find their prediction in this regard validated. The key question they would pose for America's future is: Can a nation of more than 280 million, sharing little more than a Constitution and a vast land mass, ever acquire or reacquire such a feeling? If we cannot, government will be more like the Antifederalists predicted it would become — enforced, rather than followed willingly, even happily. The need for enforcement will, in turn, foster even more resentment, necessitating firmer enforcement — a downward spiral. The Antifederalists deserve a reputation as astute political theorists for their articulation and grasp of this psychological sense of confidence, a sense required to successfully realize popular government.

The Antifederalists, more than any other political theorists with the possible exception of Rousseau and Montesquieu, had a keen sense of how the size of the polity, especially its population, affects politics. They directly articulated a premise hinted at by Machiavelli and Plato: that it is proportionally more difficult to foster the attachment required for successful governance as the regime's population grows. What is surprising is how little this principle has been articulated by scholars or appreciated in the modern age, when nations contain unprecedentedly large populations. Rarely do we stop to realize that the entire population of the United States in 1789 was smaller than that of an average state today. The political consequences of America's population increasing nearly 100-fold since the Revolution are direct and tremendous. Describing these political effects more fully is a charge that modern political theory cannot ignore.

The Antifederalists had an active hand in government during the Federalist era and beyond. As such the regime founded was not their ultimate nightmare, and "ratification did not inaugurate the countless horrors envisioned by the Anti-Federalists. Yet, the inexorable process they foresaw reached fruition."[23]

Lessons

In the last two decades particularly, there have been several commentators who have seriously plumbed the character of the Antifederalist argument in a way that had not been done in the nearly two centuries before. Herbert Storing's and Michael Lienisch's assessments, especially, demonstrate that the Antifederalists were not intellectual pushovers.[24] My research shows that the Antifederalists were not lightweights in the political arena either, even, and perhaps especially, after ratification — in part because of their key role in the Constitution's legitimation and their contributions to practical politics.

A particular strength of both Storing and Lienisch is an emphasis of the Antifederalists' conservatism. Bringing this aspect of their thought to the fore was particularly important after a few overeager Progressive and neo-Progressive scholars confused their own political hopes with those of the Constitution's critics. Staughton Lynd is the best example. Lynd argued that rank-and-file Antifederalists were radicals, committed to breaking down class distinctions. In his eyes, Antifederalist leaders failed their constituencies because of their limited commitment to radical politics. Though the Antifederalist leaders were not radical in Lynd's assessment, they should have been so: Lynd accusingly relates that Antifederalist leaders were "sunshine radicals and summer subversives, if they were really radicals and subversives at all."[25] The point Storing, Lienisch, and I drive home is that the Antifederalists never hoped, wanted, nor strove to be radicals or subversives. Instead they believed that radicals and subversives, defined as those who might work outside legally recognized bounds to obtain their political wishes, inevitably harmed the prospects for a viable government and even freedom itself.

The point has yet to fully sink in. Even now, some authors tread closer to Lynd than to Storing and Lienisch. I have cited Saul Cornell's work in several chapters, finding much of his analysis accurate and helpful in understanding the Constitution's critics. Cornell does recognize the conservatism of Antifederalist leaders, particularly in his new book *The Other Founders*, but he portrays the rank-and-file Antifederalists as much more radical. Cornell stresses that the Carlisle riot drove a deep wedge between populist Antifederalists, who were very hostile to the Constitution, and their leaders, who were so shocked by the riots that they embraced the Constitution as a means of maintaining order. "By focusing too narrowly on the delegates to the state ratifying conventions and leading Anti-Federalist politicians," writes Cornell, "studies of ratification have underestimated the depth of hostility to the new Constitution characteristic of grass-roots Anti-Federalism."[26] But if grassroots Antifederalists were so hostile to the Constitution and remained so after ratification there should have been more spontaneous popular uprisings. Yet Carlisle was a notable exception rather than an example of many towns in turmoil. Grassroots acquiescence did lag a bit behind acquiescence by Antifederalist leaders, mainly because average citizens were not as well acquainted with the details of republican political theory as were political elites. When Antifederalist leaders explained to their constituents why the Constitution was to be obeyed, the people readily did so. In truth, the public did accept the Constitution, and the relationship of Antifederalist leaders to their constituents did not turn adversarial after ratification, which it would have if the Antifederalist rank-and-file had been truly radical, as Cornell believes them to have been.

More troubling is Christopher M. Duncan's view in the conclusion of his recently published study of the Antifederalists' political thought. Duncan attempts to bring Antifederalism alive by finding the twentieth-century political group most like the critics of the Constitution. He asserts that the 1960s activists in Students for a Democratic Society (SDS) fit the bill.[27] Like the Antifederalists, those who framed the *Port Huron Statement* felt centralization had a pernicious effect on politics, stifling individual development, involvement, and control. What Duncan fails to mention, however, is how differently the leaders of SDS felt about radical thought and action. Whereas the Antifederalists did not dare act outside legal institutional bounds for fear of encouraging anarchy, the very purpose of the student activists in SDS was to break citizens out of their long-established, conventional way of thinking about politics. As a whole, the New Left movement is best characterized by a radical approach to constituted government, what has been called anarcho-Marxism, distinguishing it from the bureaucratically heavy-handed Marxist-Leninist regimes it disdained as much as the American regime. The New Left's departure from Antifederalism was, therefore, not a mere difference in tactics en route to the same end. Rather, theirs was a fundamentally different approach to the political. Accommodation and respect for legal boundaries were central to the Antifederalists' political vision; radicalism that would shake people out of their civic torpor was central to SDS.

One can imagine Antifederalists rolling in their graves at being compared to the student radicals of the 1960s. Neither, one suspects, would members of SDS savor being compared to politicians who could not find it in themselves to radically critique the constituted regime, even one formulated by their opponents. At any rate, the Antifederalists' postratification acquiescence makes clear how different they were from 1960s radicals — of whom Lynd was one, and Duncan avowedly is in spirit. This is not to say that either Antifederalism or student radicalism is a more correct political stance. The 1960s presented a far different political context than the early national period, after all, and perhaps each was appropriate in its time. But the 1960s should not be confused with the 1780s, particularly by historians and political theorists. In the early national period, the Union had little besides a mutual embrace of the Constitution holding it together. Continuing to dispute the Constitution after ratification may have ultimately resulted in governments closer to what the Antifederalists hoped for, but this could only have come at the expense of peace and union, things that the great majority of them were unwilling to risk.

Because the Antifederalists defended a form of political practice closer to the people than the Federalists, many think that they are fundamentally divorced from today's American regime and assume that they would be against it. Duncan's analysis is a case in point. In his book, Duncan stresses that the critics of the Constitution represent a "road not taken" in American politics, their arguments indicative of a "dead language" of civic republicanism. But in fact, the Antifederalists helped make the American regime what it is. Their acquiescence deeply implicates them in the present regime, for they chose to work within it rather than against it. As defective as they would find politics today, it would be entirely out of character for them to advocate radical solutions to change the constituted regime. To quote Antifederalist Elbridge Gerry, "Those who, whilst [the Constitution] was depending, were for critically examining and correcting it, will now be among the last to give it up, because they well know we cannot always be new-modelling our system."[28] Thus the story of the Antifederalists, often thought to be one of subversives and outsiders, is really about conservatives and insiders.

It is generally assumed that to qualify as "political theory," one's political outlook must be fairly comprehensive, relatively stable, and somehow, through reasoning and logic, rise above mere political preference. Certainly the more articulate individuals on either side of the ratification debate do, then, qualify as political theorists. By extension, the Antifederalists and the Federalists did have competing political theories. The extensive theorizing that preceded implementation of the Constitution occurred before practical political matters could be worked out under its auspices, though. This makes the years after implementation an excellent time to discern how political practice intersects with and affects political theory.

Attention to three groups, Federalists, Madisonians, and Antifederalists, through the year 1800 shows that political orientations were fairly stable. The Antifederalists, for instance, consistently fought to preserve state autonomy and limit the reach of the national government. After ratification they could only do so in a constrained way, within the bounds of a constitution that clearly sanctioned national solutions to certain matters. Thus the experiences of the Antifederalists show us one way in which political theory is constrained: in a constituted regime there are certain political options that are not available or defensible. The critics of the Constitution could no longer pursue true confederation and almost pure state sovereignty after ratification, as beneficial as they believed keeping sovereignty at the state level would be. Either their political theory was forced to evolve or some of its dictates were subordinated to accommodation and the pursuit of practical concerns.

The philosophies of the Hamiltonian Federalists and the Madisonians were fairly stable as well. The Hamiltonian Federalists did, of course, turn out to be more aggressively nationalist than most of their public writings of 1787–88 indicated. Yet this was not due to a change of heart so much as an unfolding of their true design, discernible through close attention to private writings. Hamilton and those like him had suppressed this preference to achieve ratification. The political philosophy they presented during the ratification debate obscured a rift that was to quickly become apparent after implementation of the Constitution and to dominate the national political scene. Hamilton, through Publius, had insisted that no one had any plans for a purely national government, even though he hoped to administrate just that kind of regime into existence. Madison also downplayed the possibility that his allies aimed at creating a much more powerful national government than the Constitution authorized, perhaps thinking that they would take the limited powers set down there as seriously as he did.

A second constraint of political theory therefore becomes apparent when observing the two Federalist factions: when political theory is employed in the quest to sanction certain political options, and it always is to some degree, its authors may not be as interested in a full airing of their views as they are in persuasion. Political theories often have an element of propaganda in them. Key questions in assessing theories must be what is left unstated? and what is assumed beneficial? Once their omissions and assumptions are recognized, to what extent is the goal being sought worthy and workable regardless of them?

Additionally, because the ratification process was defined by compromise, inaugurating a hybrid regime, no single group or person foresaw or controlled the outcome of the process in which they were involved. The Federalist project, which has been pointed to as a triumph of rationalist political theory, fell short of execution as a plan of social engineering. The American founders conducted an Enlightenment experiment in a Burkean world. The result was a surprisingly successful mix of two contrary impulses: the quest for active human control and the pull of tradition.

In any regime there are forces at work that are beyond the control and ken of even the most astute observer and powerful political actor. Republics in particular are fraught with the unforeseen and the uncontrollable, as policies are the result of compromise, including as they do many individuals and groups in the governing process. This is not a criticism of popular government. Rather, it is a lesson in humility for those who aspire to change republics through political theorizing or who passionately wish to achieve any particular political end. In a republic there are severe constraints on what any individual or group can achieve. This should not eliminate political hopes and dreams. It should make people realize that political hopes and dreams usually remain hopes and dreams, and that in a republic this is often a sign that popular government is working.

Finally, juxtaposing the political theory of the ratification debates against later political practice yields an important lesson about how the political theory of the era should be taught. Madison's embrace of partisanship and alliance with his former opponents was a result of the failure of his own prescriptive theory in Federalist #10: after ratification he found a majority faction was dominating the extended republic. Thus the idea that is often presented as the most enduring piece of political theory from the ratification debate was actually the most transient, the quickest to achieve obsolescence in the mind of its author. An accurate picture of the political legacy of ratification cannot be imparted simply by reading Federalist #10 and #51. Rather, one must be acquainted with the interplay of various actors and outside forces through time.

Many scholars believe the fundamental law has little inherent meaning. It is easy, after all, to cite examples of rights denied or court cases where the outcome seems to have been predetermined by the partisan bent of the judges involved. Pointing to modern, constitutionally sanctioned practices that would be wholly unfamiliar or distasteful to the founders is also easy. Vastly more important than the Constitution, from this neorealist perspective, are the subjective preferences of political elites or the public. In this view, constitutional law consists largely of post hoc rationalizations justifying already extant political wishes. That the Constitution itself impacts our politics is more difficult to document. Often one simply cannot tease out, except conceptually, the effect the document has had. Even when its impact is apparent, stories of cases to the contrary are more graphic than stories of the government working within its procedurally prescribed bounds.

My study reinforces the idea that the Constitution and the way we have treated it since ratification add an element to American politics outside of political preferences. After ratification the Antifederalists did not pursue state sovereignty to the extent that they did before, for instance. Additionally, the strong embrace of the Constitution by U.S. citizens has meant that it is difficult to justify major political innovations. In part, this is due to the rather cumbersome, localist institutions under which we still operate. Moreover, constitutional reverence itself can preclude major policy changes. For instance, one of the reasons that some Progressive-era legislation could be successfully struck down for so long was that the legislation itself was countermajoritarian in a certain way: it went against long-accepted constitutional doctrine. Citizens were squarely behind the Constitution, and if such laws were unacceptable under it, as judges told them was the case, then that was the way things had to be, despite policy preferences that could have sanctioned another outcome.[29]

The closeness of the American people to their Constitution is a kind of civic mythology. It is not necessarily true that the view closest to the wording or intent of the document prevails, but it is significant that the American public frequently believes this to be the case, and that constitutional doctrine is relatively stable. This, perhaps more than a tradition of local practice, is our ancient, unwritten constitution: that the Constitution provides the legitimate institutional, procedural, and even substantive bounds for politics. Though important, this belief is admittedly thin, for our embrace of the Constitution rarely definitively spells out those bounds. Indeed, modern requirements may change what had long been considered part and parcel of the Constitution.

Every nation, even one founded on Enlightenment principles, requires some belief to govern, belief in something authoritative, which forestalls potentially endless questioning of the legitimacy of governmental procedures, institutions, and policies. Finding some sort of consensual belief is especially challenging in a country without a common ethnicity, religion, social background, or conception of the good life. Mutual devotion to the Constitution helps prevent political chaos, despite American diversity and our time-honored dislike of politics. To foster belief in a sacred Constitution that preserved rights was, more than anything, Madison's vision and hope, for he knew that a consensual devotion to a constitution could provide stability that is so often lacking in politics. At this, Madison (with the help of his colleagues and the Antifederalists) succeeded brilliantly.

Many other current commentators feel that American constitutional practice has a strong influence on politics, but that this influence is, on the whole, quite negative. Michael Kammen, for instance, argues that worship of the Constitution contributes to troubling transgressions of the document, because the worship is blind. He hopes the "cult of the Constitution" will be replaced by a rational embrace. Leonard Levy faults the fiction of strict construction for stifling progressive policies. What matters far more than the intent of the framers, he says, is what might work best today. Advocates of a parliamentary model of government, like James Sundquist and Daniel Lazare, believe that the Constitution has stifled progress as well, by hindering majorities from forming policy.

Ideally, there would be neither ignorance nor impediments to beneficial innovations, of course. But politics is not an ideal thing; nor are people. We must tally the beneficial aspects of the Constitution with the negative aspects: rights are often ensured despite the limited attention paid to politics by much of the population. And, one suspects, some problematic and even dangerous innovations have been stopped in their tracks by tradition and the balance of powers. The hope for a uniformly rational embrace of the Constitution is a vain one. It comes mainly from those whose profession, academics, privileges a certain kind of overt rationality, often at the expense of what is possible or desirable for most people. Attempting to exchange belief for rationality would probably not result in an embrace of the Constitution, but rather foster dissensus.

I too am frequently frustrated by changes prevented by America's strong constitutional embrace. While I toy with the idea of a unitary parliamentary regime as a solution, I must simultaneously turn an eye to the constitutional implications of doing so. Such a major change would require renunciation of a long-functioning constitutional tradition. It would dictate relinquishing the theoretical goal of all constitutions — consensual support — in favor of reverting back several steps in constitutional time. Open for debate would be the specific contours of the new regime; if that was successfully determined, public support would need to be cultivated; if enough public support could be generated, it might be adopted; if adopted, the opposition minority would have to acquiesce to it; all of this before implementation would occur, which would produce its own challenges. That this process was successfully navigated once is no guarantee that it would again. In my view, the United States faces a dilemma. Our eighteenth-century constitution, which is almost universally revered, is not necessarily productive of the best politics, but attempting to scrap it in favor of a more responsive regime might well backfire.

That we have an unwritten constitution consisting of a traditional approach to constitutionalism means that it is difficult to replicate. Almost every nation has followed the American example in framing a written document to govern. What cannot be easily duplicated is the centrality of written constitutions in other nations' political lives. This is not to say that other attempts at written constitutions are inherently troubled; it is an acknowledgment that if written constitutions do not correspond with each particular nation's unwritten traditions and accepted practices, they will likely fail. One of the reasons that the Antifederalists' postratification argument resonated so well was that the Americans already had a century of experience in pointing to the controlling language of governmental charters during disputes. When the Antifederalists applied this concept to the national Constitution they were not making a major departure in political practice, but applying what was familiar to an altered scenario.

All written constitutions aspire to achieve what the American version has, consensual legitimacy. There is often great difficulty in making the transition from mere legality, mainly because foundings are often wrenching and divisive. At best, it seems, one can hope for majoritarian approval of a set of fundamental laws with a minimum of violence and coercion accompanying the ratification process. In the aftermath of legal acceptance, the minority must not be trampled on, but also needs to acquiesce to the will of the majority for there to be any hope of a quick transition to consensus. This acquiescence is based on a respect for the rule of law and a corresponding fear of anarchy.

Rarely do bested political minorities find themselves in the position of the Antifederalists: with incentives and the mind-set to cling to that which they had just vehemently disputed. Other fundamental laws can surely achieve consensual status, but these strivings cannot simply be patterned after a method that was once successful — favorable conditions must exist. The sine qua non of constitutional legitimacy is an acquiescent opposition. That the Antifederalists did acquiesce, and did legitimate the new Constitution, provides an additional reason why, to use the words of Elbridge Gerry, "the [present] government rests as much on the assertion of the Antifederalists as the Federalists."[30]

Ratification Chronology

1786

September	Annapolis Convention meets to promote commercial amendments; delegates meet only briefly, proposing a Constitutional Convention in Philadelphia in 1787
Fall	Debt-ridden farmers in western Massachusetts disrupt governmental proceedings

1787

February	Shays's Rebellion ends
February 21	Confederation Congress calls for Constitutional Convention
May 25	Constitutional Convention achieves quorum and begins its business
May 29	Virginia Plan introduced
July 10	New York delegates Yates and Lansing leave Philadelphia
July 16	Connecticut Compromise
September 12	Committee of Style reports final draft of the Constitution
September 17	Constitution signed by delegates at Philadelphia; transmitted to Congress
September 28	Congress transmits Constitution to states
December 7	Delaware ratifies (30–0)
December 12	Pennsylvania ratifies (46–23)
December 18	New Jersey ratifies (39–0)
December 29	Georgia ratifies (26–0)

1788

January 9	Connecticut ratifies (128–40)
February 6	Massachusetts becomes the first state to propose recommendatory amendments as it ratifies (187–168); nine amendments proposed

March 24	Rhode Island's towns vote against the Constitution
April 26	Maryland ratifies (63–11)
May 23	South Carolina ratifies (149–73)
June 21	New Hampshire becomes the ninth state to ratify (57 – 47), making the Constitution the supreme law in those states that had ratified. Twelve proposed amendments were recommended.
June 25	Virginia ratifies with recommendatory amendments (89–79)
July 2	Confederation Congress passes a resolution recognizing the legality of the Constitution and organizes a committee to suggest how to implement it
July 26	New York ratifies with recommendatory amendments (30–27)
August 2	First North Carolina convention decides not to ratify; proposes amendments
September 13	Confederation Congress passes ordinance calling for first federal elections
Fall–Winter	First federal elections held in several states

1789

Winter	First federal elections continue
March 4	Congress scheduled to meet
April 1	House of Representatives achieves quorum
April 6	Quorum reached in Senate
April 30	George Washington inaugurated as president
September 25	Congress passes twelve amendments to be sent to the states for approval, ten of which will be ratified as the Bill of Rights
October 2	President Washington transmits amendments to states
November 21	North Carolina's second convention ratifies (194–77)

1790

May 29	Rhode Island ratifies (34–32) with proposed amendments

1791

December 15	Bill of Rights ratified by three-quarters of the states

Members of the U.S. Congress
Who Voted in Ratification Conventions

In several chapters I presented data about those who voted in state ratification conventions and later served in Congress. Below is the full list of the 131 such individuals I identified. This sample was used to approximate a cross section of elite Antifederalists, Madisonians, and Federalists. Treating those who had been delegates to state ratification conventions provided a nearly foolproof indicator of one's Federalism or Antifederalism. When asked whether the Constitution should be the supreme law of the land or not, those who voted in conventions went on public record with their decision. For most other politicians of the era, the vast majority of whom are now obscure, we cannot make a perfectly reliable judgment on their position on the Constitution. This was a time when the thoughts of many politicians were guarded, either not committed to paper or presented under the cloak of anonymity. One could easily compile a list of politicians who took a clear stance one way or the other. Unfortunately such a list would likely be biased. We are more likely to know the positions of more prominent politicians; those who were most prominent tended to be more nationalist in outlook than political leaders in general. Also, selecting only those who took an unambiguous stance during the ratification debates would bias the sample toward ideological polarization. Ratification conventions presented political actors with a forced choice, allowing for the inclusion of the moderates who had to vote one way or the other, but did not definitively state their position until their vote. Thus a more accurate cross section of America's political leadership is provided by the 1,648 individuals who voted to ratify or not in the thirteen ratification conventions.[1]

As the "first branch" of government, Congress is the best place to study the interplay of politics and constitutionalism as practiced by former Federalists and Antifederalists. Given only general guidelines by the Constitution, it was largely up to the Congress to flesh out the federal government's bare bones. The debates over organizational structures and policies conducted in these years offer a rich vein of insight into the nation's early partisan struggles. All told there are 131 individuals who voted in a ratification convention and later served in Congress. Eighty-two were Federalists, while forty-nine were Antifederalists. This ratio corresponds almost exactly to the overall ratio of all those who voted in conventions.[2] If one further differentiates Federalists based on their post-ratification affiliations, there are forty-five who populated the Federalist Party and thirty-seven who joined Madison in forming the Republican Party. Among the Antifederalists are three individuals who voted for the Constitution. One of these three is Joseph Winston of North Carolina. Winston was a delegate to both the Hillsborough and Fayetteville conventions, only the latter of which ratified the Constitution. Although he voted to ratify at Fayetteville, when the new federal government was already operational, he voted against the document at Hillsborough. The other two are "ratifying Antifederalists" from New York, individuals who were elected as opponents of the Constitution in midstate New York and spoke against the document in convention, but voted to ratify so that New York would not be left out of the new Union. These two are Jonathan Nicoll Havens and John Smith.

Compiling this master list of the individuals who voted in ratification conventions and served in the federal Congress was done by checking if each one of the nearly 2,000 people who voted in ratification conventions appeared in *The Biographical Directory of the American Congress*.[3] The individuals listed below range from the well known and influential (for example, James Madison, James Monroe, and Timothy Pickering) to the utterly obscure (for example, Robert Whitehill, Samuel Earle, and Dan Ilsley). This sample of delegates appears representative of the entire population of ratification convention voters in a number of ways: every state is represented. In most states the ratio of Federalists to Antifederalists roughly reflects their overall strength at ratification. The distribution of Federalists and Antifederalists in the sample is a fair approximation of the relative strength of the two positions by region, as well as being generally indicative of relative populations.[4] In each region there were more Federalists than Antifederalists. In the North the ratio is slightly more than two-to-one.[5] In the mid-Atlantic the ratio is nearly one-to-one, while the South's ratio is right in the middle of the other two regions. There is significant representation from both sides in each region. The total number of state ratification convention delegates who served in Congress is presented in Table 5.1 in Chapter 5.

Naturally, many of these individuals served in more than one Congress. Table 6.1 in Chapter 6 compares the number of Federalists, Madisonians, and Antifederalists in the House and Senate by Congress. The Federalists are strongly represented in the initial Congresses, but after that their numbers quickly diminish. Except for a jump in the House during the Sixth Congress, the Federalist presence in Congress after the Second Congress consistently declines and after the Seventh Congress is small. Although not as strong as the Federalists initially, both the Madisonians and the Antifederalists seem more resilient. The strength of these two allied groups does not significantly diminish until the Tenth Congress. This pattern is consistent with the national trend of Federalists giving way to Republicans, who briefly held the majority in the House in the Third Congress, and then took it for good in the Seventh. Needless to say, the data presented here do not include all members of the House and Senate. During the first two Congresses roughly half of the membership had voted in ratification conventions. With the swelling of the House in subsequent years and the inevitable toll of time, the percentage of members who had voted in a ratification convention diminishes. Nevertheless, the partisan shifts in the House, and to a lesser extent the Senate, are mirrored by this sample of members.

These numbers also point to the conclusion that those who voted as Antifederalists were disadvantaged by the position they took, at least initially. In the first two Congresses the ratio of Antifederalists to Federalists in the sample is well below the overall ratio of the two groups in ratification conventions. In fact, if one compares the overall ratio of Federalists and Antifederalists who voted in state conventions with the ratio of Federalists and Antifederalists who populated the first four Congresses, the difference is statistically significant.[6]

Antifederalist weakness in the early House of Representatives probably breaks down into a number of discrete but related phenomena. First, many credible opposition candidates may not have run for fear of being defeated in the new political climate. Others ran and were defeated, partly due to their sullied reputations but also perhaps due to Antifederalist turnout being lower than that of the more interested Federalist voters. Because of the selection process of the Senate, it is easier to see the direct reason why a "critical shift" occurred between 1787 and 1789, one benefiting the Federalists at the expense of Antifederalists. With the exception of Virginia and Rhode Island, the legislatures of the states were controlled by Federalists in the years immediately following ratification. In several states, most notably New York and North Carolina, this represents a major shift in the composition of the state legislature from 1787. The Federalist-dominated state legislatures also framed election laws, several of which were biased in favor of a Federalist-dominated House delegation.

Also important to note is the total number of terms served by the three groups. The Federalists served 70 terms in the House (not all of them full terms, of course), while the Madisonians served 99, and the Antifederalists served even more, 127. In the Senate, Federalists served in fifty-eight Congresses, while the Madisonians served in significantly less, thirty-four, and the Antifederalists only twenty-eight. This disparity is striking, particularly considering the numbers of terms served in the House show precisely the opposite pattern. Part of the reason for this is the difference in the electoral structure of the two institutions. The Federalists designed the Senate, with its six-year terms and separate electoral classes, to be more insulated than the House. The effects of the critical shift that swept the Federalists into power in 1789 thus lasted longer in the Senate than in the House. Yet this does not explain why Antifederalist and Madisonian numbers do not significantly rise after the Third Congress, lagging behind the House perhaps, but still exhibiting the same general pattern. This may be partly because of the higher profile of key Federalists; but it also may indicate that the critical shift in states as a whole (and thus in their state legislatures) refused to fade even while in particular districts popular elections were more likely to put former Antifederalists in the House. Clearly there were many Antifederalists and Madisonians who were potential candidates for Senate seats, many of whom were willing to serve in national office. For whatever reason many fewer of them served in the Senate than one might expect.

Scholarship on the Federalists and Antifederalists has pointed to the possibility of some systematic differences between the groups that can be tested using this sample. Stanley Elkins and Eric McKitrick raised the question of the relative ages of Federalists and Antifederalists, drawing from a list of nine leading individuals on each side.[7] Elkins and McKitrick found "the age difference between these two groups is especially striking. The Federalists were on the average ten to twelve years younger than the Anti-Federalists."[8] They hypothesized that the Federalist movement was successful because of the boundless energy of their younger adherents, like Alexander Hamilton and James Madison. These fellows had been quite young during the Revolution and had cut their political teeth when the "nation" was acting in concert in the field against the British. The older Federalists had all distinguished themselves as national figures in the War for Independence. By contrast, most of the Antifederalists had been active in colonial politics before the outbreak of the Revolution. Despite a warning by Jackson Turner Main that "a few selected examples do not prove a point," the impression that the Antifederalists antedated the Federalists and were stuck in an older mode of thinking is commonly cited. For instance, Thornton Anderson, in his 1993 book on the ratification convention, *Creating the Constitution*, writes, "The latter

TABLE B.I

*Federalist and Antifederalist Ages at Ratification
and upon First Election to Congress*[a]

	Age at Ratification			Age when First Selected to Congress		
	Federalists	Madisonians	Anti-federalists	Federalists	Madisonians	Anti-federalists
20s	4	5	7	3	—	1
30s	17	16	16	9	11	7
40s	14	11	16	18	19	21
50s	8	3	6	11	3	11
60s	2	—	—	4	2	4
70s	—	—	—	—	—	1
N=	45	35	45	45	35	45
Mean	40.9	38.3	39.5	45.3	43.3	47.7

SOURCE: Compiled by author using data from *The Biographical Directory of the American Congress.*
[a] The birth years of four Antifederalists and two Madisonians are unknown. The data compiled here do not include these six individuals.

[Antifederalists] were generally older men whose political thinking had been shaped by the Country ideology in the struggles of the 1760s and 1770s."[9]

Elkins and McKitrick made two distinct claims, a more narrow one about the character of the top echelon of leaders on each side of the ratification debate and a general observation on political socialization during the revolutionary era. The socialization thesis pertains to all of the individuals in our sample and would lead one to believe that the state-centric Antifederalists would be those in politics prior to the Revolution, making them significantly older than the Federalists, who learned about politics (that the American "nation" was relevant political terrain) during the Revolutionary War itself.

The data, however, show that this is not the case. As a whole Antifederalists were no older than Federalists at ratification (see Table B.1). In fact, the Federalists are the oldest of the three groups here. That being said, the average ages of these three groups at ratification are not greatly different. However, it is not true that the younger one was at ratification, the more likely one was to be a Federalist. A majority of each group was in their thirties and forties when the Constitution was ratified: 69 percent of Federalists were this age, compared to 77 percent of Madisonians and 71 percent of Antifederalists. Of the three groups, the

Federalists were least likely to be in their twenties or thirties when the Constitution became law (ages ranging from eleven to twenty-seven when the Declaration of Independence was signed). Sixty percent of the Madisonians were in their twenties or thirties at ratification compared to 51 percent of Antifederalists and 47 percent of Federalists. The Federalist group also has the least number of those who were youths during the Revolution, those in their twenties at ratification (9 percent versus 14 percent of Madisonians and 16 percent of Antifederalists). Conversely, a greater percentage of Federalists were in their fifties or sixties than either of the other groups.

The criteria for the sample may slightly skew Antifederalist ages to the younger side, as many Antifederalists did not get a chance to be in Congress during the first four Congresses, when Federalists dominated. In other words, some of the older Antifederalists could have found themselves too old for Congress or may have died by the time an opportunity presented itself. However, looking at their ages when first chosen to Congress indicates any skew is not great. If it were large, then we would expect Federalist ages at first election to be significantly lower than that of Antifederalists. But the difference in age at first election is slightly more than two years, a time span that indicates only a fairly modest "crowding out" effect of older Antifederalists. In short, in this sample there is not a major difference in the ages of Federalists and Antifederalists. In fact, what is striking is how similar the two populations are. Although the criteria of the sample may bring their ages slightly closer together than in the whole population of both groups, any disparity seems small enough to conclude that one group is not significantly different in age from the other, certainly not enough to conclude that their socialization patterns are different because they are of two separate political "generations." Elkins and McKitrick's conclusion about the leading lights of the Federalist movement may still be valid, but one should not mistake this claim, based on two lists of nine names, for a more general one about the nature of Federalists and Antifederalists as a whole.[10]

The data compiled on length of tenures presented in Chapter 6 raises the question of why individuals left Congress during its early years. Reasons for the termination of tenure are listed in *The Biographical Directory of the American Congress* and several other sources. I employed these sources to determine why individuals in the sample left Congress. Table B.2 shows that only 8 percent of Federalists, 4 percent of Madisonians, and 12 percent of Antifederalists were unsuccessful in their attempt at reelection. Meanwhile 44 percent of Federalists either resigned midsession or "declined further candidacy." The percentage of Madisonians and Antifederalists who left office voluntarily is smaller, but still

TABLE B.2

Reason for Termination of Congressional Service

	Federalists	Madisonians	Antifederalists	Bogue et al.[a]
Died	3 (6%)	2 (4%)	13 (22%)	5%
Unsuccessful Reelection Attempt	4 (8%)	2 (4%)	7 (12%)	6%
Expelled	— —	2 (4%)	— —	—
Declined Further Candidacy	7 (15%)	10 (20%)	8 (13%)	18%
Resigned Midsession	14 (29%)	7 (14%)	5 (8%)	26%
No Information	20 (42%)	27 (54%)	28 (47%)	45%
Total	48	50	61	454

SOURCE: Compiled by author.
[a]Bogue et al. studied House members only, and these percentages are a compilation of all those who entered the House in the first eleven Congresses.

quite a bit larger than those who left involuntarily. One of every three Madisonians left office voluntarily compared to one of every five Antifederalists. Unfortunately there is no information on the termination of tenures for about half of each group. Although some of these "unknowns" may have tried to retain their office and lost, it seems plausible that many more from this category were content to leave the national capital behind, because an electoral loss by a sitting member of Congress was rather notable at the time and was likely to have been recorded. The number of unknowns is within five percentage points of the number Bogue et al. tallied for the entire Congress during this era.[11]

The Antifederalists had a startling streak of bad fortune with their health. Although the Federalists' and Madisonians' death rate is very close to the 5 percent that Bogue et al. find for the entire Congress from 1789 to 1810, 22 percent of Antifederalists died while serving in Congress. Thirteen of their tenures (of sixty-one overall) were ended by death. Only two of the Antifederalists who did not live out their terms were over the age of fifty-seven, and their mean age at death was fifty-three, compared to the Federalists' fifty-seven. Although reasons for expiration are, of course, as individual a matter as can be, it may not be purely a matter of "bad luck" that the Antifederalist death rate is five times higher than that of the Federalists. Since more Antifederalists hailed from rural or frontier districts, they had a longer and more arduous path to travel to and from the capital than the Federalists. In the early years of the republic traveling a far distance meant facing primitive and dangerous conditions and exposing oneself to the coastal lowland diseases prevalent in Philadelphia and Washington, but not present in mountainous or inland regions. These factors may have been enough to contribute to death in a number of cases. Further information about these deaths is, however, fairly scarce, so this hypothesis must remain somewhat speculative. The Constitution's critics found nationally oriented politics problematic not merely from a policy standpoint, they also found it deadly.

Below is the full sample of those who had voted in ratification conventions and later served in Congress, along with information about their partisan affiliation, state, and the Congresses they served.

Members of U.S. Congress Who Voted in Ratification Conventions
(Madisonians italicized)

Lemuel J. Alston	F-SC	H 10-11
Fisher Ames	F-MA	H 1-4
John Baptista Ashe	F-NC	H 1-2
Robert Barnwell	F-SC	H 2
Bailey Bartlett	F-MA	H 5-6
Richard Bassett[a]	F-DE	S 1-2
John Beatty	F-NJ	H 3
Lemuel Benton	F-SC	H 3-5
Phanuel Bishop	A-MA	H 6-9
Theodorick Bland	A-VA	H 1
Timothy Bloodworth	A-NC	H 1, S 4-6
Thomas Blount	F-NC	H 3-5, 9-10, 12
William Blount	F-NC (TN)	S 4
Benjamin Bourne	F-RI	H 1-4
Shearjashub Bourne	F-MA	H 2-3
William Bradford	F-RI	S 3-5
Nathan Bryan	A-NC	H 4-5
Aedanus Burke	A-SC	H 1
William Butler	A-SC	H 7-12
Samuel Jordan Cabell	A-VA	H 4-7
George Cabot	F-MA	S 2-4
Joseph Calhoun	A-SC	H 10-11
Isaac Coles	A-VA	H 1, 3-4
Tristram Dalton	F-MA	S 1
James Davenport	F-CT	H 4-5
John Davenport Jr.	F-CT	H 6-14
John Dawson	A-VA	H 5-13

William Johnston Dawson	F-NC	H 3
Joseph Dickson	F-NC	H 6
Samuel Earle	F-SC	H 4
Benjamin Edwards	F-MD	H 3
Oliver Ellsworth	F-CT	S 1-4
William Few	F-GA	S 1-2
William Findley	A-PA	H 2-5, 8-14
John Fowler	A-VA (KY)	H 5-9
Jonathan Freeman	F-NH	H 5-6
Frederick Frelinghuysen	F-NJ	S 3-4
George Gale	F-MD	H 1
James Gillespie	A-NC	H 3-5, 8
Christopher Gore	F-MA	S 13-14
William Grayson	A-VA	S 1
Jonathan Grout	A-MA	H 1
William Barry Grove	F-NC	H 2-7
Wade Hampton	A-SC	H 4, 8
John Andre Hanna	A-PA	H 5-9
Thomas Hartley	F-PA	H 1-6
Jonathan Nicoll Havens [bc]	F-NY	H 4-6
Benjamin Hawkins [d]	F-NC	S 1-3
John Sloss Hobart	F-NY	S 5
James Holland	F-NC	H 4, 7-11
Samuel Hopkins	A-VA (KY)	H 13
John Hunter	F-SC	H 3 S 4-5
Dan Ilsley	A-MA	H 10
Ralph Izard	F-SC	S 1-3
George Jackson	F-VA	H 4, 6-7
James Johnson	F-VA	H 13-16
William Samuel Johnson [c]	F-CT	S 1-2
Samuel Johnston	F-NC	S 1-2
Walter Jones	F-VA	H 5, 8-11
Rufus King	F-MA (NY)	S 1-5, 13-18
Martin Kinsley	A-MA	H 16
John Langdon[e]	F-NH	S 1-6
Amasa Learned	F-CT	H 2-3
Henry Lee	F-VA	H 6
Samuel Livermore [cf]	F-NH	H 1-2, S 3-7

Matthew Lock	A-NC	H 3-5
James Madison	*F-VA*	*H 1-4*
Humphrey Marshall	F-VA (KY)	S 4-6
John Marshall	F-VA	H 6
Stevens T. Mason [c]	A-VA	S 3-8
George Mathews	*F-GA*	*H 1*
Joseph McDowell	A-NC	H 5
Joseph McDowell	*F-NC*	*H 3*
Duncan McFarland	A-NC	H 9
Alexander Mebane	A-NC	H 3
John Francis Mercer	A-MD	H 2-3
Stephen Mix Mitchell	F-CT	S 3
James Monroe	A-VA	S 1-3
Andrew Moore	*F-VA*	*H 1-4, 8, S 8-10*
Frederick A. C. Muhlenberg [d]	*F-PA*	*H 1-4*
Wilson Cary Nicholas	*F-VA*	*S 6-8, H 10-11*
George Partridge	F-MA	H 1
Timothy Pickering	F-PA (MA)	S 8-11, H 13-14
Charles Pinckney	*F-SC*	*S 5-7, H 16*
William Pinkney [d]	A-MD	H 2, 14, S 16-17
Samuel J. Potter	A-RI	S 8
Richard Potts	F-MD	S 2-4
Levin Powell	F-VA	H 6
Jacob Read	F-SC	S 4-6
John Rhea	*F-NC (TN)*	*H 8-13, 15-17*
John Richards	*F-PA*	*H 4*
Cornelius Schoonmaker	A-NY	H 2
Thomas Scott	F-PA	H 1, 3
Theodore Sedgwick	F-MA	H 1-4, S 4-5, H 6
John Sevier [d]	*F-NC (NC/TN)*	*H 1, H 12-13*
Roger Sherman	F-CT	H 1, S 2-3
Thomas Joseph Skinner	*F-MA*	*H 4-5, 8*
John Smilie	A-PA	H 3, 6-12
Daniel Smith	*F-NC*	*S 5, 9-10*
John Smith [b]	F-NY	H 6-8, S 8-12
Josiah Smith	*F-MA*	*H 7*
O'Brien Smith	A-SC	H 9
Richard Dobbs Spaight	*F-NC*	*H 5-6*

Thomas Sprigg	F-MD	H 3-4
Joseph Stanton Jr.	A-RI	S 1-2, H 7-9
John Steele	F-NC	H 1-2
Michael Jenifer Stone	F-MD	H 1
Caleb Strong	F-MA	S 1-4
William F. Strudwick	A-NC	H 4
Jonathan Sturges	F-CT	H 1-2
Thomas Sumter	A-SC	H 1-2, 5-7, S 7-11
Absalom Tatom	A-NC	H 4
Thomas Tredwell	A-NY	H 2-3
Abraham Trigg	A-VA	H 5-10
John Trigg	A-VA	H 5-8
Phillip Van Cortdland	F-NY	H 3-10
Joseph Bradley Varnum[cg]	F-MA	H 4-12, S 12-14
Jeremiah Wadsworth	F-CT	H 1-3
Matthew Walton	A-VA (KY)	H 8-9
Anthony Wayne	*F-PA (GA)*	H 2
Robert Weakley	A-NC (TN)	H 11
Alexander White	F-VA	H 1-2
John Whitehill	A-PA	H 8-9
Robert Whitehill	A-PA	H 9-13
William Widgery	A-MA	H 12
Benjamin Williams	A-NC	H 3
John Williams	A-NY	H 4-5
Hugh Williamson	F-NC	H 1-2
Joseph Winston[b]	F-NC	H 3, 8-9
Henry Wynkoop	F-PA	H 1
Thomas Wynns	F-NC	H 7-9

Compiled by author based on *The Biographical Directory of the American Congress* and Kenneth C. Martis's *Historical Atlas of American Political Parties.*

[a] Although Martis does not list Richard Bassett as having served in the Second Congress, *The Biographical Directory* indicates that he served the full term.

[b] These three individuals are "ratifying Antifederalists," those who had opposed the Constitution but voted to ratify in convention to keep their state from being ostracized from the new regime. For purposes of analysis they are included among the Antifederalists.

[c] These five individuals left office before a Congress convened. Jonathan Nicoll Havens died before the Sixth Congress assembled; William Samuel Johnson resigned his Senate seat the day the Second Congress convened; Samuel Livermore resigned before the Seventh Congress convened; Stevens T. Mason died prior to the Eighth Congress's first session; and

Joseph Bradley Varnum resigned his House seat in the Twelfth Congress to move to the Senate.

[d] According to Martis, Benjamin Hawkins, Frederick Muhlenberg, William Pinkney, and John Sevier all supported the administration during their first term in Congress (later joining the Republicans). For Hawkins, Muhlenberg, and Sevier this was the First Congress, for Pinkney the Second. These designations have little meaning for Muhlenberg and Pinkney. As Speaker of the House, Muhlenberg did not vote on the floor and aimed to remain above partisanship. Because of a controversy over his eligibility for office (he had not lived in Maryland for seven years), Pinkney resigned without having voted in the Second Congress.

[e] In the first two Congresses John Langdon generally supported the Washington administration. By the Third Congress he had come to oppose it, and in the Fourth through Sixth Congresses he is classified as a Republican.

[f] According to Martis, Samuel Livermore generally opposed the Washington administration in the First Congress. In subsequent Congresses he supported the administration and was a Federalist.

[g] Joseph Bradley Varnum may have been a mild Antifederalist who was won over to the Constitution in the Massachusetts convention by the recommendatory amendments framed there. My search for reliable evidence of this stance proved fruitless, and thus I classify him as a Madisonian rather than a ratifying Antifederalist.

Reference Matter

Notes

Abbreviations Used in Notes

AC   *Annals of Congress*
DHFFC   Charlene Bangs Bickford et al., eds., *The Documentary History of the First Federal Congress*
DHFFE   Merrill Jensen et al., *Documentary History of the First Federal Elections*
DHRC   Merrill Jensen and John P. Kaminski, eds., *The Documentary History of the Ratification of the Constitution*
PAH   Harold Syrett and Jacob Cooke, eds., *The Papers of Alexander Hamilton*
PJM   William T. Hutchinson et al., eds., *The Papers of James Madison*

Preface

In recent years, most scholars writing about the critics of the Constitution have preferred "Anti-Federalists" to "Antifederalists." This change in nomenclature acknowledges that the traditional label was foisted on them by the Federalists. In doing so, the proponents of the Constitution painted their critics into a corner, as almost all who were politically literate thought of themselves as "federalist" in some way or another. All the while, the Antifederalists claimed to be the true federalists; they asserted the Federalist plan would destroy federalism by consolidating power in a centralized regime. I prefer to retain the original nomenclature. Rightly understood, it provides evidence of the political maneuvering, at times far from fair, that characterized the time. As long as it is recognized that the critics of the Constitution neither sought nor wanted this label, it strikes me as unnecessary to buck the tradition of two centuries. Political labels inevitably simplify and are often misleading. That very issue is an important component of this book and will be discussed extensively.

1. See Rakove's "Early Uses of The Federalist," 239.
2. Among the works that have aided in recovering Antifederalist thinking are Herbert Storing's multivolume documents collection, *The Complete Anti-*

federalist, 7 vols., including his analytical volume *What the Antifederalists Were For*; various works by Saul Cornell, particularly his recent book *The Other Founders*; writings of Michael Lienisch, such as "In Defence of the Antifederalists," in *History of Political Thought*; Richard E. Ellis, "The Persistence of Antifederalism after 1789," in Richard Beeman, Stephen Botein, and Edward C. Carter II, eds., *Beyond Confederation*; and other newly published documents collections, most notably *The Documentary History of the Ratification of the Constitution* (hereafter *DHRC*), 15 vols. to date, under the direction of Merrill Jensen and John P. Kaminski, eds.

3. Skowroneck, *The Politics Presidents Make*, 49–58. Also see Skowroneck's chapter "Presidential Leadership in Political Time," 125–70.

4. Viewing the founders from an unorthodox chronological angle can offer significant insights. In Drew McCoy's *The Last of the Fathers*, for instance, James Madison's retirement and old age are explored rather than his efforts as founder or president. This focus recaptures Madison's most mature thinking about American constitutionalism, the process of the founding, and the path the nation had taken forty years after ratification.

Chapter 1

1. H. L. A. Hart, in *The Concept of Law*, analyzes the difference between statutory and constitutional law he says necessarily exists in any reasonably complex society. "Primary rules," he writes, are those that obligate citizens to act a certain way, for example, rules against murder or stealing and so forth. "Secondary rules" are those of a constitutional variety that signify the proper process to make authoritative primary rules, for example, a proposal passed by a majority in parliament without veto from the king constitutes valid primary law (see particularly chapters 5 and 6). I wish to add that secondary rules (secondary really in Hart's label only) or constitutions vary in authoritativeness. Without something approaching consensual support for secondary rules, the authoritative nature of primary law becomes tenuous.

2. Hart puts it this way on p. 115 of *The Concept of Law*: "What is crucial is that there should be a unified or shared official acceptance of the rule of recognition containing the system's criteria of validity."

3. This argument applies to popular governments, not autocracies. Although the popular versus autocratic dichotomy is a simplification, it is easily recognized that despite written constitutions (many of which guarantee citizen rights) some governments rule more by force rather than consensual assent to the rules of the political game. The conceptually elegant premises of constitutionalism are nevertheless muddled by several factors: autocratic regimes may be consented to by the vast majority of inhabitants/citizens; more popular regimes contain plenty of apathetic, uninformed, or ill-informed citizens who might plausibly assent to constitutional rules for poor reasons; popular regimes usually have a greater capacity and tolerance for dissent and thus may have a more difficult time fostering consensus in that they allow/cultivate divergence of opinion. Despite these potential

shortfalls in the civic mythology of popular constitutional theory, it still seems valid to conclude that popular constitutions require broad-based popular and elite consent to be successful.

4. Elkins and McKitrick, *The Age of Federalism,* 32.

5. Bickford et al., *The Documentary History of the First Federal Congress,* (hereafter *DHFFC*), 12:764–65. In this record of a debate over whether to consider a Quaker petition condemning slavery New Jersey's Elias Boudinot declaims, "The Constitution is sacred; it is a rock that ought not to be moved." Speech delivered March 18, 1790.

6. Banning, "Republican Ideology and the Triumph of the Constitution," 167.

7. Boucher, *A View of the Causes,* lxix.

8. See generally Michael Kammen's *A Machine That Would Go of Itself*; Daniel J. Boorstin's *The Genius of American Politics*; Catherine Albanese's *Sons of the Fathers*; Jethro K. Lieberman's *The Enduring Constitution*; and Daniel Lazare's *The Frozen Republic.* The last book argues that devotion to the Constitution stifles democracy. I wish to point out an affiliated but much different concern: perhaps a constitution's ability to inspire something close to consensual support is related to the degree of connection the public perceives between the constitution and actual policies and politicians. The greater the perceived connection to politics, with its unsavory aspects — including zero-sum policy options — the less legitimate a constitution may seem. A conflict-deflecting superstructure of rules is not easy to create, particularly among a diverse, politically attentive populace well aware that a constitution inevitably sanctions policies with which they are not in full agreement. There is no assurance that a new set of decision-rules, even if more responsive than the Constitution, would be endowed with the same cast of legitimacy. Discarding the present Constitution would likely also mean setting aside consensual approval of the governing order, something of crucial importance in the successful governance of a huge, diverse polity.

9. Albanese, *Sons of the Fathers,* 217. These observations apply most directly to popular sentiments about the Constitution and how the document is treated by politicians. Though less ironclad, constitutional law scholarship and court decisions have generally hewn to this description as well. An exception is the fairly recent turn to neorealist constitutional law scholarship that views constitutional arguments mainly as post hoc rationalizations for favored political outcomes. I view the growth of this type of scholarship as an indirect product of reverence for the Constitution. The document is so long-lived and capacious that it has been used to justify countless political arrangements, even those strictly at odds with each other. Constitutional historians looking for a way to reconcile these disparate arrangements presume that skillful self-interestedness is responsible. While often true, there are many instances where one's conception of constitutionalism itself, rather than self-interestedness, is the crucial determinant of behavior. In Chapters 4 and 5 I argue that Joseph M. Lynch's neorealist view of the founding period is significantly exaggerated. Particularly in regard to James Madison,

Lynch's argument seems flawed. I revisit the subject of neorealist constitutional scholarship in my concluding chapter.

10. Powell, *The Moral Tradition*, 85 and generally.

11. Kammen, *A Machine That Would Go of Itself*, 46.

12. Ibid., 47.

13. Lienisch, *New Order of the Ages*, 160–61.

14. Ibid., 164–83.

15. The view of constitutional legitimation presented in *New Order of the Ages* is somewhat frustrating given Lienisch's own appreciation of the plausibility and significance of Antifederalist arguments. In his separate article, "In Defense of the Antifederalists," Lienisch concludes that the group's push for a bill of rights and for a meaningful role for the states in the federal system "made the constitution a sounder and stronger document. Indeed, ironic as it seems, it can be argued that without their efforts the constitutional republic could never have succeeded" (87). Perhaps Lienisch does not raise the Antifederalist role in legitimizing the Constitution in his later book because he intends it as "tunnel history," a relation of how the Federalists brought modernity to the United States. Even so, there is a chapter in the book on the Antifederalists, the theme of which is that they were bested in three crucial areas, "audacity, ambition, and adaptability."

16. Banning, "Republican Ideology and the Triumph of the Constitution," 167–88.

17. Boyd, *The Politics of Opposition*, 139.

18. Ibid., 163.

19. De Pauw, "The Anticlimax of Antifederalism," 113. That view is called into question by Bowling in "'A Tub to the Whale,'" 223–51. Bowling finds that the Federalists passed a sanitized list of amendments. The rights-oriented amendments they adopted limited the possibility that the Antifederalists' concerns about the structure of the new government could be addressed. Bowling's assessment of the Antifederalists' acceptance is similar to Banning's in that he sees the Antifederalist embrace as a reaction against Federalist policies in the new republic. In *Politics in the First Congress, 1789–91*, Bowling writes that "when the First Congress ended its sessions in March 1791, it would have been difficult not to recognize the existence of two loosely organized groups which held to opposing views about the meaning of the Constitution. Neither group attacked the Constitution; both swore by it" (243).

20. Elite Antifederalists, supporting a mixed government ideal, merely questioned whether the House of Representatives was large enough to provide the popular "estate" with adequate representation. Middling Antifederalists thought each branch of the government should be popular, without necessarily being wholly devoted to democratic control. Their problem with the Constitution was that none of its institutions was sufficiently popular, something only state institutions could accomplish. Populist Antifederalists were more devoted to democracy as we understand it, with public wishes being translated directly into public pol-

icy, and significantly more localist than the other two groups (see Cornell, *The Other Founders*).

21. Ibid., 118.

22. Ibid., 118, 139, 154.

23. Alternatively, an opposition group could fade out of existence or simply give up. As shown by my later discussion of the Antifederalists in Congress and the concluding chapter, neither was the case in the United States.

24. Unpublished Mercer manuscript of April or May 1788 contained in Storing, *The Complete Antifederalist*, 5:103. Mercer's views, as those of many Antifederalists, seem to have their roots in Montesquieu's observations in *The Spirit of the Laws*, where it was forcefully stated that only despotic regimes could range over a large land mass.

25. New York approved the Constitution with recommended amendments only after New Hampshire had effected ratification. Approximately two-thirds of the delegates at Poughkeepsie were Antifederalists. They acceded for fear New York City would no longer be the national seat of government or that it might secede from the rest of the state.

26. Morris, *The Forging of the Union*, 151. Also see Kaminski, *A Revolution in Favor of Government*.

27. From a Robert Whitehill speech in the Pennsylvania ratifying convention, November 28, 1787, in McMaster and Stone, *Pennsylvania and the Federal Constitution*, 257.

28. Of course the Carlisle rioters offer an important exception. It should be noted that Pennsylvania Antifederalists were particularly upset by events in their ratifying convention, where Federalists, with their firm majority, railroaded the Constitution through with little opportunity for debate or the possibility of recommending amendments. Federalists had hurriedly determined the meeting place of the state convention in the waning days of an Assembly, just prior to a state election they suspected might put them in the minority. To achieve the necessary two-thirds quorum for this purpose, two Antifederalists had been forcibly dragged through the streets of Philadelphia, back to the Assembly chamber. Federalists summarily dismissed their opponents' concerns, even keeping objections out of the minutes of the convention. Critics of the Constitution were verbally attacked more vehemently than in any other state, and their mail was frequently intercepted. Additionally, Pennsylvania had the most democratic state constitution in the era immediately after independence and its citizens were more accustomed to meaningful political participation than those in other states.

29. Adams quoted by Hosmer, *Samuel Adams*, 351. Also see Wells, *Life and Public Services of Samuel Adams*, 3:224–38.

30. Clinton speech to militiamen excerpted in the *New York Gazetteer*, March 12, 1787.

31. Ballagh, *The Letters of Richard Henry Lee*, 2:421. Lee letter to George Mason of May 15, 1787.

32. Massachusetts towns of any significant size were able to send delegates to

the state's ratifying convention. Certain of these towns had been the center of Shaysite actions, and some of them elected delegates who had participated in Shays's Rebellion — none were leaders of either the Federalist or Antifederalist forces. Hampshire County, the center of most of the lawless action, was by no means uniformly Antifederalist. Of its fifty-two delegates in the state ratification convention, more than one-third, nineteen, voted in favor of the Constitution. Among the Antifederalist Shaysites are Consider Arms, Malachi Maynard, and Samuel Field, who offered the reasons for their dissent in the *Hampshire Gazette*. I discuss this document briefly in Chapter 2.

33. I found only one Antifederalist who vowed not to give up the fight. Benjamin Workman, a young mathematics instructor at the University of Pennsylvania writing under the pseudonym Philadelphiensis. Storing, *The Complete Antifederalist*, 3:99–140. See particularly Letter VIII.

34. Ibid., 2:8. Gerry public letter sent to the Massachusetts legislature on October 18, 1787, and later printed in the *Massachusetts Centinel* on November 3, 1787.

35. Ibid., 2:27. Martin pamphlet printed in Baltimore on January 27, 1788.

36. Ibid., 5:165. "Republicus" letter printed by the *Kentucky Gazette* (Lexington), February/March 1788.

37. Cornell, *The Other Founders*, 117–20, 147, 156; Cornell, "Aristocracy Assailed," 1170–71.

38. Hirschman, *Exit, Voice, and Loyalty*. Consumer brand loyalty occurs largely because it takes significant time and effort to choose the optimal product from among many options. Political loyalty presents a slightly different situation. The range of polity types open to citizens are potentially endless but only hypothetical. Active pursuit of a polity fundamentally different from that in which one lives can have consequences far more grave than an investment of time and effort. Withdrawing one's loyalty and committing one's self to an alternative regime can be deadly. It also carries with it the possibility that stability will be undermined as there might be no consensually agreed on rules of the political game.

39. Michael Lienisch writes convincingly of the Antifederalists' conservatism in his article "In Defense of the Anti-Federalists" and his book *New Order of the Ages*. In chapter 6, he offers the observation that one of the most important reasons Federalists triumphed over the Antifederalists during the ratification fight was because of the former's "audacity," which the critics of the Constitution utterly lacked (140–45).

40. Banning, *The Sacred Fire of Liberty*, chaps. 6–8.

41. Federalist #37. Cooke, *The Federalist*, 269. Jack N. Rakove highlights this passage from *The Federalist* to stress that none could know how the Constitution would work in practice until implemented. He also points out that Madison's thoughts on how to properly interpret the Constitution were evolving well into the 1790s (*Original Meanings*, 341, 345–62).

42. The labels I use are based on two factors: positions on the Constitution and subsequent political affiliation during the 1790s. The Antifederalists are, quite obviously, those who opposed the Constitution. Almost all of them remained in the

same coalition, becoming Republicans in the 1790s. "Madisonians" are those who favored the Constitution, but later followed Madison's lead in splitting with the remaining Federalists led by Hamilton, who form the third group and were members of the Federalist Party. My terms are at once simpler than Anderson's and more accurate. Not all Antifederalists were wholly committed to state sovereignty, as Anderson implies. Anderson also counts Madison among the nationalists at the convention, which makes his later split with Hamilton very difficult to explain. In Chapter 4 I show that Madison's position toward the national government was more equivocal than Hamilton's, leading quite naturally to their falling out.

43. Anderson, *Creating the Constitution*, 83.

44. Jillson, *Constitution Making*, particularly chap. 2.

45. Beard believed the motivation for this quest to be self-interest.

46. Claiming that a group of politicians is less than fully forthright should not come as a surprise, as part of the art of politics is "spin" and shrewd restraint. Surely many Antifederalists shaded things as well, particularly in their sureness that the Constitution would be problematic.

47. Pocock, *The Machiavellian Moment*, chap. 15; and Storing, *What the Antifederalists Were For*, the opening volume of *The Complete Antifederalist*.

48. James Wilson holds the distinction of having the argument on the Constitution that was most widely known. He said that it was a document only of expressed powers. Part of the reason for its wide dissemination was its simplicity, something that Madison in Federalist #10 did not have going for it. In Chapter 3 I demonstrate that this speech of Wilson's was co-opted by the Antifederalists after ratification.

49. Kramer, "Madison's Audience," 611–79.

50. Matthews, *If Men Were Angels*. The subtitle of this book is *James Madison and the Heartless Empire of Reason*.

51. Wolin, *The Presence of the Past*. Kramnick's introduction to the Penguin edition of *The Federalist Papers*, esp. 47–54. Wolin calls the American regime "a meritocracy with a human face" that has so much difficulty "representing the remarkable diversity of American society" that it is better described as a "parody of equalitarianism" than a functioning democracy (4–5).

52. Banning, *The Sacred Fire of Liberty*; and Read, *Power versus Liberty*, chaps. 2 and 4.

53. Wood, "Interests and Disinterestedness in the Making of the Constitution," 102, 109.

54. Ibid., 69.

Chapter 2

Letter of Patrick Henry to James Monroe, January 24, 1791, in Henry, *Patrick Henry*, 2:460. Portions of this chapter were first published in the fall 1998 issue of *Studies in American Political Development* under the same title.

1. To keep the relationship between events and evolving positions straight, it is crucial to keep a rough timeline in mind. Pennsylvania ratified on December 12,

1787. The ninth state (New Hampshire) did so on June 21, 1788, making the Constitution the fundamental law of the states that had ratified, according to its own criteria. The first federal elections were held in the fall and winter of 1788–89, while the first meeting of the U.S. Congress and President Washington's inauguration took place in April 1789. The first session of the First Congress debated amendments to the Constitution beginning in June. Most Antifederalists' discomfort continued at least through September 1789, when Congress proposed amendments to the states. It took more than two years for ten of the twelve amendments to be ratified by the states and added to the Constitution as the Bill of Rights. The contemporaneous sources I quote in this chapter are mainly from June 1788 to April 1789, a time in which the Antifederalists could not know what kind of amendments would be adopted or even if there would be any. A more detailed ratification chronology is included as Appendix A.

2. Since each state ratified the Constitution on a different day, it is necessary to clarify my use of the term *ratification*. If I write of ratification in a particular state (for example, Pennsylvania) or "in the several states" I am referring to the specific date(s) on which that state (or those states) ratified. If I speak generically of ratification, then I am referring to the time when New Hampshire became the ninth state to ratify, thus fulfilling the requirement of Article VII of the Constitution that would allow implementation among the ratifying states. The Antifederalists' fears that the national government would not work out is why Cecelia Kenyon dubbed them "Men of Little Faith" in her well-known *William & Mary Quarterly* article of the same name. My view is significantly different. Given their deep skepticism about the new government, they showed great forbearance in acquiescing to the Constitution. For more on my view, see chapter 1 of my *The Antifederalists: Men of Great Faith and Forbearance* (forthcoming).

3. Jensen et al., *The Documentary History of the First Federal Elections, 1788–1790* (hereafter *DHFFE*), 1:250. Letter written to John Vandegrift, Nathan Vansant, and Jacob Vandegrift, August 15, 1788.

4. A near-unanimous norm in the ten states that had ratified the Constitution (including Virginia, which did so just four days after New Hampshire). In a qualified way the Antifederalists of New York may also be included here. I discuss New York more fully later in this chapter, explaining why its Antifederalists changed their stance while North Carolina and Rhode Island continued to hold out against ratification (see below, note 25).

5. Western Pennsylvanian Richard Bard estimated the ratio of men willing to take up arms in defiance of the Constitution at nine out of ten (February 1, 1788, *DHRC*, 2:712). In addition to the anti-Constitution riot in Carlisle, a petition urging the legislature not to verify the convention's ratification netted more than 6,000 signatures in the first three months of 1788, an astounding number for the time (see pp. 642, 692–93, 709–16, 718–25). Had Antifederalist leaders been unwilling to acquiesce to the Constitution after New Hampshire's ratification, they likely could have torn the state in two.

6. *DHFFE*, 1:262, 250. Hanna letter of August 15, 1788.

7. North Carolina and Rhode Island had yet to ratify at the time the new

government met for the first time. If a single state could have derailed the Federalists' constitutional revolution it is a certainty that one of these states or New York would have done so, as they had done during the confederation period. From June 1788 to April 1789 the nation continued to function under the Articles of Confederation at the same time that the Constitution was technically the law of the land, awaiting implementation. Refer to the ratification chronology in Appendix A.

8. Cornell, *The Other Founders*, 142–43.

9. Ibid., 200–18; Cornell, "Aristocracy Assailed," 1172.

10. The Whiskey Rebellion and later political events like the Nullification Crisis and the Civil War indicate that deep, lawless conflicts occur even with something approaching constitutional consensus. Even if self-restraint in pursuing the extralegal does not always result from constitutional consensus, it seems that it can be used to effectively mobilize power and public opinion to enforce what is legal, as was done in the Whiskey Rebellion.

11. Zaller, *The Nature and Origins of Mass Opinion*, chaps. 8, 9, 11.

12. Ibid., 270–72, 285.

13. Ibid., 267. This model of opinion leadership applies without too much difficulty to the earlier American context. In both contexts there are recognizable elites and opinion leaders, as well as active "media" sources that disseminated information. Although the documentary record from the late eighteenth century is less complete than something as contemporary as the Vietnam War (particularly in serial measurements of public opinion), this relative lack of information does not indict the theory, just its authoritative validation.

14. Although the Pennsylvania Antifederalists acted in a manner representative of Antifederalists in all the states that had ratified, one must take care not to assume that these professions were uniformly distributed throughout the nation, or even were so in the ratifying states. Since three state conventions had unanimously endorsed the Constitution, there were few Antifederalist leaders in those states to acquiesce. It has already been noted that acquiescence did not strictly apply to the states that had not yet ratified. Finally, because population and the press were unevenly distributed, more testimonials come from places like Massachusetts than Maryland. The number of professions varies from state to state just as the number of Antifederalists did.

15. Elbridge Gerry letter to the Massachusetts General Court, October 18, 1787. *DHRC*, 13:548–50.

16. *DHRC*, 14:220. John Quincy Adams diary entry of February 7, 1788. Letter to William Cranch of February 16, 1788.

17. Ibid.

18. *DHFFE*, 2:160. Mercer circular letter of December 20, 1788.

19. Ibid.

20. Meleney, *The Public Life of Aedanus Burke*, 145.

21. *DHRC*, 15:290. Quote of Boston tradesmen's resolves, January 7, 1788.

22. Ibid.

23. "Reasons for Dissent," in Storing, *The Complete Antifederalist*, 4:265.

24. *DHRC*, 10:1482, 1537, 1562, 1669, 1698, 1701–2, 1703n., 1715–16. Immediately after Virginia's ratification, Henry was asked to preside over a meeting of die-hard Antifederalists who wished to continue the fight against the Constitution. "He accepted, but once in the chair told his supporters that although he had opposed the Constitution, he had done so 'in the proper place.' The question was now settled, said Henry, and he advised those present that 'as true and faithful republicans,' they had all better go home" (Smith, *John Marshall*, 141). Also see De Pauw, "The Anti-Climax of Antifederalism," 108, 109.

25. Antifederalists in the holdout states of New York, North Carolina, and Rhode Island did not feel the same need to acquiesce as their counterparts in the states that had already ratified, because by the Constitution's own stipulation, it became the fundamental law only in the states that had ratified. Nevertheless, the New York Antifederalists did ratify quickly after New Hampshire and Virginia did so. In order to prevent Federalist New York City from breaking with the rest of the state and to keep it as the seat of government, Antifederalists chose to ratify with recommendatory amendments. See *DHFFE*, 3:207–9.

26. Heideking, "Federal Processions of 1788 and the Origins of American Civil Religion," 367–88. David Waldstreicher finds that Federalists used parades and other rituals "to ally their cause with that of the people and the nation." Such seemingly apolitical events helped to form a national consciousness, one that treated the Antifederalists rather schizophrenically. On the one hand, it threatened to leave Antifederalists "outside the magic circle of agreement and benevolence." But on the other, they "held out the promise of regeneration to Antifederalists" that "may help explain why Antifederalists were so quickly reconciled to the national government" (*In the Midst of Perpetual Fetes*, 90–98).

27. *DHFFE*, 1:55–56.

28. *DHFFE*, 3:206.

29. *DHFFE*, 2:397. Although the *Independent Gazetteer* had been strongly Antifederalist during the ratification debates, Philadelphia had been solidly Federalist.

30. Ibid., 258. Letter of August 31, 1788.

31. Given the Antifederalists' extremely poor showing in the first federal elections, it is apparent that the Federalists succeeded in their endeavor to win broad-based public support. In addition to the Antifederalist acquiescence, the continuation of the Federalist newspaper campaign after ratification was a major contributor to the "apotheosis" of the Constitution.

32. For example, *DHFFE*, 1:243–44. July 16, 1788, article in the *Pennsylvania Chronicle*, and pp. 251–52, an anonymous letter to James Hopkinson of August 17, 1788.

33. "Centinel" continued to write even after the ninth state ratified, trying to persuade readers that they should elect Antifederalists to Congress because they would secure the necessary amendments. Centinel did not dispute the Constitution's legal status after June 1788. He continued to employ strident language, however, still claiming the document was an aristocratic conspiracy. For this reason and his highly democratic principles, Centinel became something of an

embarrassment to other Antifederalists and easily fell prey to this Federalist lampooning.

34. *DHRC*, 16:134.

35. Yates, *The Secret Proceedings and Debates*, 306–7.

36. *DHFFE*, 1:548. December 8, 1788. These kinds of arguments were also made by candidates on their own behalf. Virginia's Arthur Lee, for instance, declared his candidacy for the U.S. Congress by writing, "In my Mind, it is the Duty of every good Man to submit to the Determination of the Majority of his Fellow-Citizens; and therefore, although in my Judgment, the Constitution required Amendments, previous to its Adoption, yet I shall always think it incumbent on me to support what the Convention — after a full and fair Discussion — has adopted, until it shall be altered in the Mode which the Constitution itself points out. For the same Reason, I shall deem it my Duty to use every Effort for obtaining those Amendments which have been sanctioned by so great a Majority of the Convention" (*DHFFE*, 2:352. Circular letter of January 1789).

37. New Hampshire's "A Friend to the People," for instance, made an impassioned plea against consideration of Samuel Livermore for the Senate because he opposed amendments. *DHFFE*, 1:776–77. November 1, 1788.

38. See, for example, the essay by "Truth" from the *Boston Gazette*, September 1, 1788. Ibid., 452–53.

39. Ibid.

40. On the seriousness with which the founding generation took oaths see Levinson, *Constitutional Faith*, chap. 3. New York's anti-Constitutional party even tried to stave off ratification by passing an oath that would have disqualified those who took it from ever changing the state's sovereign status. Letter of Philip Schuyler to Stephen Van Rensselaer, January 27, 1788, New York State Library Manuscript.

41. Levinson, *Constitutional Faith*, 91–92.

42. See Harold M. Hyman's 1959 book, *To Try Men's Souls: Loyalty Tests in American History*; and Milton Greenberg's 1955 Ph.D. dissertation, "The Loyalty Oath in the American Experience."

43. *Journal of the House of Delegates*, 3.

44. Maryland's *Votes and Proceedings of the House of Delegates*, November 4, 1788.

45. Batchellor, *Early State Papers of New Hampshire*, 367, 567, 726.

46. Bartlett, *Records of the State of Rhode Island and Providence Plantation in New England*, 380.

47. *Minutes of the Supreme Executive Council of Pennsylvania*, 16:96. June 16, 1789. Apparently these two left for their homes in the western part of the state very soon after June 16.

48. I used the last vote to approximate total attendance because some legislators arrived late to the session. With the legislative term lasting just seventeen days and held during the middle of winter, it is likely that very few left early, so this tally should serve as a fair approximation of total attendance.

49. Labaree, *Public Records of the State of Connecticut*, 7:71. Wadsworth

had been a delegate to the Confederation Congress in the legislative session of 1783–84 and again in 1785–86. He was also a former member of Connecticut's council. Also see *DHRC*, 3:563.

50. See Wadsworth letter of October 15, 1789, to Governor Samuel Huntington, in the microfiche supplement, *DHRC*, 3:365.

51. Yates, "History of the Movement for the United States Constitution," 223–45. The history is introduced by Staughton Lynd. Yates is quoted in Bielinski, *Abraham Yates, Jr. and the New Political Order in Revolutionary New York*, 50.

52. Bielinski, *Abraham Yates, Jr. and the New Political Order in Revolutionary New York*, 52. Needless to say, Yates was convinced that the Constitution, entrusted to Federalists, would never be amended. But just as his short history was being finished in June 1789, the Federalist-dominated U.S. Congress began discussing amendments. Perhaps this event, "so unexpected from Yates's bitter and suspicious viewpoint," brought him back to reality. For whatever reason, Yates decided against publication. See Lynd's introduction of Yates's history, 227. At least one other Antifederalist, Aedanus Burke, planned to write a history of the ratification process intended to convince the people that they had made a mistake. In preparation for his history, the South Carolinian sent a detailed questionnaire to two prominent Antifederalists, Elbridge Gerry and Samuel Bryan. Gerry was unable to respond, as the trunk in which he had placed the questionnaire was stolen before he read it. Bryan, the young Pennsylvanian who had penned the incendiary letters of "Centinel," seemed not to provide Burke the response he had anticipated, and in fact rejected the notion that a systematic conspiracy had taken place. See Saul Cornell's introduction of Bryan's response to Burke's questionnaire in the *Pennsylvania Magazine of History & Biography*, 103–30.

53. Lynd, "Abraham Yates's History of the Movement for the United States Constitution," 223.

54. The failure to adequately explain the postratification behavior of Antifederalists other than Yates (that is, almost all of them) further exposes the grave flaws in the early Progressive analysis. If the Constitution was formulated by and for the advantage of a small minority, and the Antifederalists, who did not hold government securities, adamantly argued against the proposed system, then after ratification they should uniformly have cried foul in the manner of Yates. There was no reason to acquiesce if the Constitution was an elite economic conspiracy. If the vast majority of people did not benefit, but in fact suffered, from the new aristocratic government, the Antifederalists should have continued trying to convince the people that they had been duped, precisely what Yates was attempting in 1789. In this scenario, the Antifederalists should have gone to their graves crying foul about the Constitution, but they did no such thing.

Surely many Federalists believed they would reap great economic benefits from the new system. But their personal windfall was not to come at the expense of others so much as along with the nation, as they believed that breaking down barriers to interstate commerce would yield greater general prosperity. When the Antifederalists focused on economics they also were not thinking primarily in terms of personal benefits or losses. Instead, they concentrated on economic rights and the potential danger in which the Constitution put those rights. Even someone whose analysis turned on economics like Yates was more concerned about safeguarding a constellation of rights than in protecting his individual or group economic status. The strong pull of political principles on both Federalists and Antifederalists is lost in the Progressive view; there is little appreciation that Antifederalists felt a sense of duty to law ratified by proper procedural means. It is no wonder that Lynd was so pleased to find an Antifederalist who thought in something resembling a Progressive manner after ratification. It is telling that this thinker was extremely atypical.

Other neo-Progressive historians, like Jackson Turner Main and Merrill Jensen, present a much more nuanced and accurate take on the economic incentives for and against ratification than Beard and Lynd. Main and Jensen convincingly show that regional economic interests were a prime determinant of stances for and against ratification. But after ratification, as I show, the Antifederalists pledged to abide by the Constitution despite their continuing concerns over the type of political economy it could usher in. Therefore, explaining Antifederalist stances after ratification requires one to focus more on ideology than on economics.

55. Volume 1 of the *DHFFE* points out that along with Atherton, Thomas Person of North Carolina "suggested that the state legislatures might refuse to hold federal elections until amendments were assured" (1:16).

56. *DHFFE*, 1:839. Letter of February 23, 1789.

57. Banning, *Jefferson & Madison*, 73.

58. Ibid.

59. Knupfer, *Union as It Is*, x, 1. The dissertation on which this book was based is titled "The Union as It Was." The latter title better expresses Knupfer's finding that mutual accommodation faded as the proper "template" for American politics. By 1861, the accommodationist spirit of the founding generation had given way, and citizens were willing to fight over a divisive issue like slavery, formerly considered the province of accommodationist politics. Drew R. McCoy nicely portrays this trend on a personal level in his comparison of James Madison and Edward Coles (*The Last of the Fathers*, chap. 7). While Madison decried slavery's existence every bit as much as Coles (younger by a generation), he did not pursue the same course because of disparate norms about politics. Madison sublimated his own disgust for the peculiar institution to the accommodative determinations of the polity, which continued to recognize its existence. Coles left his native Virginia when it became clear that it was not on a course to abolish slavery, moving to Illinois, where he freed his slaves. By comparison, Madison's stance seems hypocritical to us. Madison's position only becomes understandable, if not defensible, when one realizes how fragile he felt the new American polity was. The founding generation literally felt it needed to accommodate — even, or perhaps especially, on the issue of slavery — or there would not be a nation.

60. At least two scholarly articles have been written detailing the situation and plight of Antifederalists whose political careers were ended because of their

efforts at moderation. See Robin Brooks's "Alexander Hamilton, Melancton Smith, and the Ratification of the Constitution in New York," 339–58; and John P. Kaminski's "Political Sacrifice and Demise — John Collins and Jonathan J. Hazard, 1786–1790," 91–98. In the aggregate Antifederalists made a very poor showing in the first federal elections and may not have fully recovered electorally until 1800 (see Chapter 6 of this work and my chapter called "The Electoral Dynamics of Ratification" in *The House and the Senate in the 1790s*, Kenneth R. Bowling and Donald R. Kennon, eds.).

61. John Locke, with whom the founding generation was very familiar, warned in *The Second Treatise on Civil Government* that obtaining relief from government outside legal bounds was not to be undertaken on "slight occasions." Among other criteria, "where the injured party may be relieved, and his damages repaired by appeal to the law, there can be no pretense for force" (paragraphs 208, 207).

62. Originally published in Boston, this pamphlet was distributed and reprinted in New York.

63. Mercy Otis Warren quoted in Storing, *The Complete Antifederalist*, 4:281.

64. Ibid., 4:286.

65. Ibid.

66. Ibid., 6:215.

67. Ibid., 6:242.

68. Ibid.

69. Ibid., 6:240.

70. Bowling, "'A Tub to the Whale,'" 223–51.

Chapter 3

1. Billias, *Elbridge Gerry*, 215. Letter of July 28, 1788.

2. Gerry employed this extended metaphor in a letter to John Hancock: "The body politic . . . is not unlike a patient recovering from an acute disease," and that the patient's health was still "exceedingly delicate" (*DHFFE*, 1:658. Letter of February 26, 1789).

3. Ibid., 1:647. Circular Letter of January 22, 1789.

4. *DHFFC*, 11:831. From floor speech of June 8, 1789.

5. Prohibiting the outlaw of the foreign slave trade until 1808 was designed to calm fears in the deep South. By the 1780s the overworked land of Virginia and Maryland contained a "surplus" of slaves. Many slave owners in these two states would have been quite content with a prohibition of the African slave trade, as they would become the primary source for slaves bought by the expanding plantation culture of the deep South, Kentucky, and Tennessee. The resulting migration would reduce the burdens resulting of having too many slaves (food shortages, increased possibility of rebellion, and so on) and provide sellers with much needed cash.

6. John Walker was selected by Virginia's legislature as a temporary replace-

ment for Grayson. Walker served in the second session. Meanwhile, Monroe lobbied for the position and was made Grayson's "permanent" replacement, serving in the third session.

7. *DHFFE*, 2:347. Letter to Thomas Jefferson, February 15, 1789.

8. During the ratification debates, Monroe wrote a pamphlet detailing these views. Although advance copies were printed, they were never publicly distributed. Monroe blamed "printing errors" for his reluctance to distribute them, but it is more likely that the always politic Monroe suppressed the pamphlet to avoid alienating Federalists like Madison and Washington. See Storing, *The Complete Antifederalist*, 5:279.

9. Hamilton, *The Writings of James Monroe*, 1:184–88. Letter to Thomas Jefferson, July 12, 1788.

10. Ibid., 1:201. Letter of April 26, 1789.

11. During the ratification debate, many Antifederalists hoped that a second convention would be called to frame amendments. But in the months after ratification, support for a second convention dwindled. As implementation grew nearer, Antifederalists realized that framing amendments in Congress itself could be accomplished much more quickly than if they held out for a second convention. Before a second convention could meet, two-thirds of the states would have to petition Congress for it. Then elections would have to be held to select delegates. See generally Linda Grant De Pauw's "The Anti-Climax of Antifederalism," 98–114.

12. *DHRC*, 18:55. Burke's hunch about malapportionment has received quantitative backing from Charles W. Roll Jr. In a *Journal of American History* article "We, Some of the People," Roll documented the unevenness of apportionment in state ratification conventions. His conclusion was that apportionment in only two states would satisfy the modern Supreme Court's dictum of "one man, one vote." South Carolina had the second worst apportionment problem. Roll figured that delegates representing as few as 13.1 percent of the free population could have formed a majority at the ratification convention (22).

13. *DHRC*, 18:56.

14. This was a rather odd statement for Burke to make, as he was a lifelong bachelor. Though he never married, Burke did court the daughter of New York Governor George Clinton while the First Congress met in New York City. He also fathered a child by another woman during this time. Those inclined can take this as confirming evidence that politicians were much the same during the founding era as they are now. See *DHFFC*, 14:837, 838; and Meleney's *The Public Life of Aedanus Burke*, 196.

15. Meleney, *The Public Life of Aedanus Burke*, 149.

16. *DHFFE*, 2:267. Letter of October 28, 1788.

17. Ibid., 2:359. Letter to St. George Tucker, February 8, 1789.

18. Bland reached New York two days before the House achieved a quorum, but by that time, Frederick Augustus Muhlenberg had already been chosen by those present to act as secretary until a quorum could vote on a Speaker. The secretary was apparently unofficially understood to be the Speaker-designate. Muh-

lenberg's selection had the advantage of putting a Pennsylvanian in a key leadership position. Bland carried the stigma of being an ardent Antifederalist and was from Virginia, the same state as Washington. His ill health may also have been a factor.

19. The biographical sketch of Gerry contained in vol. 14 of *The Documentary History of the First Federal Congress* notes, "In mid-March, [1789,] his colleagues offered [Gerry] the responsibility of keeping the House Journal, pending the arrival of a quorum to select an official Clerk. It was largely an honorary duty, but whoever performed it was expected to be promoted to the speakership once Congress actually convened. Gerry declined, and the post went to Frederick A. Muhlenberg" (620–21).

20. During the first session of the First Congress, Burke advocated delay in discussing amendments. Burke correctly figured that the Antifederalists were in a very weak position, and that Federalists would co-opt the amending process to make sure that only "safe" amendments would be adopted. Delaying the process would allow people nationwide to see the defects of the new system and seriously agitate for reforms. The end result would be much stronger amendments, according to Burke.

21. For a full account of the electoral shift away from the Antifederalists after ratification, see my "The Electoral Dynamics of Ratification."

22. I am using the label "Federalist" rather loosely here. Since the term did not gain wide currency before mid-1787, I am applying it to state politicians anachronistically. The only states immune from this critical shift were those that had ratified the Constitution unanimously, and Virginia, where those allied with Patrick Henry retained their narrow majority through the late 1780s.

23. Georgia changed its constitution in 1789, Pennsylvania and South Carolina followed suit in 1790, New Hampshire and Delaware changed theirs in 1792. The ratification of the national Constitution and the subsequent "critical shift" in political power directly contributed to these constitutional changes.

24. *DHRC*, 3:600.

25. Figures from the 1790 census indicate that Federalists William Loughton Smith and Daniel Huger represented 23,035 and 16,468 free white inhabitants, respectively. Antifederalists Burke, Thomas Sumter, and Tucker represented 17,099, 29,400, and 62,630 white inhabitants, respectively. Not only did districting allow Federalists to be elected as South Carolina's representatives, but apportionment was tilted in favor of the coastal, Federalist-oriented districts. Data compiled from the first census, *Return of the Whole Number of Persons Within the Several Districts of the United States.*

26. *DHFFE*, 1:438.

27. Elkins and McKitrick, *The Age of Federalism*, 234.

28. After 1778, the British adopted a Southern strategy in fighting the Revolutionary War. They had left Massachusetts altogether, were in firm control of New York City and environs, and eschewed battles in the middle Atlantic states, concentrating their forces in the Southern theater. South Carolina was devastated by this strategy. Given its relatively small population and the crushing debt

incurred during these years, South Carolina's outstanding debt was the greatest of any state in 1789. The first state delegation to Congress was instructed by the state legislature to approve assumption.

29. Originally, the states' debts had been owed primarily to in-state inhabitants. As years went by without repayment in many states, the individuals who held debt certificates despaired of payment. Many of them sold their debt certificates to Northern speculators at a fraction of their face value just to recoup some value. By the late 1780s those to whom state debts were owed resided mainly in the North. The abundance of debt certificates owed to Massachusetts residents helps to explain the votes of Gerry and Grout.

30. McIlwain, *Constitutionalism*, 21. Also see Burke's *Reflections on the Revolution in France*, in which he emphasized the importance of precedent, but also reminded readers that the "state without the means of some change is without the means of its conservation," and that the ideal state acts "[a]t once to preserve and to reform" (28, 19, 148); Adams, *The First American Constitutions*, 18; and Levy, *Original Intent and the Framers' Constitution*, 143.

31. Government by royal charter should not be confused with government by proprietary charter, like the one issued to William Penn. Although Penn is known for his policy of religious toleration, proprietary governments in general were not as liberal in acknowledging rights and allowing for self-government as those with royal charters.

32. Labaree, *Royal Government in America*, 177–78.

33. Because New Hampshire and New York did not have royal charters they were more easily brought under strict crown control.

34. Even though charters were considered the colonists' best defense, they were not foolproof. Tiny Plymouth Bay's incorporation into the Massachusetts colony turned out to be permanent, despite the fact that Plymouth had had its own charter before King James's consolidation. Massachusetts was also issued a modified charter in 1691, one that placed a royal governor at the head of the colony. For a general history of the progress and aftermath of the Glorious Revolution in America, see Lovejoy, *The Glorious Revolution in America*.

35. From a petition of the people of Weymouth, Mass., circulated during the Stamp Act crisis. Quoted in Reid, *Constitutional History of the American Revolution*, 2:97. The American concept that constitutions were static rights-granting entities was bolstered by natural-right theories. Locke and others had argued that rights were a suprapolitical phenomenon — humans inherently had a static set of rights, regardless of their political situation. The Americans felt that written constitutions could best approximate these unchanging natural rights in a legal sense.

36. Nevins, *The American States during and after the Revolution*, 117–18.

37. Conley and Kaminski, *The Bill of Rights and the States*, xii.

38. Reid, *Constitutional History of the American Revolution*, 3:127.

39. Ibid., 2:5.

40. For most eighteenth-century Britons, the idea of a written constitution was an absurdity. The 1792 *Oxford Dictionary* entry under "constitution"

quoted Arthur Young scoffing at the idea, "as if a constitution was a pudding to be made by a receipt [recipe]." See McIlwain, _Constitutionalism_, 2.

41. Cesare Beccaria's treatise _On Crimes and Punishments_ was a highly influential work that emphasized that law should be clear and accessible. In chapter 4, Beccaria argues that if laws require interpretation, they are prone to the "petty tyrannies" of judges who will interpret the law in accord with their own prejudices. He begins chapter 5 by writing, "If the interpretation of laws is an evil, another evil, evidently, is the obscurity that makes interpretation necessary." Written laws were the sine qua non of good government for Beccaria, for "without writing, a society can never acquire a fixed form of government with power that derives from the whole and not from the parts, in which the laws, which cannot be altered except by the general will, are not corrupted in their passage through the mass of private interests" (14–18).

42. Interestingly, the states that had governed under royal charters did not adopt new constitutions. They simply expunged all references to England and the king. All other newly independent states framed written constitutions. Constitutional formulation by state legislatures, though much better than monarchical authorship, ultimately became unacceptable to many Americans, James Madison included. As noted in the next chapter, Madison and others like him felt that legislative formulation of a constitution did not sufficiently separate the fundamental law from statute law. In theory, a legislature that could form its own constitution had unlimited power, which contradicted the American ideal of charters only providing limited powers.

43. See Smith's _John Marshall_, 94.

44. Reid, _Constitutional History of the American Revolution_, 3:19.

45. James Wilson's speech was the best-known Federalist defense of the Constitution during the ratification period due to its early appearance, simplicity, widespread dissemination in the press, and numerous Antifederalist responses. The speech was delivered just three weeks into the ratification process. It was reprinted in newspapers at least thirty-four times before the end of the year, across the nation, from Portland, Maine (then Massachusetts), to Augusta, Georgia. The Antifederalists who responded to him and his claims were: "A Democratic Federalist," "An Old Whig" Letters II–III, "An Officer of the Late Continental Army," "Plain Truth," "Centinel" Letter II, "A Federal Republican," "A Republican" Letter I, "Brutus" Letter II, "Cincinnatus" Letters I–VI, "Timoleon," "Brutus, Junior," "A True Friend," "Impartial Examiner," "John DeWitt," "Republican Federalist" Letters II, V, "Hampden," "Junius," and "Agrippa." Because it was a single item that could be easily reproduced and digested, the October 6 speech was much more well known than any of "Publius's" essays. Only as the ratification process wore on was Wilson's commentary eclipsed by the sheer weight of argument in _The Federalist_, now easily the most celebrated Federalist defense of the Constitution (_DHRC_, 13:337–38).

46. _DHRC_, 13:337–44.

47. After ratification, Antifederalists became experts at this "boomeranging," turning Federalist arguments against their originators. As discerned by Jack N.

Rakove, this is how the opposition treated *The Federalist* ("The Early Uses of *The Federalist*"). Saul Cornell extends Rakove's argument to Federalist texts in general, noting that "former Anti-Federalists made liberal use of the writings of Federalists" and that the authors of ratification debate materials "no longer were the masters of them" (*The Other Founders*, 222, 224). My own wrinkle is to add that James Wilson's argument was by far the best-known defense of the Constitution's limited powers and on its face gave rise to a plausible line of Antifederalist constitutional argument after ratification.

48. Madison's argument is often mistaken for a defense of constitutional elasticity and implied powers. The text itself makes no such claims. For example, in the First Congress, Elias Boudinot felt that Federalist #44 justified the constitutionality of the Bank Act. Four days earlier, James Jackson more accurately argued from its premises that the Bank Act was not constitutional. Many commentators, including Stanley Elkins and Eric McKitrick, repeat Boudinot's error (*The Age of Federalism*, 105–6, 231–34).

49. Hamilton in Cooke, *The Federalist*, 204.

50. Ibid., 205.

51. Ibid., 303, 304.

52. Ibid. Though their arguments about the necessary and proper clause are remarkably similar, Hamilton and Madison could still disagree over the extent of power the new Constitution authorized by harboring different conceptions of the extent of powers implied by particular clauses. Hamilton consistently took a much broader view of what clauses authorized than Madison — sufficiently broad to call into question the seriousness of his public statement in Federalist #33.

53. Until recently, such a comprehensive search was not possible. From 1992 to 1995, all recorded documentary evidence of the inaugural House's floor debates was issued in five volumes by the Documentary History of the First Federal Congress project. These volumes contain more than twice as much material as the previous standard reference work, the *Annals of Congress*, and they are meticulously indexed. From the indexes I compiled a list of the hundreds of references to the Constitution made in each of three legislative sessions. I read each speech where such a reference was made and those necessary to put the issue into context. I deal exclusively with the House here for two reasons: there was a sufficient Antifederalist presence there to draw meaningful conclusions about their constitutional thought, and the House's decision to authorize published accounts stands in stark contrast to the Senate's penchant for secrecy, yielding a fuller and more reliable documentary record.

54. Rakove's *Original Meanings* stresses that there was no single way to understand or interpret the Constitution at the founding and that interpretive philosophies were only developed during the politically charged atmosphere of the 1790s. Currie's *The Constitution in Congress* provides a comprehensive treatment of constitutional arguments of the Federalist era, but remains agnostic about the political scene, choosing to focus exclusively on developments in constitutional law. Jaffa's *Original Intent and the Framers of the Constitution* points out that the Federalists wished to set a dynamic process in motion whereby natural

rights would come to be realized as fully as possible in the United States. Powell's essay in Rakove's edited volume, *Interpreting the Constitution*, titled "The Original Intent of Original Intent," is supplemented by thoughts in his later book, *The Moral Tradition of American Constitutionalism*. Together these works describe the tension between Enlightenment political theory, which privileged written clarity in the law to preclude the need to interpret it, and the English common law tradition, which consisted largely of unwritten precedents and required interpretation in practice. Lynch's *Negotiating the Constitution* emphasizes that the Philadelphia Convention intentionally wrote a document that could be interpreted different ways because taking a decisive stance on that issue would have prohibited agreement on the Constitution. The early representatives battled over several plausible versions of how to properly interpret the document.

55. In 1784 Tucker had written a pamphlet under the name of Philodemus, arguing for a new state constitution in South Carolina. In "Conciliatory Hints" (1784) he argued that constitutional provisions should be approved by a specially convened ratifying convention rather than the legislature. The convention would frame specific powers to be granted to the legislature. The legislature itself could not be expected to limit its own power. Tucker's views are dealt with more extensively in Chapter 4, where I compare his thinking with Madison's and Hamilton's.

56. *DHFFC*, 10:220.

57. *DHFFC*, 14:65–70; 12:70, 73, 137.

58. See generally Currie's *The Constitution in Congress*.

59. Sherman called Churchman's discovery "ingenious" and supported his claim to its benefits. Protecting the inventor's ability to benefit from his discovery was "as far as proper to go at this time," though, and probably "as far as warranted by the Constitution" (*DHFFC*, 10:213). Some Federalists, like William Loughton Smith of South Carolina, were often in the minority, and it was not unusual for them to resort to the same type of argument used by the Antifederalists, based on the constitutional theories of James Wilson and Publius. See, for example, Theodorick Bland and Smith on their mutual opposition to taxing coastal shipping (*DHFFC*, 10:239–40). New York Federalist John Laurance and New Jersey Federalist Elias Boudinot joined them (*DHFFC*, 10:243, 255, 396); Smith and Alexander White agreed with Elbridge Gerry on the unconstitutionality of presidential power to fire cabinet officers without Senate approval (*DHFFC*, 11:727, 738–39, 876–79, 900–902); Smith and White agreed with Theodorick Bland in arguing the unconstitutionality of committing petitions asking Congress to pass unconstitutional acts (Quaker petitions regarding slavery); Sherman and Bloodworth together make the case that though Congress has some power over state militias, it cannot determine their composition (*DHFFC*, 14:84, 92–93, 114, 118). Federalist uses of Wilson's constitutional thought included James Madison's and Michael Jenifer Stone's speeches against the national bank (*DHFFC*, 14:374, 424). James Jackson cited Federalist #44 to bolster his argument that the national bank was unconstitutional (*DHFFC*, 14:363–64, 376), and Roger Sherman quoted Publius.

60. *DHFFC*, 10:453.

61. Ibid., 11:831.
62. Ibid., 11:1278.
63. Ibid., 10:481.
64. Ibid., 11:1232, 1235, 1241; 13:830–31.
65. Ibid., 11:974.
66. Ibid., 11:1021.
67. See, for example, Gerry (ibid., 11:976, 1022); Baldwin (ibid., 13:776); and Boudinot (ibid., 14:440–41). Interestingly, none of these claims that the federal judiciary had the right to declare federal legislative acts unconstitutional was greatly contested. Judicial review may have been more accepted than previously thought, long before it was employed in practice.
68. Because of their reticence, it is not entirely clear whether the Antifederalists agreed with Tucker and Gerry (ibid., 14:413–14, 371). The phrases "natural construction" and "forced construction" were used by John Laurance and James Madison, respectively, to describe Hamilton's proposed Bank of the United States. Similar phrases had been used throughout the First Congress and during the Continental Congress as well.
69. Ibid., 10:394. Bland quoted part of Article I, section 9, paragraph 6.
70. Ibid., 10:410.
71. Ibid., 14:222.
72. Ibid., 13:576, 949.
73. Madison doubted that a majority at the convention backed assumption. Even if there were enough votes to pass such a clause, the delegates had thought better of including it because of the divisiveness of the issue. Since the convention had refused to authorize assumption there could be no inference made about their intent to do so (ibid., 13:1160–61, 1176).
74. Cornell, *The Other Founders*, 225.
75. *DHFFC*, 10:472–73.
76. Ibid., 14:368.
77. Ibid., 14:459–60.
78. Farrand, *The Records of the Federal Convention of 1787*, 3:372–75, excerpt of Madison's House floor speech of April 6, 1796. The occasion that prompted Madison's statement was that President Washington cited the framers' intent in his State of the Union message. Madison "acknowledged his surprise" at this occurrence, thinking that the issue was settled against employing the intent of the Philadelphia Convention. Rakove deftly treats Madison's developing sense of constitutional interpretation in his *Original Meanings*, 340–70.
79. *DHFFC*, 14:474.
80. Ibid., 14:424–25.

Chapter Four

1. Alexander Hamilton, John Jay, and James Madison, in Cooke, *The Federalist*, 6–7; Hamilton italicized his entire plan for the series, meaning that the specific emphasis here is mine.

2. Ibid., 146.

3. Ibid., 231.

4. It is often thought that Madison's push for a national veto on state legislation was intended to make the national government more vigorous. Madison himself did not view it this way. The negative on state laws was purely a defensive power in his mind, something that would prevent states from encroaching on national prerogatives. Before the Philadelphia Convention met, Madison related to Jefferson that "without this defensive power experience and reflection have satisfied me that however ample the federal powers may be made, or however clearly their boundaries may be delineated on paper, they will be easily and continually baffled by the Legislative sovereignties of the States" (*The Papers of James Madison* [hereafter *PJM*], 9:318). The way Madison attempted to make the government more vigorous was in enumerating powers that were not ultimately included in the Constitution. Among these powers: the ability to grant charters of incorporation, authorization to found a national university, the power "to establish seminaries for the promotion of literature and the arts & sciences, and the wherewithal to promote agriculture, commerce, trades, and manufactures" (see Farrand, *The Records of the Federal Convention of 1787*, 2:325–26). Had Madison persuaded a majority of the convention to think likewise, there would have been no constitutional impediment to the national bank. Madison's push for these powers no doubt confused Hamilton and other Federalists when he argued against a national bank in the First Congress.

5. Banning, *The Sacred Fire of Liberty*, 199. Evidence that Madison's and Hamilton's differences were long-standing comes from the Confederation Congress. In 1783 both were members, and along with the other delegates, their preferences based on roll-call votes were systematically measured by Calvin C. Jillson and Rick K. Wilson. Though Jillson and Wilson group the two together in one of three loose factions, Hamilton and Madison are at extremes of the faction, indicating significant, even systematic differences in their voting records (*Congressional Dynamics*, 246).

6. Though Alpheus T. Mason provided the first extensive commentary on the "split personality" of *The Federalist*, he acknowledged that the division was not entirely lost on the contemporaries of Madison and Hamilton. Mason points out that John Quincy Adams found it "not difficult to perceive [in *The Federalist*] that diversity of genius and character which afterwards separated them so widely from each other on questions of public interest, affecting the Constitution which they so ably defended, and so strenuously urged their country to adopt" ("The Federalist — A Split Personality," 625). After Mason, Dietze argued that the essays of Hamilton were "state-inimical," while Madison's were "state-friendly" (*The Federalist: A Classic on Federalism and Free Government*, 260–71). More recently, Banning writes of "The Personalities of Publius" in *The Sacred Fire of Liberty*, 396–402.

7. Rakove, "Early Uses of The Federalist," 234–49.

8. *PJM*, 10:259–60; *The Papers of Alexander Hamilton* (hereafter *PAH*), 4:288.

9. *PJM*, 11:227.

10. Ibid., 10:304; *PAH*, 4:377–78.

11. *PAH*, 2:403.

12. Farrand, *The Records of the Federal Convention of 1787*, 1:287.

13. Federalist #17, Cooke, *The Federalist*, 107.

14. *PAH*, 2:401.

15. Ibid., 2:407.

16. Ibid., 2:409. Congress did, in fact, commission several single-headed executive departments not long after Hamilton wrote his letter, in early 1781. Robert Morris was selected as superintendent of finance on February 20 of that year. True to Hamilton's expectations, Morris aggressively pursued nationalizing measures in order to stabilize the country's finances. While several of his suggestions were adopted, many others were thought too aggressive and rejected by the Confederation Congress, which granted him "little policy-making authority," according to Jillson and Wilson, *Congressional Dynamics*, 112–16, 247–54. Hamilton did not view Morris's failed attempt to nationalize the power over finance as a failure of his theory that the national government could be administered into full sovereignty. The Confederation Congress simply maintained too close control over Morris, rejecting so many of his proposals that his presence made only marginal differences in how citizens perceived the national government.

17. *PAH*, 2:415.

18. Read, *Power versus Liberty*, 84.

19. Farrand, *The Records of the Federal Convention of 1787*, 1:282–93.

20. Ibid., 1:645–46.

21. *PAH*, 5:221.

22. Ibid., 4:276–77.

23. Farrand, *The Records of the Federal Convention of 1787*, 1:306, 299.

24. Cooke, *The Federalist*, 117.

25. Ibid., 128–29.

26. Farrand, *The Records of the Federal Convention of 1787*, 1:165, 316, 356–57; *PJM*, 10:209.

27. Federalist #42, Cooke, *The Federalist*, 284–85.

28. Despite this strong bias, Madison understood that the inherent vagueness of language made a perfectly clear delineation of powers an impossibility and thus expressed reservations about the success of such an endeavor both in the Philadelphia Convention and in *The Federalist*; Farrand, *Records of the Federal Convention of 1787*, 1:53; Federalist #37, Cooke, *The Federalist*, 235–38.

29. *PJM*, 10:208.

30. Ibid., 10:209.

31. Farrand, *The Records of the Federal Convention of 1787*, 1:314–15; *PJM*, 10:209–12.

32. Farrard, 2:324–26.

33. Often obscured, perhaps because of his rather arrogant nationalism, is the fact that Hamilton was no disrespecter of individual rights; see Read's *Power versus Liberty*, 65–70.

34. Federalist #38, Cooke, *The Federalist*, 248.

35. Farrand, *The Records of the Federal Convention of 1787*, 1:464.

36. Rosen, *American Compact*, 154.

37. Farrand, *The Records of the Federal Convention of 1787*, 1:122–23; *PJM* 9:318; Federalist #43, Cooke, *The Federalist*, 297.

38. Farrand, *The Records of the Federal Convention of 1787*, 3:534.

39. Elkins and McKitrick, *The Age of Federalism*, 233–34.

40. Lynch, *Negotiating the Constitution*, 61–69, 75–83, 104–5, 133.

41. Ibid., 68–69.

42. Rakove, *Original Meanings*, 364 and 342–66 generally.

43. There are interpreters who do not fit neatly in either category. John Zvesper, for instance, has written that Madison alternated between two ultimately contradictory impulses, one consolidationist, the other pluralist. Madison himself understood the limits of these two protean systems of thought, though he was loath to admit them in public and did not fully appreciate their contradictory nature. Zvesper's interpretation does not stress Madison's consistency, but neither does he posit a transformation from one to the other through time. Zvesper's contextualism places him closer to James H. Read's argument than the others, but his assessment of Madison's overall thinking as contradictory hews closer to those who believe Madison underwent a major change. I appreciate Zvesper's idea that much of Madison's thought was not fully articulated, at least in public, and his assessment of Federalist #10 as problematic within the entire corpus of Madisonian thought but wish to point out in rebuttal that Madison's explicitly *constitutional* thought shows much greater consistency and coherence than Zvesper admits.

44. Banning, *The Sacred Fire of Liberty*, 22, 14.

45. Ibid., 205. Also see 7–10, 295–98, 329–33.

46. Read, "'Our Complicated System,'" 457.

47. Swift, *The Making of an American Senate*, 111.

48. Ibid., 81.

49. Myers, *The Mind of the Founder*, xlii.

50. McDonald, *Novus Ordo Seclorum*, 204, emphasis in original.

51. Banning, *The Sacred Fire of Liberty*, 22.

52. *DHFFC*, 1:270. April 22, 1789.

53. Recall that Madison argued that the bank proposal was a "forced construction" in February 1791. Reminding representatives that the necessary and proper clause did not grant any powers in and of itself, Madison pointed out that the bank could only be justified if it was a logical method of pursuing a specifically enumerated power. One properly "condemn[ed] the exercise of any power, particularly a great and important power, which is not evidently and necessarily involved in an express power." The only specific enumeration that Federalists were using to justify the bank was the borrowing clause. Madison pointed out that the bank was not designed to lend the national government money and therefore was not a natural legislative construal of the clause: "It never could be deemed an accessory or subaltern power, to be deduced by implication, as a

means of executing another power" (*DHFFC*, 3:371–73). By contrast, two days later John Laurance argued that the bank was a "natural construction," basing his argument less on a specific clause than that fiscal concerns had generally been ceded to the national government and that there was no express prohibition on incorporating a bank (ibid., 3:412–16).

54. Kramer, "Madison's Audience," 623–36.

55. Ibid., 628.

56. After hearing of Madison's intention to fight for a national veto on all state laws in the convention, Jefferson expressed deep-seated reservations that Madison was overreacting: "The negative proposed to be given them on all acts of the several legislatures is now for the first time suggested to my mind. Prima facie I do not like it. It fails in an essential character, that the hole & patch should be commensurate. But this proposes to mend a small hole by covering the whole garment" (*PJM*, 10:64).

57. Cooke, *The Federalist*, 60–61.

58. Ibid., 63.

59. Ibid., 60.

60. Ibid., 59

61. Ibid., 60.

62. Ibid., 318, my emphasis.

63. One of the things Madison failed to account for was that an increase in national powers and the ability of representatives to vote individually without ever needing to rotate out of office would create incentives for a more stable kind of politics than that of the Confederation Congress. Absent much power, the delegates to the ratification conventions did not wish to risk the stigma of partisanship to accomplish what little they could by banding together in parties. In the new Congress much could be accomplished, including deciding the critical question of "just how strong and active the new federal government was to be." Madison failed to realize that "transaction costs in salvaging half loaves case by case are high," to use the words of John Aldrich, and that with much serious decision-making to be done in the new Congress, proceeding in the manner of the old confederation would seriously overburden representatives (*Why Parties?* 70, 76). I deal with Aldrich's argument on party formation in the early Congress extensively in Chapter 6.

64. Boyd et al., *The Papers of Thomas Jefferson*, 19:242.

65. Tucker [writing under the pseudonym "Philodemus"], *Conciliatory Hints Attempting by a Fair State of Matters, to Remove Party Prejudices*, Evans #18731.

66. Ibid., 12.

67. Ibid., 22.

68. Nadelhaft, "South Carolina: A Conservative Revolution," 162.

69. Tucker, *Conciliatory Hints*, 11.

70. Cooke, *The Federalist*, 250–51.

71. *PJM*, 10:29–30.

72. Ibid., 10:44. In chapter 14 of *The Creation of the American Republic*,

Gordon Wood portrays Adams's estate-based representational scheme as quite out of step with American sentiment. This seems to me a fair statement if by "American sentiment" popular sentiment is meant. Among the Federalist elite, however, there were those who believed as Adams did — and that is part of what alienated the Madisonians.

73. *DHFFC*, 11:1300.

74. Cooke, *The Federalist*, 303–6.

75. *PJM*, 17:476.

Chapter Five

1. *PJM*, 14:375.

2. Ibid., 14:377.

3. Ibid., see editorial notes on Madison's responses to letters from George Nicholas, December 31, 1790 (13:337–38); from Thomas Jefferson, August 1, 1791 (14:56–57, 61); from Henry Lee, January 8, 1792 (185), all of which are missing.

4. Allen, *The Works of Fisher Ames*, 1:638.

5. Ketcham, *James Madison*, 293.

6. Unlike most elections of the time, there actually was a public campaign in the Madison-Monroe contest. The two future presidents met each other in debates at several courthouses and churches in the district. If we had better accounts of these meetings they might rank with the Lincoln-Douglas debates in historical importance (see vol. 2 of *The Documentary History of the First Federal Elections*).

7. Madison had opposed enumerating rights because it could prove problematic in two ways. First, any item omitted from a listing of rights would be fair game for government intrusion. Second, bills of rights were most vulnerable precisely at times of crisis when they were most needed. The susceptibility of a bill of rights to transgression at these times would expose a constitution's words as less than definitive (see letter to Thomas Jefferson, *PJM*, 11:297–99).

8. Unlike France, which did have a commercial treaty with the United States and whose exports would thus have been granted a primitive form of "most favored nation" status.

9. Letter to Thomas Jefferson of May 27, 1789, *PJM*, 12:186.

10. Ibid., 13:66

11. Ibid., 13:104.

12. Ibid., 13:151.

13. This was not an idle concern. States no longer had the power to levy taxes on imports, which had been used by other states to relieve their debts. This being the case, states already in a weak financial position would have to heavily burden their own citizens to repay war debts, an option that could have caused financial collapse.

14. Some have disputed that this agreement took place over dinner at Jefferson's home, but there seems to have been such a dinner and voting patterns sup-

port rather than contradict this version of events (see Elkins and McKitrick, *The Age of Federalism*, 156–60). Although Madison himself did not in the end vote for assumption, a few members of his coalition did, enough to allow for assumption to pass the House.

15. *PJM*, 13:252.
16. Ibid., 13:261–62.
17. Although the variety of arguments he used to win representatives to his side easily misleads one into thinking that Madison is against it on practical grounds.
18. *PJM*, 13:390.
19. Ibid., 13:384.
20. Letter to Richard Peters, ibid., 12:347; letter to Henry Lee, ibid., 14:193.
21. Ibid., 14:69.
22. On the rough-and-tumble partisan nature of the nation's press see Stewart's *The Opposition Press of the Federalist Period*; and Kaminski's "The Role of Newspapers in New York's Debate over the Federal Constitution," 280–92.

23. *PJM*, 13:90.	24. Ibid., 13:137.
25. Ibid., 13:147.	26. Ibid., 14:278.
27. Ibid., 14:355.	28. Ibid., 14:360.
29. Ibid., 13:48.	30. Ibid., 13:166.
31. Ibid., 13:222.	32. Ibid., 14:43.
33. Ibid., 14:47.	34. Ibid., 14:197.
35. Ibid., 14:198.	36. Ibid., 14:3.
37. Ibid., 14:373.	38. Ibid., 14:56–57, 73.
39. Ibid., 14:373.	40. Ibid., 14:403.
41. Ibid., 14:367, 451.	42. Ibid., 14:367.
43. Ibid., 14:138–39.	44. Ibid., 14:170.
45. Ibid., 14:117–22.	46. Ibid., 14:257–59.
47. Ibid., 14:274–75.	48. Ibid., 14:371.
49. Ibid., 14:372.	50. Ibid., Jan. 18, 1792.

51. Bogue et al., "Members of the House of Representatives and the Processes of Modernization," 282. Bogue et al.'s study aggregates members by the decade they entered Congress. Of those who entered Congress from 1789 to 1800, 40.9 percent went to college; for those entering in the next decade 36.6 percent attended college.
52. Brown's *Charles Beard and the Constitution* and McDonald's *We the People* amply and convincingly establish this point.
53. Bogue et al.'s ("Members of the House of Representatives and the Prospects of Modernization") percentages by decade of entry are as follows:

1789–1800: Law, 44.8 percent; Agriculture, 12.9 percent; Business, 13.3 percent; Unknown, 19.2 percent; Other, 9.4 percent

1801–1810: Law, 41.6 percent; Agriculture, 17.6 percent; Business, 15.4 percent; Unknown, 12.2 percent; Other, 12.2 percent

54. *Annals of Congress*, 35:388–417. Also see Benton, *Abridgment of the Debates of Congress, from 1789 to 1856*, 6:435–50.

55. Benton, *Abridgment of the Debates of Congress, from 1789 to 1856*, 6:435–50. Also see Ernst's *Rufus King, American Federalist*, 369–75; and *Annals of Congress*, 35:372–73.

56. Pinckney's speech was delivered on February 14, 1820 (*Annals of Congress*, 35:1310–29). Among his questionable claims is that the South made the only real sacrifice in the adoption of the 3/5 compromise. Rather than a mutual concession, Pinckney relates that the North got full representation while the South graciously acceded to a representation less than what its population dictated. Pinckney's defense of slavery as an institution moves beyond the questionable to the offensive ("During the whole of his life [the slave] is free from care, that canker of the human heart") and is more characteristic of Southern arguments of the mid-nineteenth century than the founding generation's apologetic but hand-tied attitude.

57. Ibid., 35:1320.

Chapter Six

1. Letter of March 4, 1790. Sedgwick Papers, Massachusetts Historical Society. Madison does sound like an Antifederalist in many of his writings and speeches from this time. For instance, in an article written for Freneau's *National Gazette* an anonymous Madison writes of the Hamiltonians that they are "more partial to the opulent than to the other classes of society; and having debauched themselves into a persuasion that mankind are incapable of governing themselves, it follows with them, of course, that government can be carried on only by the pageantry of rank, the influence of money and emoluments, and the terror of military force. Men of those sentiments must naturally wish to point the measures of government less to the interest of the many than of a few, and less to the reason of the many than to their weaknesses" (*PJM*, 14:371, from the *National Gazette* essay "A Candid State of Parties").

2. Adams to Tufts, May 30, 1790. Files of the First Federal Congress.

3. Elkins and McKitrick, *The Age of Federalism*, 26.

4. During the course of this chapter more will be said on the Francophile versus Anglophile dynamic in early American politics. The reach of these two approaches went beyond the bounds of foreign policy to encompass a way of thinking about government that greatly contributed to the divisions I write about here.

5. Sharp, *American Politics in the Early Republic*, 5–10 and epilogue.

6. Wood, *The Radicalism of the American Revolution*. One difference is how involved the Federalists themselves were in cultivating a politics of popular opinion. Stanley Elkins and Eric McKitrick imply that the Federalists were more closely tied to this development than Wood and Sharp suggest (*The Age of Federalism*).

7. Chambers, *Political Parties in a New Nation*, 17–31. Also of interest is Chambers's *The First Party System*, the title of which indicates that Chambers views the Federalist-Republican divide as a true party system.

8. Bell, *Party and Faction in American Politics*, chap. 3.

9. Hoadley, *Origins of American Political Parties*, 29, 93–99.

10. Aldrich and Grant, "The Antifederalists, the First Congress, and the First Parties," 296.

11. Ibid., 319.

12. Aldrich, *Why Parties?* 73.

13. Ibid., 74, 80.

14. Hoadley, *Origins of American Political Parties*, 173. Many others who write on the formation of parties during this era concur. For example, Joseph Charles remarks on p. 96 of *The Origins of the American Party System* that "anti-Federalism was at no time their [the Republican's] dominating principle."

15. Aldrich, *Why Parties?* 72, 73.

16. Martis, *The Historical Atlas of Political Parties in the United States Congress*, 27–29.

17. Even though the Federalists were not a major force on the national political scene after 1800, they were still relevant in certain states and retained a distinctive way of thinking. Linda K. Kerber nicely draws a portrait of "articulate Federalism" as it existed after 1800 in *Federalists in Dissent*, and Shaw Livermore explains how many of the Federalists, strangely, wound up supporting Andrew Jackson's candidacy in 1828 in *The Twilight of Federalism*.

18. This measure is akin to the party-unity score used frequently in political science. Another typical measure of partisanship is the percentage of "party votes" there are, where a majority of one party opposes a majority of the other party. The majority-alignment analysis I present approximates that measure under conditions where there are three recognizable groups instead of two.

19. By comparison, Rohde calls the increase in partisanship that occurred in the U.S. Congress from 1970 to the mid-1980s a "remarkable resurgence." Democrats bottomed out at 70 percent cohesion in 1972, but reached 88 percent by 1987. In 1969 and again in 1974 Republicans voted together 71 percent of the time, but by 1988 that figure was up to 80 percent (*Parties and Leaders in the Postreform House*, 14–15).

20. That consensual votes persisted into Congresses that have been described as almost perfectly partisan indicates the crude nature of roll-call analysis. Many of these votes are on trivial matters of personal business or parliamentary procedure. Given roll calls such as "a bill for the relief of Amy Darden, so as to enable the settlement on this claim, for the value of her horse, Romulus, pressed into service of the U.S. and killed," we must qualitatively discriminate between those that are more important and those that are less so, as I do in the subsequent section on the contours of congressional politics to 1800. Still other consensual votes are substantive and important, indicating that the groups' ideologies were related and may be accurately thought of as different strains of republicanism. For an in-depth discussion of the foibles and possibilities of employing roll-call data in political analysis see Van Doren, "Can We Learn the Causes of Congressional Decisions from Roll-Call Data?" 311–40.

21. Whether those votes did indeed bring the Federalists and Madisonians

back into alignment will be discussed in the next section, where I reconstruct Bell and Hoadley's categorization of individual votes. These votes are not exclusively what Bell called "government power" votes, as I will make clear in Table 6.6.

22. The dividing line between percentage differences which are "low" or "high" is inevitably somewhat arbitrary. I have set the bar at 40 percent, which means, for example, if 88 percent of Federalists support a bill and only 28 percent of Antifederalists do, the difference between them is high. If 67 percent of the Madisonians vote in favor, then the difference between them and the Antifederalists is the greatest it can be without being high.

23. In the First Congress most Anomalous Alignment votes are over the seat of the national capital, the votes for which tended to be almost purely sectional, rather than based on ideology. Similarly, in the Second Congress there was an issue that divided representatives on a state-by-state basis, the issue of apportionment, and it is over apportionment that most of these types of votes occurred.

24. Aldrich's evidence (*Why Parties?*) "clearly implies that parties were not voting coalitions in the First Congress but had emerged as central coalitional features in the Third Congress" (87).

25. Bell did not list into which category each vote fell. I attempted to obtain this information, but it was no longer at hand. Bell did relate how many roll calls were in each category, though. On the basis of this information I was able to categorize the votes according to his instructions. I cannot be sure that my categorizations are exactly the same, but they are at least very close.

26. The votes are roll calls 4, 11, and 12 taken in the First Congress.

27. Aldrich, *Why Parties?* 77.

28. *PJM*, 14:56.

29. Aldrich, *Why Parties?* 45.

30. Ibid., 72.

31. The votes are the 2d, 5th, 6th, 7th, 13th, and 48th recorded in the Second Congress.

32. These votes are the 29th and 31st, respectively, taken in the Second Congress.

33. The question of Hamilton's misconduct was the last major issue the Second Congress addressed. The six votes taken were the 95th through the 100th roll-call votes.

34. The embargo votes are numbers 12–16, 23, 25, and 40. The two proposals on augmenting the nation's military are votes 36 and 44 of the Third Congress.

35. These measures were votes 55 through 57 of the Third Congress.

36. The eight votes involved are the 3d, 6th, 10th, 11th, 12th, 13th, 20th, and 21st of the Fourth Congress.

37. The disparity in the number of votes cast is due to a particularly small number of Federalists, compared with Madisonians and Republicans, who had voted in ratification conventions populating the Fourth Congress: 6 against 22. That ratio is not indicative of the overall party composition of the Congress, though the Republicans were a majority when all members of the House were accounted for.

38. Vote 144 from the Fifth Congress. There had also been a series of votes on how to discipline Lyon earlier in the Congress, prior to the passage of the Sedition Act.

39. To give some idea of how widespread calls for rotation were among the Antifederalists, the critics of the Constitution who suggest them in Herbert Storing's (*The Complete Antifederalist*) far from complete record are: Centinel, 2:142; a Federal Farmer, 2:283, 288–94; Brutus, 2:444–45; Montezuma, 3:54 (pretending to be a Federalist in favor of continuous reappointment); An Officer of the Late Continental Army, 3:94; Charles Turner, 4:218–19; a Columbian Patriot, 4:278; Republicus, 5:163; and Melancton Smith, 6:164–65.

40. In transit to the third session of the First Congress, for instance, Aedanus Burke was delayed by a shipwreck at the mouth of the Delaware.

41. For a general discussion of the early sanitary and medical conditions in the nation's capitals, see the foreword and first five chapters of R. Marx's *The Health of the Presidents.*

42. Young, *The Washington Community*, 89.

Chapter Seven

1. If not for the few Antifederalists there and its secrecy, the Senate would be a good forum for this research as well. The Senate's initial organizational structure lasted even longer than the House's. Until 1816 the Senate directed legislation as an entire body without any standing committees. With the Senate firmly in Federalist hands until 1801, my claim that the Federalists as well as Republicans preferred that legislative action take place in the whole assembly seems bolstered by the Senate's legislative procedures. The most comprehensive treatment of early Senate organization is that offered recently by Swift in *The Making of an American Senate.*

2. Had the founders realized how much and in what way institutional arrangements would affect political outcomes, the organization of Congress's subordinate structures surely would have been a matter of lively debate.

3. See generally Cooper's *Congress and Its Committees.* Cooper studies committee structures and the policy process in three different eras, including the years 1789–1825. For an excellent treatment of the effects of post-Watergate reforms on the legislature and partisanship, see Rohde, *Parties and Leaders in the Postreform House.*

4. McConachie, *Congressional Committees*, 7–9. This procedural innovation was originally designed by the British House of Commons as a means of reserving to itself the right of unlimited debate when James I threatened to curb it in Parliament proper.

5. Ibid., 92.

6. Ibid., 92–93.

7. Ibid., 95.

8. Harlow, *The History of Legislative Methods in the Period Before 1825*, chap. 6. Representatives from the Carolinas were familiar with the proceedings of

the committee, though its use had recently declined, mainly as a result of the increasingly tight hold majority parties were able to keep on legislation. Still other states rarely found use for this parliamentary device, and the Committee of the Whole was all but unknown in New England's state legislatures.

9. Ibid., 103.

10. Ibid., 126.

11. Cooper, *Congress and Its Committees*, 11.

12. Ibid., 51–60. Also see Cooper and Young's "Bill Introduction in the Nineteenth Century," 67–105.

13. This is true except in the first session of the First Congress, when by rule the House as a whole determined who would be on committees of more than three. Apparently this kind of balloting was not worth the time it took, because in the first days of the second session, the Speaker was given appointment power for all committees, barring a special determination by the House to the contrary.

14. McConachie, *Congressional Committees*, 97.

15. Ibid., 133.

16. Ibid., 124, 133. The decisions made by the two committee types were also distinguishable. For example, the standing Committee on Claims was overburdened with work, and petitions referred to it stood little chance of success compared with those for which a select committee was specially convened (ibid., 148–49).

17. Cooper, *Congress and Its Committees*, 30.

18. Jefferson quoted in Cooper, *Congress and Its Committees*, 30.

19. In "The House Goes to Work: Select and Standing Committees in the U.S. House of Representatives, 1789–1828," Skladony does for the early select committees what Richard Fenno did for modern standing committees in his *Congressmen in Committees*. There Fenno masterfully emphasized the difference in the purpose and role of committees and how those differences affected business and outcomes.

20. Risjord, "Partisanship and Power," 647, 650.

21. Ibid., 635.

22. Stewart et al., "Taking Care of Business," 28–29.

23. Ibid., 34. This exception resulted from poor Republican attendance and coordination in the Third and Fourth Congresses. If and when all the Republicans showed up in these two Congresses, they could have formed a majority, or at least outvoted the Federalists (a few independent souls remained). Indicative of Republican difficulties, though, a Federalist Speaker was selected to preside during these years. So a Federalist Speaker appointed members of his own minority party to a majority of committee positions.

24. Jillson and Wilson, *Congressional Dynamics*, 289, also see chap. 4 and conclusion. Interestingly, they find that the Confederation Congress experimented with standing committees and later rejected their use.

25. Ibid., 300. I find that Jillson and Wilson's own observation about intrainstitutional rules are thus better applied to attitudes about rules than rules themselves. They write, "Rather than conceiving institutions to be malleable, we regard them as remarkably sticky. That is, they are unlikely to be smoothly bent

and reshaped. Instead, once created, they are changed infrequently and only with difficulty" (ibid., 299). If one replaces "institutions" with "rule preferences" in the above sentences, one gets a more accurate sense of what transpired in the early republic, despite it no longer fitting the "new institutional" perspective of Jillson and Wilson.

26. Stewart et al., "Taking Care of Business," Table 3.

27. McConachie, *Congressional Committees*, 131.

28. Ibid., 138–42.

29. Ibid., 144–49.

30. Harlow, *The History of Legislative Methods in the Period Before 1825*, 225–26; Cooper, *Congress and Its Committees*, 57–58. For an account of standing committee formation from 1810 to 1825, see Gamm and Shepsle, "Emergence of Legislative Institutions."

31. McConachie, *Congressional Committees*, 144.

32. Ibid., 124.

33. Harlow, *The History of Legislative Methods in the Period Before 1825*, 128–29; Cooper, *Congress and Its Committees*, 12; McConachie, *Congressional Committees*, 95.

34. Furlong, "The Evolution of Political Organization in the House of Representatives, 1789–1801," 85–86.

35. Allen, *Works of Fisher Ames*, vol. 1.

36. Martis, *The Historical Atlas of Political Parties in the United States, 1789–1989*, chap. 1.

37. Allen, *Works of Fisher Ames*, 1:61.

38. Furlong, "The Evolution of Political Organization in the House of Representatives, 1789–1801," 38.

39. For example, see Livermore's "Irrelevance of Federalist Ideas," 106–11.

40. Elkins and McKitrick, *The Age of Federalism*, 703.

41. *Annals of Congress*, 1:592.

42. Ibid., 3:699.

43. Harlow, *The History of Legislative Methods in the Period Before 1825*, 147; Stewart et al., "Taking Care of Business," 6; Caldwell, *The Administrative Theories of Hamilton & Jefferson*, 34–46.

44. Furlong, "The Evolution of Political Organization in the House of Representatives, 1789–1801," chap. 5.

45. Elkins and McKitrick, *The Age of Federalism*, 627–28.

46. See, for example, *Annals of Congress*, 3:438–52, where pro-administration forces proposed that Hamilton file a report on how to alleviate the public debt. Opposition forces were adamantly against this referral, polarizing the two sides far more than committee references themselves seem to have.

47. Cooper, *Congress and Its Committees*, 19.

48. Ibid., 54.

49. Standards of evidentiary documentation were not as stringent when McConachie wrote in 1898, so the number of footnotes in *Congressional Committees* is understandably minimal. Harlow's work, written nearly twenty years later, has extensive footnotes, but unfortunately they do not document the claim

that Federalists and Republicans were consistently at odds over legislative reference.

50. Examples of Federalists favoring deliberation in the Committee of the Whole include: Sherman, Vining, and Lee (*Annals of Congress*, 1:448–50); Smith, Ames, and Fitzsimons (*AC*, 3:686–87); Sedgwick, Dayton, and Smith (*AC*, 4:941–42); Parker (*AC*, 4:975); Smith and Sedgwick (*AC*, 4:1141); Tracy and Hillhouse (*AC*, 5:248–49); Smith (*AC*, 6:1598), Smith (*AC*, 7:242). Note Ames's call for further deliberation in the Committee of the Whole, evidence that after the First Congress he became accustomed to and at least sometimes favored this procedure. Republicans preferred referral of a legislative subject to a select committee over the Committee of the Whole in the following instances: Bland (*AC*, 1:119); Madison, Baldwin, and Williamson (*AC*, 3:686–87); Nicholas (*AC*, 4:614); Baldwin (*AC*, 4:933); Claiborne (*AC*, 4:975); Greenup (*AC*, 5:338).

51. Cooper, *Congress and Its Committees*, 329, n. 44.

52. See *Annals of Congress*, 1:424–31. Just as importantly for Madison, he was able to help exclude amendments that would significantly change the institutional structure of the new government.

53. Furlong, "The Evolution of Political Organization in the House of Representatives, 1789–1801," 25–28.

54. See generally Stewart's *The Opposition Press of the Federalist Period*.

55. Elkins and McKitrick, *The Age of Federalism*, 240.

56. In the early years of Congress's existence, select committees were often referred to as "subcommittees," a linguistic reminder of the primacy of the Committee of the Whole. See Cooper, *Congress and Its Committees*, 326, n. 36, and the early volumes of the *Annals of Congress* generally.

57. Stewart et al., "Taking Care of Business," 9.

58. This is the classic "two Congresses" thesis at work. Most cogently stated by Davidson and Oleszek in *Congress and Its Members*, the thesis emphasizes that the American Congress aims both to represent (a more "Antifederalist" approach) and legislate (requiring a more "Federalist" mind-set).

59. Harlow, *The History of Legislative Methods in the Period Before 1825*, 123; Stewart et al., "Taking Care of Business," 34.

60. Harlow, *The History of Legislative Methods in the Period Before 1825*, 129.

61. The only member of Congress that questioned the legitimacy of the Committee of Elections to look into the matter was Samuel Livermore, a Federalist from New Hampshire. His qualms were apparently quieted by his appointment to chair the committee. See *Annals of Congress*, 3:144–45.

62. Ibid., 3:880.

63. Risjord, "Partisanship and Power," 635.

64. *Annals of Congress*, 5:141.

65. Furlong, "The Evolution of Political Organization in the House of Representatives, 1789–1801," 116–18; Harlow, *The History of Legislative Methods in the Period Before 1825*, 157.

66. *Annals of Congress*, 5:144.

67. In fact, during the later part of Hamilton's service as secretary of the treas-

ury some Federalists became troubled by his extensive influence, and these individuals came to agree with Republicans that the House should maintain more control of economic affairs.

68. Elkins and McKitrick, *The Age of Federalism*, 14–19.
69. Ibid., 19.
70. Cooper, *Congress and Its Committees*, 60.
71. Young, *Washington Community*, 202–4.

Chapter Eight

1. Cullen, *The Papers of Thomas Jefferson*, 23:538–39.
2. Findley, *A Review of the Revenue System* (1794), Evans #26973, 116.
3. Findley, *History of the Insurrection in the Four Western Counties of Pennsylvania*, 300.
4. Ibid., 54.
5. Dawson, untitled broadside printed in Philadelphia on July 19, 1798. Evans #33610.
6. Elkins and McKitrick, *The Age of Federalism*, 722.
7. Young, *The Washington Community*, 153.
8. Livermore, *The Twilight of Federalism*, 273.
9. Tilden quoted in Carpenter, *The South as a Conscious Minority*, 116.
10. Elkins and McKitrick, *The Age of Federalism*, 749. As vice president, Burr killed his longtime nemesis Alexander Hamilton in a duel, after which he fled west, hoping to become the leader of a new nation by liberating territory from Spanish control. Because some thought his designs extended to the American Southwest he was tried for treason, but acquitted.
11. The other politician who was vice president for two different presidents was John C. Calhoun, who served under John Quincy Adams and Andrew Jackson.
12. Beeman, Botein, and Carter, *Beyond Confederation*, 305.
13. Kaminski, *George Clinton*, 161–66.
14. Rose, "The Ancient Constitution vs. the Federalist Empire," 74–105.
15. The Supreme Court case preventing states from imposing term limits on U.S. representatives and senators is *U.S. Term Limits, Inc., et al. v. Thornton et al.* (1995). A public opinion poll conducted in 1996 found that 74 percent of adult Americans favored term limits for elected officials. The groundswell of support in favor of term limits has subsided somewhat since, but not before more than twenty states imposed limits on state legislators.
16. Bartlett, *John C. Calhoun*, 34.
17. Niven, *Martin Van Buren*, 6.
18. Cole, *Martin Van Buren and the American Political System*, 12.
19. Seagar, *And Tyler Too*, 51.
20. Ibid., 50.
21. Roane as quoted in Carpenter, *The South as a Conscious Minority*, 46. Roane's statement was originally printed in the paper he had founded (in 1804), the *Richmond Enquirer*, on April 2, 1819. Roane served as a judge on Virginia's highest court for more than twenty years and would have been selected by Jeffer-

son to serve as chief justice had John Adams's replacement of Oliver Ellsworth not been hastily approved in the waning days of his administration. Adams's appointment was John Marshall, who served as chief justice until 1835.

22. Harry Scheiber quoted by Cornell in "The Changing Historical Fortunes of the Anti-Federalists," 57.

23. Ibid., 58.

24. Storing's commentary is contained in vol. 1 of *The Complete Anti-federalist*. Michael Lienisch's 1983 article is entitled "In Defense of the Anti-federalists," 65–87.

25. Lynd, *Anti-Federalism in Dutchess County, New York*, 87.

26. Cornell, "Aristocracy Assailed," 1148.

27. Duncan, *The Anti-Federalists and Early American Political Thought*, xiii, 182–83.

28. Gerry quoted in *DHFFC*, 13:952.

29. Gillman, *The Constitution Besieged*, 199 and generally.

30. Elbridge Gerry quoted in *DHFFC*, 2:1102.

Appendix B

1. Vermont, the first new state admitted after the original thirteen, also held a ratification convention. Because it ratified in 1791, convention positions in Vermont more accurately reflect the near-universal esteem in which the Constitution was held after ratification, rather than a true division of Federalists and Antifederalists. Of 109 voting delegates, 105 voted for adoption, 4 voted against.

2. The total number of delegates who voted was 1,648. Of these 1,071 (65 percent) voted for the Constitution, and 577 (35 percent) voted against. This tally considers "ratifying Antifederalists" as ratifiers. Their numbers are fairly small and would not raise the actual number of Antifederalists by more than a percentage point. Of those delegates later elected to Congress, 65 percent voted to ratify (again considering "ratifying Antifederalists" as ratifiers), and 35 percent voted against. If we include Havens, Smith, and Winston as Antifederalists, the percentages are 63 percent in favor, 37 percent against. Unless noted otherwise these three are considered as Antifederalists in all analyses. The number 1,648 does not include those who voted in North Carolina's second convention. I do, however, include those who voted there and later served in Congress in the analysis.

3. Also helpful in this regard was Congressional Quarterly's *American Leaders, 1789–1987: A Biographical Summary*. Of about two hundred name matches, some were easily confirmed, as *The Biographical Directory of the American Congress* entry stated that that person had served in a ratification convention. For others, confirmation or elimination was less easy. In these cases I turned to the files of the Center for the Study of the Constitution. Their biographical files allowed me to confirm or reject all but one possible match. In the stubborn case of William Smith of South Carolina a judgment call was made to exclude him from the sample, primarily because the residence of Congressman William Smith was in an entirely different part of the state than the residence of the William

Smith who was a delegate to the ratification convention. Neither should be confused with the prominent Federalist Congressman William Loughton Smith, who served in the first five Congresses.

4. Two states that are overrepresented compared to their populations are North and South Carolina. Both had very large conventions, so that there was a greater pool of individuals who met the first criteria of inclusion than in any other state but Massachusetts. North Carolina also was the only state to hold two distinct conventions. At the first Antifederalists dominated, at the second Federalists won handily. This being the case, most of the public figures who were considered for congressional office had been at one or both of the conventions, and there are more North Carolinians in the sample than individuals from any other state.

5. I have included Delaware, often considered in the mid-Atlantic group, among the Northern states. The reason for this is that Delaware's politics were closely tied to Pennsylvania's during the colonial and early national period. See chapter 1 of Conley and Kaminski's, *The Constitution and the States.*

6. At the $p < .05$ level.

7. Elkins and McKitrick, "The Founding Fathers," 181–216. The list of nine key leaders from each side they cite is Merrill Jensen's. The Federalists are Robert Morris, John Jay, James Wilson, Alexander Hamilton, Henry Knox, James Duane, George Washington, James Madison, and Gouverneur Morris. The Antifederalists are Samuel Adams, Patrick Henry, Richard Henry Lee, George Clinton, James Warren, Samuel Bryan, George Bryan, George Mason, and Elbridge Gerry. The list seems to have originated with early-twentieth-century historian Charles Warren (see Main, *The Antifederalists,* 259).

8. Elkins and McKitrick, "The Founding Fathers," 203.

9. Main, *The Antifederalists,* 259; Anderson, *Creating the Constitution,* 175.

10. The standard deviation of Federalist ages when ratification occurred is 9.7 years, that of the Madisonians is 8.0 years, and the Antifederalists is 9.4 years. The standard deviation in ages when first selected to Congress is 8.5 years for Federalists, 7.1 years for Madisonians, and 10.0 years for Antifederalists. This last figure (the largest of these standard deviations and the only "age at selection" deviation not lower than the group's "age at ratification" deviation) is a result of their electoral demise and subsequent comeback: although solidly Antifederalist districts were able to select young critics of the Constitution to populate the early Congresses, many others were not elected until many years after ratification.

11. Bogue et al. ("Members of the House of Representatives and the Process of Modernization") found the following reasons for termination, again by decade of entry to Congress:

1789–1800: Died, 5.0 percent; Involuntary Retirement, 5.5 percent; Voluntary Retirement, 29.4 percent; Did not seek reelection, 15.6 percent, Reason Unknown, 44.5 percent.

1801–1810: Died, 5.5 percent; Involuntary Retirement, 5.9 percent; Voluntary Retirement, 23.7 percent; Did not seek reelection, 20.3 percent; Unknown, 44.5 percent.

Works Cited

Adams, Willi Paul. *The First American Constitutions.* 1973. Reprint, Chapel Hill: University of North Carolina Press, 1980.

Albanese, Catherine L. *Sons of the Fathers: The Civil Religion of the American Revolution.* Philadelphia, Pa.: Temple University Press, 1976.

Aldrich, John H. *Why Parties? The Origin and Transformation of Political Parties in America.* Chicago: University of Chicago Press, 1995.

Aldrich, John H., and Ruth Grant. "The Antifederalists, the First Congress, and the First Parties." *Journal of Politics* 55 (1993): 295–326.

Allen, W. B., ed. *Works of Fisher Ames.* Indianapolis, Ind.: Liberty Classics, 1983.

American Leaders, 1789–1987: A Biographical Summary. Washington, D.C.: Congressional Quarterly, 1987.

Anderson, Thornton. *Creating the Constitution: The Convention of 1787 and the First Congress.* University Park: Pennsylvania State University Press, 1993.

Annals of Congress. Joseph Gales, ed. 42 volumes, Washington, D.C.: Gales and Seaton, 1834–56.

Ballagh, James Curtis, ed. *The Letters of Richard Henry Lee.* 2 vols. 1911. Reprint, New York: Da Capo Press, 1970.

Banning, Lance. "Jeffersonian Ideology Revisited: Liberal and Classical Ideas in the New America Republic." *William & Mary Quarterly,* 3d series, no. 43 (1986): 3–19.

———. *Jefferson & Madison: Three Conversations from the Founding.* Madison, Wisc.: Madison House, 1995.

———. "Republican Ideology and the Triumph of the Constitution, 1789–1793." *William & Mary Quarterly,* 3d series, no. 31 (1974): 167–88.

———. *The Sacred Fire of Liberty: James Madison and the Founding of the Federal Republic.* Ithaca, N.Y.: Cornell University Press, 1995.

Bartlett, Irving H. *John C. Calhoun: A Biography.* New York: W. W. Norton & Company, 1993.

Bartlett, John Russell, ed. *Records of the State of Rhode Island and Providence Plantations in New England.* 1790. Reprint, Providence, R.I.: Providence Press Company, 1865.

Batchellor, Albert Stillman, ed. *Early State Papers of New Hampshire.* 1788–90. Reprint, Concord, N.H.: Ira C. Evans, 1892.

Beard, Charles A. *An Economic Interpretation of the Constitution*. 1913. Reprint, New York: The Free Press, 1986.

Beccaria, Cesare. *On Crimes and Punishments*. 1763. Reprint, New York: MacMillan Publishing Company, 1963.

Beeman, Richard, Stephen Botein, and Edward C. Carter II, eds. *Beyond Confederation*. Chapel Hill: University of North Carolina Press, 1987.

Bell, Rudolph M. *Party and Faction in American Politics*. Westport, Conn.: Greenwood Press, 1973.

Benton, Thomas Hart, ed. *Abridgment of the Debates of Congress from 1789 to 1856*. Vol. 6. New York: D. Appleton & Company, 1858.

Bernstein, Richard B., with Jerome Agel. *Amending America*. New York: Times Books, 1993.

Bickford, Charlene Bangs et al., eds. *The Documentary History of the First Federal Congress, 1789–1791 (DHFFC)*. 14 vols. Baltimore, Md.: Johns Hopkins University Press, 1972–.

Bielinski, Stefan. *Abraham Yates, Jr. and the New Political Order in Revolutionary New York*. Albany: New York State Revolution Bicentennial Commission, 1975.

Billias, George Athan. *Elbridge Gerry: Founding Father and Republican Statesman*. New York: McGraw-Hill Book Company, 1976.

The Biographical Directory of the American Congress, 1774–1987. Washington, D.C.: Government Printing Office, 1987.

Bogue, Allan G., Jerome M. Clubb, Carroll R. McKibbin, and Santa Traugott. "Members of the House of Representatives and the Processes of Modernization, 1789–1960." *Journal of American History* 63 (1976): 275–302.

Boorstin, Daniel J. *The Genius of American Politics*. Chicago: University of Chicago Press, 1953.

Boucher, Jonathan. *A View of the Causes and the Consequences of the American Revolution*. 1797. Reprint, New York: Russell and Russell, 1967.

Bowling, Kenneth R. *Politics in the First Congress, 1789–91*. New York: Garland Publishers, 1990. Reprint of a University of Wisconsin Ph.D. dissertation, 1968.

———. "'A Tub to the Whale': The Founding Fathers and the Adoption of the Bill of Rights." *Journal of the Early Republic* 8 (1988): 223–51.

Bowling, Kenneth R., and Donald R. Kennon, eds. *The House and the Senate in the 1790s: Petitioning, Lobbying, and Institutional Development*. Athens: Ohio University Press, 2002.

Boyd, Steven R. *The Politics of Opposition*. Millwood, N.Y.: KTO Press, 1979.

Brooks, Robin. "Alexander Hamilton, Melancton Smith, and the Ratification of the Constitution in New York." *William & Mary Quarterly*, 3d series, no. 24 (1967): 339–58.

Brown, Robert E. *Charles Beard and the Constitution*. Princeton, N.J.: Princeton University Press, 1956.

Burke, Edmund. *Reflections on the Revolution in France*. 1790. Reprint, Indianapolis, Ind.: Hackett Publishing, 1987.

Caldwell, Lynton K. *The Administrative Theories of Hamilton & Jefferson*, 2d edition. 1944. Reprint, Westport, Conn.: Greenwood Press, 1988.

Carpenter, Jesse T. *The South as a Conscious Minority, 1789–1861.* 1930. Reprint, Columbia: University of South Carolina Press, 1990.

Chambers, William N. *Political Parties in a New Nation.* Oxford: Oxford University Press, 1963.

———, ed. *The First Party System: Federalists and Republicans.* New York: John Wiley and Sons, 1972.

Cole, Donald B. *Martin Van Buren and the American Political System.* Princeton, N.J.: Princeton University Press, 1984.

Conley, Patrick T., and John P. Kaminski, eds. *The Bill of Rights and the States.* Madison, Wisc.: Madison House, 1992.

———, eds. *The Constitution and the States.* Madison, Wisc.: Madison House, 1988.

Cooke, Jacob E., ed. *The Federalist.* Cleveland, Ohio: World Publishing, 1961.

Cooper, Joseph. *Congress and Its Committees: A Historical Approach to the Role of Committees in the Legislative Process.* New York: Garland Publishers, 1988. Reprint of a Harvard University Ph.D. dissertation, 1960.

Cooper, Joseph, and Cheryl D. Young. "Bill Introduction in the Nineteenth Century: A Study of Institutional Change." *Legislative Studies Quarterly* 14 (1989): 67–105.

Cornell, Saul. "Aristocracy Assailed: The Ideology of Backcountry Anti-Federalism." *Journal of American History* 76 (1990): 1148–72.

———. "The Changing Historical Fortunes of the Anti-Federalists." *Northwestern University Law Review* 84 (1989): 39–73.

———. *The Other Founders: Anti-Federalism and the Dissenting Tradition in America, 1788–1828.* Chapel Hill: University of North Carolina Press, 1999.

———, ed. "'Reflections on the Late Remarkable Revolution in Government': Aedanus Burke and Samuel Bryan's Unpublished History of the Ratification of the Federal Constitution." *Pennsylvania Magazine of History & Biography* 112 (1988): 103–30.

Cullen, Charles T., ed. *The Papers of Thomas Jefferson.* Vol. 23. Princeton, N.J.: Princeton University Press, 1990.

Currie, David P. *The Constitution in Congress: The First Congress, 1789–1791.* Chicago: University of Chicago Press, 1994.

Davidson, Roger H., and Walter Oleszek. *Congress and Its Members.* 4th ed. Washington, D.C.: CQ Press, 1994.

Dawson, John. Untitled broadside regarding laws passed in the last Congress. Philadelphia, 1798. Evans #33610.

The Debates and Proceedings in the Congress of the United States [Annals of Congress]. 42 vols. Washington, D.C.: Gales and Seaton, 1834–56.

De Pauw, Linda Grant. "The Anticlimax of Antifederalism: The Abortive Second Convention Movement, 1788–89." *Prologue* 2 (1970): 98–114.

Dietze, Gottfried. *The Federalist: A Classic on Federalism and Free Government.* Baltimore, Md.: Johns Hopkins University Press, 1960.

Duncan, Christopher M. *The Anti-Federalists and Early American Political Thought.* DeKalb: Northern Illinois University Press, 1995.

Elkins, Stanley, and Eric McKitrick. *The Age of Federalism: The Early American Republic, 1788–1800.* Oxford: Oxford University Press, 1993.

———. "The Founding Fathers: Young Men of the Revolution." *Political Science Quarterly* 76 (1961): 181–216.

Ellis, Richard E. "The Persistence of Antifederalism after 1789." In *Beyond Confederation,* ed. Richard Beeman, Stephen Botein, and Edward C. Carter II. Chapel Hill: University of North Carolina Press, 1987.

Ernst, Robert. *Rufus King, American Federalist.* Chapel Hill: University of North Carolina Press, 1968.

Farrand, Max, ed. *The Records of the Federal Convention of 1787.* 4 vols. 1911. Reprint, New Haven, Conn.: Yale University Press, 1966.

Fenno, Richard F. *Congressmen in Committees.* Boston: Little, Brown. 1973.

Findley, William. *History of the Insurrection in the Four Western Counties of Pennsylvania.* 1796. Reprint, Spartanburg, S.C.: The Reprint Company, Publishers, 1984.

———. *A Review of the Revenue System Adopted by the First Congress Under the Federal Constitution.* Philadelphia, Pa.: T. Dobson, 1794. Evans #26973.

Furlong, Patrick Joseph. "The Evolution of Political Organization in the House of Representatives, 1789–1801." Ph.D. dissertation, Northwestern University, 1966.

Gamm, Gerald, and Kenneth Shepsle. "Emergence of Legislative Institutions: Standing Committees in the House and Senate, 1810–1825." *Legislative Studies Quarterly* 14 (1989): 39–66.

Gillman, Howard. *The Constitution Besieged: The Rise and Demise of Lochner Era Police Powers Jurisprudence.* Durham, N.C.: Duke University Press, 1993.

Goodman, Paul. *The Federalists versus the Jeffersonian Republicans.* New York: Holt, Rinehart and Winston, 1967.

Greenberg, Milton. "The Loyalty Oath in the American Experience." Ph.D. dissertation, University of Wisconsin, 1955.

The Papers of Alexander Hamilton. Ed. Harold C. Syrett and Jacob E. Cooke. 26 vols. New York: Columbia University Press, 1961–79.

Hamilton, Stanislaus Murray, ed. *The Writings of James Monroe.* Vol. 1. 1898. Reprint, New York: AMS Press, 1969.

Harlow, Ralph Volney. *The History of Legislative Methods in the Period Before 1825.* New Haven, Conn.: Yale University Press, 1917.

Hart, H. L. A. *The Concept of Law.* 1961. Reprint, Oxford: Clarendon Press, 1994.

Heideking, Jürgen. "The Federal Processions of 1788 and the Origins of American Civil Religion." *Soundings* 77 (1994): 367–88.

Hoadley, John F. *Origins of American Political Parties.* Lexington: University Press of Kentucky, 1986.

Hosmer, Samuel K. *Samuel Adams.* 1898. Reprint, New York: Chelsea House, 1980.

Hyman, Harold M. *To Try Men's Souls: Loyalty Tests in American History.* Berkeley and Los Angeles: University of California Press, 1959.

Inter-University Consortium for Political and Social Research. Data set #0004, U.S. Congressional Roll Call Voting Records, 1789–1990.

Jaffa, Harry V. et al. *Original Intent and the Framers of the Constitution.* Washington, D.C.: Regnery Gateway, 1994.

The Papers of Thomas Jefferson. Ed. Julian P. Boyd et al. Princeton, N.J.: Princeton University Press, 1950–.

Jensen, Merrill et al., eds. *The Documentary History of the First Federal Elections (DHFFE).* 4 vols. Madison: University of Wisconsin Press, 1976–89.

Jensen, Merrill and John P. Kaminski, eds. *The Documentary History of the Ratification of the Constitution (DHRC)* plus microfiche supplements. Madison: State Historical Society of Wisconsin, 1976–.

Jillson, Calvin C. *Constitution Making: Conflict and Consensus in the Federal Convention of 1787.* New York: Agathon Press, Inc., 1988.

Jillson, Calvin C., and Rick K. Wilson. *Congressional Dynamics: Structure, Coordination, and Choice in the First American Congress, 1774–1789.* Stanford, Calif.: Stanford University Press, 1994.

Journal of the House of Delegates of the Commonwealth of Virginia. 1789. Reprint, Richmond, Va.: Thomas H. White, 1828.

Journals of the Continental Congress, 1774–1789. 34 volumes. Washington, D.C.: Government Printing Office, 1904–37.

Kaminski, John P. *George Clinton: Yeoman Politician of the New Republic.* Madison, Wisc.: Madison House, 1993.

———. "Liberty versus Authority: The Eternal Conflict in Government." *Southern Illinois University Law Journal* 16 (1992): 213–31.

———. "Political Sacrifice and Demise—John Collins and Jonathan J. Hazard, 1786–1790." *Rhode Island History* 35 (1976): 91–98.

———. *A Revolution in Favor of Government: The Ratification of the United States Constitution.* Collegeville, Minn.: St. John's University Press, 1987.

———. "The Role of Newspapers in New York's Debate over the Federal Constitution." In *New York and the Union*, ed. S. Schechter and R. Bernstein, 280–92. Albany: New York State Commission on the Bicentennial of the United States Constitution, 1990.

———, ed. *A Necessary Evil?: Slavery and the Debate over the Constitution.* Madison, Wisc.: Madison House, 1995.

Kammen, Michael. *A Machine That Would Go of Itself.* New York: Alfred A. Knopf, 1986.

Kenyon, Cecilia. "Men of Little Faith: The Anti-Federalists on the Nature of Representative Government." *William & Mary Quarterly*, 3d series, no. 12 (1955): 3–43.

Kerber, Linda K. *Federalists in Dissent.* Ithaca, N.Y.: Cornell University Press, 1970.

Kessler, Charles R., ed. *Saving the Revolution: The Federalist Papers and the American Founding.* New York: The Free Press, 1987.

Ketcham, Ralph. *James Madison*. Charlottesville, Va.: University Press of Virginia, 1990.

Knupfer, Peter B. *The Union as It Is*. Chapel Hill: University of North Carolina Press, 1991.

Kramer, Larry D. "Madison's Audience." *Harvard Law Review* 112 (1999): 611–79.

Labaree, Leonard Woods, ed. *Public Records of the State of Connecticut*. 1789. Reprint, Hartford: State of Connecticut, 1948.

———. *Royal Government in America*. 1930. Reprint, New York: Frederick Ungar Publishing Company, 1958.

Lazare, Daniel. *The Frozen Republic: How the Constitution Is Paralyzing Democracy*. New York: Harcourt Brace and Company, 1996.

Levinson, Sanford. *Constitutional Faith*. Princeton, N.J.: Princeton University Press, 1988.

Levy, Leonard W. *Original Intent and the Framers' Constitution*. New York: MacMillan Publishing Company, 1988.

Lieberman, Jethro K. *The Enduring Constitution*. New York: Harper & Row, 1987.

Lienisch, Michael. "In Defense of the Anti-federalists." *History of Political Thought* 4 (1983): 65–87.

———. *New Order of the Ages: Time, the Constitution, and the Making of Modern American Political Thought*. Princeton, N.J.: Princeton University Press, 1988.

Livermore, Shaw. "The Irrelevance of Federalist Ideas." In *The Federalists versus the Jeffersonian Republicans*, ed. P. Goodman, 106–11. New York: Holt, Rinehart and Winston, 1967.

———. *The Twilight of Federalism*. Princeton, N.J.: Princeton University Press, 1962.

Locke, John. *The Second Treatise on Civil Government*. 1690. Reprint, Buffalo, N.Y.: Prometheus Books, 1986.

Lovejoy, David S. *The Glorious Revolution in America*. New York: Harper & Row, 1972.

Lynch, Joseph M. *Negotiating the Constitution: The Earliest Debates over Original Intent*. Ithaca, N.Y.: Cornell University Press, 1999.

Lynd, Staughton, ed. "Abraham Yates's History of the Movement for the United States Constitution." *William & Mary Quarterly*, 3d series, no. 20 (1963): 223–45.

———. *Anti-federalism in Dutchess County, New York*. Chicago: Loyola University Press, 1962.

Maddex, Robert L. *Constitutions of the World*. Washington, D.C.: Congressional Quarterly, Inc., 1995.

The Papers of James Madison. Ed. William T. Hutchinson et al. Chicago and Charlottesville: University of Chicago Press and University Press of Virginia, 1962–.

Main, Jackson Turner. *The Antifederalists*. Chapel Hill: University of North Carolina Press, 1961.

Martin, James Kirby, ed. *The Human Dimensions of Nation Making: Essays on Colonial and Revolutionary America*. Madison: State Historical Society of Wisconsin, 1976.

Martis, Kenneth C., ed. *The Historical Atlas of Political Parties in the United States Congress*. New York: MacMillan Publishing Company, 1989.

———. *The Historical Atlas of U.S. Congressional Districts*. New York: Free Press, 1982.

Marx, Rudolph. *The Health of the Presidents*. New York: G. P. Putnam's Sons, 1960.

Mason, Alpheus Thomas. "The Federalist — A Split Personality." *American Historical Review* 57 (1952): 625–43.

Matthews, Richard K. *If Men Were Angels: James Madison and the Heartless Empire of Reason*. Lawrence: University Press of Kansas, 1995.

McConachie, Lauros Grant. *Congressional Committees: A Study of the Origins and Development of Our National and Local Legislative Methods*. 1898. Reprint, New York: Burt Franklin Reprints, 1973.

McCoy, Drew R. *The Last of the Fathers: James Madison and the Republican Legacy*. Cambridge: Cambridge University Press, 1989.

McDonald, Forrest. *Novus Ordo Seclorum: The Intellectual Origins of the Constitution*. Lawrence: University Press of Kansas, 1985.

———. *We the People: The Economic Origins of the Constitution*. Chicago: University of Chicago Press, 1958.

McIlwain, Charles Howard. *Constitutionalism: Ancient and Modern*. Ithaca, N.Y.: Cornell University Press, 1947.

McMaster, John Bach, and Frederick D. Stone. *Pennsylvania and the Federal Constitution, 1787–1788*. 1888. Reprint, New York: Da Capo Press, 1970.

Meleney, John C. *The Public Life of Aedanus Burke*. Columbia: University of South Carolina Press, 1989.

Mercer, John Francis. *An Introductory Discourse to an Argument in Support of the Payments Made of British Debts into the Treasury of Maryland during the Late War*. Annapolis, Md.: Frederick Green, 1789. Evans #21958

Minutes of the Supreme Executive Council of Pennsylvania. Vol. 16. 1789. Reprint, Harrisburg: Tho. Fenn & Company, 1853.

Montesquieu, Baron de. *The Spirit of the Laws*. 1748. Reprint, Cambridge: Cambridge University Press, 1989.

Morris, Richard B. *The Forging of the Union, 1781–1789*. New York: Harper & Row, 1987.

Myers, Marvin. *The Mind of the Founder: Sources of the Political Thought of James Madison*. Hanover, N.H.: University Press of New England, 1981.

Nadelhaft, Jerome. "South Carolina: A Conservative Revolution." In *The Constitution and the States*, ed. Patrick T. Conley and John P. Kaminski. Madison, Wisc.: Madison House, 1988.

Nevins, Allan. *The American States during and after the Revolution: 1775–1789*. New York: Augustus M. Kelley, 1969.

Niven, John. *Martin Van Buren: The Romantic Age of American Politics*. Oxford: Oxford University Press, 1983.

Pocock, J. G. A. *The Machiavellian Moment: Florentine Political Thought and the Atlantic Republican Tradition.* Princeton, N.J.: Princeton University Press, 1975.

Powell, H. Jefferson. *The Moral Tradition of American Constitutionalism.* Durham, N.C.: Duke University Press, 1993.

Rakove, Jack N. "Early Uses of The Federalist." In *Saving the Revolution: The Federalist Papers and the American Founding,* ed. Charles R. Kessler. New York: The Free Press, 1987.

———. *Original Meanings: Politics and Ideas in the Making of the Constitution.* New York: Alfred A. Knopf, 1996.

———, ed. *Interpreting the Constitution: The Debate over Original Intent.* Boston: Northeastern University Press, 1990.

Read, James H. "'Our Complicated System': James Madison on Power and Liberty." *Political Theory* 23 (1995): 452–75.

———. *Power versus Liberty: Madison, Hamilton, Wilson, and Jefferson.* Charlottesville: University Press of Virginia, 2000.

Reid, John Phillip. *Constitutional History of the American Revolution.* 4 vols. Madison: University of Wisconsin Press, 1986–93.

Return of the Whole Number of Persons within the Several Districts of the United States (the first census). 1802. Reprint, New York: ARNO Press, 1976.

Risjord, Norman K. "Partisanship and Power: House Committees and the Power of the Speaker, 1789–1801." *William & Mary Quarterly,* 3d series, no. 49 (1992): 628–51.

Rohde, David W. *Parties and Leaders in the Postreform House.* Chicago: University of Chicago Press, 1991.

Roll, Charles W., Jr. "We, Some of the People: Apportionment in the Thirteen State Conventions Ratifying the Constitution." *Journal of American History* 56 (1969): 21–40.

Rose, Carol M. "The Ancient Constitution vs. the Federalist Empire: Antifederalism from the Attack on 'Monarchism' to Modern Localism." *Northwestern University Law Review* 84 (1989): 74–105.

Rosen, Gary. *American Compact.* Lawrence: University Press of Kansas, 1999.

Seagar, Robert, II. *And Tyler Too: A Biography of John and Julia Gardiner Tyler.* New York: McGraw-Hill Book Company, Inc., 1963.

Sharp, James Roger. *American Politics in the Early Republic.* New Haven, Conn.: Yale University Press, 1993.

Siemers, David J. *The Antifederalists: Men of Great Faith and Forbearance.* Lanham, Md.: Rowman & Littlefield. Forthcoming.

———. "Electoral Dynamics of Ratification." In *The House and Senate in the 1790s: Petitioning, Lobbying, and Institutional Development,* ed. Kenneth R. Bowling and Donald R. Kennon. Athens, OH: Ohio University Press, 2002.

———. "'It is Natural to Care for the Crazy Machine': The Antifederalists' Post-Ratification Acquiescence." *Studies in American Political Development* 12 (1998): 383–410.

Skladony, Thomas W. "The House Goes to Work: Select and Standing Committees in the U.S. House of Representatives, 1789–1828." *Congress and the Presidency* 12 (1985): 165–87.

Skowroneck, Stephen. *The Politics Presidents Make*. Cambridge, Mass. and London: The Belknap Press of Harvard University Press, 1993.

———. "Presidential Leadership in Political Time." In *The Presidency and the Political System*, 6th ed., ed. Michael Nelson. Washington, D.C.: Congressional Quarterly Press, 2000.

Smith, Jean Edward. *John Marshall: Definer of a Nation*. New York: Henry Holt, 1996.

Stewart, Charles, III, et al. "Taking Care of Business: The Evolution of the House Committee System Before the Civil War." Paper delivered at the annual meeting of the American Political Science Association, Chicago, August 1995.

Stewart, Donald H. *The Opposition Press of the Federalist Period*. Albany: State University of New York Press, 1969.

Storing, Herbert J. *The Complete Antifederalist*. 7 vols. Chicago: University of Chicago Press, 1981.

Sumter, Thomas. Personal papers in the Draper Collection, housed at the State Historical Society of Wisconsin.

Swift, Elaine K. "The Making of an American Senate: Reconstitutive Change in Congress, 1787–1841." Ann Arbor: University of Michigan Press, 1995.

Swift, Elaine K. et al. "Collaborative Research on a Relational Database on Historical Congressional Statistics, 1788–1992." James Madison University computer file.

Tocqueville, Alexis de. *Democracy in America*. 1835. Reprint, ed. Richard D. Heffner, New York: Mentor, 1956.

Tucker, Thomas Tudor. *Conciliatory Hints, Attempting, by a Fair State of Matters, to Remove Party Prejudices*. Charleston, S.C.: A. Timothy, 1784. Evans #18731.

Van Doren, Peter. "Can We Learn the Causes of Congressional Decisions from Roll-Call Data?" *Legislative Studies Quarterly* 15 (1990): 311–40.

Votes and Proceedings of the House of Delegates [Maryland]. Annapolis: Frederick Green, 1789–1790. Evans #22641, 23538.

Waldstreicher, David. *In the Midst of Perpetual Fetes: The Making of American Nationalism, 1776–1820*. Chapel Hill: University of North Carolina Press, 1997.

Warren, Mercy Otis. *History of the Rise, Progress and Termination of the American Revolution*. 1805. Reprint, Indianapolis, Ind.: Liberty Classics, 1988.

Wells, William V. *Life and Public Services of Samuel Adams*. 3 vols. Boston: Little, Brown, & Company, 1866.

Wolin, Sheldon S. *The Presence of the Past*. Baltimore, Md.: Johns Hopkins University Press, 1989.

Wood, Gordon S. *The Creation of the American Republic, 1776–1787*. New York: W. W. Norton & Company, 1969.

———. "Interests and Disinterestedness in the making of the Constitution." In *Beyond Confederation*, ed. Richard Beeman, Stephen Botein, and Edward C. Carter. Chapel Hill: University of North Carolina Press, 1987.

———. *The Radicalism of the American Revolution*. New York: Vintage Books, 1991.

Yates, Abraham. "History of the Movement for the United States Constitution." *William & Mary Quarterly*, 3d series, no. 20 (1789/1963): 223–45.

Yates, Robert. *The Secret Proceedings and Debates of the Convention to Form the U.S. Constitution.* 1821. Reprint, Birmingham, Ala.: Southern University Press, 1987.

Young, James Sterling. *The Washington Community, 1800–1828.* New York: Columbia University Press, 1966.

Zaller, John R. *The Nature and Origins of Mass Opinion.* Cambridge: Cambridge University Press, 1992.

Zvesper, John. "The Madisonian Systems." *Western Political Quarterly* 37 (1984): 236–56.

Index